RESEARCH METHODS
IN CLINICAL PSYCHOLOGY
Second Edition

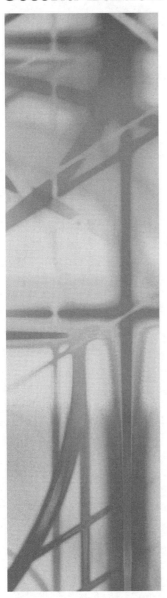

RESEARCH METHODS IN CLINICAL PSYCHOLOGY

An Introduction for Students and Practitioners

Second Edition

Chris Barker and Nancy Pistrang
University College London, UK

Robert Elliott
University of Toledo, Ohio, USA

JOHN WILEY & SONS, LTD

Copyright © 2002 John Wiley & Sons, Ltd,
The Atrium, Southern Gate, Chichester,
West Sussex PO19 8SQ, England

Telephone (+44) 1243 779777

Email (for orders and customer service enquiries): cs-books@wiley.co.uk
Visit our Home Page on www.wileyeurope.com or www.wiley.com

Reprinted September 2003, August 2005, July 2007, September 2008, March 2010

This publication is designed to provide accurate and authoritative information in regard to the subject matter covered. It is sold on the understanding that the Publisher is not engaged in rendering professional services. If professional advice or other expert assistance is required, the services of a competent professional should be sought.

Other Wiley Editorial Offices

John Wiley & Sons Inc., 111 River Street, Hoboken, NJ 07030, USA

Jossey-Bass, 989 Market Street, San Francisco, CA 94103-1741, USA

Wiley-VCH Verlag GmbH, Boschstr. 12, D-69469 Weinheim, Germany

John Wiley & Sons Australia Ltd, 33 Park Road, Milton, Queensland 4064, Australia

John Wiley & Sons (Asia) Pte Ltd, 2 Clementi Loop #02-01, Jin Xing Distripark, Singapore 129809

John Wiley & Sons Canada Ltd, 22 Worcester Road, Etobicoke, Ontario, Canada M9W 1L1

Library of Congress Cataloging-in-Publication Data
Barker, Chris, 1948–
  Research methods in clinical psychology : an introduction for students and practitioners
  / Chris Barker and Nancy Pistrang and Robert Elliott.– 2nd ed.
      p. cm.
  First ed. published under title : Research methods in clinical and counselling psychology. Chichester : Wiley, 1994.
  Includes biblographical references and index.
  ISBN 0-471-49087-3 (cased) – ISBN 0-471-49089-X (pbk.)
  1. Clinical psychology–Research–Methodology. 2.
Counselling–Research–Methodology. 3. Psychotherapy–Research–Methodology. I.
Pistrang, Nancy. II. Elliott, Robert, 1950– III. Barker, Chris, 1948–. Research methods in clinical and counselling psychology. IV. Title.

RC467.8 .B37 2002
616.89′0072–dc21   2002069167

British Library Cataloguing in Publication Data
A catalogue record for this book is available from the British Library

ISBN 13: 978-0471-49087-6 (HB)
ISBN 13: 978-0471-49089-0 (PB)

Typeset in 10/12pt Palatino by Dobbie Typesetting Limited, Tavistock, Devon
Printed and bound in Great Britain by TJ International Ltd, Padstow, Cornwall

TABLE OF CONTENTS

ABOUT THE AUTHORS

Chris Barker and Nancy Pistrang
Sub-Department of Clinical Health Psychology,
University College London,
Gower Street, London, England, WC1E 6BT

email: c.barker@ucl.ac.uk and n.pistrang@ucl.ac.uk

Robert Elliott
Department of Psychology, University of Toledo,
Toledo, OH, USA, 43606-3390

email: robert.elliott@utoledo.edu

All three authors obtained their PhDs in clinical psychology from UCLA, where they acquired a taste for psychological research in general and studying interpersonal processes in particular.

Chris Barker and *Nancy Pistrang* are Senior Lecturers in Clinical Psychology at University College London and Honorary Clinical Psychologists in the Camden and Islington Mental Health NHS Trust, London.

Robert Elliott is Professor of Psychology and Director of the Center for the Study of Experiential Psychotherapy at the University of Toledo, Ohio. He is a former editor of *Psychotherapy Research* and a past president of the Society for Psychotherapy Research.

There is a dedicated website for this book on www.wileyeurope.com/go/barker containing supplementary material on clinical psychology research methods for instructors, students, and general readers.

PREFACE

The first edition of this text was written in the early 1990s. Since then, the field of clinical research methods has continued to develop rapidly, and this second edition has been extensively updated to reflect these developments. We have also tried to make the whole book more user friendly, both in layout and in content. All chapters now have summaries and boxes highlighting the key points, and we have provided many more illustrative examples.

The biggest area of change is in our treatment of qualitative methods. There have been massive changes in clinical psychologists' attitudes to qualitative research over the last decade. When we wrote the first edition, qualitative methods were seen as rather daring and controversial; now they have become much more part of the mainstream. The first edition tried to give a balanced account of both quantitative and qualitative methods within a unifying framework. We espoused a methodological pluralism: a philosophy of fitting the research method to the research question. We still adhere to this pluralist position. However, new approaches to qualitative research have been developed, and old ones have become more clearly articulated. On a personal level, all three of us have now got several more qualitative research projects under our belts, and also have read more broadly in the area, so we are much more aware of the theoretical and practical issues in this genre of research. The present edition, therefore, has a new chapter on the fundamentals of qualitative research (Chapter 5), and a revised discussion of qualitative interviewing (Chapter 6) and analysis (Chapter 12).

Other recent ideas that we have tried to reflect include the topics of evidence-based practice, empirically supported therapies, and the like. Writings on these topics raise the issue of the relative value of effectiveness versus efficacy studies, which we consider in Chapters 8 and 11. In line with the emphasis on evidence-based practice, we have also expanded the treatment of psychometric theory, in particular to give a clearer treatment of validity issues. However, we have not neglected the important philosophy of science issues raised by these approaches and their critics.

Preparing the first edition of the book, as a transatlantic cooperation, was made much simpler by the use of email. However, at that time, the world wide web was barely functioning: there is not a single website mentioned in the first edition of the book. The internet has changed how research is approached, and at the time of writing, new technologies are being announced weekly. So we have made this edition more internet friendly, by including useful websites where possible.

We have continued to focus exclusively on examples from English-language publications and clinical examples from the US and the UK, not out of choice but because these sources represent our primary knowledge base. We are aware that the first edition was used widely around the world, in many non-English speaking countries. We hope that international readers will continue to forgive our anglocentrism; we only wish that we had more international experience to draw upon.

Another aspect of the book's being a transatlantic enterprise is that we have had to struggle with terminology and forms of expression. As George Bernard Shaw was reported to have said, the US and the UK are divided by a common language. This is certainly true in psychology as well as in everyday speech. Where different US and UK terms exist for the same things (e.g., "mental retardation" in the US is equivalent to "intellectual disabilities" in the UK), we have tried to use them both. However, it is possible that in trying to satisfy readers from both sides of the Atlantic, we may have ended up by not satisfying anyone!

We have simplified the title of the book for this edition, having reluctantly dropped the word "counseling". We obviously still welcome counseling psychologist readers, as we do readers from other applied areas: e.g., community, health, or occupational psychologists. The first edition of the text also ended up being used by members of other professions, such as doctors and nurses, and by graduate students in other disciplines, such as anthropology or architecture. So it seemed simpler to focus it around clinical psychology, our primary professional allegiance, but to state clearly that we intend this second edition to be used by counseling psychologists, and by other types of applied psychologists, and by colleagues and students in related disciplines. We always welcome a dialogue with our readers; do email us with your comments, criticisms, and suggestions.

Many friends, colleagues, and students, too numerous to mention individually, gave us encouraging and constructive feedback on the first edition. Many thanks to the following colleagues who helped us with this second edition: Chris Brewin, John Cape, Kate Cheney, Pasco Fearon, Dick Hallam, David Shapiro, and Jonathan Smith. We are indebted to Anna Barker for saving us hours of work with the indexing. Thanks also to Vivien Ward, Lesley Valerio, and the rest of the team at John Wiley for all their encouragement and assistance in helping us to make the book as user friendly as possible. However, any errors or omissions still lurking in the text remain our responsibility alone. Emory Cowen, a prominent American psychologist, once said that he was well qualified to write about errors in research, since he had committed most of them himself (Cowen, 1978). It is a sentiment that we all echo.

Finally, thanks once again to our families for putting up with our authorship travails and especially for providing a welcome relief from the world of psychology.

PREFACE FROM THE FIRST EDITION

This book has grown out of our experience in teaching research methods, advising mental health professionals who were struggling to conduct research, and carrying out research projects ourselves. It aims to help readers become both better consumers and better producers of research in clinical and counseling psychology. We hope that, at a minimum, it will encourage and enable practitioners to read research reports critically and to evaluate a study's strengths and weaknesses. We further hope to inspire at least some of our readers to produce research themselves. In addition to teaching the tools of the trade, we will try to convince readers that doing research can be stimulating, challenging, and fun.

The book presents a practical description of the research process, using a chronological framework. It takes readers through the sequence of steps involved in executing a project: groundwork, measurement, design, analysis, and interpretation. In addition to these technical aspects of research, the book also addresses some essential background issues, such as the underlying philosophy of the various research methods. We also look at sociopolitical issues, since clinical and counseling research is often conducted in working service settings and it is potentially threatening as well as illuminating. For simplicity, the book has been written from the perspective of producers rather than consumers of research, but we intend it to be of equal use to both audiences.

We have tried to be comprehensive in terms of breadth, but not in terms of depth: there are entire books covering material which we encompass in a chapter. We cover the essential areas and guide the interested reader towards more specialized literature as appropriate. Most of the statistical aspects of research methods are omitted, since this is a separate field in itself. We have aimed the book at clinical and counseling psychology students and practitioners; others who might find it useful are students and practitioners in health and community psychology, counselling, psychiatry, psychiatric nursing, and social work.

The terms therapy, psychotherapy and counseling will mostly be used interchangeably to refer to face-to-face work with clients. Where a broader sense of the psychologist's role is intended, e.g., to encompass prevention or consultation, we will use the terms clinical work or psychological intervention. All three of us have worked in both clinical and counseling settings and we publish in both clinical and counseling journals. We regard the different labels as more indicative of differences in training and professional allegiance than differences in the work done with clients. However, for even-handedness, we tend to use the phrase clinical and counseling psychologists, except where it is too cumbersome, in which case we say clinician, counsellor or therapist alone for convenience. Whatever, the language, we always have in mind anyone engaged in clinical, counseling or psychotherapeutic work.

The book addresses those issues faced by clinical and counseling psychologists who do research that are not covered in the more general social and behavioural science research texts. The advantage of having a clinical or counseling psychology training is that you are likely to conduct research with more practical relevance, to ask less superficial questions and to have a strong sense of the complexities of human experience and behaviour. The interviewing skills acquired in clinical and counseling training are also helpful in doing research, but research and therapeutic interviews have crucial differences; therefore researchers may need to unlearn certain interventions used in therapeutic settings. Being trained in clinical or counseling psychology also makes one aware of the tension between the scientific and the therapeutic stance: in the former case looking for generalities, in the latter uniqueness. Throughout the book, we have tried to place research methods in the clinical and counseling context.

Two central assumptions inform our work. The first is methodological pluralism: that different methods are appropriate to different problems and research questions. Until recently, research methods were largely segmented along the lines of academic disciplines. Sociologists and anthropologists tended to use qualitative methods, such as ethnography or participant observation, whereas psychologists stuck almost exclusively to quantitative methods. Now, however, a significant change is under way, in that psychologists are beginning to regard a variety of research methods, including qualitative ones, as part of their toolkit. For each topic area, such as interviewing or observation, we present the strengths and weaknesses of the various methodological options, quantitative and qualitative. We have tried to be even-handed, to present the arguments and let readers decide for themselves what is best for their particular application. As in our work with clients, we hope to be empowering, to give skills, present options, and let our readers make informed choices.

Our second assumption is the importance of the scientist-practitioner model: that clinical and counseling psychologists should be trained to be both competent clinicians and competent researchers (although we hold a broader view of what is scientific than was implicit in the original discussion of the scientist-practitioner model). This model encapsulates the unique contribution psychologists can make to service settings and to the academic development of the field. In practice, many applied psychologists feel that they do not have sufficient research skills, and good intentions to conduct research fail to come to fruition. This book aims to help such practitioners.

The three of us met in the mid-1970s as graduate students on the UCLA clinical psychology PhD program, where we worked together in the Interpersonal Process Research Group. The book bears the hallmark of the excellent eclectic scientist-practitioner training we received at UCLA, but also evidences our struggles against some of the constraints of our professional socialisation. Our own research has continued to be broadly focused on interpersonal processes: such areas as client-therapist interaction, informal helping and couples' communication are what we get excited about. We have inevitably drawn heavily on these areas for our examples, but have tried to make the discussion of general relevance. Our approach to research is strongly influenced by humanistic values: we believe that it is possible to do rigorous psychological research without being reductionist or making a travesty of the phenomenon under study.

We would like to thank the friends and colleagues who helped us by discussing ideas, supplying references and commenting on drafts: John Cape, Lorna Champion, Linda Clare, Neil Devlin, Jerry Goodman (for the slogan "research is fun"), Les Greenberg, Dick Hallam, Maria Koutantji, David Rennie, Laura Rice, Joe Schwartz, and Pam Smith. Mark Williams and Connie Hammen provided incisive and helpful reviews of the manuscript. The team at Wiley were consistently supportive: Michael Coombs helped us to get the project off the ground, and Wendy Hudlass, our publishing editor, was a constant source of encouragement and help as the project progressed. Thanks also to our students, who inspired us to develop and clarify our thinking about clinical research and whose encouraging comments on early drafts helped to sustain us. In addition we are grateful to the research participants with whom we have sought to understand the workings of psychological helping processes. Our interactions with them and the data that they have provided have stimulated and challenged us to broaden our scope as researchers. And finally, many thanks to our children, for constantly reminding us that play is at least as important as work.

CHAPTER 1

INTRODUCTION: THE RESEARCH PROCESS

KEY POINTS IN THIS CHAPTER

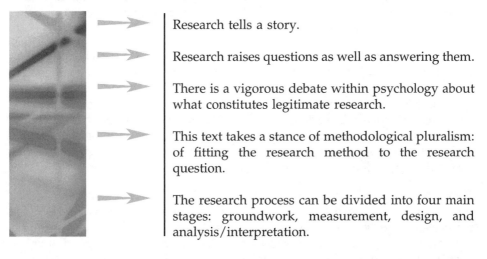

Research tells a story.

Research raises questions as well as answering them.

There is a vigorous debate within psychology about what constitutes legitimate research.

This text takes a stance of methodological pluralism: of fitting the research method to the research question.

The research process can be divided into four main stages: groundwork, measurement, design, and analysis/interpretation.

Research tells a story. Ideally, it resembles a detective story, which begins with a mystery and ends with its resolution. Researchers have a problem that they want to investigate; the story will reach its happy ending if they find a solution to that problem.

In practice, however, things aren't quite that simple, and the actual picture is closer to an adventure story or traveler's tale (Kvale, 1996), with many unexpected twists and turns. Often, the resolution of a research project is uncertain: it doesn't answer your initial research question, rather it tells you that you were asking the wrong question in the first place, or that the way that you went about answering it was misconceived. You struggle with discouragement and frustration; perhaps you come out of it feeling lucky to have survived the thing with your health and relationships (mostly) intact. So, if you enjoy research and are determined to make a contribution, you organize a sequel, in which you try out a better question with a better designed study, and so it goes on. Another way of putting it is that there are stories within stories, or a continuing series of stories. Each individual research project tells one story, the series of projects conducted by a researcher or a research team forms a larger story, and the development of the whole research area a yet larger story. And this progression continues up to the level of the history of science and ideas over the centuries.

How a research area develops over time is illustrated in an article by Hammen (1992), whose title, "Life events and depression: The plot thickens", alludes to the mystery-story aspect of research. Her article summarizes her 20-year-long research program into depression. She discusses how her original research drew on rather simplistic cognitive models of depression (e.g., that depression is caused by negative appraisals of events). The findings of early studies led her to modify these models (e.g., to take into account that people's appraisals of events may be negative because the events themselves are negative) and thus to ask more complex questions. Her team is currently working with more sophisticated models, which take into account that individuals may play a role in bringing about the life events that happen to them.

Another way that things are not so simple is that not all researchers agree on what constitutes a legitimate story. The situation in psychology is analogous to developments in literature. On the one hand is the traditional research story, rather like a Victorian novel, which has a clear beginning, middle, and end, and is expected to provide a more or less faithful reflection of reality. On the other hand, in this modern and postmodern age, we encounter narratives that do not follow an orderly chronological sequence or tie up neatly at the end. Furthermore, they may not claim to represent, or may even reject the idea of, reality.

These developments in literature and psychology reflect general intellectual developments during the last century, which have ramifications across many branches of European and English-speaking culture, both artistic and scientific. Our own field of interest, psychology in general and clinical psychology in particular, is currently going through a vigorous debate about the nature of research—that is, which of these narratives we can call research and which are something else. Scholars from various corners of the discipline of psychology (e.g., Carlson, 1972; Richardson, 1996; Rogers, 1985; Sarbin, 1986; Smith et al., 1995) have questioned the validity and usefulness of psychology's version of the traditional story, which has been called "received view" or "old paradigm" research: essentially a quantitative, hypothetico-deductive approach, which relies on linear causal models. These and other critics call for replacing, or at least supplementing, the traditional approach with a more qualitative, discovery-oriented, non-linear approach to research.

This debate, as Kimble (1984) points out, is a contemporary manifestation of William James's (1907) distinction between tough-minded and tender-minded ways of thinking, which is itself a translation into psychological terms of the old debate in philosophy over rationalism (Plato) versus empiricism (Aristotle). However, it is simplistic to view this debate as two-sided, with researchers being either in one camp or the other. It is better viewed as reflecting multiple underlying attitudes, for example, preferences for quantitative versus qualitative methods, attitudes towards exploratory versus confirmatory research questions, experimental control versus real-world relevance, and so on (Kimble, 1984).

One consequence of the lack of consensus about acceptable approaches to research is that people who are doing research for the first time may experience considerable anxiety—rather like the existential anxiety that accompanies a loss of meaning (Yalom, 1980). Undertaking a research project without being clear about what standards are to be used to evaluate it is an unsettling experience. Furthermore, there is a political dimension, since people in powerful positions in the academic world—journal editors, grant reviewers, and university professors —often adhere to the more traditional models.

This anxiety is exacerbated because the rules are not always made explicit, which may make beginning researchers feel like Alice in Wonderland: that they are in a strange land with mysterious and arbitrary rules that are continually being changed. Researchers are constantly reminded, in various ways, to behave themselves properly according to these scientific rules; as the Red Queen said to Alice, "Look up, speak nicely and don't twiddle your fingers all the time!" This experience can be understandably off-putting for people trying to enter the research wonderland for the first time.

We will reconsider these issues in Chapters 2, 4, and 5, which address the conceptual underpinnings of research. However, it is worth stating at the outset that our own stance is one of methodological pluralism. We don't think that any single approach to research (or indeed that psychological research itself) has all the answers; thus, we believe that researchers need to have at their disposal a range of methods, appropriate to the problems being investigated. We have considerable sympathy with the critics of the received view, but are not convinced that the consequence of accepting their criticisms is to abandon traditional quantitative methods, or even research in general. Indeed, we feel that to do so would be a disaster for psychology and for society. Fortunately, we see increasing signs that it is possible to articulate a synthesis of the old and new paradigm traditions, that there are general principles common to rigorous research within whatever paradigm, and that it is possible to lay out an overall framework which organizes different approaches to research and clarifies the ways in which they can complement one another. Learning to do psychological research is partly a process of learning disciplined enquiry according to these principles within this general framework.

At the same time, there are rules of good practice specific to each type of research. We will base our methodological pluralism on a principle of appropriate methodologies (by analogy to the catch phrase "appropriate technology" in the economics of development). By this, we mean that the methods used should flow out of the research questions asked. Different questions lend themselves to different methods. To resume our literary analogy, like the different literary genres (mystery, romance, science fiction, autobiography, etc.), we can think of different research genres, such as survey research, randomized clinical trials, systematic case studies, and in-depth qualitative interviewing. Each of these research genres has different stories to tell and different rules of good practice.

We will attempt to clarify these general principles and specific rules of good practice, so that you will be in a better position to appreciate other people's research. We hope that this will help you feel less intimidated about the prospect of conducting your own research. Also, there is value in making the rules of research explicit, so that one can challenge them more effectively, and thus contribute to the debate about how psychological research should be conducted.

Research is demanding: it does require clear and rigorous thought, as well as perseverance and stamina, but it is also fascinating and exciting, and, we hope, beneficial to the public that psychologists ultimately profess to serve.

The Research Process

This book is structured around a simple chronological framework, which we call the *research process*: that is, the sequence of steps that researchers go through during a project. The steps can be grouped into four major stages. Like all such frameworks, it is idealized, in that the stages are not always distinct and may interact with each other. However, we find it a useful way of thinking about how research is conducted, both one's own and other people's.

1. *Groundwork* (Chapter 3). This stage involves both scientific issues—choosing the topic, specifying the conceptual model, reviewing the literature, formulating the research questions—and also practical issues—resolving organizational, political, financial, or ethical problems. Sometimes researchers give the groundwork short shrift, being anxious to get on with the business of running the project itself. However, we will argue that devoting careful thought at this stage repays itself with interest during the course of the project.

2. *Measurement* (Chapters 4 to 7). Having formulated the research questions, the next step is to decide how to measure the psychological constructs of interest. We are here using the term "measurement" in its broadest sense, to encompass qualitative as well as quantitative approaches to data collection.

3. *Design* (Chapters 8 to 11). Research design issues concern when and from whom the data will be collected. For example: Who will the participants be? Will there be an experimental design with a control group? How many pre- and post-assessments will there be? What ethical concerns need to be addressed? These design issues can usually be considered independently of measurement issues.

The research questions, measurement procedures, and design together constitute the *research protocol*, the blueprint for the study. Having gone through these first three stages, researchers will usually conduct a small pilot study, whose results may cause them to rethink the protocol and possibly to conduct further pilots. Eventually the protocol is finalized; the last stage then consists of implementing it.

4. *Analysis, interpretation, and dissemination* (Chapter 12). The data are collected, analyzed, interpreted, written up, possibly published, and, let us hope, acted upon.

These stages in the research process constitute our framework for the book. However, we will also examine some key philosophical, professional, and political issues that are central to thinking about the whole research enterprise (Chapters 2, 4, and 5). Although following these arguments is not necessary for learning purely technical research skills, it is important to understand the wider context in which research is being conducted, as doing so will lead to more focused, coherent, and ultimately useful research programs. It is also important to keep in mind that doing research is much more than the exercise of a set of techniques; carrying out research involves imagination and empathy, problem-solving skills and critical thinking, ethical reflection and social responsibility.

The first part of this background material is given in the next chapter, which analyzes the meaning of some of the terms we have so far left undefined, such as research itself. We will also discuss why anyone might want to engage in research at all.

CHAPTER 2

PERSPECTIVES ON RESEARCH

KEY POINTS IN THIS CHAPTER

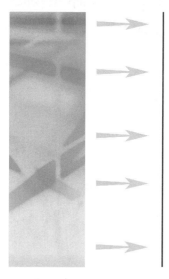

The process of psychological research is similar to that of open-minded enquiry in everyday life.

Several philosophers have attempted to characterize the essence of scientific progress: Popper, Kuhn, and Feyerabend are central figures.

Social and political forces shape the development of science.

The scientist-practitioner model is a central part of clinical psychology's professional ideology, but there is often a gap between rhetoric and reality.

Practicing clinical psychologists may choose to do research, or not to, for a variety of reasons.

This chapter examines some important background issues, in order to give you a sense of the context in which research is conducted. These include the philosophical framework (i.e., the underlying set of assumptions about the research process), the professional context (i.e., how research fits in to clinical psychology's professional viewpoint), and also the personal context (i.e., each individual researcher's own attitudes towards research).

Understanding these issues is helpful both in reading other people's research and also in conducting your own. It helps make sense of other people's research if you understand the framework within which it was conducted. If you are doing research yourself, it follows that the more you are aware of your assumptions, the more you are able to make informed choices about what methods to use, rather than following available examples blindly. This is similar to clinical work, where clients who have greater insight into their motivating forces are generally better able to live freer and more productive lives, and therapists who are able to step outside of their own perspective are better able to understand and help their clients (Rogers, 1975). However, again as in clinical work, making decisions can become a burden as you become aware of the multiple possibilities of action instead of making automatic choices.

The chapter has three sections, covering philosophical, professional, and personal issues. Another important "P," political, is addressed in all three sections.

PHILOSOPHICAL ISSUES

This section examines what is meant by two key terms: research and science. It is worth starting out with a couple of disclaimers. Several of the ideas are complex and require philosophical expertise to appraise them properly. We do not possess such expertise, nor do we expect the great majority of our readers to. Furthermore, we are concerned that grappling with difficult issues, such as what is the nature of reality, at this early stage can be heavy going. As is the case in all philosophy, there are more questions than answers. We attempt to give an overview of some interesting contemporary issues; it is not necessary to follow them in detail in order to conduct or critique research. However, having a broad grasp of them will help you understand (perhaps more clearly than the researchers themselves do) what a piece of research is attempting to achieve.

Philosophical issues that relate more specifically to psychological measurement (namely discussion of the positivist, phenomenological, and social construc-tionist positions) are covered in Chapters 4 and 5.

What is Research?

- Research can be depicted as a circular process.

- Research requires psychological flexibility and open-mindedness.

- Research is not the only way to acquire psychological understanding: literature, life experience, and supervised clinical work are also important.

- The main reason for following rigorous research methods is to minimize bias and reduce errors in drawing conclusions.

- A rudimentary understanding of epistemology (the theory of knowledge) helps to elucidate some basic procedures and distinct stances towards research (e.g., critical realism and constructionism).

Conducting research is essentially a circular activity, which in simplified form looks something like this (see Figure 2.1).

As the figure suggests, this activity is potentially everlasting. The human propensity to understand oneself and the world we live in has been noted since ancient times. Plato had Socrates say (in the *Apology*, 38) that "the unexamined life is not worth living." Some writers, e.g., Cook and Campbell (1979), consider that the psychological roots of research have evolutionary significance: that there is survival value in our attempts to understand the world and ourselves.

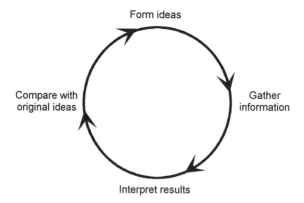

Figure 2.1   The research cycle

Note that this model does not attempt to explain where we get our ideas from in the first place. There is a long-standing debate in philosophy and developmental psychology, which we will sidestep for the moment, about whether acquiring knowledge of the world is possible without some previous understanding. Our emphasis is on how the educated adult discovers and tests ideas.

Research demands a degree of psychological flexibility, that is, an ability to modify one's ideas if they are not supported by the evidence. It may be helpful to view various sorts of disruptions in the circular model as corresponding to various maladaptive psychological styles. For instance, a refusal to interact with the world at all, elaborating theories without ever testing them against the "real world" (i.e., never moving down off the first stage of our circular model), is a solipsistic stance of building dream castles with no basis in reality—a stance captured in the epithet used to describe out-of-touch academics: "the ivory tower." This refusal to gather information also characterizes someone who is overconfident in the value of their ideas, and does not see any need to put them to any kind of empirical test (politicians often seem to fall into this category).

Problems in the lowest quadrant of the circle include biases in analyzing or interpreting the data: allowing what you want to get from a research project to distort how you report what actually happened. Our data are always influenced to some extent by our values and preconceptions; after all, these determine what we choose to study in the first place, what we count as data, and how we select among our findings in drawing out the implications of our research. However, in extreme cases, our personal and ideological commitments may lead us to ignore or suppress unwanted findings, or even to fabricate results. While such extreme cases of scientific dishonesty are relatively rare, each of us is subject to self-deception, which may lead to distorting our results in subtle ways. Similar problems exist in the final step of the circular model: the refusal to modify one's ideas, by dismissing or distorting the evidence, which characterizes a rigid, dogmatic stance. This can be seen in people who cling to various kinds of orthodoxies and fundamentalist beliefs.

While passions and personal feuds make science more interesting, and have always helped drive it forward, we believe that an inquiring, open-minded research attitude is one aspect of good psychological functioning. It is similar to Jahoda's (1958) concept of "adequate perception of reality" as one criterion for positive mental health.

Thus far, our characterization of research applies to everyday life as much as to organized science. We all do research informally; it is one way that we form our mental representations of the world. This is what Reason and Rowan (1981) call "naive enquiry." George Kelly (1955) elaborated the metaphor of the person as a scientist into an entire theory of personality: that people are continually building and testing their set of "personal constructs." However, cognitive and social scientists have also shown that people display pervasive biases in the way that they process information (Fiske & Taylor, 1991; Mahoney, 1976; Nisbett & Ross, 1980). The fundamental reason for the development of rigorous research methods is to attempt to minimize biases in drawing conclusions from evidence.

Finally, we should make it clear at the outset that we do not see research as being the only, or even an especially privileged, route to knowledge. One can learn much of relevance to being a good clinical psychologist from the works of Shakespeare, Tolstoy, George Eliot, or James Joyce (to name a few of our own favorites). Great works of art or literature will often have a ring of truth that will immediately resonate with the reader or viewer. Furthermore, everyday life experiences also help build a knowledge base. In Morrow-Bradley and Elliott's (1986) survey on sources of psychotherapeutic knowledge, therapists reported that they learned most from experience with their clients, followed by theoretical or practical writings, being a client themselves, supervision, and practical workshops. Research presentations and research reports were ranked first by only 10% of the sample of practicing therapists (in contrast to experience with clients, which was ranked first by 48%).

However, the strength of formal research is that it is a systematic way of looking at the world and of describing its regularities, and it provides knowledge that can allow us to decide between conflicting claims to truth that may be put forward by rival proponents. New approaches to treatment are constantly being developed, and usually the person who develops the therapy will offer some preliminary evidence on its effectiveness. Two examples of new therapies that gained attention in the 1990s were dialectical behavior therapy (DBT) for personality disorders (Linehan, 1993) and eye movement desensitization and reprocessing (EMDR) therapy for post-traumatic stress disorder (Shapiro, 1999). Each therapy has its advocates and its critics (see, e.g., Herbert et al., 2000). However, until several rigorous studies have been conducted, preferably by groups with varying theoretical allegiances and using different research designs, we will not be able to know the effectiveness and mechanisms of action of each approach.

Furthermore, because research is a shared, public activity, it has a crucial role in contributing to the development of theory and professional knowledge. Interactions with clients, conversations with fellow professionals, and personal growth experiences are all useful ways of educating oneself individually, but research, theoretical writings, and published case reports are public documents and therefore contribute to the development of the profession as a whole.

We will explore such professional issues more fully in the next section, and then, in the final section, discuss why individual psychologists might (or might not) want to do research. However, before we can do this, we need to examine the meaning of some of our core terminology in greater depth.

Definition of "Research"

The Oxford English Dictionary's definition of "research" serves as a good working definition. It is: "A search or investigation directed to the discovery of some fact by careful consideration or study of a subject; a course of critical or scientific enquiry." Five aspects of this definition are noteworthy.

First, the definition stresses the *methodical* aspect of research, that research is careful and disciplined. It is a craft that requires considerable dedication and attention to detail. There is also, however, a chance element to research: not all discoveries are necessarily planned (Merbaum & Lowe, 1982). A classic example of an accidental scientific discovery is Fleming's isolation of penicillin, when he noticed that some mould in a dish stopped the growth of bacteria he was attempting to cultivate. However, to take advantage of a chance discovery, you must have the knowledge and insight to appreciate its significance, and then the persistence to follow it up.

Second, the definition specifies a *critical or detached* attitude. This attitude is an important feature of the clinical psychology discipline. Clinical psychologists are trained to question the basis of professional practice, e.g., "What's going on here?", "How do you know that?", "What's the evidence for that assertion?" This sceptical attitude does not always endear them to their colleagues from other mental health disciplines, and may contribute to the common perception of psychologists as standing at one step removed from the other professionals in a team or service.

Third, the definition does not specify the method of research, suggesting the value of both *rational and empirical* investigation. While conceptual research is sometimes denigrated in psychology as "speculation" or "armchair philoso-phizing," it is essential in other disciplines, especially the humanities, and is the method of choice in mathematics (the "queen of the sciences") and theoretical physics, both of which proceed from axioms to deductions. Psychology is primarily an empirical science, concerned with systematically gathering data, which are then used, in ways we will discuss below, to develop and test its theories. However, there is also an important role for conceptual research, to formulate theories, to explicate underlying principles, and to identify the assumptions underlying research (Slife & Williams, 1995). This issue of research method relates back to the centuries-old philosophical debate between rationalists and empiricists over the sources of human knowledge (Russell, 1961).

Fourth, the definition states that research is a process of *discovery*. This raises the distinction between exploratory research, which sets out to find something new, and confirmatory research, which sets out to evaluate existing theory (see Chapter 3). Philosophers of science use parallel language to distinguish between the context of discovery and the context of justification of a particular finding (Reichenbach, 1938). We include both exploratory and confirmatory approaches under the definition of research.

Finally, the definition says that research is directed towards the discovery of *facts*. The Oxford English Dictionary defines a fact as "something that has really occurred or is the case." However, this definition begs some difficult philosophical questions about how we come to know what is true, and requires some consideration of the philosophical basis of truth and knowledge.

Epistemology

The theory of knowledge is known as *epistemology*; it is the area of philosophy devoted to describing how we come to know things or believe them to be true or real. In fact, when psychologists talk about validity and reliability, in either quantitative psychometrics or qualitative research (Packer & Addison, 1989), they are talking in epistemological terms. According to Hamlyn (1970), there are four fundamental epistemological positions, or criteria of truth:

1. The *correspondence theory* of truth, the basis of realist philosophies, holds that a belief is true if it matches reality.

2. *Coherence theory*, the basis of rationalist philosophies, holds that a belief is true if it is internally consistent or logically non-contradictory.

3. The *pragmatist or utilitarian criterion* holds a belief is true if it is useful or produces practical benefits.

4. The *consensus criterion*, the basis of sociological theories of knowledge (see below), holds a belief is true if it is shared by a group of people.

None of these theories is completely adequate: all have serious logical flaws. For example, correspondence theory involves an infinite regress, because reality must be measured validly before the degree of correspondence can be assessed. (This is referred to as the criterion problem in measurement.) Furthermore, counter-instances of each of the other three criteria can readily be imagined (e.g., an elegant, coherent theory which has no bearing on reality; a false belief which nevertheless proves useful; and a false consensus or collective delusion). On the other hand, all four theories have some value, as practical, but fallible guidelines (Anderson et al., 1986), suggesting the importance of a pluralist epistemology. Optimally, one would attempt to realize all four truth criteria in one's research (cf. Elliott et al., 1999).

Realism and Constructionism

Physical scientists often implicitly work from a *realist* position, which is based on a correspondence theory of truth. Realism posits that there is a real world out there, independent of whoever may be observing it (Bhaskar, 1975). Thus the rocks of the moon have a geological composition that is, at least in principle, discoverable: that some people may believe the moon to be made of green cheese is irrelevant. Within this realist framework, the task of the scientist is to understand as accurately as possible the properties of the real world. Scientists themselves might say that they are trying to understand Nature.

For most of the past 100 years, psychologists have also emphasized a correspondence theory of truth, although in the latter half of the 20th century this evolved into a *critical realist* position (Cook & Campbell, 1979). This assumes that there exists a real world out there that has regularities. However, we can never know it with certainty: all our understandings are essentially tentative. The critical realist position emphasizes the replicability of research: that other researchers should be able to repeat your work and get approximately the same results, or in more technical language, that knowledge should be "intersubjectively testable" (Cook & Campbell, 1979; Popper, 1959). This means that researchers must be explicit about how they collect their data and draw their conclusions, so that other researchers can evaluate their conclusions or replicate the study themselves. Beyond this, it suggests that researchers should approach the same topic using different methods, with complementary strengths and weaknesses, a strategy of "triangulation." Thus, critical realists go beyond correspondence theory to include consensus and coherence truth criteria.

In the last two decades of the 20th century, various challenges to realist and critical realist philosophies emerged. These approaches emphasize either coherence or consensus theories of truth and try to eliminate correspondence criteria. The major current alternative to the critical realist position can be found in the various forms of *constructionism* and *constructivism*, some of which overlap considerably with *postmodernism* (Gergen, 2001; Guba & Lincoln, 1989; Lyotard, 1979/1984; Neimeyer, 1993). These are fairly imprecise terms, but they share a common stance of dispensing with the assumption of an objective reality and instead studying people's interpretations (see Chapter 5 for further discussion). Postmodernists are impatient with what they call "grand theory"; instead they present a more multifaceted, fractured world view, some taking the extreme point of view that there are no true and false stories, only different stories. The central problem with such radical constructionist or postmodernist views is that not all constructions are equally accurate, consistent, consensually replicable, or useful. That smoking causes lung cancer or that poverty reduces one's quality of life, though not unassailable propositions, seem to describe important consistencies in the world.

Social constructionists emphasize the social construction of reality and see the research setting as a specialized form of social interaction. They argue that researchers are not detached observers, but actively play a part in what they are studying and how they make sense of it. Thus, the collection, analysis, and interpretation of data involve processes of active construction. A related point is the interdependence of the knower and the known. That is to say, in coming to know a thing, both the state of our knowledge and the thing itself may be changed; what we call facts are a joint construction of the things themselves and our knowing process. For example, the process of interviewing a client about her reactions to a recent therapy session may change the way that she feels about the session, her therapist, or herself.

Pure and Applied Research

There are many ways to classify research, e.g., according to content, setting, population, or method. One important distinction is between basic academic research and applied (including evaluation) research. Although often presented as a dichotomy, the two positions are better thought of as two ends of a continuum (Milne, 1987; Patton, 2002).

Basic (or pure) research addresses the generation and testing of theory. What are the underlying processes that help us understand the regularities in nature? Basic research emphasizes processes common to most people. Because clinical psychology is an applied discipline, basic research is rare, but examples of research toward the basic end of the spectrum include the relative contributions of relationship versus technique factors in therapy outcome in general, and the neuropsychological mechanisms involved in recalling traumatic memories.

Applied research addresses practical questions, e.g., whether a particular intervention works for a particular client group. At the far applied end of the spectrum is *action research* (Patton, 2002), carried out to address a particular local problem, such as the high dropout rate at a local psychotherapy clinic. *Evaluation research* also resides near the applied end of the spectrum, as it primarily addresses the general needs or outcomes of a particular agency or service, but may have a broader relevance. Evaluation is often motivated by pragmatic concerns, such as the need to maintain funding for a particular service. Although the methods used in pure and applied research overlap considerably, we will address some issues particular to evaluation in Chapter 11.

In actual practice, pure and applied research blend into each other. As the above two examples of pure research demonstrate, there is often an element of application in clinical research: that is what makes it clinical. Many examples of clinical research lie on the middle ground. For instance, psychotherapy outcome research addresses questions of both theory and application. Since we see the pure/applied distinction as a continuum rather than a dichotomy, we adhere to a definition of research that encompasses the full spectrum, and can even be extended to clinical practice (a point we take up later in this chapter).

What is Science?

We have used the word "science" up to now without questioning its meaning. Yet there is a lively debate about what science consists of, a debate that goes to the heart of some enduring controversies within psychology and related fields. It addresses the question of how knowledge is acquired and which methods of research are "scientific" (and therefore respectable). In a much-used example,

Key points:

- There is a lively debate within psychology about which methods are scientific and which are not.

- Philosophers of science have attempted to define the unique characteristics of science.

- Induction is the process of deriving theories from careful observations. The central problem with induction is the theory-dependence of observation.

- Deduction is the process of making testable predictions from theories. It is the basis of the hypothetico-deductive model of science.

- Popper proposed that good scientific theories should be testable and therefore potentially falsifiable.

- Kuhn analyzed the historical progression of scientific thought in terms of his concepts of paradigms and scientific revolutions.

- The sociology of knowledge examines the role of social and political forces in the development of scientific thought.

how can we distinguish between legitimate science and voodoo, or astrology? Or is such a distinction only a social construction? Closer to home, in what sense is psychoanalysis a science? Or, indeed, psychology in general?

The literature on this area is enormous: philosophy of science is an entire academic specialty in itself. Here we briefly review some central ideas. Since much undergraduate psychology education is implicitly based on a traditional view of science, it is important for psychologists to know about the positions presented here and in Chapters 4 and 5, in order to understand the context of the traditional view and to be aware of its alternatives.

Induction

An initial, common-sense way of attempting to characterize science is that it is based on careful observation, from which theories are then formulated. The derivation of theory from observation is known as *induction*, that is, going from the particular to the general. Astronomy is the classic example: astronomers gaze at the heavens, record what they see, and then try to spot the general pattern underlying their observations. Kepler's 17th century laws of planetary motion were derived in such a way, using the accumulated data of his predecessor, Tycho Brahe. Within psychology, clinical observation also uses induction. For example, the psychoanalyst carefully observes a number of patients within the analytic setting, and then attempts to formulate his or her impressions into a theory. This was the basis of Freud's methods when he enunciated psychoanalytic theory at the beginning of the 20th century.

Unfortunately, there are two insuperable problems with induction as a guiding principle of science (Chalmers, 1982). The first is that it is impossible to have pure observations: what we observe and how we observe it are, implicitly or explicitly, based on theory. This phenomenon is known as the *theory-dependence of observation*. For example, a psychoanalyst, a Skinnerian behaviorist, and a lay person will notice very different things in a videotape of a therapy session. The second problem is that there is no logical basis for the principle of induction. Because something has been observed to happen on 10 occasions, it does not necessarily follow that it will happen on the eleventh. This means that theories can never be conclusively verified, only temporarily corroborated by scientific evidence, resulting in probabilistic rather than necessary truths. The philosopher, Karl Popper, who was a contemporary of Freud and Adler in 1920s Vienna, has put this point of view forcefully. It is worth giving an extended quotation, which is of enduring relevance to psychologists:

> I found that those of my friends who were admirers of Marx, Freud, and Adler, were impressed by a number of points common to these theories, and especially by their apparent *explanatory power*. These theories appeared to be able to explain practically everything that happened within the fields to which they referred . . . .
>
> The most characteristic element in this situation seemed to me the incessant stream of confirmations, of observations which 'verified' the theories in question; and this point was constantly emphasized by their adherents.... The Freudian analysts emphasized that their theories were constantly verified by their 'clinical observations'. As for Adler, I was much impressed by a personal experience. Once, in 1919, I reported to him a case which to me did not seem particularly Adlerian, but which he found no difficulty in analyzing in terms of his theory of inferiority feelings, although he had not even seen the child. Slightly shocked, I asked him how he could be so sure. 'Because of my thousandfold experience', he replied; whereupon I could not help saying: 'And with this new case, I suppose, your experience has become thousand-and-one fold.'
>
> What I had in mind was that his previous observations may not have been much sounder than this new one; that each in its turn had been interpreted in the light of 'previous experience', and at the same time counted as additional confirmation.... I could not think of any human behavior which could not be interpreted in terms of either theory. It was precisely this fact—that they always fitted, that they were always confirmed—which in the eyes of their admirers constituted the strongest argument in favor of these theories. It began to dawn on me that this apparent strength was in fact their weakness. (Professor K. R. Popper, 1963: 34–35, reproduced by permission)

This quotation illustrates several important issues: (1) the limits of a verificationist approach (i.e., the approach taken by Adler of supporting his theory by looking for confirming instances)—good theories should be potentially capable of discomfirmation; (2) problems of post-hoc explanation (it is easy to fit a theory to facts after the event); (3) the theory-dependence of observation (e.g., Adlerians tend to interpret everything in terms of inferiority complexes); and, finally, (4) the temptation for scientists to jump to conclusions without careful data gathering—Adler might have been more convincing if he had actually seen the child in question!

However, despite these major problems with induction, we are not suggesting that it be abandoned altogether, rather that it be conducted within a rigorous framework and complemented by other approaches, such as deduction and falsification. We will return to this in several subsequent chapters, especially in the section on systematic case studies in Chapter 9.

Deduction and Falsification

Having rejected the principle of induction as a sole, secure foundation for science, Popper attempted to turn the problem on its head: he looked at solutions based on deduction rather than induction, on falsification rather than verification. *Deduction* is the converse of induction: it means going from the theory to a testable prediction, known as a hypothesis. This approach to research, which is the traditional scientific approach within psychology, is known as the *hypothetico-deductive method*.

Popper's landmark volume, *The Logic of Scientific Discovery* (1934/1959), set out to establish a demarcation between science and non-science (or "pseudo-science"). His central criterion was that a science must be able to formulate hypotheses that are capable of *refutation* or, in his preferred terminology, *falsification*. For example, Newtonian physics generates the proposition that a ball thrown up in the air will come down to land again. If tennis balls started shooting out into space, the theory would have a lot of explaining to do. In a more technical example, Newtonian physics also generates the proposition that light travels in a straight line. Although this proposition seems almost self-evident, it was ultimately falsified in a spectacular way by Eddington's expedition to observe a solar eclipse in Africa, in order to test a deduction from Einstein's theory of relativity that light will bend in the presence of a gravitational field.

In psychology, such unequivocal falsifications of theoretically derived predictions are less common. One area where they can be found is in neuropsychological case studies of patients with acquired brain damage. The presence of certain patterns of dysfunction in a single case can be used to refute general theories of mental structure (Shallice, 1988).

As an example of a non-falsifiable theory, consider this statement, by the painter Mondrian: "The positive and the negative break up oneness, they are the cause of all unhappiness. The union of the positive and negative is happiness" (quoted by Wilson, 1990: 144). This certainly appears to be some sort of psychological theory, but it is not clear to what extent it could generate falsifiable propositions, and thus what could be done to test its validity. According to Popper, a statement that cannot be falsified is unscientific (though it is not necessarily meaningless— religion and poetry may have meaning, but they are not falsifiable).

For Popper, good science is characterized by a series of bold conjectures, which will be ultimately falsified. This approach is encapsulated in the title of one his books, *Conjectures and Refutations* (1963). A good theory is one that makes a large number of falsifiable propositions. A bad theory, or an unscientific one, is incapable of falsification. However, all theories must be considered to be tentative; it is impossible to know the world exactly. Every theory in its time will be falsified and replaced by another (as Newtonian mechanics were supplanted by Einstein's theory of relativity).

The falsifiability criterion places those fields which rely on post-hoc explanatory methods outside the boundaries of science. In particular, it rules out psycho-analysis and Marxism, fashionable theories in Popper's Vienna of the 1920s, which he explicitly pointed to as his main targets (Popper, 1963). On the other hand, operant behavioral approaches, with their philosophy of "prediction and control" (Skinner, 1953), would be included as scientific.

This version of falsificationism has a number of problems. The main one is that no theory ever completely accounts for all the known data. Inconsistencies always exist, but the theory may well be retained in spite of them, as they could be explained in other ways than the falsification of the theory, e.g., measurement error or unexplained extra variables. Refutation is never cut and dried: there is always scope to deny that it has occurred. One example is in the extended debate in the psychotherapy outcome literature over the effectiveness of psycho-dynamically oriented therapy. Comparative outcome studies have now demonstrated beyond reasonable doubt that psychodynamically oriented therapy, and other forms of therapy too, have, on average, beneficial effects (e.g., Lambert & Bergin, 1994; Stiles et al., 1986). However, some critics fought a long rearguard action against this conclusion, which was possible to do if the evidence was appraised in a partisan way (Shapiro & Shapiro, 1977), by emphasizing supportive findings while discounting the validity of contradictory data.

Paradigms and Scientific Revolutions

Thus it becomes a central problem to explain how one theory is replaced by another. Since there are always unexplained or contradictory observations within a scientific field, what determines when one theory is rejected and replaced by another? This issue is the point of departure for the work of Thomas Kuhn, one of the central figures of 20th century philosophy of science. In *The Structure of Scientific Revolutions* (1970), he applies the tools of historical analysis to address these questions.

Kuhn proposed the concept of a *paradigm*, that is, the central body of ideas within which the great majority of scientists is working at any given time. The paradigm determines what phenomena scientists consider important and the methods that they use to make their observations. Scientists working within a paradigm are said to be doing *normal science*: they are elaborating theories rather than attempting to refute them. Eventually, the accumulated deficiencies of a paradigm lead to its overthrow and replacement by another paradigm, in what Kuhn labels a *scientific revolution*. For example, the replacement of Aristotelian cosmology (that the earth was the center of the universe) by Copernican theory (that the earth moves around the sun) was a scientific revolution.

The concept of a paradigm is central to Kuhn's work. It fits well with the physical sciences, but there is much debate about how well it can be applied in the social sciences (Lambie, 1991). Is there a guiding paradigm in clinical psychology? Or are there multiple paradigms, indicating that we are still in what Kuhn referred to as a *pre-paradigmatic* state? Arguably, cognitive-behavioral, psychodynamic, and humanistic approaches may be considered as concurrent competing paradigms, although this is perhaps overlooking the large amount of theoretical overlap between competing approaches (Goldfried, 1980).

Kuhn's views and their relationship to those of Popper were hotly debated when they first appeared (Lakatos & Musgrave, 1970). Lakatos accused Kuhn of propounding a "mob psychology" of scientific revolutions (Lakatos, 1970: 178).

The problem in Kuhn's work is that it proposes no criteria for considering one theory better than another, and thus no sense in which scientific understanding could be said to be progressing. Feyerabend's (1975) anarchistic view takes this to an extreme. Under a slogan of "anything goes," Feyerabend appears to be claiming that different theories are "incommensurable" and that there are therefore no rational grounds for preferring one to another. For example, psychoanalysis and experimental psychology may be incommensurable since they have different criteria for what evidence is acceptable: psychoanalysis derives its evidence from the consulting room, experimental psychology from the laboratory (Fonagy, 1982). So the anarchistic view would accord astrology, voodoo, and Babylonian astronomy the same scientific status as quantum mechanics or relativity (Chalmers, 1982). This viewpoint is pithily summed up in a piece of doggerel from the late poet and musician Moondog (1991): "What I say of science here, I say without condition/ That science is the latest and the greatest superstition" (Louis Hardin, Managarm; reproduced by permission).

It seems as though the views of Popper and of Kuhn are themselves "incommensurable" in that they are each using different concepts to discuss somewhat different phenomena. Popper takes a logical approach, Kuhn a historical one. While trying to avoid the danger of falling into a relativist, "anything goes" position ourselves, we contend that much of value can be taken from both writers.

From Popper, researchers can take the central admonition of making bold theories that lead to clear and risky predictions, and being ready to give these theories up in the face of contradictory evidence. Popper also urges researchers to put their thoughts into clear and precise language. As an example, Rogers' (1957) seminal paper on the necessary and sufficient conditions of therapeutic personality change is written with admirable clarity, and makes bold hypotheses about the central mechanisms of therapeutic change.

Kuhn also encourages taking intellectual risks, though from a different standpoint. By clearly delineating the constrictions of "normal science," he provides an implicit critique, helping researchers to be aware of and to question the assumptions of the paradigm within which they work, and to ask whether that paradigm is worth challenging. His work also leads scientists to look ahead to the next paradigm revolution and to ask whether their work will have any enduring value.

Finally, the methodological pluralist stance that informs this book owes something to the spirit that animates Feyerabend's writing. We agree with his stress on the value of diversity and the dangers of scientific conformity. We do, however, strongly disagree with his rejection of the canons of scientific method. As we hope to show, it is possible to articulate criteria to evaluate work conducted within the very different scientific traditions in clinical psychology.

Social and Political Issues

As Kuhn (1970) illustrates, science is not conducted in a cultural and political vacuum. It is carried out by scientists working within a particular scientific, professional, and cultural community at a specific moment in history. Sociologists of knowledge (e.g., Berger & Luckmann, 1966) and social constructionists (e.g., Gergen, 1985) look at how social factors influence the development of thought. For example, what is seen as abnormal behavior varies from culture to culture, and within cultures over time.

Sociological and historical methods can be applied to examine science itself, to look at how socio-economic and political forces shape the kind of science that is practiced within a given culture (Chalmers, 1990; Schwartz, 1992): how one set of ideas gains prominence over another. These analyses have often been carried out within a Marxist framework, which examines the influence of class interests on scientific thought (Albury & Schwartz, 1982). For example, genetic explanations of individual differences in IQ scores fit in well with racist and fascist ideologies, and some of the impetus behind the development of IQ tests undoubtedly arose from such a background (Gould, 1981; Rose et al., 1984).

An example within clinical psychology is the debate about "empirically supported therapies"—the attempt to produce a list of therapies that have been systematically researched and found to be beneficial. Proponents of this project argue that it is a valuable attempt to summarize the state of scientific research on the psychological therapies, and it will ultimately benefit clients; its opponents argue that it is driven by the needs of the US managed care industry to have short-term treatments, and by factions within clinical psychology itself that are seeking to advance their own favored orientations at the expense of other approaches (Elliott, 1998).

Rigid rules for what is and is not science sometimes serve political purposes (e.g., fighting for limited funds from government or universities), and may have the unfortunate consequence of restricting healthy diversity in studying complex clinical phenomena (Elliott, 1998). On the other hand, psychology in general now seems more secure as a discipline, and as a consequence it seems that more psychologists are now freer to work within a broader definition of science and to use a wider range of methods.

One other important source of socio-political influence on scientific activity stems from the fact that research is conducted within an organized professional context. The official pronouncements of the clinical psychology profession have stressed the value of conducting research and have also sought to prescribe what type of research is regarded as legitimate. The various ways that this is expressed are examined next.

PROFESSIONAL ISSUES

It now seems almost uniformly accepted that research should be part of clinical psychologists' training and practice. How did this idea arise? What is the relationship between clinical practice and research? Several models of how practitioners might produce or consume research have been proposed, among them the scientist-practitioner model and the applied-scientist model. It is also worth considering, as a kind of baseline, a model of a psychologist who does not use research, which we have labeled the intuitive practitioner model.

There are several models of how practitioners might produce or consume research:

- The intuitive practitioner, who conducts clinical work on the basis of personal intuition and knowledge from sources other than research.

- The scientist-practitioner, who is competent as both a researcher and a practitioner.

- The applied scientist, who conducts clinical work as a form of applied research.

- The local clinical scientist, who applies a range of research methods and critical thinking skills to solve local problems in clinical settings.

- The evidence-based practitioner, who systematically searches the literature to obtain the best evidence on which to base clinical decisions.

- The clinical scientist, who draws on general psychology to produce research on clinical problems for the evidence-based practitioner to use.

The Intuitive Practitioner

The intuitive practitioner is the therapist who does not conduct research and does not consciously use research findings in their clinical work. Intuitive practitioners conduct clinical work mostly on the basis of knowledge drawn from personal experience, supervision, or reading clinical case reports; they are often highly skilled but are sometimes unable to articulate their implicit knowledge. Most clinical psychologists have probably encountered examples of skilled colleagues or supervisors who fit this description.

It is impossible to say what proportion of psychologists come under this heading. It has often been observed that many clinical psychologists do not do research, nor even consume it (Hayes et al., 1999; Morrow-Bradley & Elliott, 1986; O'Sullivan & Dryden, 1990). A much cited statistic is that the modal number of publications among practicing clinical psychologists is zero. This statistic may give a misleading impression, as psychologists are often involved in research that does not reach the publication stage (Milne et al., 1990). However, it is a salutary reminder to academically oriented clinical psychologists, who have been at the forefront of articulating the more mainstream models of research and practice, that, despite all their earnest pronouncements, research and research findings are generally not at all salient in practicing psychologists' minds. If intuitive practitioners do research at all, it is in the form of clinical observation and narrative case studies.

The Scientist-Practitioner

Since its inception, psychology has been a university-based discipline. It originally emerged out of philosophy in the 19th century and was later aligned with the natural sciences in order to give it increased respectability in the academic world. The profession of clinical psychology started life in the first decades of the 20th century and was initially concerned with "mental testing" as an aid to selection and diagnosis; it was only after World War II that its role expanded to include treatment (Korchin, 1976). However, during its transition from university to clinic, the profession sought to retain its academic roots, in that the distinctive role of the psychologist was seen to lie in his or her academic, scientific, or scholarly viewpoint. As we have mentioned, this academic viewpoint may lead to tensions with other colleagues in multidisciplinary clinical teams.

This scientific role has received somewhat different emphases in the USA and the UK. In the USA it is known as the *scientist-practitioner* (or Boulder) model, in the UK the *applied scientist* model.

The post-war expansion of US clinical psychology, especially in the Veterans Administration Hospitals, led to an upgrading of training from the Masters to the Doctoral level, and to an examination of what such training should consist of (Hayes et al., 1999). The consensus view at the time was expressed in a conference at Boulder, Colorado, in 1949, and became known, naturally enough, as the *Boulder model*. The field was then in its infancy, its knowledge base was tiny, and there was a great need for placing the profession on a firm scientific footing, in order to know whether its procedures worked. The conference concluded that clinical psychologists should be able to function both as scientists and practitioners, capable of conducting research as well as clinical work. A quotation from an article slightly prior to the Boulder conference gives the flavor:

Participants [in doctoral training programs] should receive training in three functions: diagnosis, research, and therapy, with the special contributions of the psychologist as research worker emphasized throughout. (American Psychological Association, 1947: 549)

Thus the scientist-practitioner model emphasizes research and practice as separate, parallel activities. Clinical psychologists are seen as both productive researchers and productive clinicians.

The main limitation of the scientist-practitioner model is that it is hard to put into practice. It demands a high level of skill and motivation in two distinct areas—research and practice—and clinicians who are equally comfortable in both of these areas are rare. Furthermore, the pressures of many clinical psychologists' jobs make it hard to find the time and resources to do research.

The Applied Scientist

In the UK, the applied scientist model took a slightly different emphasis to the American scientist-practitioner model: less on research and clinical work as separate activities, more on the systematic integration of scientific method into clinical work. Monte Shapiro, one of the founders of British clinical psychology, set out the three aspects of the applied scientist role (Shapiro, 1967, 1985):

1. Applying the findings of general psychology to the area of mental health.

2. Only using methods of assessment that had been scientifically validated.

3. Doing clinical work within the framework of the scientific method, by forming hypotheses about the nature and determinants of the client's problems and collecting data to test these hypotheses.

Thus, in Shapiro's applied scientist model, research and practice are not dichotomized but integrated. This approach is also manifested in the behavioral tradition of single case experimental designs (see Chapter 9, this volume, and Hayes et al., 1999).

In sum, the applied scientist is principally a clinician; the scientist-practitioner is both a clinician and a researcher.

The limitations of the applied scientist approach are that, like the scientist-practitioner model, it can be hard to put into practice. It works better within some types of therapy than others (e.g., it is hard to fit psychodynamically oriented therapies into this approach). Also, the intensive collection of session-by-session data can be burdensome for both therapist and client.

The Local Clinical Scientist

Trierweiler and Stricker (1998) have recently put forward the *local clinical scientist* model, a more flexible version of the applied scientist model. Their formulation is worth quoting here:

The local clinical scientist is a critical investigator who uses scientific research and methods, general scholarship, and personal and professional experience to develop plausible and communicable formulations of local phenomena. This investigator draws on scientific theory and research, general world knowledge, acute observational skills, and an open, sceptical stance toward the problem to conduct this inquiry. (pp. 24–25)

Thus, in their formulation, Trierweiler and Stricker emphasize both quantitative and qualitative methods of inquiry, as well as critical thinking skills, all adapted to the local needs and culture of the particular agency within which the clinical psychologist is working. For them, the local clinical scientist is anthropologist, detective, and experimentalist, all rolled into one. While this is clearly a tall order, it can be understood as an aspirational goal.

The scientist-practitioner, applied scientist, and local clinical scientist models all try to encompass research and practice within the same person. At their best, these models all set up a creative tension between practice and research; at their worst, they set up an impossible ideal leading to role strain and, ultimately, cynicism. The final two models, presented next, are recent attempts to resolve the tension by shifting the balance toward either practice or research.

The Evidence-based Practitioner

On the one hand, practitioners can be regarded as consumers rather than producers of research. The notion of basing one's practice on the systematic use of research findings has been part of clinical psychology's ethos since its inception. It has recently found renewed currency within the medical profession. Sackett et al.'s (1997) book, *Evidence-based medicine*, has been influential in articulating how this might work for individual doctors in practice.

Evidence-based medicine is defined as "the conscientious, explicit, and judicious use of current best evidence in making decisions about individual patients" (Sackett et al., 1997: 2). Thus, when faced with a difficult clinical decision, whether it be about diagnosis or treatment, doctors are urged to consult the research literature for an answer. Sackett et al.'s book gives rules for how to judge good research. Evidence from well-conducted randomized controlled trials and meta-analyses are regarded as being especially valuable.

Within clinical psychology, there is a parallel, contemporary movement to identify "empirically supported treatments," which we mentioned earlier in this chapter. This movement has grown out of the understandable need for health-care purchasers (usually insurance companies in the US; the National Health Service in the UK) to be reassured that they are paying for the most cost-effective care. However, there is considerable controversy about whether it is desirable, or even possible, to specify preferred treatments in this way, and particularly about the methods and standards used to designate certain therapies as "efficacious" or not (Elliott, 1998).

The evidence-based practitioner model also leaves aside the question of who will produce new research findings, an issue addressed by the final model.

The Clinical Scientist

At the opposite extreme from the intuitive practitioner is the *clinical scientist* model (not to be confused with the *local* clinical scientist model described above), which has recently emerged in North America (Cherry et al., 2000). In this model, clinical psychologists are first and foremost researchers who study clinical phenomena, usually with substantial background in one or more areas of experimental psychology, and may not be involved in delivering clinical services at all (e.g., Clinical Science Program, Indiana University, n.d.). This is actually not a new model, but has only recently been distinguished from the traditional scientist-practitioner model. In a way, because of its emphasis on general psychology, this model is the opposite of the local clinical scientist. Clinical scientists are portrayed as producers of research for evidence-based practitioners to consume.

This overall division of labor sounds logical, but has several potential drawbacks, all of which stem from the loss of the creative tension between research and practice. First, clinical scientists may be too divorced from clinical practice to produce research that is meaningful to practitioners. Second, in this model, practitioners may be relegated to the role of passive consumers or even technicians. Third, the actual relation between research and practice is more often the opposite to that portrayed in the clinical scientist/research-informed practitioner model: innovations are more likely to emerge out of clinical practice than out of research (Stiles, 1992). Researchers are thus more likely to be consumers of practice (e.g., subjecting clinical hypotheses to rigorous tests) than the other way around.

Comparison of Models

These models each have a different orientation towards research, and emphasize different types of research (see Table 2.1).

Producing Versus Consuming Research

The models can be ranked in terms of how much they regard the practitioner as a producer and as a consumer of research. As we have noted, the scientist-practitioner model assumes that the clinician will be producing research (as well as consuming it), whereas the evidence-based practitioner model emphasizes only the use of research. The applied scientist and local clinical scientist models take a middle position, focusing on doing research within a clinical context. The intuitive practitioner does not produce or consume research, except in the form of case studies. Clinical scientists produce research as their main function.

Type of Research

The scientist-practitioner model places no restriction upon the type of research that psychologists are expected to conduct. The applied scientist model, as its

Table 2.1 Characteristics of professional models

Model	Orientation to research	Research emphasized
Intuitive practitioner	Nonconsumer or indirect consumer	Narrative case studies
Scientist-practitioner	Producer and consumer	Basic and applied
Applied scientist	Integrated with clinical work	Applied small-N
Local clinical scientist	Integrated with clinical work	Evaluation and action
Evidence-based practitioner	Consumer	Controlled trials
Clinical scientist	Producer	Controlled trials

name implies, emphasizes applied research, often single case research or at least research using small sample sizes (see Chapter 9), while the local clinical scientist model emphasizes evaluation and action research. The evidence-based practitioner and clinical scientist models give preference to high-quality randomized controlled trials and meta-analyses.

Current Developments

With the benefit of hindsight, the scientist-practitioner and the applied scientist models appear as ideals that have not been universally adopted or that may not even be universally desirable (Hayes et al., 1999; Peterson, 1991; Shapiro, 1985). Many psychologists have called for a reassessment of the role of research in training. There seems to be some recognition that a broader definition of research needs to be adopted, one that can be more easily integrated with practice (Corrie & Callahan, 2000; Hoshmand & Polkinghorne, 1992; Peterson, 1991). In the USA, this has led to the establishment of "professional schools" of clinical psychology, which award the degree of PsyD (Doctor of Psychology) rather than the PhD, and have a more practice-oriented research dissertation. The local clinical scientist model emerged from this context.

The clinical psychology profession in the UK has recently upgraded its postgraduate qualification from a Masters to a Doctoral level (the Doctorate in Clinical Psychology). This involved a strengthening of the research component of the training, though the D.Clin.Psy. does not require as extensive research as a PhD, which has become a qualification for those who aspire to an academic or research career. It is still too early to appraise the effects of this change on the profession's view of research, but it does seem that the greater stress on teaching research skills has resulted in more of a scientist-practitioner emphasis in training programs; whether this will affect the research productivity of clinical psychologists once they graduate remains to be seen.

PERSONAL ISSUES

Having considered philosophical and professional issues, we now make a transition to the individual level. What motivates the individual clinical psychologist to engage in research—or not to, as the case may be?

> • There are several different reasons that individual clinical psychologists might have for being involved, or not being involved, in research.
>
> • Each psychologist will weigh each one differently.
>
> • It is important for clinical psychologists to reflect on where research fits in to their own practice.

Why do Clinical Psychologists do Research?

We have already mentioned the benefits of conducting research as a systematic way of developing knowledge and theory for the profession and science of clinical psychology. There are also a variety of personal reasons why clinical psychologists may wish to engage in research (Milne, 1987). Some of the more common ones are:

• *Curiosity.* Research exists to answer questions: it must add something to knowledge at the end, otherwise there is no point in doing it. For many researchers, this is an end in itself: they want to make sense of the world and see research as a way of doing so.

• *Personal pleasure.* Some psychologists do research purely for the intrinsic satisfaction. They may enjoy the challenge of research, feel a need to maintain their intellectual sharpness (especially in the middle or later stages of their career), value the contact it brings with other colleagues, or simply see research as a break from everyday routine. There is also the satisfaction of seeing one's work in print and of feeling one is shaping the development of one's profession.

• *Professional and social change.* Ideally, research should not just lead to an accumulation of knowledge, but also to some change in professional practice, or social or legal reforms. Karl Marx's epitaph puts this point forcefully: "Philosophers have interpreted the world, the point, however, is to change it." Many clinicians want to know which interventions work and which do not, and to change their practice, or that of their profession, accordingly. Others are disturbed by the manifest inequalities in western societies, and want to make social or political changes that will alleviate psychological distress (e.g., Joffe & Albee, 1981).

• *Competition between professions and theoretical orientations.* Similarly, some people may be drawn to research as a way of advancing their professional field or favored theoretical orientation. Research is a way of legitimizing existing professional practices and of developing new ones. A large part of applied psychology's claim to professional status is that its procedures were legitimized by research. In marketing jargon, one of psychology's "unique selling points" is that its practitioners possess research expertise.

- *Individual career needs.* The career structure of one's employing institution may dictate that in order to advance up the hierarchy one must conduct research. There are research requirements for clinical psychology students wanting to obtain a professional qualification, and a research track record may be required for appointment to senior positions in the profession.

- *Institutional demands.* In service settings, there is often pressure from management to conduct evaluation or other forms of applied research. For example, the recent move towards "clinical governance" in the British National Health Service calls for practitioners to systematically monitor their treatment outcomes.

- *Research as avoidance.* There may also be negative reasons for conducting research, such as using research to retreat from the stresses of personal contact with clients. Parry and Gowler (1983) look at how psychologists' involvement in research may be a strategy for coping with their occupational stress (if it provides a justification for reducing large caseloads).

Why don't Clinical Psychologists do Research?

Although there are many positive reasons for doing research, psychologists at all levels of experience also voice several reasons to explain why they do not conduct, or draw upon, research (Hayes et al., 1999; Morrow-Bradley & Elliott, 1986):

- *Irrelevance.* Research is seen as not saying anything useful about practice. It is seen as being over-concerned with rigor at the expense of relevance (i.e., journals are filled with rigorous but irrelevant studies). The main source of learning is felt to be clinical practice, rather than research studies.

- *Emphasis on generalities.* There is a tension between the scientific stance, which looks for generalities and lawfulness, and the clinical stance, which stresses human individuality. Most research has been done within the nomothetic tradition, which emphasizes pooling people together to look for commonalities, rather than the idiographic tradition, which emphasizes individual uniqueness (Allport, 1962).

- *Mistaken paradigm.* The positivist paradigm (see Chapter 4), under which much research is conducted, is seen as being reductive and simplistic. This paradigm may be linked with macro-political structures, e.g., feminists have critiqued the patriarchal nature of traditional psychological research and Marxists have critiqued psychology's emphasis on individualism at the expense of collectivism (see Chapter 5).

- *Intrusiveness.* Research is seen as a blunt instrument that crushes the phenomenon under study. Much as zoologists may kill a butterfly to study it, so, for example, the intrusion of research procedures into a therapeutic relationship is felt to damage that relationship. For instance, therapists often fear that the act of tape recording a session might severely distort the therapy process, e.g., by making the client apprehensive about confidentiality issues.

- *Time demands*. Research is time consuming and often has a low priority compared to service demands. Also, it is often not supported or valued by managers or colleagues.

- *Technical expertise*. Research is seen as requiring considerable technical expertise, with journal editors and other gate-keepers setting prohibitively high standards that discourage beginning researchers.

- *Ethics*. Research in general is felt to dehumanize participants subtly (or not so subtly in some cases) by turning them into "subjects." In addition, there are ethical problems with some psychological studies, e.g., those using deception.

- *Bad training experiences*. For various reasons, during their training many clinical psychologists experience research as a painful, alienating process. For example, some may feel forced to study something they find uninteresting, or may feel inadequate for not being research-oriented. Others fail to receive sufficient direction or support for their research, and therefore find it to be a lonely or unmanageable activity.

- *Being scrutinized*. Research participants can feel scrutinized, which may arouse great anxiety. This may make the conduct of the research project very difficult, particularly in evaluation studies, where the continuation of a service may depend on the findings.

- *Disturbing conclusions*. Research may come up with findings that you do not like. It can lead to a painful re-examination of your cherished ideas if they do not match up to the facts. It may challenge your assumptions and ways of working, and this can be an uncomfortable process.

The last two reasons have to do with the threatening aspects of research. Sometimes, these feelings of threat may not be directly acknowledged, but instead find their expression in the form of some of the other reasons listed. For example, practicing therapists may, understandably, feel sensitive about being scrutinized, and therefore may be reluctant to participate in a project which involves tape recording their sessions. However, they may argue against the project because of intrusiveness for the client, rather than admitting their own sense of vulnerability.

Summary

Different individuals will weigh each of the above positive and negative considerations differently. Some concentrate entirely on being a practicing clinician and never conduct research again once their training is completed. Others concentrate on an academic career and do little if any practice. Many, however, take a middle road, combining the two activities in their professional work, although perhaps only consuming research and not conducting it. We hope to show, in the remainder of this book, that doing research need not be a formidable challenge and that it is possible to conduct research even if you work primarily in a service setting. We will also offer practical advice aimed at making your research experience more interesting and less painful.

CHAPTER SUMMARY

In one sense, there is nothing special about doing research, in that the process of psychological research is similar to that of open-minded enquiry in everyday life. However, research is a disciplined and self-conscious activity that can be quite demanding. Clinical psychology considers itself to be scientific, but it is not easy to pin down exactly what science consists of. Several philosophers have attempted to characterize the essence of scientific progress: Popper, Kuhn, and Feyerabend are central figures. Science is a human enterprise, and its development is shaped by social and political forces. The scientist-practitioner model, and the closely related applied scientist model, are a central part of clinical psychology's professional ideology. However, there is often a gap between the rhetoric and the reality: many clinical psychologists do not do research once they have qualified. Practicing clinical psychologists may choose to do research, or not to, for a variety of personal reasons. This chapter has attempted to shed light on the research process from three perspectives: philosophical, professional, and personal. It is useful to keep these background issues in mind while planning, conducting, and reading research.

FURTHER READING

The Oxford Companion to Philosophy (Honderich, 1995) is a magnificent resource for anyone needing to know what all those troublesome "-isms" actually mean (and indeed for anyone at all curious about Life, the Universe and Everything). Alan Chalmers, in his two books *What is This Thing Called Science?* (1982) and *Science and its Fabrication* (1990), explains complex philosophy of science issues with admirable clarity. However, he draws most of his examples from the natural sciences. Polkinghorne's (1983) *Methodology for the Human Sciences* gives a thorough review of the range of philosophy of science positions, including alternatives to the traditional views, as applied to the social sciences. Since Popper and Kuhn are so often referred to, it is worth reading them both in the original. The obvious choice from Kuhn's work is *The Structure of Scientific Revolutions* (1970). For Popper the choice is wider. Perhaps his most accessible work is *Conjectures and Refutations* (1963), especially the chapter of the same title.

Research in the context of professional issues is surveyed in Hayes et al. (1999) and Korchin (1976) from an American perspective, and by Pilgrim and Treacher (1992) from a British one. Roth et al. (1996) give an interesting discussion of the relationship between research and practice.

CHAPTER 3

DOING THE GROUNDWORK

KEY POINTS IN THIS CHAPTER

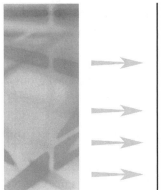

This chapter focuses on practical issues in getting a research project started:

choosing a topic and formulating the research questions or hypotheses;

searching the literature;

writing a proposal and applying for funding; and

dealing with the organizational politics of research in clinical settings.

In sharp contrast to the previous chapter, this one focuses on practical rather than theoretical issues. It covers the first stage of the research process, which we label the groundwork stage. The researcher's primary task at this stage is to formulate a set of research questions, often including specific hypotheses; the secondary task is to tackle organizational or political issues, in order to prepare the ground for data collection. Researchers often apply for ethics committee approval and for funding at this stage.

In practice, as we noted in Chapter 1, the groundwork stage overlaps with the other two planning stages: selecting the measures and specifying the design. We are separating them here for didactic reasons, but assume that readers who are actually planning a project are working concurrently on measurement and design. For example, we cover funding issues here, but if you are applying for funding, the grant-giving committee will want a full plan of your research. Similarly, when you are applying for ethics approval, you will also need to submit a detailed plan of the project.

Planning the study is usually quite anxiety provoking, both because you are grappling with difficult intellectual and organizational problems, and also because researchers often feel that they are not being productive if they are not collecting or analyzing data. You may be tempted to get the planning over and done with as soon as possible. This is usually a mistake. We have been involved with many studies, including some of our own, which have suffered because of inadequate planning. A poorly planned study can cause hours of frustration at the analysis and interpretation stage, and, at an extreme, may produce worthless results because of design faults or poorly thought-out research questions. Furthermore, such studies can be confusing to read, as the research questions and the research methods are often not fully consistent with one another. Time put in at the early stages often repays itself with interest later on, so it is worth trying to contain your anxiety and take time over the planning.

This chapter has two sections. The first considers how the research questions are formulated and specified in a research proposal. The second looks at the politics of research in clinical settings and other organizations, in particular how research in such settings can easily come to grief. Ethical issues, which often need to be addressed at this stage, are covered in Chapter 10, where we discuss the topic of research participants.

FORMULATING THE RESEARCH QUESTIONS

Key points:

- The process of planning research is painstaking and often anxiety provoking, but effort put in here usually pays off later.

- Research questions can be either exploratory (open-ended) or confirmatory (hypothesis testing).

- Various databases can be used to locate relevant literature.

- The planning process is iterative: feedback from colleagues, and one's own second thoughts, mean that it is usual to take proposals through several drafts.

- Research should generally be question-driven rather than method-driven. The essence of planning good research is making the procedures fit the questions, rather than the other way around.

The first step in undertaking a piece of research is obviously to select a topic to investigate. By topic we mean a broad area of interest, such as "depression in children," "marital communication," or "something in the area of therapy process." This is all that is needed at the beginning of the project. As the planning progresses, the topic will become more and more focused, until you eventually arrive at some specific research questions.

It is valuable to start keeping a personal research journal from the time you begin to think about your research questions. In it you can record the development of your ideas as the project progresses. You can also note your thoughts, feelings and general reactions to the research process. For example, it is useful at the end of the project to have a record of where you've come from and why you took the decisions that you did (sometimes it's hard to remember!). You might also use the research journal during data collection and analysis, especially with qualitative projects, to record your thoughts about the meaning of your data. Such "research memos" (Strauss & Corbin, 1998) can be incorporated into the analysis and write-up of the project.

Choosing the Topic

Ideally, the topic will arise naturally out of an intrinsic interest in the area, perhaps stimulated by clinical work, reading, or issues that have arisen in your personal life. (However, it may be unwise to research a topic that is too close to you personally, as it makes it hard to attain the necessary critical detachment. If you're in the middle of a divorce, you may want to avoid doing research on marital satisfaction. On the other hand, doing research on an issue that you are personally involved in does give you give you the benefit of experiential knowledge that an outside researcher cannot possess.) All things being equal, it is better to choose a topic that excites or interests you, as you may have to live with it for a long time and the personal interest will help keep you going. In the case of PhD research, your choice of topic may influence the direction of your subsequent career.

If the research is being done for extrinsic reasons (the prime example being when it is undertaken to fulfil a degree requirement), the problem arises of what to do when inspiration fails to strike. In this case, there are several possibilities. The first is to talk to a colleague or potential supervisor, ideally someone whose work you admire, to see if they can suggest a topic. The second is to go to the library and browse through some current books and journals until something takes your fancy. The third is to choose a topic on practical grounds. Is there some research going on in your institution that you could slot into? Is someone conducting a large project that you could take a part of? The disadvantages of working on a large project are that you may have less sense of ownership and achievement, as the study will not be directly yours; compensating advantages are being able to work with a team and often having some assistance with data collection and analysis.

Developing the Questions

Having chosen your general topic area, the next step is to narrow it down into specific research questions or hypotheses. This step is important to get right, because, as we shall often argue, the methods of the research will flow naturally from the questions that are asked. Similarly, when you read a research article, the first thing to look for is precisely what questions the study is trying to answer. Some papers will clearly state their questions or hypotheses, usually at the end of the introduction section, others will leave the reader to infer them from the general drift of the paper. It makes it much easier for the reader to understand and evaluate the study if its questions are clearly spelled out.

The first step is to formulate a few initial questions that encapsulate what you wish to find out from the study. It is a good idea to ask yourself what is the most important thing that you intend the project to tell you. Keeping this in mind helps you make choices later on if the study starts to become overly complicated. The number and complexity of the research questions will depend upon the time scale and the available resources. Practitioners doing service-oriented research on their own, or students carrying out a supervised project, will need to ask circumscribed questions. Funded research teams undertaking multi-year projects can set themselves much more ambitious targets.

Always bear in mind that the research must be able to teach you something: there is no point in doing a project if it simply confirms what you knew before you started it. As we noted in the previous chapter, research should put one's expectations or beliefs at risk, in the sense that it could falsify cherished ideas. It is worth trying to "game out" the study (Horowitz, 1982; Patton, 1997): in other words, ask yourself what are its possible outcomes, what would you learn from each of them, and which ones would make a difference in how you think about or what you do about the topic you are studying. Good studies yield useful information whatever their outcome, even if they fail to confirm initial predictions.

It is not usually possible to formulate clear and useful research questions at the beginning of the planning phase of the study. You need to pose an initial question, and then refine it by reading the literature, consulting with colleagues, deciding what is feasible in your intended research setting, considering what is practicable in terms of measurement and research design, and conducting pilot studies. This process of refining the research questions often takes several months. In their final form, the questions should be clear and concise, so that there is no ambiguity about what the study is aiming to achieve.

It is important to begin by formulating the research questions in advance of developing your procedures. Beginning researchers often rush into selecting the measures that they will use before considering clearly what they really want to find out. This inevitably muddles their thinking and limits the range of questions they consider. For example, we have often seen researchers use measures simply because they are easily available and well known (locus of control springs to mind as an example). The essence of planning good research is *appropriate methods*: making the research procedures fit the questions rather than the other way around. In other words, the study should generally be question-driven rather than method-driven.

Hypothesis-testing versus Exploratory Research Questions

A *hypothesis* is a statement of a proposition that will be tested by the research (although in practice it can be phrased either as a statement or as a question). It expresses a tentative prediction of the results that are expected to emerge. For example, a study of whether clients fare better with culturally similar therapists hypothesized that "ethnic or linguistic matches between therapists and clients

Table 3.1   Hypothesis-testing and exploratory approaches to research

	Hypothesis-testing	Exploratory
Logic	Hypothetico-deductive	Inductive
Scientific context	Confirmatory	Discovery-oriented
Example 1: Recovery from alcohol abuse	Is the first month of sobriety more difficult (in terms of psychological symptoms) than the sixth month?	How does the experience of sobriety evolve over the first six months?
Example 2: Wearing a nicotine patch (adapted from Tiffany et al., 2000)	Does wearing a transdermal nicotine patch reduce craving when a smoker is exposed to a smoking cue (seeing someone else light up a cigarette)?	What is the experience of wearing a nicotine patch (including emotions, cognitions, perceptions)?

result in less premature termination...and better client outcomes than do mismatches" (Sue et al., 1991: 534).

The advantages of a carefully formulated hypothesis are that it gives an immediate clarity and focus to the investigation and it enables you to know immediately whether or not the findings of the study support its predictions. It is part of the *hypothetico-deductive* view of science, which emphasizes the use of theory and previous research to generate testable hypotheses (as in Popper's view of the scientific method: see Chapter 2). Using hypotheses also has the merit of increasing precision and fitting in more closely with the theory of statistical inference (Howell, 2002).

On the other hand, stating the research questions in open-ended question form allows an *exploratory, discovery-oriented* approach (e.g., Elliott, 1984; Mahrer, 1988), in contrast to the *confirmatory* approach of the hypothetico-deductive model (see Table 3.1). There may not be sufficient theory or previous research to be able to make meaningful hypotheses, or you may not want to constrain your investigation early on. What is important is to be clear about what you are trying to investigate. Exploratory, discovery-oriented research questions are typically descriptive. The research questions that guide exploratory research should be clearly delineated, in order to narrow the research topic to workable size and to provide a central focus for data collection and analysis. The question "What is the nature of clients' experiences in therapy?" would be too broad (at least for a student research study; but see Rennie, 1990); a more narrow question such as "What is the nature of clients' experiences of withholding their negative reactions from therapists?" would be more workable (Rennie, 1994). If you take the attitude, "I want to study x, so I'll just collect some data and see what is interesting," you are likely to end up with an incoherent mishmash of findings.

Open-ended, discovery-oriented research questions are typically most appropriate under the following circumstances:

• When a research area is relatively new or little is known about it, making it difficult or premature to ask more specific questions.

• When a research area is confusing, contradictory, or not moving forward. This may be due to narrow conceptualization or premature quantification prior to adequate open-ended descriptive work.

• When the topic is a highly complex event, process, or human experience, requiring careful definition or description.

The Role of Theory

As we noted in Chapter 2, research is always conducted within an explicit or implicit theoretical framework. Therefore, it is almost always useful to work at developing that framework and making it more explicit. For one thing, conducting your research within an explicit theoretical framework will guide the formulation of research questions. As Kurt Lewin famously said, "There is nothing so practical as a good theory" (quoted in Marrow, 1969). Thus, it is an excellent idea to devote time early in the research process to locating an existing theoretical model or to formulating your own model. You can do this by trying to map out the likely relationships between the variables you are studying. For example, if you are studying the relationship between therapist empathy and client outcome, you might think about what some of the intervening processes might be, as well as variables that might affect both empathy and outcome. Therapist empathy might facilitate client self-exploration which might lead to better outcome, or client pretreatment self-awareness might facilitate both therapist empathy and client outcome (see Chapter 8). From a different theoretical perspective, therapist empathy might act as a reinforcer for client disclosure of feelings or statements of positive self-esteem. The theoretical model could then guide the selection of specific correlational or comparative research questions, suitable for quantitative investigation.

Even in exploratory research, it is good practice for researchers to try to be as explicit as possible about their implicit theories or "preunderstandings" (Packer & Addison, 1989), in the form of expectations, hunches or possible biases. The difference is that in exploratory research these implicit theories are set aside (referred to as "bracketing": see Chapter 5) rather than explicitly tested. After an exploratory study is completed, the researcher may find it useful to compare the actual results to these original expectations, in order to determine what has been learned.

Some Types of Research Questions

There are a number of different types of research question, which are often associated with different approaches to research. For example, questions about description often lend themselves to discovery-oriented qualitative research, while questions about correlation and causality usually lead to quantitative methods. Since we have not yet discussed these specific procedures, we will not pursue this notion of appropriate methods here; we will return to it in subsequent chapters. We present some common types of questions below (see Elliott, 2000; Horowitz, 1982; Meltzoff, 1998 for a more extensive treatment).

Description

What is X like? What are its features, characteristics, or variations? How frequent or common is it?

Examples:

What are patients' experiences of personal safety on psychiatric inpatient units?

What do people with bipolar affective disorder find helpful about mutual support groups?

Which verbal response modes are most frequently used by cognitive therapists?

How common is borderline personality disorder?

Descriptive questions usually aim to provide a full picture of an experience or condition, including its variations. They might focus on its origin and development, or seek to provide examples of typical cases. Descriptive questions might also focus on amount or frequency, such as in epidemiological survey research.

Descriptive-comparison

Does group X differ from group Y?

Examples:

Do men and women differ in emotional expressiveness?

What kinds of interactions occur in families with aggressive boys, compared to those with non-aggressive boys?

Is childhood sexual abuse more common in bulimic than in non-bulimic individuals?

This type of question extends the simple descriptive question. Note that it does not address issues of causality, although causality may be implied, as in the last example on bulimia. These questions aim to compare two or more groups of people who are defined in terms of some pre-existing differences, such as gender, socioeconomic status, or diagnostic category. However, questions addressing differences resulting from an experimental intervention (e.g., a therapeutic intervention) come under the heading of causality questions, below.

Correlation

Do X and Y covary, i.e., is there a relationship between them? Is that relationship affected by a third variable Z?

Examples:

Is degree of marital support associated with speed of recovery from depression?

Is burnout among psychiatric nurses related to their experience of physical assault?

Does ethnic background affect the relationship between school achievement and children's self-esteem?

Correlational questions focus on investigating a possible association between two or more variables. These associations are often ones that have been predicted on the basis of theory or previous research. Although correlational questions may arise from an interest in causal explanations, they cannot be used to investigate causality.

Causality

Does X cause change in Y? Does X cause more change in Y than does Z?

Examples:

Do parent training groups lead to more effective parenting?

Does family therapy prevent relapse in patients diagnosed as schizophrenic?

Does taking Ecstasy lead to impairments in memory?

Is cognitive therapy more effective than treatment as usual for clients with borderline personality disorder?

This type of question goes beyond the descriptive-comparison and correlation questions in attempting to look at causal influences. Establishing causal influence usually requires some sort of experimental design (Cook & Campbell, 1979; see also Chapters 8 and 9). Some of these questions are phrased with an explicit comparison; e.g., in the final example above, cognitive therapy is explicitly compared to treatment as usual. In other questions, the comparison is implicit; e.g., in the first example, parent training is implicitly compared with no parent training. More elaborate questions can also be asked, concerning interactions between variables (Meltzoff, 1998), e.g., "Is cognitive therapy more effective than treatment as usual for male clients with borderline personality disorder, but not for female clients?"

Measurement

How well (reliably, validly, and usefully) can X be measured by means of measure M?

Examples:

Can subtypes of marital conflict be measured reliably and distinguished from one another?

How consistent are clients' ratings on the Working Alliance Inventory over the course of therapy?

Is the Group Environment Scale a good way to measure the climate of multidisciplinary team meetings?

These questions often have some overlap with other question types. For example, the second question, on the working alliance, is similar to a descriptive-comparison question (comparing clients' views at two or more time points), and the third question, on group climate, implies a question about correlation (how well does this measure correlate with other similar measures). However, the distinguishing feature is that these questions focus on the performance of a specific measurement instrument, rather than the construct underlying the measure.

Literature Review

Once the topic area has been chosen, the process of reviewing the literature starts, proceeding in parallel and in interaction with the process of formulating the research questions. The literature review is done for several reasons:

- To assess how well developed the literature is, what kinds of gaps there are in it, and whether there has been sufficient preliminary descriptive research to define the phenomena of interest.

- To see how far the existing literature answers the research questions. What can the proposed study add to the existing literature? Is there a need for another study? Has the study been done before? However, study duplication is rarely a great problem, because no two people ever seem to design a study in the same way and because it is always easy to devise variations on something that has already been done before.

- To help formulate the research questions in the light of theory or previous research, and possibly to give a theoretical or conceptual framework to work within.

- To help with measurement and design issues. To see what measures and approaches have been used in previous studies, and what are the strengths and weaknesses of previous designs.

In established research areas, there may be an enormous amount of literature, which can seem daunting to get to grips with. Several information sources can help speed up the process of reviewing psychological literature:

- Library catalogues can be used to locate books by author, title, or subject. Also, the low-tech method of just browsing along library shelves, especially new acquisitions shelves, can often yield a useful collection of books to help start your search.

- Handbooks. Current editions of handbooks in the topic area, e.g., Baum et al. (2001) for health psychology, Bergin & Garfield (1994) for psychotherapy research, and Hess & Weiner (1999) for forensic psychology, all have chapters by expert authors providing comprehensive reviews of focused topic areas.

- *PsycINFO* (a computerized version of *Psychological Abstracts*) is an American Psychological Association database which indexes journal articles, books, and technical reports. Literature searches can be conducted by selecting terms from the Thesaurus of Psychological Index Terms, or text from titles and abstracts, as well as authors' names.

- *MedLine* (a computerized version of *Index Medicus*), is a national Library of Medicine database which indexes journals across the whole field of biomedicine. It is available on the internet at http://www.ncbi.nlm.nih.gov/entrez/

- *Science Citation Index* and *Social Science Citation Index* from the Institute for Scientific Information index a broad range of science and social science journals. Their unique feature is the cited reference search, to see which articles have cited (or have been cited by) a particular author or work. If a field has a few key papers, it can quickly show who is citing them. (It is also useful for established researchers who want to know who is citing their own publications. Aside from giving narcissistic pleasure, this can also be useful to see who is working in the same research area.)

- Web searches, utilizing a reliable search engine such as Google (http://www.google.com), on the topic area, or on the names of some key authors, can often be useful. It is wise to exercise caution when evaluating the validity of information on the world wide web. Gateways such as SOSIG (Social Sciences Information Gateway at http://www.sosig.ac.uk/), BIOME (http://biome.ac.uk/), or BUBL (http://link.bubl.ac.uk/) are an excellent starting point for identifying good-quality internet sites.

- Current journals of interest in your area. It is worthwhile browsing through the last few years' issues of the three or four most important journals covering your topic area. *Current Contents,* from the Institute for Scientific Information, is a current awareness resource, listing the contents pages of journals in specified fields.

- *PsycSCAN* is a quarterly journal, published by the American Psychological Association, containing abstracts of journal articles covering specific specialties. For example, there are *PsycSCANs* in clinical psychology, psychoanalysis, etc.

- Review publications. *Clinical Psychology Review, Clinical Psychology: Science and Practice*, and *Evidence-Based Mental Health* are journals that publish review articles on major areas of research that are relevant to clinical practice. The *Annual Review of Psychology* has authoritative reviews of contemporary developments across the whole of psychology (and there are also *Annual Reviews* in related disciplines, e.g., public health and sociology).

- The *Cochrane Collaboration* (http://www.cochrane.org) is another excellent source of authoritative, contemporary reviews of clinically relevant topics.

Also remember that librarians are there to be helpful. They are experts in locating information and can help you to find the best sources of reference, or to use sources that you have difficulty with. Since new sources are appearing frequently, especially on the web, it is very useful to have specialist help in your search.

The Proposal

As your ideas start to become clearer, it is worth setting them down on paper. This will help you show other people what you are planning to do (if you can bear exposing your less than perfect ideas to other people) and it will also help you develop your thoughts yourself, as it is much easier to re-think something that is down on paper rather than just in your head.

At the very least, prepare a one- to three-page summary of your proposed research questions, the theoretical model, and your measures and design. You can use this to get some initial feedback, recruit research supervisors (in the USA, doctoral committee members) and get early consultations. You can then expand it into a longer proposal.

Often (e.g., for PhD research and grant applications) a formal research proposal is required. This is usually not wasted effort, as the proposal will form the core of the introduction and method sections of your final report. It is best approached by successive approximations. The first step is to draft a rough outline, to get something down on paper, no matter how sketchy. Proposals evolve through multiple drafts—six or seven is common—as you continue to read, talk and think about the project.

The structure of the proposal is similar to the introduction and method section of a journal article. It should state what the research topic is and why it is important, briefly review what has already been done and what psychological theory can be brought to bear on the problem, and summarize the intended study and its research questions or hypotheses. The method section describes in detail the proposed design and measurement aspects of the study. A typical proposal has the following structure:

Outline of a research proposal

Introduction
    Statement of the research topic and its importance
    Focused literature review (covering previous research and psychological theory)
    Rationale for and overview of the proposed study
    Research questions or hypotheses
Method
    Participants
    Design
    Measures
    Ethical considerations
    Data analysis procedures
    Expected results and implications (optional)
    Timetable (optional; see below)
References
Costings (for grant proposals)

You may want to give an estimated timetable for the project in your proposal. Even if you do not include one, it is usually helpful at this stage to map one out for your own consumption. List each of the major tasks that comprise the project and try to estimate how long each one will take and what other tasks need to be completed before it can be done. However, one rule of thumb, especially in doctoral research, is to double any time estimate: expect everything to take twice as long as you think it will (Hodgson & Rollnick, 1996). In our experience, the most common causes of problems in student projects are a slow initial start and unexpected delays later on, often out of your control (e.g., ethics committees, access to participants, and data collection problems).

Table 3.2 gives a possible timetable for a two-year student project.

Table 3.2 Possible timetable for a two-year student project

Month 1	Start reading the background literature in your general area of interest.
Months 2–4	Decide on the topic and formulate preliminary research questions. Find a supervisor. Continue the literature review.
Months 5–6	Draft a one- or two-page proposal. Discuss the project in the setting in which you will carry it out.
Month 7	Apply to your local ethics committee for approval.
Month 8	Finalize the research plan and prepare for data collection.
Month 9	Begin data collection.
Month 10	Write the first draft of the introduction and method sections.
Months 11–18	Data collection continues. Re-draft the introduction and method sections.
Month 19	Finish data collection. Begin data analysis.
Months 20–21	Complete the data analysis. Write the first draft of the results and discussion sections.
Months 22–23	Complete the write-up. Give the final draft to your supervisor for comments. Make any advance arrangements for duplication and binding.
Month 24	Make final corrections. Duplicate, bind, and submit the polished version.

Consultations

It is a good idea to get a variety of opinions on your proposal from people of different backgrounds: for example, colleagues who know the research area, potential research supervisors, psychologists outside of your area, non-psychologists, and clients or ex-clients from the population that you are studying. No research is carried out in isolation: it is always helpful to get input from lay people and from colleagues in the scientific community. Even if many of their suggestions cannot be implemented, you will often find that something of value emerges each time you present your ideas to someone else.

You may also want to email some key researchers in the field, to ask for measures, reprints, or details of current work. Also, consider attending a conference, as this is an excellent way to meet people with similar interests in order to exchange ideas, learn about work that has not yet reached the journals, and generally make connections.

Piloting

Pilot studies are small-scale try-outs of various aspects of your intended protocol. Initial pilots may be done with colleagues or friends role-playing participants. This will help you get the administrative procedures roughly right and reveal any gross errors in measurement or design. Subsequent pilots can be with people closer to the target population that you intend to study.

The importance of piloting cannot be stressed enough. Just as a jumbo jet is not built straight from the drawing board without extensive testing, it is rarely possible to design a study in your armchair and then translate it straight into action. You always need to test out procedures, measures, and design. Some things that look good on paper just do not work in practice: they are not understandable to participants or they do not yield useful information. It is also worthwhile performing a few crucial analyses on the pilot data to try out coding and analysis procedures and to see whether the data can actually be used to answer the research questions. A few hours here can save you weeks or months of anguish later on.

Funding

It is often possible to get funding for clinical psychology research, if you plan your application in advance. The major expense in most psychological research projects is research assistant time. (Grants will rarely support the principal investigator, on the assumption that they are earning a salary from the sponsoring institution.) A secondary expense will be equipment (e.g., for computing or tape recording) and supplies (e.g., printing, photocopying, and postage), although this part of the budget will usually be small, in contrast to biomedical research, where equipment is often a major part of the budget.

The format for proposals varies from agency to agency; it is important to obtain applicants' guidelines from potential agencies before starting work on the proposal. However, most proposals will follow the broad outline we have discussed above, with a final section on the proposed costs and timetable of the research (Brooks, 1996). The goal of the proposal is to convince the awarding body that you have a well thought-out plan for innovative and valuable research. The opinions of nonspecialist colleagues can help predict how the agency might react to your proposal.

Grant-giving bodies often employ a multi-stage screening process. Administrative staff will first read your proposal to check that it falls within the mission of the funding body and that its estimated costs are reasonable. Then it will be sent out to professional reviewers, who will be familiar with the area of research that you are proposing. They will give it an overall rating and supply a detailed report. These will be considered by a meeting of the grant-giving committee, who will be professionals in the field, though probably not specialists in your area. They will be looking to support proposals that demonstrate scientific excellence and have a realistic estimate of costs and timetable.

Specific sources of funds are too numerous and rapidly changing to list here. They can be classified into central and local government agencies, charities, businesses, universities, and health service bodies. Many universities, especially in the USA, have officials that can help you identify funding sources for your research. Competition is great, and even if your project is turned down, it does not mean that it was not worthwhile. It is worth asking to see the referees' reports, if they are available, to identify any weaknesses in your proposal before revising and resubmitting it elsewhere.

THE POLITICS OF RESEARCH IN APPLIED SETTINGS

Key points:

- A good relationship between the researcher and the setting is vital to the success of the project.

- A poor relationship can complicate, delay, or thwart the project.

- Access to research settings is often controlled by official or unofficial gatekeepers.

- It is important to get people in the setting on your side and to respond honestly to their doubts about the research.

Researchers often underestimate the organizational difficulties of conducting research in field, as opposed to laboratory, settings. Obtaining access, especially to highly bureaucratic settings such as hospitals, schools, and mental health agencies, may require months. It is vital to start doing your groundwork early on, in order to establish whether it is viable to do the study in your proposed setting. You need to develop a relationship with the gatekeepers and managers, as well as with the clients, staff, etc. Although some people will be supportive of your research, others will oppose it, not always openly.

Access

Negotiating access often requires considerable flexibility, political savvy, and interpersonal skills. Many researchers simply avoid the whole process by creating their own settings, which they can more thoroughly control (Cook & Campbell, 1979). However, if you want to study settings outside the laboratory or research clinic, access problems are hard to avoid.

The first step is to identify and approach the *gatekeepers* of the setting (Taylor & Bogdan, 1998), that is, those who control access and help protect it from disruptive outside interests. Gatekeepers vary in their apparent social and political power, from receptionists who screen out unwanted inquiries to managers, senior doctors, head teachers, or school principals. An initial working knowledge of the role structure and formality of the setting greatly facilitates the access process and may prevent disasters or wasted effort. Cowen and Gesten (1980) recommend starting at the top of the setting and working your way down (otherwise, leaders are likely to be insulted or suspicious and refuse permission on general principles). They also note that newer programs tend to be less formal and more flexible. It is generally useful to have a prior association with the setting or the support of someone who is trusted (Cook & Campbell, 1979; Taylor & Bogdan, 1998).

If you have not already, it is important to begin your research journal at this point and, in addition, qualitative researchers may start keeping detailed field notes. The access process often yields essential information about how the setting functions and how it protects itself, which is worth describing in its own right.

The next step is to present your request to conduct research in the setting. Be clear about what you are proposing to do. It often helps to avoid misinterpretation if you put things in writing, stating the general aim of the research and how the data will be collected. This is an adaptation of the brief proposal that we suggested above, in everyday, jargon-free language; you might do it as a kind of press release, such as would be given out to a local newspaper. A draft participant information sheet and informed consent form (see Chapter 10) is often needed. It is advisable to make your own presentations to the administration or staff, rather than giving in to the temptation to let someone else do it for you, as they will often forget or do a poor job of it (Cowen & Gesten, 1980). Presentations to staff meetings should also be supplemented with personal meetings, especially with resistant individuals, preferably in their own setting rather than yours.

In addition, there is often a formal screening process, such as a human subjects review or research ethics committee. We will address ethical issues in Chapter 10, but it is worth anticipating substantial delays, which may be difficult if you are a student trying to complete your research within a tight timetable. Delays may occur for two reasons. First, ethics committees may meet infrequently or at intervals that do not fit in well with your plans. Second, they may raise objections about your research, which you will need to respond to (sometimes involving substantial changes to the protocol) before you proceed with the study.

Responding to Doubts

You often have to work to get people's goodwill and to get them on your side. They may not be convinced by your research topic—people in applied settings may have little understanding of psychological research—but at least they should trust you. A senior doctor once said to one of us, "I'm allergic to anything beginning with psych!", but he was still willing to cooperate with our project because he trusted us.

People might oppose your project for rational, practical reasons, as even the best-run projects inevitably cause disruption, and some services are constantly being asked permission to conduct studies. They might also oppose it in order to protect patients, who may be in danger of being over-researched, even with adequate informed consent procedures. For example, we are aware of projects that have been turned down in services for post-traumatic stress disorder because of patients being on the receiving end of too much research. There are also instances of researchers who exploit the people in the setting by, for example, failing to keep them informed or not acknowledging their contribution when the research is published.

In addition to these rational, practical concerns, research in service settings often arouses feelings of threat and suspicion (Hardy, 1993; Weiss, 1972). It can be seen as intrusive, critical, and a challenge to the established way of doing things. Be sensitive to such opposition: if you do not listen to and attempt to meet people's fears at the planning stage, the likelihood is that the study will be undermined later on. Often these fears may be expressed indirectly: medical and nursing staff may appear overly protective of "their" patients, forms may be mysteriously lost, and so on.

Furthermore, your research may become embroiled in the internal politics of the setting. It is important to be aware of existing organizational tensions, as your study may be used as part of a power struggle: different factions may gain from seeing it carried out or from blocking it (Hardy, 1993).

Your clinical and consulting skills are often valuable in both understanding and in responding sensitively to the doubts of other people about the research. In responding to their often complex feelings it is important to be open about what you intend to do and why. Goodman (1972) describes how he put the client-centered principles of disclosure, empathy, and acceptance into action in a large community psychology project which evaluated the effects of companionship therapy for emotionally troubled boys:

> . . . A careless procedural mistake or two, showing cause for mistrust and generating serious community complaint, could close down the project. We therefore sought to reduce risks by establishing some global operating principles that would simultaneously protect our participants and our research goals.
>
> Eventually, the principles took the form of a general approach, or a 'clinical attitude' toward the community, consistent with the client-centered theory of effective therapist–client relationships. That is, we would try to empathize with any complaints about us, accept community apprehension and protective activities, and disclose our own needs and plans—including the global intervention strategy . . . Sometimes we also disclosed the motives for our disclosures (meta-disclosure). Implementing this approach took extra time initially, but it brought trust and proved efficient in the long run. (Goodman, 1972: 2)

The central issue is what the members of the setting get out of being involved in your research. From their point of view, research has a high nuisance factor. You need to minimize such nuisances and help them realize any possible gains, e.g., possible helpful feedback on procedures, the opportunity for patients to talk about their concerns, the increased status of being part of an academic setting, and so on. In Hardy's (1993) terms, you need to align the goals of the research with the goals of the setting. Where possible, it can be useful to include a staff member as part of the research team and to ask the staff to contribute to the design of the research (Cowen & Gesten, 1980; Patton, 1997). However, some clinicians will not want any involvement, while others will want to be kept closely informed. It is wise to provide information to all important staff members: circulate updates, show drafts of papers, etc.

Through these contacts, the researcher, gatekeepers and prospective participants engage in a process of negotiation, in which the research contract is developed (Taylor & Bogdan, 1998). This agreement, which can be formal or informal, makes clear what the researcher is asking for, as well as spelling out the researcher's obligations in regard to confidentiality, avoiding disruption, and feedback.

Authorship

If you are intending to publish the study, it is worth considering authorship issues from the outset. In applied settings, such issues can be complicated because several people may be involved in different ways in the research. Senior staff sometimes ask to have their name on a paper simply because the research is being done in their unit. Unless they have made a significant contribution to the research, this is inappropriate and, for psychologists, unethical (American Psychological Association, 1992). Appreciation for permission to work in a setting should be mentioned in the Acknowledgements section of the research paper. (We discuss authorship issues further in Chapter 12.)

CHAPTER SUMMARY

The first stage of the research process involves doing the groundwork. There are two major tasks here: formulating the research questions or hypotheses and resolving any organizational or political issues, in order to prepare the ground for data collection. Researchers may also need to apply for ethics committee approval and for funding at this stage.

Planning research begins with developing a set of research questions for which you would like to find answers. After this, you can consider what type each question is and the appropriate method that goes along with it. As you progress through the groundwork phase of your research, you are likely to revise your questions substantially. Specifying useful, intellectually coherent, and realistic research questions is an iterative process that involves system-atically appraising the existing literature, consulting with expert colleagues, and conducting small-scale pilot studies. The research questions can be formulated from either an exploratory, discovery-oriented or a confirmatory, hypothesis-testing approach.

Successfully dealing with the organizational politics of the research setting requires considerable skill. A good relationship between the researcher and the setting is vital to the success of the project, whereas a poor relationship can complicate, delay, or thwart the project. Access to research settings is often controlled by official or unofficial gatekeepers, with whom the researcher must negotiate at the start of the project. People in applied settings often have justified reservations about having research conducted in their organizations. It is important to get people on your side and to respond honestly to their doubts.

FURTHER READING

Hodgson and Rollnick's (1996) amusing chapter entitled "More fun, less stress: How to survive in research" is well worth reading, especially their tongue-in-cheek laws of research (sample: "A research project will change twice in the middle"). Rudestam and Newton's (2000) book *Surviving your dissertation* is especially useful for students and has some good material on planning and writing.

Several specialist texts have material on the politics of working in field settings, e.g., from the point of view of evaluation research (Weiss, 1972), participant observation (Taylor & Bogdan, 1998), and randomized experiments (Cook & Campbell, 1979).

CHAPTER 4

FOUNDATIONS OF QUANTITATIVE MEASUREMENT

KEY POINTS IN THIS CHAPTER

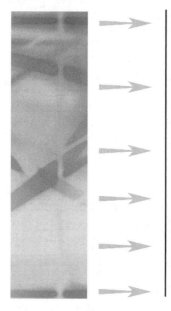

How to measure a psychological construct depends on the research questions, the theoretical framework, and the available resources.

Measures can be classified into self-report and observation, and also according to whether they are qualitative or quantitative.

The quantitative approach partly derives from the philosophy of positivism.

Psychometric theory is the study of the properties of quantitative measures.

Reliability concerns the reproducibility of measurement.

Validity assesses the meaning of measurement.

We have now reached the second of the four stages of the research process, the measurement stage. It consists of deciding how to assess each of the psychological concepts that are to be studied. Before examining actual methods of measurement (which are covered in Chapters 6 and 7), we will first consider the underlying theory of psychological measurement. The present chapter will concentrate on the conceptual foundations of quantitative approaches; qualitative approaches are covered in Chapter 5.

Furthermore, as we noted in Chapter 3, developing psychometrically sound quantitative measures is an important research activity in itself, especially for new research areas. If the absence of adequate measures looks like an obstacle to your research, it may mean that the logical first step is measure development research, in which case the issues we present in this chapter are at the heart of your study.

The previous, groundwork, stage will have culminated in the formulation of a set of research questions or hypotheses, involving various psychological constructs.

The measurement stage of the project then consists of specifying how each of these constructs is to be assessed. For example, the research questions might be about the role of social support in psychological adjustment to stressful life events. The researcher then needs to decide how to assess social support, how to capture emotional adjustment, and what constitutes a stressful life event. There are two separate but interdependent issues to be considered: how each construct is defined and how it is measured.

The boundary between the groundwork and measurement stages (and also the design stage, which we cover in Chapter 8) is not, of course, as watertight as we are implying. For instance, measurement considerations may shape the formulation of the research questions. If an investigator knows there is no valid method for measuring something, it would be difficult to study it. For example, it would be fascinating to study the content of dreams as they are happening during sleep, but there is presently no conceivable method to do this; therefore research about real-time dream images cannot be conducted, and we can only rely on people's recall of dreams after they wake up. Furthermore, some types of measurement may be beyond the time constraints or the financial resources of the researcher. For example, in research on the process of family therapy, transcribing interviews and training raters to code them is time consuming and expensive, and therefore it may be inappropriate for a project with little or no funding.

However, it does not greatly distort the research process to treat groundwork, measurement, and design as three separate, sequential stages. For the rest of this chapter, we will assume that the research questions have already been decided upon (at least for the time being) and that we are now solely concerned with translating them into measurement procedures.

Separating the groundwork and measurement stages is also helpful in beginning to think about the study. Novice researchers often worry prematurely about measurement. As we argued in Chapter 3, it is better to think first about what to study and only secondarily about how to do so. Ideas about measurement will often flow from clearly formulated research questions: measurement will be less problematic if you've thought through the questions you are asking.

As in the previous, groundwork, stage, there are several important conceptual issues, some of which are controversial. We are including this material to give essential background information and in order to help you think more broadly about the framework within which research is conducted. The present chapter and Chapter 5 cover this conceptual background material, whereas Chapters 6 and 7 deal with practical issues in selecting or constructing measures. The first section of this present chapter defines some key terms and looks at the general process of measurement, the second section examines the conceptual foundations of the quantitative approaches, and the third addresses psychometric theory, in particular the concepts of reliability and validity.

THE PROCESS OF MEASUREMENT

Domains of Variables

Variables studied in clinical psychology research can be grouped into five general domains:

- *Cognitive*: thoughts, attitudes, beliefs, expectations, attributions, memory, reasoning, etc.

- *Affective*: feelings, emotions, moods, bodily sensations, etc.

- *Behavioral*: actions, performance, skill, speech, etc.

- *Biological*: physiological and anatomical, e.g., heart rate, blood pressure, immune functioning, etc.

- *Social*: acute and chronic stressors, social supports, family functioning, work, etc.

These variables form the content of psychological research: the research questions will have been framed in terms of several of them. However, each must be clearly defined and translated into one or more practical measurement methods.

Measuring Psychological Constructs

We will use the term "measurement" in a general sense to refer to the process of finding indicators for psychological concepts. Virtually all psychological concepts can have multiple possible indicators, for example:

- *Phobia*: observed avoidance; self-report of fear; physiological measures of sympathetic nervous system arousal in presence of phobic stimulus.

- *Pain*: self-report of intensity; pain behaviors (flinching, crying, avoidance of painful stimuli); clinician's judgement.

- *Death anxiety*: semi-structured qualitative interview; standardized question-naires.

The underlying psychological concept (phobia, pain, death anxiety) is known as a *construct*; the indicator, or way of observing it, is known as a *measure* of that construct. Although this language is associated with quantitative methods, it can usefully be applied to qualitative methods as well, though in this case researchers may speak of a *phenomenon* rather than of a construct.

The process of going from a construct to its associated measure is often called *operationalization*.

Operationalization

Construct $\longrightarrow$ Measure

Operationalization is, however, more complex than this simple diagram implies. As the above three examples show, there are often several different ways to operationalize a given construct. Which one(s) to use depends on the research questions, the theoretical framework, and on the resources available for the study. A second, related difficulty is that no single measure can perfectly capture a construct. Finally, the relationship between a construct and its measure(s) is usually not a linear process: how the construct is measured can shape how we understand or define it. Thus, the process of measurement is more complex than implied by the traditional view of operationalization, as there is rarely a clear-cut, direct mapping of constructs onto measurement operations.

In order to facilitate the process of operationalization, the construct may be given an *operational definition*, i.e., it may be defined so that it can be easily measured. Thus, empathy may be initially conceptualized as "Entering the private perceptual world of the other and becoming thoroughly at home in it" (Rogers, 1975), but for psychotherapy process research it may be operationally defined as how accurately the therapist responds to the client's expressed feelings, which then leads to its being measured using expert ratings of audiotaped interactions.

It is not always possible or desirable to develop an operational definition for every construct. Earlier generations of researchers were taught the doctrine of *operationism* (Stevens, 1935), which stated that a concept is identical to its measurement operations, for example, intelligence is what IQ tests measure. This doctrine was subsequently rejected by philosophers, and replaced by the critical realist strategy of *converging operations* (Grace, 2001), which advocates using multiple indicators to measure underlying constructs. In the clinical context, we often cannot adequately capture many important constructs by our current measures. Social skills may be operationalized by such indicators as good eye contact, smiling, etc., but performing only these behaviors does not produce socially skilled interactions; rather the reverse, it tends to produce people who act like robots (or breakfast TV presenters). In line with the critical realist position, we are arguing that most psychological constructs are only partially captured by their associated measures. We will take up these issues again in the following two sections when we discuss positivism and construct validity.

The operational definition of a construct clearly depends on how it is conceptualized theoretically. For example, two ways of measuring social support—by counting the number of people in a person's social network or by assessing the quality of relationships within that network—have different implications for what is meant by the social support construct itself: whether good social support means several potentially supportive relationships available or just a few good ones. This issue is known as the *theory dependence of measurement* (see also Chapter 2). Any way of measuring a concept presupposes a view of what that concept consists of: it is impossible to have pure observations. Similarly, qualitative researchers highlight the influence of the researcher's preconceptions on the measurement process: the concept of the hermeneutic circle (e.g., Packer & Addison, 1989) encapsulates the mutual feedback between our current ideas and our understanding of the data.

A further complication is that the act of measurement often changes the person or situation being measured, a phenomenon known as *reactivity of measurement*. For example, people may behave differently if they know that they are being observed, and asking a client to monitor the day-to-day frequency of her anxious thoughts may in itself affect the frequency of those thoughts. Research participants are often influenced by their perception of what the researcher is trying to find out.

Measurement Sources and Approaches

Sources of measurement can be categorized into self-report and observation: you can either ask people about themselves or look at what they are doing. (Strictly speaking, self-report data should be called verbal-report, since it can be gathered from several perspectives, for example, the person of interest, a significant other, or a therapist or teacher. Similarly, observational data could be gathered from an observer, a psychological test, or a physiological measure.) Data may be collected from either source using either qualitative or quantitative methods (see Table 4.1).

The distinction between quantitative and qualitative methods raises a number of fundamental epistemological issues and visions of what science is (as discussed in Chapter 2). Each method derives from contrasting academic and philosophical traditions.

Quantitative methods are identified with the so-called "hard science" disciplines, principally physics; qualitative methods, with the "soft" social sciences, such as sociology and anthropology, and the humanities. In the early decades of the 20th century, many influential psychologists felt that the road to academic prestige and legitimacy lay with being considered "hard science," and thus sought to identify psychology with physics and quantitative methods (Polkinghorne, 1983; Lincoln & Guba, 1985; Packer & Addison, 1989). This issue has been a continuing struggle within psychology, with its roots in older philosophical traditions (idealism and realism) and early schools of psychology (e.g., introspectionism and associationism). The structure of the present chapter and the following one reflect this debate. They have a thesis, antithesis, synthesis form: we will attempt

Table 4.1 Examples of measures classified by source and approach

	Self-report	Observation
Quantitative	Attitude questionnaires	Behavioral observation
	Symptom checklists	Psychological tests of ability
		Physiological measures
Qualitative	Qualitative interviews	Participant observation
	Diaries, journals	Projective tests

to set out the underlying issues for each approach, and then suggest in the final section of Chapter 5 how they might be integrated in practice.

FOUNDATIONS OF QUANTITATIVE METHODS

Quantitative methods are useful both for precise description and for comparison. They fit in well with the hypothetico-deductive view of science.

There are well-developed procedures for the analysis of quantitative data.

The philosophical position of positivism seeks to model psychology and the social sciences on the methods used in the physical sciences.

The positivist approach was taken up in psychology in the form of methodological behaviorism.

Positivism has been heavily critiqued, especially by qualitative researchers.

Quantitative methods, by definition, are those which use numbers. The main advantages of quantitative measurement are as follows:

- Using numbers enables greater precision in measurement. There is a well-developed theory of reliability and validity to assess measurement errors; this enables researchers to know how much confidence to place in their measures.

- There are well-established statistical methods for analyzing the data. The data can be easily summarized, which facilitates communication of the findings.

- Quantitative measurements facilitate comparison. They allow researchers to get the reactions of many people to specific stimuli and to compare responses across individuals.

- Quantitative methods fit in well with hypothetico-deductive approaches. Hypothesized relationships between variables can be specified using a mathematical model, and the methods of statistical inference can be used to see how well the data fit the predictions.

- Sampling theory can be used to estimate how well the findings generalize beyond the sample in the study to the wider population from which the sample was drawn.

The development of science would have been impossible without quantification. The necessity of the ancient Egyptians to preserve the dimensions of their fields after the flooding of the Nile led to the development of geometry (Dilke, 1987). If the fields could be measured and mapped out, their boundaries could be restored once the waters had subsided. However, it was not until the late Renaissance that quantification and mathematics began to become an integral part of science. In the 17th century, Newton's laws of motion employed fairly simple algebra to provide a tool of great power and beauty that enabled scientists to predict the behavior of falling apples and orbiting planets.

Positivism

The success of quantitative methods in the physical sciences, especially that of Newtonian mechanics, led to an attempt to extend them into other areas of enquiry. The 19th-century philosopher, Auguste Comte (1830) articulated the doctrine of *positivism*, which has been much elaborated by succeeding scholars. These elaborations have not always been consistent with each other or with Comte's original formulation (see Bryant, 1985; Bryman, 1988; Polkinghorne, 1983), making it difficult to formulate precisely what is meant by positivism. However, its three main tenets are usually taken to be:

1. That scientific attention should be restricted to observable facts ("positive" in this sense means dealing with matters of fact); "inferred constructs," such as beliefs or motives, have no place in science. This is a version of *empiricism* (the belief that all knowledge is derived from sensory experience).

2. That the methods of the physical sciences (e.g., quantification, separation into independent and dependent variables, and formulation of general laws) should also be applied to the social sciences.

3. That science is objective and value free.

A related 20th-century development was *logical positivism*. It is associated with the "Vienna circle" group of philosophers, such as Carnap and Wittgenstein. They sought to analyze which propositions have meaning and which do not, and then to restrict philosophical discourse to those things that can properly be talked about. Wittgenstein's famous dictum captures the flavor: "What can be said at all can be said clearly, and what we cannot talk about we must pass over in silence" (Wittgenstein, 1921/1961: 3). The logical positivists' central criterion, that all philosophical statements should be reducible to sensory experience, rules out discussion of metaphysical concepts. They contend that it is pointless arguing about things like the ultimate nature of the universe, since such propositions can never be proved or disproved.

Methodological Behaviorism

The positivist doctrine was incorporated into psychology in the form of *methodological behaviorism*, whose best-known proponents are Watson and Skinner. They sought to restrict psychology to a "science of behavior," eschewing consideration of any "inner variables," e.g., cognitions and affects. For instance, Watson urged: "Let us limit ourselves to things that can be observed and formulate laws concerning only those things" (Watson, 1931: 6). In other words, methodological behaviorists would not say that a rat was hungry, as hunger is an inferred construct; instead, they would say it had been deprived of food for eight hours, or that it was at three-quarters of its initial body weight.

Similarly, they would not talk about aggression, but rather such specific behaviors as kicking, punching, or insulting someone. As we noted in our discussion of operationism, the meaning of psychological constructs was limited to the operations or procedures used to measure them.

This attitude was a reaction to the perceived limitations of the introspectionism that had preceded it. *Introspection* consisted of the investigator observing the contents of his or her own consciousness and attempting to expound general theories therefrom. The virtue of sticking to observable behavior is that it is clear what you are talking about and your conclusions can be replicated by other investigators.

Another important manifestation of methodological behaviorism was found in clinical work, in the behavioral assessment movement (e.g., Goldfried & Kent, 1972). This called for clinical assessment to be tied closely to observable behavior, to remove the inferences that clinicians make when, for example, they label a client as having a "hysterical personality."

However, the distinction between high-inference and low-inference measures may be less useful than it seems at first, since inference must occur sooner or later in the research process to give psychological meaning to the data. There is a kind of conservation of inference law: the lower the level of inference in the measurement process, the higher the level of inference needed to connect the observed data to interesting variables or phenomena. Conversely, high inference measures often do much of the researcher's work early on, requiring less inference to make sense of the data obtained. For example, a measure of non-verbal behavior in family therapy might use a low level of inference, but the researcher may need to make further inferences in order to make sense of the data, such as interpreting certain body postures as indicating detachment from the family. On the other hand, a measure of transference in psychotherapy might require a high level of inference in rating clients' verbal statements, but no further inferences may be needed to interpret the data.

Criticisms of Positivism

The positivist, methodological behaviorist stance has been severely criticized both from within and outside of psychology (e.g., Bryman, 1988; Guba & Lincoln, 1989; Harré, 1974; Koch, 1964; Polkinghorne, 1983; Rogers, 1985). The central criticism is that, when carried through rigorously, it leads to draconian restrictions on what can be studied or talked about. Psychological constructs that attempt to capture important aspects of experience, e.g., feelings, values, and meanings, are ruled out of court. It leads to a sterile and trivial discipline alienated from human experience. Although few researchers today adopt a strict methodological behaviorism, some articles in mainstream psychological journals still seem to lose sight of the people behind the statistics.

The rise of quantitative methods has also been associated with the rise of capitalism. Young (1979) argues that reducing everything to numbers is a manifestation of a balance sheet mentality. A brilliant fictional indictment of such a mentality was made a century ago in Dickens's novel *Hard Times*, which starkly depicts the loss of humanity that comes from reducing all transactions into quantitative terms. This criticism is still timely, in the light of managed care in the US and the culture of performance indicators, clinical audit, and cost-effectiveness in the British National Health Service. Emphasizing easily measurable indices of workload often leaves out the less tangible—and arguably more important—aspects of quality.

Conclusions

In our view, the important message to take from the positivists is the value of being explicit about how psychological constructs are measured. It reminds researchers and theorists to be conscious of measurement issues, to tie their discourse to potential observations, and, when speculating about more abstract constructs, to have an awareness of what measurement operations lie behind them. For example, if you are attempting to study complex constructs such as defense mechanisms, you need to specify what would lead you to conclude that someone is using denial or projective identification. Cronbach and Meehl's (1955) notion of construct validity, which we discuss below, is an attempt to place the use of inferred constructs on a sound methodological basis.

It is worth noting that, although quantification and positivism are often treated as equivalent, the stress on quantification is actually only a small part of the positivist package, and possibly not even a necessary part. For example, qualitative methods can be used purely descriptively, without using inferred constructs. Also, the role of quantification in science may have been overstated by the positivists. Schwartz (1999) points to examples in the physical and biological sciences, e.g., the double helix model of DNA, that use mainly descriptive qualitative methods.

Having described the rationale for quantification, we can now look at the underlying theory of measurement, including the important question of how to evaluate particular measures.

PSYCHOMETRIC THEORY

Psychometric theory refers to the theory underlying psychological measurement in general. In particular, it leads to a framework for evaluating specific measurement instruments. Although developed in the context of quantitative measurement, some of its ideas can, arguably, be translated into qualitative methods. They are essential for all would-be researchers to grasp, whatever approach they ultimately plan to adopt.

Key points:

- Psychometric theory is the theory of psychological measurement.

- Classical test theory leads from a simple set of assumptions to useful concepts for evaluating specific measurement instruments, notably reliability and validity.

- Reliability refers to the reproducibility of measurement: its principal subtypes are test-retest, equivalent forms, internal consistency, and inter-rater reliability.

- Validity assesses the meaning of measurement. It can be divided into content, face, criterion, and construct validity.

- Utility refers to how easy the measure is to administer and to how much information it adds.

- Two alternatives to classical test theory are generalizability theory and item response theory.

Definitions

Scales of Measurement

Measurements may have the properties of nominal, ordinal, and interval scales (Stevens, 1946). *Nominal scales* consist of a set of mutually exclusive categories, with no implicit ordering. For example, researchers in a psychiatric day hospital might use a simplified diagnostic system consisting of three categories: 1 = schizophrenia; 2 = affective disorder; 3 = other. In this case, the numbers are simply labels for the categories: there is no sense in which 2 is greater than 1, etc., and thus the diagnostic system forms a nominal scale.

Scales of measurement:

- Nominal: no ordering

- Ordinal: ordering only

- Interval: ordering plus distance

An *ordinal scale* is like a nominal scale but with the additional property of ordered categories, that is, it measures a variable along some continuum. For example, psychiatric day hospital patients might be rated on a scale of psychosocial impairment, consisting of three categories: 1 = slightly or not at all impaired; 2 = moderately impaired; 3 = highly impaired. On this scale, someone with a score of 3 is defined to be more impaired than someone with a score of 2, and thus it has ordinal properties. However, there is no assumption that the distance between successive ordinal scale points is the same, that is, the distance between 1 and 2 is not necessarily the same as that between 2 and 3.

An *interval scale* is like an ordinal scale with the additional property that the distances between successive points are assumed to be equal. For example, the Beck Depression Inventory (Beck et al., 1988), a self-report measure of depression, is usually treated as an interval scale. This assumes that the increase in severity of depression from a score of 10 to a score of 15 is equivalent to the increase in severity from 20 to 25.

The importance of distinguishing between these types of measurement is that different mathematical and statistical methods are used to analyze data from the different scale types. A scale needs to have interval properties before adding and subtracting have any meaning. Thus it makes no sense to report the arithmetic average of nominal scale data: the mode must be used instead. Nominal and ordinal scales also require non-parametric or distribution-free statistical methods, whereas interval scales can potentially be analyzed using standard methods such as the t-test and the analysis of variance, provided that the data are normally distributed (Howell, 2002).

Type of Measure

Measures are either nomothetic or idiographic. *Nomothetic measures* compare individuals with other individuals; most psychological tests and inventories fall into this category. The scores on a nomothetic measure can be *norm-referenced*, when they have no absolute meaning in themselves, but are simply indicative of how the individual stands with respect to the rest of the population. For example, the scores on the Wechsler Adult Intelligence Scale (WAIS) are norm-referenced: they are constructed in such a way as to have a population mean of 100 and a standard deviation of 15. A *criterion-referenced* measure, on the other hand, compares individuals against an absolute standard. For example, a typing speed of 40 words per minute denotes a certain degree of skill at the keyboard; scores on the Global Assessment Scale (Endicott et al., 1976) denote specific levels of psychological functioning.

The contrasting approach, *idiographic measurement*, focuses solely on a single individual, without reference to others (Korchin, 1976). No attempt at comparison is made. Some examples of idiographic methods are repertory grids (Winter, 1992), Q-sorts (e.g., Jones et al., 1993), and the Shapiro Personal Questionnaire (Phillips, 1986; Shapiro, 1961a). Such measures are often used within small-N research designs, and are discussed further in that context in Chapter 9.

Reliability

How do we go about evaluating specific measures? The two main criteria, reliability and validity, are derived from a set of assumptions known as classical test theory (Nunnally & Bernstein, 1994). We will first describe them within that framework, and then reconceptualize them in terms of a newer approach, generalizability theory.

The original idea in classical test theory was that in measuring something, one is dealing with consistency across repeated measurements. The consistent part of the score, the part that is the same across measurements, is known as the *true score*. It is conceived of either as an ideal score or as the mean of an infinitely large set of scores. The observed score is the sum of the true score and error, which is conceived of as a random fluctuation around the true score.

Expressed as an equation, this relationship is $x = t + e$ (where x is the observed score, t is the true score, and e is the error); this is called the fundamental equation of classical test theory. From this simple equation, and a few assumptions about how the error score behaves, the theory of reliability can be constructed.

Reliability refers to the degree of reproducibility of the measurement. If you repeat the measurement in various ways, do you get the same results each time? The more consistent the measurement, the greater the reliability and the less error there is to interfere with measuring what one wants to measure. It is analogous to the signal to noise ratio in electronics. To put it the other way around, unreliability is the amount of error in the measurement: mathematically speaking, the proportion of error variance in the total score. For example, if you were measuring couples' marital satisfaction using a questionnaire, you would expect the score to stay roughly stable, at least over short time periods. If people's scores fluctuated widely over a two-week interval, the measure would be unreliable and probably not worth using.

Reasonably high reliability is important because it enables you to measure with precision, and therefore allows you to discover relationships between variables that would be obscured if too much error were present. At the other extreme, if the measurement is totally unreliable, you are simply recording random error, not whatever it is you want to measure.

If you are examining how two variables correlate, the effect of unreliability is to attenuate their observed relationship, making their underlying relationship more difficult to detect. Any relationship between measures of two variables is a joint function of the true underlying relationship of the variables and the weakening effect of the unreliability of the measures (Nunnally & Bernstein, 1994). For example, if you are studying the correlation between social support and depression, and your measures of each of those two constructs are somewhat unreliable, the correlation which you obtain may be low, even though the underlying relationship between the variables is large. The reliability of your measures can have a huge impact on your ability to find what you are looking for, especially with small samples.

However, reliability says nothing about what the measure actually means. It simply says that the measurement is repeatable. A thermometer with insufficient liquid in it will give very reliable readings, but they will be wrong. The meaning of the measure is assessed by its validity, which we will discuss later under a separate heading.

Reliability types:

- Test-retest
- Equivalent forms
- Internal consistency (including split-half)
- Inter-rater

Methods for assessing reliability depend on the scale of measurement (nominal or interval), the type of measure (self-report or observation), and the type of consistency that you are interested in. The most common methods are as follows.

Test-retest reliability examines consistency over time. The measure is administered to the same set of people on two or more separate occasions (e.g., a week or a month apart). Its test-retest reliability (sometimes called the stability coefficient) is assessed by the correlation between the scores from the different time points. There may be a problem with practice effects, unless these are uniform across individuals (in which case the overall mean would be affected, rather than the correlation). This is the most appropriate type of reliability when you are considering change over time, or when you are combining repeated measurements to produce a single index (e.g., therapeutic alliance over the first three sessions of treatment).

Equivalent forms reliability examines reliability across different versions of the same instrument. This is an extension of test-retest reliability, where instead of re-administering the same measure on the second occasion, you use an alternate (or "equivalent" or "parallel") form. (Some instruments have a Form A and a Form B to facilitate this.) Again, the reliability coefficient is the correlation between the scores on the two administrations.

Internal consistency is the standard way of assessing the *inter-item reliability* of a scale that is composed of multiple similar items (many self-report measures fall into this category). The assumption is that the items are *equivalent* or *parallel*, i.e., that they all aim to tap the same underlying construct. For instance, two parallel items on the Client Satisfaction Questionnaire (CSQ-8: Larsen et al., 1979), a widely used self-report scale assessing clients' satisfaction with psychological and other healthcare services, are "Did you get the kind of service you wanted?" and "Overall, in a general sense, how satisfied are you with the service you received?" Even though these items ask slightly different questions, they are assumed to be tapping the same psychological construct: satisfaction with the service. Internal consistency, figuratively speaking, is a way of assessing how well all the items of the scale hang together: are they all measuring the same thing (high consistency) or different things (low consistency)? Overall scale reliability is estimated from the covariances of all the items with each other, typically assessed using *Cronbach's alpha* (see below).

Split-half reliability is an older form of internal consistency used prior to the development of high-speed computers, because it was easier to calculate. Split-half reliability is assessed by dividing a measure into two equivalent halves (e.g., odd and even items), then correlating the two halves with each other. It has been replaced by Cronbach's alpha.

Inter-rater reliability is used for observational rather than self-report measures, in order to check the reliability of observations. For example, researchers may be interested in measuring therapist empathy in a therapeutic interaction, or in estimating children's mental ages from their drawings. The researchers making the ratings may be referred to as coders, raters, or judges; their inter-rater reliability is the extent to which their ratings agree or covary with each other (see the next section for computational details). There are two separate issues: how good is the rating system as a whole and how good are individual raters—for example, should one be dropped?

Reliability Statistics

A variety of different statistics are used to measure reliability. For some reason, confusion continues to surround their selection and use (Tinsley & Weiss, 1975). The first step is to establish which scale of measurement is involved, since this determines the reliability statistic. For practical purposes only nominal and interval scales need be considered: ordinal scales are generally analyzed as if they were interval scales.

Nominal Scales

As psychologists frequently need to calculate the reliability of nominal scale data, we will illustrate the calculations using a simple example. Suppose that two psychologists who work in a psychiatric day hospital each categorize patients into three diagnostic groups—schizophrenia, affective disorder, and other—and they want to know how similar their judgements are. Since there is no ordering implied in the categories, it is a nominal scale.

The first thing to do with two sets of categorical measurements (e.g., judgements across raters, occasions, instruments or settings) is to display the data in a two-way classification table. Table 4.2 gives some possible data from the diagnostic classification study with 100 patients.

The obvious initial thing to do is to calculate the *percentage agreement* between the clinicians. This is computed from the total number of observations in the agreement cells of the table (indicated by underlining in the table), divided by the total number of observations. In the example, the agreement is $(10 + 20 + 20)/100 = 0.50$, or 50% agreement.

Table 4.2   Simplified example of a two-way classification table

	Rater 2			
Rater 1	Schizo	Affective	Other	Total
Schizophrenia	<u>10</u>	20	0	30
Affective disorder	10	<u>20</u>	10	40
Other	0	10	<u>20</u>	30
Total	20	50	30	100

However, since raters categorizing patients at random would still agree by chance part of the time, a way to control for chance agreement is desirable. *Cohen's kappa* is used to accomplish this (Cohen, 1960). The formula is:

$$\kappa = (p_o - p_c)/(1 - p_c)$$

where p_o is the proportion of agreement observed (i.e., the total of the numbers in the agreement cells of the table divided by the grand total), i.e., 0.50 in the example above. p_c stands for the proportion of agreement expected by chance alone. To calculate p_c, first calculate the proportion of observations in each row and column, by dividing each row and column total by the grand total. Then p_c is calculated by multiplying corresponding row and column proportions by each other and adding the resulting numbers together. In the example, p_c is given by 0.3*0.2 + 0.4*0.5 + 0.3*0.3 = 0.06 + 0.20 + 0.09 = 0.35.

Using the above formula for Cohen's kappa, the corrected agreement statistic is therefore $\kappa = (0.50 - 0.35)/(1 - 0.35) = 0.23$.

With nominal scale data it is further possible to analyze the reliability of any particular category within the scale. That is, you can determine which categories have good agreement and which do not. This is done by collapsing the scale into two categories: the category of interest and all other categories combined. In the example above, the researchers might be interested in the reliability of the schizophrenia category. They would then form a smaller, two-by-two table, amalgamating the two non-schizophrenia categories, and calculate Cohen's kappa for that table.

Ordinal and Interval Scales

With ordinal and interval scale measurements, there are several choices for assessing reliability. To begin with, if you are using a cut-off point on an interval scale (e.g., an observational rating scale for depression), you may turn it into a binary nominal scale (e.g., "depressed–nondepressed"). You could then use Cohen's kappa to compute reliability.

More commonly, however, the researcher calculates the association between the two measurements using Pearson's correlation coefficient, *r*. This statistic is usually robust enough to use in most applications (Nunnally & Bernstein, 1994; Tinsley & Weiss, 1975). If more than two raters are involved, Cronbach's alpha can be used with raters treated as items, or a more complicated statistic known as the *intraclass correlation* can be used (Shrout & Fliess, 1979).

In the common situation where a scale is formed from multiple items that are averaged or totaled together, *Cronbach's alpha* is the standard index of the reliability of the pooled observations (overall score across items, pooled judges' ratings, or observations pooled over time). The SPSS Reliability procedure (or any other reasonably complete statistics software package) can usually be used to perform the computations. The reliability of the whole scale will be higher than the average inter-item correlation, because adding together multiple measures averages out the errors in each of them.

Since the internal consistency of a scale increases with the number of items in the scale, it is easier to get higher reliabilities with, say, a 24-item scale than with an 8-item one. Thus you might want to see how much increasing your scale by various amounts would improve its reliability. The reliability of such combined measurements can be calculated using the Spearman-Brown Prophecy Formula (Nunnally & Bernstein, 1994):

$$r_{kk} = k(r_{11})/(1 + (k - 1)r_{11})$$

where r_{kk} refers to the reliability of the combined measurements; $k =$ the factor by which you are increasing the scale (a fraction if you are making it shorter); and r_{11} is the original reliability coefficient. (This formula yields the same results as the standardized Cronbach alpha statistic.)

Two examples of common uses of this formula may clarify its application. In the first example, suppose that you have an 8-item scale with a reliability of 0.6, and you want to know how reliable a 24-item version made up of similar items would be. In this case, r_{11} is equal to 0.6 and k is 3 (because the new scale is three times as long as the original one). Then the new reliability would be $3*0.6/(1 + 2*0.6) = 0.82$.

In the second example, suppose that you wish to combine 20 parallel items with an average intercorrelation of only 0.3 into a scale. Surprisingly, the scale thus formed would have an excellent reliability of 0.89 ($ = 20*0.3/(1 + 19*0.3)$), proof that, statistically speaking, if you just have enough sow's ears, it is possible to make quite a nice leather purse (even if it isn't silk!).

Dimensionality

The above discussion has assumed that the measure is attempting to assess a single construct. If, instead, you suspect that it may be capturing several different dimensions, e.g., on a psychological symptom checklist like the SCL-90-R (Derogatis, 1994), then factor analysis should be used to investigate the internal structure of the measure. The procedure for this is beyond the scope of the present text: readers should consult specialist references (e.g., Floyd & Widaman,

1995; Nunnally & Bernstein, 1994; Tabachnik & Fidell, 2001). However, Cronbach's alpha should also be used to assess the internal consistency of the resulting subscales.

Validity

Validity is a more difficult concept to understand and to assess than reliability. The classical definition of validity is "whether the measure measures what it is supposed to measure." For example, does a depression scale actually measure depression, or does it measure something else, such as self-esteem, or willingness to admit problems?

In this chapter we are discussing validity of measurement. However, Cook and Campbell (1979) have articulated a highly influential, broader conception of validity which involves design as well as measurement. We will address this in detail in Chapter 8.

There is a two-step process in developing and evaluating measures: first you look at reliability, then validity. Reliability is a necessary but not sufficient condition for validity. To be valid, a measure must first be reliable, otherwise it would consist mainly of error. For example, if two expert raters cannot agree on whether transcripts of a therapy session show evidence of client denial, then the validity of the denial category cannot be established. On the other hand, a measure can be highly reliable but still invalid, e.g., head girth as a measure of intelligence.

Validity may be assessed in several different ways, and a thoroughly researched measure will report all of them in its manual.

Content Validity

Content validity assesses whether the measure adequately covers the different aspects of the construct that are specified in its definition. For example, does a self-report depression scale have items which capture the components of lowered mood, decreased motivation, sleep disturbance, etc.? This is a qualitative judgement: there is no such thing as a content validity coefficient.

Face Validity

Face validity is similar to content validity and assesses whether the measure looks right on the face of it, that is, that it self-evidently measures what it claims to measure. For instance, the items of a depression scale should ask about low mood, but not about attitudes to authority. The Hogan Empathy Scale has the item "I prefer a shower to a bath"—it is not at all obvious, on the face of it, how this relates to empathy. Face validity is usually desirable, but not always so, e.g., the Minnesota Multiphasic Personality Inventory (MMPI) has a number of "subtle items," which were designed to make the test more difficult to fake (Weiner, 1948).

Face validity is partly a public relations concept, to make sure that the scale looks right to potential respondents, who will become alienated if it does not appear relevant to the purpose at hand. For example, a symptom checklist asking about such abnormal experiences as psychosis or suicide may be inappropriate for research in family practice settings because it will put people off. Like content validity, face validity is a qualitative concept: there is no face validity coefficient. Face validity, in the sense of "resonance" with the reader, is a key criterion for evaluating qualitative research findings (see Chapter 5).

Criterion Validity

Criterion validity is a central validity consideration. It assesses how well the measure correlates with an established criterion or indicator of the construct it is measuring. It is divided into concurrent and predictive validity, depending on whether the criterion is measured at the same time or later on. For *concurrent validity*, the scale is correlated with a current criterion, e.g., a depression scale could be correlated with clinicians' ratings of depression. For *predictive validity*, the scale is correlated with a future criterion, e.g., a hopelessness scale could be used to predict future suicide attempts. The validity coefficient in both cases is the correlation between the measure and the criterion.

Note that seeing whether a measure can predict membership of two separate criterion groups (e.g., can a depression scale distinguish between depressed and non-depressed patients?) also falls under this heading. It is an example of concurrent validity, though it is often wrongly referred to as discriminant validity, which is a different concept altogether (see below).

If the measure is being used for diagnostic reasons, it is useful to specify its sensitivity and specificity. *Sensitivity* is an index of how well the measure picks out those patients who have the target condition (i.e., how few false negatives there are); *specificity* is an index of how well it avoids picking out those patients who do not have the target condition (i.e., how few false positives there are). Thus a depression scale, with a given cut-off point, would have high sensitivity if it identified almost all of the depressed patients in the sample, and high specificity if it did not identify any non-depressed people as being depressed. In practice, when one is developing a test and deciding where to place the cut-off points, there is a trade-off between sensitivity and specificity.

For criterion validity, the measurement that is being used as the criterion must be well established and of unquestionable validity itself. It is often referred to as a "gold standard" (a clear application of the correspondence theory of truth). In cases where there is no established gold standard criterion, then considerations of construct validity are adopted instead.

Criterion validity is basically about the usefulness of the measure: how well it performs in predicting the criterion. It is less concerned with the underlying construct that the measure is capturing. The Beck Hopelessness Scale may have good predictive validity for suicide attempts, but that does not necessarily imply that it is a good measure of hopelessness. To establish whether a measure is actually assessing the psychological construct it was intended to assess, considerations of construct validity must be addressed.

Construct Validity

Construct validity is a complex consideration. As its name suggests, it examines the validity of a construct rather than of individual methods of measuring that construct, which the previous validity types look at (Cronbach & Meehl, 1955). It asks whether the pattern of relationships between measures of that construct and measures of other constructs is consistent with theoretical expectations: how it fits with what Cronbach & Meehl (1955) termed the "nomological net." Construct validity is established by accumulating studies which test predictions about how the construct in question should relate to other constructs and measures.

In one classical type of construct validity study, the relevant associations are displayed in a *multitrait-multimethod matrix* (Campbell & Fiske, 1959). This is a table that sets out the correlations between several ways of measuring several different constructs. For example, if a researcher were interested in the construct validity of public-speaking anxiety, she might measure it by using, say, two different self-report scales, in addition to an observational measure and measures of heart rate and galvanic skin response taken while the person is speaking. In addition she would collect comparable self-report and observational measures from the same people on different constructs, such as IQ, trait anxiety, extraversion, and self-esteem. The multitrait-multimethod matrix displays the correlations among all of these variables.

The matrix reveals the extent to which measures of the construct of interest are positively correlated with measures of related constructs (*convergent validity*) and uncorrelated or weakly correlated with measures of unrelated constructs (*discriminant validity*). In the above example, all of the different measures of public-speaking anxiety would be expected to correlate at least moderately with each other. They would also be expected not to correlate significantly with age or IQ, and to correlate only moderately with trait anxiety and self-esteem, but more highly with extraversion.

The multitrait-multimethod matrix also reveals the extent of *method variance*, the tendency of measures of a similar type to correlate together. For example, scores from self-report measures are often moderately intercorrelated, even though they were designed to assess quite different constructs. This is why it is desirable, where possible, to use different measurement methods within a study or research program, and not to rely on any one viewpoint or type of measure.

Generalizability Theory

An alternative to classical test theory is generalizability theory, which was developed by Cronbach et al. (1972). It uses a multifactorial model rather like analysis of variance (see Shavelson et al., 1989; Wiggins, 1973). It asks, "To which conditions of observation can a particular observation be generalized?" or "Of which other situations can a measurement be considered to be representative?" It de-emphasizes the concept of the true score in favor of the central activity of analyzing sources of variations in the scores. The theory deliberately blurs the

Table 4.3 How reliability and validity correspond to generalizing across measurement facets

Facet to generalize across	Traditional psychometric concept
Observers: across raters, judges	Inter-rater reliability
Occasions: across time	Test-retest reliability
	Predictive validity
Instruments: across various ways of measuring the same thing (including individual items)	Equivalent forms reliability
	Internal consistency
	Concurrent validity
	Convergent validity
Settings: across situations (usually going from more to less controlled situations)	Criterion validity
	Convergent validity

distinction between reliability and validity, a distinction that is not clear cut even within classical test theory (Campbell & Fiske, 1959).

Generalizability theory assumes that measurement comprises three elements: persons, variables, and facets (or conditions) of measurement. Four facets can be distinguished: observers, occasions, instruments, and settings. Generalization across these facets corresponds to several of the traditional psychometric concepts (see Table 4.3).

In other words, generalizability theory examines the confidence with which you can generalize measurements to other observers, occasions, instruments, or settings. If you are developing a test or scale, it is a good idea to define these conditions, and determine generalizability across the desired range. Such an examination is referred to as a generalizability study, and is typically set up as a multifactorial research design (see Chapter 8) that incorporates each relevant facet as a factor. However, even if you do not actually carry out such a study, the conceptual framework of measurement facets is still useful for understanding the factors important to your instruments.

The more conceptual forms of validity, i.e., content, face, and more complex forms of construct validity, do not fit neatly into the generalizability theory framework. They can be treated separately, or could be considered as aspects of a fifth facet, level of abstraction: generalization from the specific working definition of the variable to other representations—theoretical, empirical and pheno-menological—inferred on the basis of what it is theorized *not* to be as well as what it *is* related to.

Item Response Theory

A second alternative to classical test theory is item response theory. Like generalizability theory, it is quite complicated mathematically. It works best for tests of knowledge or ability, though it can be applied more generally. The basic idea is to plot the probability of correctly responding to an item (usually one that has a yes–no or pass–fail response) against levels of the underlying trait that the test is trying to assess. This graph, which has an elongated S-shape, is known as the item-characteristic curve. For example, it could plot the proportion of correct answers to the item "who wrote *War and Peace*?" against the respondent's verbal IQ.

The item-characteristic curve demonstrates the difficulty level of the item for various levels of the latent construct being measured, and is a rapid way to summarize its performance. There are various mathematical models of the relationship between the latent construct and the probability of passing the item: the one parameter (or Rasch) model, and the two and three parameter models. For technical details, see Embretson and Prenovost (1999), Fox and Jones (1998), or Rust and Golombok (1999).

One clinical example of item response theory is Santor et al.'s (1994) detailed investigation of potential gender bias in the Beck Depression Inventory. They found that depressed men and women responded equivalently to the majority of items; the only exception being that women endorsed the item on body image distortion more strongly than men. Item response theory is also particularly useful for computerized psychological testing, as it enables the computer to present items that are determined by the participant's previous performance, thus greatly increasing the efficiency of the testing procedure.

Utility

In addition to reliability and validity, measures also vary in their utility or practical value. Measures which are easy to complete, or take little time to administer or score, are more convenient than measures which require more skill and time. Another aspect of utility is the incremental value of the information provided. Does the instrument yield information which has not been obtained from other measures and which therefore adds something or can be put to good use?

For example, the utility criterion weighs against using the Rorschach projective test as a measure of pre-post change in therapy, because it is time consuming and difficult to administer and score—except in circumstances where the Rorschach provides critical information that can be gathered in no other way. On the other hand, piling on additional easy-to-administer self-report outcome measures may also violate utility considerations (in addition to imposing an unacceptable burden on the participants), because such measures are typically highly intercorrelated and thus do not add useful information.

Standards for Reliability and Validity

Reliability and validity calculations are useful both for off-the-shelf measures and for measures that you are constructing yourself. The usual practice is to report the reliability of new or uncommon measures in the Method section of a research paper. Table 4.4 gives some suggested standards for evaluating the reliability and validity of measures. These have no logical basis; they are simply rules of thumb

Table 4.4 Suggested reliability and validity standards

	Reliability	Validity
Good	0.80	0.50
Acceptable	0.70	0.30
Marginal	0.60	0.20
Poor	0.50	0.10

that represent current standards in the research community (although there are variations between different researchers and journals). We have drawn from the recommendations of Kraemer (1981) and Nunnally and Bernstein (1994), in addition to our own experience in scale development and editorial reviewing.

Statistical significance tests of reliability coefficients are usually irrelevant, since they are too lenient, as the null hypothesis of no agreement at all should be easily rejected in most cases. What matters is the magnitude of the coefficient, not whether it attains statistical significance.

Generally speaking, the higher the reliability the better. However, it is possible to have too much of a good thing. Reliabilities greater than 0.90 may indicate either overkill (i.e., too many items or raters) or triviality (selection of superficial but readily ratable variables).

Values in validity research (i.e., research which attempts to test predicted relationships among constructs) are typically substantially lower than in reliability research (i.e., research which attempts to generalize across raters, occasions or within measures). In this case, values of 0.70 or higher generally mean that one is really tapping reliability instead of validity (i.e., that the two measures are really measuring the same thing instead of two different things that are supposed to be related). Validity values of 0.50 can be considered good, and 0.30 acceptable, but these recommendations are much more tentative, as they depend considerably on the particular application area. In particular, validity coefficients in epidemiological research tend to run much smaller than in clinical or personality research.

CHAPTER SUMMARY AND CONCLUSIONS

This chapter has examined the theory and philosophical background of psychological measurement, looking at how to conceptualize the measurement process and how to evaluate the quality of particular measures. The process of going from an underlying construct to the measurement of that construct is known as operationalization. There are typically several ways to measure any given construct; how it is done depends on the research questions, the theoretical framework, and the available resources.

The quantitative approach to measurement partly derives from the philosophical position of positivism, which seeks to model psychology and the social sciences on the methods used in the physical sciences. The positivist approach has been heavily critiqued, especially by qualitative researchers.

The central framework for conceptualizing the properties of quantitative measures is known as psychometric theory. Making some simple assumptions within psychometric theory allows us to develop a set of ideas, known as classical test theory, about how to evaluate measures. The central concepts are reliability and validity. Reliability concerns the reproducibility of measurement: its principal subtypes are test-test reliability, internal consistency, and inter-rater reliability. Validity assesses the meaning of measurement. It can be divided into content, face, criterion, and construct validity. Reliability is a necessary, but not sufficient, condition for validity. Finally, there is the concept of utility, which asks: how easy is the measure to administer and what information does it add? Two alternatives to classical test theory are generalizability theory and item response theory; however they are both more complicated mathematically.

The measurement criteria of reliability, validity, and utility relate to the four epistemological truth criteria discussed in Chapter 2. Criterion validity is an instance of the correspondence criterion of truth, while construct validity and internal consistency are examples of the coherence criterion. Furthermore, inter-rater reliability is an example of the consensus criterion, and utility fits the pragmatist criterion. Thus, the different principles of quantitative measurement are all part of a "system of inquiry" (Polkinghorne, 1983) into the truth of psychological phenomena.

Considerations of reliability and validity are central to evaluating quantitative measures, but whether they can be extended to qualitative methods is still being debated. We will address these issues at the end of the next chapter, after examining the rationale behind qualitative approaches in general.

FURTHER READING

For an extensive but accessible treatment of the quantitative versus qualitative research issue, see Bryman (1988). For general psychometric theory, Nunnally and Bernstein's (1994) text gives a thorough treatment, and Rust and Golombok (1999) cover recent approaches. It is worth becoming acquainted with two classic papers in psychometric theory: Cronbach and Meehl (1955) on construct validity and Campbell and Fiske (1959) on convergent and discriminant validity. They are both difficult to read in their entirety, but dipping into the first few pages of each will provide a flavor of the reasoning. The June 1995 special issue of *Psychological Assessment* has several articles reviewing contemporary approaches to psychometrics.

CHAPTER 5

FOUNDATIONS OF QUALITATIVE METHODS

KEY POINTS IN THIS CHAPTER

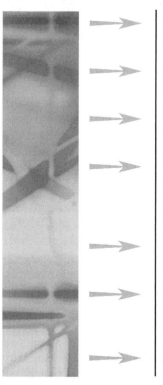

Qualitative research uses language as its raw material.

It aims to study people's thoughts, experiences, feelings, or use of language in depth and detail.

The main advantage of qualitative methods is that they allow a rich description.

There are two main traditions, phenomenology and constructionism, although there is considerable diversity within, and overlap between, these traditions.

Phenomenologists attempt to understand the person's perceptions and experiences.

Constructionists focus on how language is used in social interactions, and how discourse is affected by culture, history, and social structure.

It is possible to specify criteria for evaluating qualitative research studies.

The raw material for qualitative research is ordinary language, as opposed to the numbers that are the raw material for quantitative research. The language may be obtained in many ways. It may be the participant's own descriptions of him or herself, recorded during a qualitative interview. Or it could be words transcribed from a conversation, such as that between a client and a therapist during a session of therapy. Or it could be something printed, such as a newspaper article or the operational policy statement of a hospital's management committee. It could also take the form of the researcher's field notes of the participants' behavior, as written down after a qualitative observation session. Whatever source it may come from, linguistic data can give the researcher rich, deep, and complex information, sometimes referred to as "thick description" (Geertz, 1973).

This can be used to understand people's feelings, thoughts, ways of understanding the world, or ways of communicating with others.

A simplified illustration of the difference between the quantitative and the qualitative approach is shown in the differing responses to the question "How are you feeling today?" A quantitatively oriented researcher might ask the participant to respond on a seven-point scale, ranging from 1 = "Very unhappy" to 7 = "Very happy," and receive an answer of 5, signifying "Somewhat happy." A qualitative researcher might ask the same person the same question, "How are you feeling today?", but request an open-ended answer, which could run something like "Not too bad, although my knee is hurting me a little, and I've just had an argument with my boyfriend. On the other hand, I think I might be up for promotion at work, so I'm excited about that." In other words, the quantitative approach yields data which are relatively simple to process, but are limited in depth and hide ambiguities; the qualitative approach yields a potentially large quantity of rich, complex data which may be difficult and time consuming to analyze.

However, the difference between quantitative and qualitative approaches to research is about more than the difference between numbers and words; it is also about epistemology, the theory of what knowledge consists of (see Chapter 2). As we noted in Chapter 4, quantitative research is largely based on the philosophy of positivism. Qualitative researchers usually reject positivism, often quite vehemently, instead preferring non-realist epistemological positions based on developing understanding rather than on testing hypotheses (Bryman, 1988). We will describe these positions more fully below.

It is worth noting in passing that there is one potential source of confusion over the meaning of the word "qualitative," as it also has a second distinct meaning in research terminology. In quantitative research, the term "qualitative data" is used to refer to nominal scale data, to distinguish it from ordinal or interval scale data (see Chapter 4 on psychometric theory). Thus, census categories measuring ethnic background (white European, black African, etc.) may be referred to as a "qualitative" variable (because they have no ordering property), even though the data are analyzed by quantitative methods. However, in this book we will reserve the term "qualitative" for data that are collected by open-ended questions or by observations that yield verbal descriptions. Simple yes–no responses or nominal categories will be considered as a form of quantitative data, since they are narrowly delimited. The qualitative–quantitative distinction, as we are using it, boils down to whether the data are collected and analyzed as words or numbers (including counts, proportions, multiple choice, and yes–no responses).

Advantages

The main advantages of using qualitative methods are:

- They avoid the simplifications imposed by quantification, since some things cannot be easily expressed numerically. That is, they enable more complex aspects of experience to be studied and impose fewer restrictions on the data or the underlying theoretical models than quantitative approaches.

- They allow the researcher to address research questions that do not easily lend themselves to quantification, such as the nature of individual experiences of a psychological condition (e.g., eating disorders) or event (e.g., being a victim of crime).

- They enable the individual to be studied in depth and detail.

- The raw data are usually vivid and easy to grasp: good qualitative research reports make the participants come alive for the reader. In general, the reports of qualitative studies are often more readable than those of quantitative studies (except that some qualitative researchers, especially those with postmodernist or existential-phenomenological leanings, tend to write in an impenetrable jargon all of their own).

- Qualitative methods are good for hypothesis generation, and for exploratory, discovery-oriented research. They permit a more flexible approach, allowing the researcher to modify his or her protocol in mid-stream. The data collection is not constrained by pre-existing hypotheses.

- Qualitative self-report methods usually give more freedom to the participant than structured quantitative methods. For example, open-ended questions give interviewees a chance to respond in their own words and in their own way.

- Since the data collection procedures are less constrained, the researchers may end up in the interesting position of finding things that they were not originally looking for or expecting.

Historical Background

Qualitative methods can be traced back to the ancient Greek historians. For example, Herodotus, who is often called the father of history, traveled widely in the ancient world and recounted in his *Histories* the stories he had heard from the people he met. His successors down the ages recorded their observations of people that they encountered in their travels. These kinds of observations eventually became formalized in the discipline of anthropology.

In their modern form, qualitative methods were first used in ethnographic fieldwork. In the early decades of the 20th century, the founders of cultural anthropology, such as Malinowski and Boas, conducted ethnographic observations on cultural groups that were remote from their own: Malinowski in the Trobriand Islands in Papua New Guinea and Boas with the Kwakiutl tribe in the Pacific Northwest Coast of North America. They spent many months living with and observing the cultures they were studying. In the 1920s and 1930s, sociologists adapted these methods to study subcultures within their own society. For example, the "Chicago school" of sociology tended to focus on people at the fringes of society, such as criminals and youth gangs. A classic example of this genre is Whyte's (1943) *Street corner society*, which was based on fieldwork with an Italian-American youth gang in Boston, Massachusetts. Ethnographic methods started out being used to study the "weird and wonderful" (from a Eurocentric viewpoint), e.g., Pacific Island tribal cultures, and have been brought progressively closer to bear on the investigators' own culture, culminating in such contemporary specialties as medical anthropology, which use anthropological methods to study health and illness in our own culture (Helman, 1990).

Some ethnographic work is located on the rather fuzzy boundary between social science and journalism. A good example is Blythe's (1979) *The view in winter*, a moving account of people describing how they experience being old. The distinction is that journalism seeks to report accurately and produce an engaging story, whereas social science brings a body of theory to bear on the subject matter, or seeks to develop theory from the data, and it articulates its assumptions and procedures in order to enable replication.

In clinical research, qualitative methods were first used in case histories (see Chapter 9), for instance, Breuer and Freud's (1895/1955) first cases, which began the psychoanalytic tradition, and Watson and Rayner's (1920) study of "Little Albert," which helped establish the behavioral tradition. There is also a tradition of participant observation methods in mental health research, though they are more often conducted by sociologists than by psychologists. Classic examples of participant observation studies are Goffman's (1961) *Asylums* and Rosenhan's (1973) "Sane in insane places" study.

The two main qualitative data collection methods currently used in clinical psychology research are in-depth interviewing (see Chapter 6) and qualitative observation (see Chapter 7). Common data analytic methods are grounded theory, various types of phenomenological analysis, and discourse analysis (general principles of qualitative data analysis are covered in Chapter 12).

Traditions of qualitative research

Qualitative research is unfortunately not immune to the usual kinds of factions that bedevil most academic enterprises. Although qualitative researchers are united by their wish to move beyond the perceived limitations of the quantitative approach, they dispute the underlying epistemology and philosophy of science that characterizes their endeavors. Broadly speaking, we will consider qualitative approaches under two headings: the phenomenological tradition and the social constructionist tradition. However, other writers would find this dichotomy simplistic. For example, Willig (2001) depicts the approaches as being arranged on a continuum, ranging from realist to relativist. Much like in qualitative analysis generally, there is no one best way to organize the material, just various possible constructions.

It is also worth noting that, whichever way they are classified, there is considerable diversity within, and overlap between, the various qualitative approaches. Also, some approaches have different variants under the same label: for example, there is more than one version of grounded theory and of discourse analysis.

Phenomenologists attempt to understand the person's thoughts, feelings, perceptions, and interpretations of the world. Social constructionists, and the postmodernists with whom they are often allied, look at language as a social product in itself, questioning many of the familiar concepts, such as reality, truth or the person, that are taken for granted in other branches of the discipline. The next two sections of this chapter describe each of these traditions in more detail.

PHENOMENOLOGICAL APPROACHES

Central tenets of phenomenology:

- The objects of study are people's experiences, "life worlds," and underlying assumptions.

- Understanding is the true end of science.

- Multiple valid perspectives are possible.

The word "phenomenology" is itself a bit of a mouthful, and some of the underlying theory is couched in off-putting existentialist jargon. However, phenomenology is simply the study of phenomena (singular: phenomenon), and "phenomenon" is simply a fancy word for perception (that is, what appears to us). In any case, the essence of phenomenology is relatively simple: it is the systematic study of people's experiences and ways of viewing the world.

Sometimes the approach is known as "phenomenological-hermeneutic," to stress its interpretive aspect. ("Hermeneutic" is a fancy word for interpretive, and can be used interchangeably with it.) However, there is a potential source of confusion here, as there is a brand of phenomenological research known as "Interpretative Phenomenological Analysis" (Smith et al., 1999), which we will discuss below. (Interpretative is given here in its British spelling, because the approach originated in the UK.) Here, we will use the term "phenomenological" in its general sense, to also encompass phenomenological-hermeneutic methods.

Philosophical Background

Phenomenological approaches in psychology derive from the phenomenological movement in philosophy, which developed in the late-19th and early-20th centuries. It in turn is descended from the rationalist, idealist philosophical tradition of Plato and Kant. Husserl was its founder; Brentano, Heidegger,

Merleau-Ponty, and Sartre were key figures in its development (Jennings, 1986; Spinelli, 1989). Their ideas were introduced into psychology by Giorgi, Laing, May, and others (e.g., Giorgi, 1975; Laing, 1959; May et al., 1958), and were a major influence on the client-centered, humanistic, and existential approaches to psychological therapy.

Assumptions

We can distinguish four central assumptions of phenomenology. First, perception is regarded as the primary psychological activity, since our perceptions give rise to what we do, think, and feel. Because of this, *perceived meaning* is more important than objective reality, facts, or events.

Second, *understanding* is regarded as being the true end of science (in contrast, for example, to the aim of prediction and control that more traditional hypothetico-deductive approaches espouse). The goal is to produce explanations of the person's experiences and actions in terms of intentions, purposes, and meanings.

A third key assumption is that of *multiple perspectives*, also known as "epistemological pluralism." Each person's perspective has its own validity (i.e., it is how they see things); therefore, multiple, differing perspectives are equally valid and of interest for study. These multiple perspectives constitute different life-worlds (in German, *umwelten*). For example, the same aging oak tree is radically different when perceived by the forester, the lost child, the fox, or the wood beetle. These life-worlds are the object of study for the phenomenologist (Pollio, 1982).

Fourth, individuals' perceptions of their life-worlds are based on implicit assumptions or *presuppositions*, which phenomenologists also try to understand. That is, what we perceive is built on multiple assumptions about ourselves, others, and the world. These assumptions are the taken-for-granted, unquestioned context for our actions and perceptions. For example, if an acquaintance greets you with "How are you?", you are not usually expected to give an accurate or detailed answer; in fact, to anyone but a close friend, it would seem quite odd to do so—the underlying assumption is that we respond with a brief, positive answer. Although we accept these underlying assumptions, we are not generally aware of them and do not question them. In other words, they are believed to be "known to all" and part of what "everybody knows that everybody knows" (Garfinkel, 1967).

A key set of underlying assumptions is known as the "natural attitude" or "mundane reason" (Pollner, 1987). This is made up of the unquestioned belief that things are what they appear to be, and that all sane persons share the same world. In fact, in everyday life, it is considered strange or deviant to talk about many of these presuppositions, so that their very obviousness at the same time hides them or prevents them from being noticed.

Table 5.1 Types of phenomenological research

Type of research	Sample references
Client-centered research	Rogers, 1985; Shlien, 1970
Consensual qualitative research	Hill et al., 1997
Ethnography	Fetterman, 1989
Empirical phenomenology (Duquesne school)	Giorgi, 1975; Wertz, 1983
Field and participant observation	Taylor & Bogdan, 1998
Grounded theory	Henwood & Pidgeon, 1992; Strauss & Corbin, 1998
Hermeneutic-interpretive research	Packer & Addison, 1989; Terwee, 1990
Interpretative phenomenological analysis	Smith et al., 1999
Life history or biographical research	Denzin, 1989; Taylor & Bogdan, 1998
Protocol analysis	Ericsson & Simon, 1993

Types of Phenomenological Research

The explosion of interest in phenomenological research in the past 20 years has given rise to a bewildering number of variations, the more important of which are listed in Table 5.1. However, it is worth bearing in mind that, in practice, they have much more in common than separates them. We will briefly describe four approaches that are commonly encountered by clinical psychologists: empirical phenomenology, grounded theory, hermeneutic approaches, and interpretative phenomenological analysis.

Empirical Phenomenology

The oldest systematic approach to phenomenological psychology is associated with Duquesne University (Pittsburgh, USA), and published in the *Journal of Phenomenological Psychology* (see also *Duquesne studies of phenomenological psychology*, 1971 to 1983). Giorgi, Wertz, and Fischer are three of the better known proponents. The approach stresses in-depth analysis, often at first of single cases, aiming to describe the main defining features of an experience (e.g., that of being criminally victimized), and the different variations that the experience may have in the population (analogous to the statistical ideas of mean and standard deviation). Carrying out research in this tradition involves the practice of the phenomenological method, a rigorous procedure that is based on two key processes: bracketing and describing.

Bracketing is an attempt to set aside one's assumptions and expectations, as far as is humanly possible. However, because one's underlying assumptions are often hidden, it requires a special act of reflection to identify them. This act has been described in several different ways. The most common is "bracketing the natural attitude" (or "bracketing" for short). It involves a process of stepping back from the phenomenon in order to see it as if from the outside, as if we were the proverbial observer from Mars. Bracketing involves a special kind of turning away from the natural attitude, in which the researcher does not accept a description as a statement about the world, but simply as a statement about an experience of the world.

In the clinical context, bracketing is one aspect of the process of empathy in such exploratory psychotherapies as client-centered and experiential therapy. When a client says that she is "trapped" in a situation, the therapist is not interested in determining whether this is factually the case; what is important is that the client feels trapped (Rogers, 1975). In contrast, beginning therapists generally prefer to stay "within the natural attitude" by trying to talk the client out of such presumed irrational beliefs, often questioning the facts of the situation. One important component of empathy is letting go of one's own presuppositions, in order to understand what the client is trying to say. A similar idea is found in the ideal therapist state of "evenly hovering, free-floating attention" referred to in the psychoanalytic literature (e.g., Greenson, 1967).

A naive approach to bracketing might be to mentally steel oneself and promise to give up one's biases. However, a more fruitful alternative is to begin by carefully investigating one's assumptions. At the beginning of a study, the researcher can conduct a thought experiment of carrying out the study in imagination in order to identify expectations of what it might find. This thought experiment might also be repeated at the end of the study in order to identify additional expectations that only became clear in the course of the study. These expectations take the place of hypotheses in traditional research, but they are not the same. In phenomenological research, expectations are not given a place of honor at the end of the introduction, instead, they are figuratively locked in a drawer until the study is over. Phenomenological research is perhaps most exciting when it uncovers understandings that are unexpected or even startling.

The second step in the empirical phenomenological method is *describing*. Several principles are involved (see, for example, Spinelli, 1989). First, good descriptions focus on concrete or specific impressions, as opposed to the abstract or general. Second, they avoid evaluative terms such as "good or bad" and their many synonyms and euphemisms (e.g., "ineffective," "helpful"), except where these are part of the experience itself. Third, they tend to avoid explanations, particularly early in the research. The task is to discover meaning, not invent it. This means avoiding "why" questions or anything that encourages the informant to speculate on causes or reasons: such questions encourage intellectualization and interfere with the slow, careful process of attending to concrete experience.

Grounded Theory

Grounded theory is probably the most common form of qualitative analysis used today. It was developed by two North American sociologists, Glaser and Strauss, in their 1967 book, *The discovery of grounded theory: Strategies for qualitative research.* As the title suggests, Glaser and Strauss were attempting to articulate how qualitative data could be used not just to provide rich descriptions, but also to generate theory. Grounded theory can be used with a range of qualitative material, such as semi-structured interviews, focus groups, participant observation, and diaries.

The term "grounded theory" is potentially confusing, as it refers both to a method—a set of systematic procedures for analyzing data—and also to the outcome or product of the analysis, which is theory "grounded" in the data. The basic process involves identifying categories at a low level of abstraction and then building up to more abstract theoretical concepts. The end point is often one or more core categories, which capture the essence of the phenomenon (see Chapter 12). This process of analysis occurs concurrently with the process of data collection, and the developing theory guides the sampling strategy ("theoretical sampling": see Chapter 10).

The original Glaser and Strauss (1967) volume was more theoretical and polemical rather than practical; it was aimed at challenging the prevailing quantitative paradigm in American sociology. The practical implications for researchers, i.e., the steps in actually carrying out a grounded theory study, are developed in Glaser (1978) and Strauss and Corbin (1998).

The grounded theory method was taken up by psychologists in the 1980s and 1990s. Articles by Rennie et al. (1988) and by Henwood and Pidgeon (1992) were aimed at introducing the grounded theory approach to an audience of psychologists. Rennie and Brewer's (1987) study entitled "A grounded theory of thesis blocking" (i.e., writer's block among research students) may well be of personal interest to some readers of this text! As more psychologists have taken up the invitation of Rennie et al., and of Henwood and Pidgeon, grounded theory has become a popular approach to qualitative research.

One example of the method in clinical psychology is Bolger's (1999) study of the phenomenon of emotional pain. The participants were women in a therapy group for adult children of alcoholics; they were interviewed on several occasions following group therapy sessions in which they had explored painful life experiences. The interviews focused on how pain was experienced and what was significant in that experience for them. The core category that emerged from the analysis was labeled the "broken self," characterized by four sub-categories of woundedness, disconnection, loss of self, and awareness of self.

Another, well-known, example of a grounded theory study, in a more popularized book format, is Charmaz's (1991) analysis of the experience of living with chronic illness (see box).

Hermeneutic Approaches

A somewhat more flexible approach to qualitative research is represented by approaches that bill themselves as hermeneutic (e.g., Packer & Addison, 1989). Researchers who describe themselves in this way find grounded theory and empirical phenomenology too restrictive and use a wider range of methods. They argue that it is important to go beyond the surface meaning of research

---

Grounded theory example: Charmaz (1991)

The sociologist Kathy Charmaz conducted in-depth qualitative interviews with people who had a chronic illness. The results, written up in her book *Good days, bad days* (1991), give compelling accounts of the impact of chronic illness on people's lives. In accordance with the grounded theory approach, she also used the data to construct a theory of how the person's experience of time changes, and how this impacts on their sense of self.

---

protocols, in order to identify the implicit or even unconscious meanings embedded in texts.

A recent example is a study by Walsh et al. (1999), which used a hermeneutic approach to explore "good moments" within a videotaped psychotherapy session. They identified the differing values of professionals and students at various stages of training about what constituted good psychotherapy.

Interpretative Phenomenological Analysis

A final example of the phenomenological approach, which often appeals to newcomers to qualitative research, is Interpretative Phenomenological Analysis (Smith et al., 1999). This is an accessible and clearly presented procedure for conducting qualitative research, set out with a minimum of theoretical baggage. Interpretative Phenomenological Analysis is basically a systematic and practical approach to analyzing phenomenological data. It articulates the steps involved in conducting an investigation: e.g., how to generate meaningful lower order and higher order categories from the data. Smith et al.'s (1999) chapter sets out the basis of their method, illustrating its steps using examples of data drawn from clinical and health psychology. Hill and colleagues (1997) have also described a comparable highly structured, easy-to-follow method of qualitative analysis, which they refer to as Consensual Qualitative Research.

SOCIAL CONSTRUCTIONIST APPROACHES

Social constructionists (constructionists, for short) are interested in how language is used to order and manage the world. In contrast to phenomenologists, constructionists do not see language as necessarily reflecting the individual's underlying thoughts and feelings; rather they are interested in how people use language to structure things, or to get things done. For example, constructionist researchers have examined psychiatric diagnostic systems from the point of view of how diagnosis may be used by mental health professionals to impose a particular view of the world on people's experience (e.g. Georgaca, 2000; Harper, 1994).

Central features of social constructionism:

- Part of the postmodernist and poststructuralist movements.

- Non-realist.

- "Radical pluralism."

- Often focuses on language in text or speech.

- Stresses the indeterminacy (ambiguity) of language and meaning.

- Interested in language as social action.

- Does not assume that language reflects cognition.

- Emphasizes the reflexivity (circular nature) of psychological theory.

Background to Social Constructionism

The basis of the constructionist approaches is an opposition to the realist approach to social science, in particular as articulated by adherents of positivism (see Chapters 2 and 4). Social constructionists reject, or at least dispense with, the assumption of an underlying, independent reality (Gergen, 1985; Madill et al., 2000; Willig, 2001). They may speak in terms of multiple realities—that each individual constructs their own personal reality. This rejection of realism is to some extent shared by the phenomenologists, although the constructionist position tends to be more forcefully expressed and may be more thorough going: phenomenologists do not explicitly reject realism, they just accept that different people may have different concepts of what reality is.

However, as we have mentioned above, there is a diversity of views within many qualitative approaches, and social constructionism is no exception. There is a radical version of constructionism that completely rejects any notion of reality. Thus Guba and Lincoln (1989) write that their constructivist paradigm "denies the existence of an objective reality, asserting instead that realities are social constructions of the mind, and that there exist as many such constructions as there are individuals (although clearly many constructions will be shared)" (p. 43). Such radical constructionists also do not wish to "privilege" one world view over any other. Thus they see traditional scientific methods as one possible way of understanding the world, but would not necessarily regard them as being any more valid than other systems of belief, such as shamanism or astrology. However, they would accept that scientists' own criteria for validity are meaningful within the scientists' own domain of discourse.

Social constructionists pay close attention to language, spoken and written. However, they analyze language in a different way to researchers working within traditional realist approaches, who are usually concerned with whether statements expressed in language are true or not. Thus if a psychiatrist says, "This patient is paranoid", a realist approach would be to see whether the statement was accurate—i.e., is the patient paranoid or not? In constructionism the focus shifts towards looking at how people construct their arguments and what work their constructions do: for example, what rhetorical devices does the psychiatrist use to convince us of the validity of her position, that the patient is indeed paranoid (see Harper, 1994)?

The type of focus on language also distinguishes the constructionist approach from the phenomenological one. Phenomenologists and social constructionists may share the assumption that objective reality is not of primary concern. Furthermore, phenomenologists also use spoken language, in the form of qualitative interviews, as their primary medium of research. However, the phenomenologist is using the language to understand the thoughts and feelings of the participants—to try and understand their inner world. For radical constructionists, this act of understanding, too, is a social construction, leaving us with only the process of construction to study, especially as this plays out in

---

Social Constructionism versus Constructivism—What's the difference?

The terms "constructionism" and "constructivism" are often used interchangeably, but they are not identical. Constructionism usually refers to the view that the concepts we use—e.g., madness or masculinity—are socially determined, that is, they don't refer to an independent reality but may vary across cultures or over time. Constructivism is a more psychological concept; it refers to the process by which individuals arrive at the constructs they use. One important example of constructivist thinking is Kelly's (1955) personal construct theory, which looks at the central constructs each individual uses in order to make sense of their world.

Another example of constructivism can be found in contemporary cognitive therapy. Historically, cognitive therapists have viewed the external world as less important than how clients make sense of the world. The ancient Stoic philosopher Epictetus is often quoted: "Men are not disturbed by things, but by the view which they take of them." However, as Neimeyer (1993) points out, most cognitive therapists follow in the realist tradition, in that thoughts are viewed as rational (and therefore healthy) if they correspond to reality. This realist stance is similar to that adopted by traditional psychiatry, in which the prime criterion for psychosis is loss of contact with reality. However, some contemporary cognitive-behavioral therapists have begun to move toward a constructivist position, which is, as we have noted, more internally consistent with its philosophical roots.

language use. As Reicher (2000) puts it ". . . language is a form of social action which we use in order to create our social world. The focus is on how apparent descriptions serve to manage our social relations. Psychological categories such as beliefs, desires, and even experience, are only of interest in so far as participants themselves put them to use in their discourse" (pp. 3–4).

The other feature of many constructionist theories is that they stress the *reflexivity* (from "reflection," a function of mirrors) of psychological theorizing. By this is meant that psychologists are doing the theorizing, but the psychologists themselves, as human beings, are also the object of the theory. Psychological research is thus a circular process, which is what the reflexivity metaphor is attempting to capture. Some constructionists maintain that the existence of reflexivity fatally undermines any claims of psychology to be an objective science.

Postmodernism

Social constructionism is closely aligned with the body of thought known as postmodernism, or sometimes poststructuralism (the two terms overlap, but are not synonymous). This can be rather difficult territory. One major difficulty is that it is often hard to pin down exactly what many of the authors writing in this tradition are actually saying, as their prose style is often opaque, and the ratio of useful ideas to verbiage can seem frustratingly low. However, postmodern thought is currently fashionable and much discussed within several fields of study, so it is important to come to grips with it.

A second difficulty, however, is that the term "postmodernism" itself is hard to define. It refers to a rather loose collection of ideas that have found expression in a number of different fields, e.g., literary theory, sociology, and architecture. The key figures are all French: the literary theorist Derrida, the historian Foucault, the psychoanalyst Lacan. Some of its central themes are:

- *A rejection of "grand theories"* that provide overarching explanations, such as psychoanalysis or Marxism; instead micro- or composite theories are favored. This is coupled with a questioning of the personal and social interests that lie behind scientific theories, particularly where those theories seem to serve the interests of those in power (Prilleltensky, 1997).

- *An intellectual playfulness*, that borrows from many different traditions within the same piece of work. For example, postmodernist architecture often "quotes" from earlier traditions, inserting a Gothic turret here, a Georgian window there. This is exemplified in the image of the qualitative researcher as "*bricoleur*," a sort of handy-person who uses whatever is at hand to construct things that are useful but not elegant (Levi-Strauss, 1958/1963; McLeod, 2001).

- *A focus on language*. Lyotard (1979) borrows Wittgenstein's phrase, "language games," to capture both the aspect of playfulness and the idea that language is governed by rules.

- *The indeterminacy (ambiguity) of language*. Post-modernists stress that all communication carries multiple meanings, so that understanding is always an act of interpretation, and what one reader makes of a text may differ from another reader's understanding. Eagleton (1983) gives the example of a sign seen in the London Underground: "Dogs must be carried on escalators." Does this mean one cannot step on the escalator unless one is carrying a dog?

Constructionism is not identical to postmodernism, and it was first articulated before postmodernism became popular (e.g., Berger & Luckmann, 1966). However, the postmodernist viewpoint has been adopted by many social constructionists (e.g., Gergen, 1994, 2001), and it provides a useful framework in which to understand their ideas.

Critiques of Postmodernism

The postmodernist position (and also the extreme versions of constructionism) have been fiercely criticized, in a debate which has generated much heat, and perhaps a little light. The main lines of argument are:

- The lack of interest in people's mental states is open to the same criticisms that were earlier leveled at the methodological behaviorists, who adopted an identical stance for completely different reasons (i.e., to become, as they saw it, more scientific). A psychology that sidesteps the role of inner experiencing is severely limited, and ultimately presents an alienating view of the person.

- Likewise, the non-realist emphasis can make research into an ivory tower exercise. Reality is important, especially unpleasant reality. Studying rape, child abuse, racism, or genocide purely from a discursive viewpoint can easily seem to diminish their importance or even appear to deny their existence or the need to prevent them.

- The underlying model of the person is that of a fragmented, unintegrated self; it is not the model that many psychological therapists, who are trying to help their clients feel more whole, would endorse. Likewise, the person can be viewed as a manipulator of language, whose goal is to manage the impression they make or to get others to act in a certain way. This is not an image of human beings that can support the enterprise of helping people lead more fulfilling, meaningful lives.

- The language that postmodernists employ is often riddled with impenetrable jargon, which seems designed to convey an impression of erudition and profundity. Sokal and Bricmont (1999) exposed the ridiculousness of much postmodernist writing, especially its use of scientific metaphors, in their critique, *Intellectual impostures*.

Conclusion

In summary, the strong points of the constructionist position are that they remind us to look closely and critically at how language is used to construct reality and to accomplish practical purposes. What "position" is the speaker or writer trying to adopt, how is their language being used to bolster this position, and what is

Table 5.2 Main types of social constructionist approaches

Type of research	Sample references
Conversation analysis	Sacks (1995); Schegloff (1999)
Critical approaches	Lather (1991); Reason and Rowan (1981)
Deconstructionism	Slife and Williams (1995)
Discourse analysis	Potter and Wetherell (1987)
Radical feminist research	Belenky et al. (1986)
Social representations	Farr and Moscovici (1984)

finally achieved by this? It also stresses the theory-dependent nature of scientific observation: a view that the constructionists share with Popper (see Chapter 2), who reached this position from a completely different philosophical standpoint. Finally, it stresses the social nature of psychological concepts. Instead of treating a concept such as "racism" or "mental illness" as an individual trait, constructionists urge us to look at the term in its wider social and political context.

Types of Social Constructionist Research

Like the phenomenological branch of qualitative research, several different strands of constructionist research can be identified (see Table 5.2). The most popular with psychologists is discourse analysis; other approaches include conversation analysis, social representations theory, critical and feminist approaches, and deconstructionism.

Discourse Analysis

Example of discourse analysis:

Madill and Barkham (1997) examined the transcripts of a single case of time-limited psychodynamic therapy. They showed how, during the course of therapy, the client took on three different subject positions—which they labeled as the dutiful daughter, the bad mother, and the damaged child—and the discourses that she drew upon which exemplify each of these. For instance, they argued that the dutiful daughter position "draws on 18th and 19th century discourses of female subjectivity. During this period, subject positions were provided for women based primarily upon their domesticity..." (p. 242). Thus they were able to analyze the client's talk within the context of its historical and social antecedents.

There are many kinds of discourse analysis (see van Dijk, 1997a, 1997b); it is an interdisciplinary field spanning psychology, sociology, communication, linguistics, and literature. Within psychology, the most popular approach is that articulated by Potter and Wetherell (1987). In general, discourse analysis involves rigorously examining texts, in order to analyze the repertoires of discourse that a speaker is drawing upon, and the kinds of "subject positions" that the speaker is adopting (see box for an example).

Conversation Analysis

Although sometimes grouped with discourse analysis, conversation analysis has its own tradition and its own particular methods. An outgrowth of the work of sociologists Garfinkel and Goffman, it was developed by Harvey Sacks (1995) as a rigorous method for identifying the common conversational sequences and strategies used by people to accomplish practical purposes. Conversation analysis attempts to study how speakers perceive each other's utterances, based on how they respond to each other. Although it attempts to develop general models of the strategies people use to accomplish practical work in conversation, it emphasizes the ad hoc, contextually embedded nature of "talk-in-interaction" (Schegloff, 1999). Over the past 25 years, conversation analysis has built up a large repertoire of provisional understandings of everyday and professional speech, including many investigations of psychotherapy (see Mondada, 1998, for a review).

One interesting clinical application of conversation analysis is Rapley and Antaki's (1996) British study of how psychologists administered a standardized quality-of-life instrument to people with learning disabilities (mental retardation in US terminology). They demonstrated how the interviewers' questioning strategies and reformulations shaped the answers that respondents produced. Their analysis challenged the traditional notion of acquiescence in this population (see Chapter 6) and suggested a more complex picture of the conversational strategies used by both interviewers and respondents.

Social Representations Theory

Example of research based on social representations theory:

Joffe (1996) examined how HIV/AIDS was discussed within various cultural groups. She adopted an interesting sampling strategy, interviewing black and white, heterosexual and homosexual participants in both Britain and South Africa. Using ideas drawn from psychoanalytic theory, she found that people in the various groups tended to represent HIV/AIDS in a way that enabled them to blame the members of an "outgroup" for the problem.

Social representations theory is influential within social psychology, but has not yet been widely taken up outside that sub-field. Originally articulated by

Moscovici and promulgated by Farr (e.g., Farr & Moscovici, 1984), social representations research involves the examination of how new ideas, especially scientific ideas, are perceived and assimilated within the culture at large. For instance, social representations researchers might examine the metaphors that people use to understand psychological disorders and their treatment.

Critical Approaches

Critical researchers attempt not only to understand but also to emancipate their research participants; they try to minimize the distinction between researcher and "subject" in order to create research in which participant and researcher are co-researchers who interact as equals. They argue that the act of studying another human being establishes an alienated relationship between them: the researcher treats the "subject" like an object.

This viewpoint is forcefully articulated by Reason and Rowan (1981). Their approach is sometimes described as the human inquiry approach and sometimes as new paradigm research (they use both labels in the title of their book). As McLeod (2001) notes, human inquiry research emphasizes disciplined subjectivity, respect for the whole person, linking research to action, and creative forms of presenting the results of research (e.g., in the form of art or poetry). An example is an investigation that Wilshaw (1996) carried out in collaboration with a support group for individuals who had been sexually abused as children. In this study, he acted as a co-participant in the support group and as a research consultant; members of the group selected the research questions, methods, and means of presenting the results (which consisted in part of group members' paintings, depicting the impact that their abuse had had on them).

Other critical research approaches include neo-Marxist approaches, as well as participatory action research and Freirian research (Lather, 1991).

Radical Feminist Approaches

There are several different strands of thinking within feminist psychology (Campbell & Wasco, 2000). Some feminists conduct their research largely within traditional quantitative approaches, others use more phenomenological methods, and some (e.g., Belenky et al., 1986; Carlson, 1972; Riger, 1992; Wilkinson, 1986) make a similar argument to the critical researchers. These latter see traditional paradigms, where the researcher is in charge of the relationship, as replicating patriarchal power relationships. Their critique is not only aimed at quantification and experimental manipulation, but also at more traditional forms of qualitative interviewing (Oakley, 1981).

Radical feminist researchers argue that to empower women one must listen directly to what they are saying and respond personally without hiding behind the facade of the objective researcher. Several authors (e.g., Carlson, 1972; Wilkinson, 1986) draw on P. Bakan's (1966) distinction between "agentic" and "communal" approaches. Agentic research, involving separating, ordering and controlling, is seen as a masculine activity; communal research, involving sensitivity and personal participation, is seen as feminine. However, in a feminist critique of this stance, Peplau and Conrad (1989) argue that attempts to identify a distinctive set of feminist research methods are mistaken, and that feminist researchers should avail themselves of the full range of research methods, including quantitative and experimental approaches.

Deconstructionism

Finally, deconstructionist researchers engage in self-critique, embracing a postmodern view of the research process. They see the major task of researchers as being "deconstruction" of the cultural, social, or epistemological assumptions of their work and that of others. They embrace radical pluralism, and attempt to speak or give air to multiple voices while eschewing any attempt to bring these voices together into a single message. In essence, they attempt to mirror fragmented, postmodern, multicultural society in their research. For example, a deconstructionist researcher such as Lather (1991) might present her findings as a kind of research collage.

Perhaps most importantly, deconstruction is an essential component of the process of evaluating research, in which one attempts to identify the implicit assumptions that drive a research study. Slife and Williams (1995) provide an excellent introduction to this approach. In our view, deconstructionism is less useful as a primary research method than as a method for reflecting on and critiquing research. This takes us to our final topic.

WAYS OF EVALUATING QUALITATIVE STUDIES

As must be obvious from the above discussion, the traditional psychometric criteria of reliability and validity do not easily carry over to qualitative approaches. The concepts of face and content validity can be used without much stretching, and a case can be argued for adapting some of the other concepts. However, it appears that a more fruitful approach is to articulate specific criteria for evaluating qualitative studies. Several scholars have recently attempted to do this (e.g., Elliott, Fischer, & Rennie, 1999; Stiles, 1993; Yardley, 2000).

We are partial to the Elliott, Fischer et al. (1999) version, not only because Elliott is a co-author of this text, but also because their guidelines, although having a broad applicability, were mainly developed and published within a clinical psychology context. Elliott et al. are attempting to help journal reviewers and editors evaluate qualitative studies that have been submitted for publication, but their framework is relevant to any readers of qualitative studies, as well as to researchers themselves. They describe some common guidelines shared by both quantitative and qualitative approaches, for example respect for participants and use of appropriate methods, and then guidelines specific to qualitative approaches (see Table 5.3). They describe each one and then give examples of

Table 5.3 Summary of Elliott et al.'s (1999) evolving guidelines

---

A. Publishability guidelines shared by both qualitative and quantitative approaches
1. Explicit scientific context and purpose
2. Appropriate methods
3. Respect for participants
4. Specification of methods
5. Appropriate discussion
6. Clarity of presentation
7. Contribution to knowledge

B. Publishability guidelines especially pertinent to qualitative research
1. Owning one's perspective
2. Situating the sample
3. Grounding in examples
4. Providing credibility checks
5. Coherence
6. Accomplishing general versus specific research tasks
7. Resonating with readers

Note. This table has been reproduced with permission from the *British Journal of Clinical Psychology* © The British Psychological Society.

good and bad practice under each. In summary, their guidelines for qualitative studies are:

Owning one's perspective. The authors describe their theoretical orientations and biases, in order to help readers evaluate the researchers' interpretation of the data. For example, they would state if they were coming to the research from a psychoanalytic, or from a feminist, perspective.

Situating the sample. The authors describe the research participants so that readers can judge how widely the findings might apply.

Grounding in examples. The authors provide enough examples of their raw data to illustrate the analytic procedures used and to allow the reader to evaluate their findings. They also stay close to the data; any speculations that exceed the data are clearly labeled as such.

Providing credibility checks. The researchers use methods for checking the credibility of the results, for example, *analytic auditing* (e.g., using multiple researchers or an additional person who checks the results against the data), *triangulation* (examining the phenomenon from multiple, varied perspectives) and *testimonial validity* (checking the results with the original informants or similar others).

Coherence. The interpretation of the data is coherent and integrated, but at the same time it does not oversimplify the data.

Accomplishing general versus specific research tasks. If the research aims to achieve a general understanding, then the appropriate range of people or situations is sampled. If it aims to achieve a specific understanding of a particular case, that case is described thoroughly enough for the reader to gain a full understanding.

Resonating with the reader. From the point of view of the reader, the results are not only believable but seem to capture or make sense of the phenomenon, enabling the reader to understand the phenomenon more fully.

CONCLUSIONS

Qualitative methods have now become much more fully accepted within psychology, and the heat seems to be dying out of the old quantitative versus qualitative debate. Research methodologists are now focusing their attention on when best to use either a quantitative or a qualitative approach, what is the appropriate qualitative method for any given research question, and how best to appraise qualitative studies. However, given that we have now described the fundamentals of both quantitative and qualitative approaches, it is worth briefly considering how researchers might decide between them.

How do you choose between a Qualitative and a Quantitative Approach?

We espouse the notion of *methodological pluralism*: that different research methods are appropriate for different types of research question (see Chapter 3). For example, qualitative methods are good for descriptive questions within a discovery-oriented framework—e.g., when you are trying to learn about a phenomenon that has not been previously researched. Quantitative methods are good for delimited questions of covariation and comparison, e.g., looking for relationships between variables.

On the other hand, all methods have weaknesses or limitations, so if possible it is better to use multiple methods of measuring important variables, an approach known as *triangulation*. In other words, it is unwise to rely solely on one perspective, source or approach (Campbell & Fiske, 1959; Cronbach & Meehl, 1955; Patton, 2002), because all of these have their limitations. For example, in psychotherapy outcome research it is useful to assess client change from the perspective of the client, the therapist, and a clinical interviewer. Moreover, a qualitative study focusing on how change occurred would complement the quantitative data (McLeod, 2001).

Clinical psychology may be gradually entering a more pluralist phase for pragmatic reasons. A variety of publications have urged psychologists to adopt a qualitative approach to research (e.g., Elliott, Fischer, & Rennie, 1999; Henwood & Pidgeon, 1992; Patton, 2002; Richardson, 1996; Smith, in press). However, the acid test—whether qualitative studies get published in prestigious journals—still reveals a strong quantitative bias in the field. There is still a residual attitude that qualitative methods are second class: the saying of Rutherford, the eminent physicist, that "qualitative is bad quantitative" (quoted in Stewart, 1989: 219) expresses this viewpoint succinctly. However, one sign that a pluralist attitude may be taking root is the interest among the newer generation of researchers. Qualitative methods seem to appeal particularly to graduate students in applied social sciences, because they allow much closer contact with clinical phenomena. In the institutions we are familiar with, an increasing number of dissertations and theses now employ qualitative methods, perhaps so much so that there is a danger in some places that traditional quantitative skills are no longer being acquired. We believe that clinical psychologists should be competent in both quantitative and qualitative methods.

Combining Qualitative and Quantitative Methods

It is possible to do research that combines both quantitative and qualitative methods; the two approaches can often complement each other. This can take several forms:

1. Beginning research in a new area with qualitative studies, either pilot research or more elaborate qualitative investigations.

2. Building quantitative studies on earlier qualitative research.

3. Using qualitative methods such as interviews and focus groups to develop quantitative measures.

4. Using qualitative data to elucidate or explore quantitative findings, either as an adjunct to a primarily quantitative study or as a follow-up investigation.

5. Using quantitative data to elucidate qualitative findings, i.e., the reverse of point 4, often found in sociology articles.

6. Using both kinds of data in a complementary fashion in the same study (e.g., case studies by Elliott, 1984; Parry et al., 1986).

7. Carrying out separate qualitative and quantitative studies of the same participants, either to address different questions, or to address the same question from different angles (e.g., Madill & Barkham, 1997; Patton, 2002).

As we hope to have made clear, choosing the approach depends largely on the question you are trying to answer. The next two chapters examine practical issues in selecting and constructing measures, covering the two major approaches to psychological measurement: self-report and observation, looking at each from both qualitative and quantitative points of view.

We hope that this chapter has given readers a taste of the range of available qualitative methods, and an understanding of their underlying philosophies, particularly the distinction between phenomenological and constructionist methods. This chapter has been mostly theoretically oriented; Chapter 12 will look in more detail at practical issues in analyzing qualitative data.

CHAPTER SUMMARY

This chapter has looked at the varieties of qualitative research. Qualitative approaches use language as their raw material, in order to examine the participants' thoughts, feelings, behavior, or linguistic strategies. Their main advantage is that they allow a rich description of the phenomena in depth and detail, sometimes called "thick description" (Geertz, 1973). There are two central traditions in qualitative research: phenomenology and constructionism. Phenomenologists attempt to understand the person's perceptions and experiences— their inner world. Constructionists, on the other hand, focus on how language is used in social interactions. The criteria of reliability and validity do not translate easily to qualitative research, but it is nevertheless possible to specify criteria for how qualitative research studies can be evaluated.

FURTHER READING

Many treatments of qualitative methods have recently been published. Richardson (1996), Smith (in press), and Willig (2001) give accessible treatments of the theory and practice of the commonly used approaches. Some of the old stalwarts, such as Lincoln and Guba (1985) and Patton (2002), still hold up, and Taylor and Bogdan's (1998) sociologically oriented text includes some illustrative studies, although their current edition omits the fascinating and moving single case account (originally published in Bogdan & Taylor, 1976) of an articulate "mentally retarded" man, "Ed Murphy", who describes his life in state institutions. Potter and Wetherell (1987) is a core reference for the social-psychological approach to discourse analysis. For an extensive but accessible treatment of the quantitative versus qualitative debate, see Bryman (1988) and Polkinghorne (1983). Since many qualitative approaches have their roots in literary theory, it is also worth reading about them in that context. Eagleton (1983) gives an excellent exposition and critique of, among other things, phenomenology, hermeneutics, and poststructuralism as applied to the analysis of literary texts.

CHAPTER 6

SELF-REPORT METHODS

KEY POINTS IN THIS CHAPTER

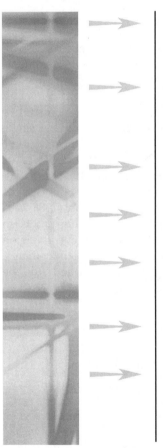

Self-report methods, such as interviews and questionnaires, ask the person for information directly.

Their advantage is that they give you the person's own perspective; their disadvantage is that there are potential validity problems (i.e., people may deceive themselves or others).

The main qualitative self-report approach is the semi-structured interview.

Qualitative interviewing is a distinct skill, related to but different from clinical interviewing.

The main quantitative self-report approach is the written questionnaire, but structured interviews and internet surveys are also used.

There are several principles to follow in constructing quantitative self-report instruments.

Response sets, such as acquiescence and social desirability, refer to tendencies to respond to items independently of their content. They need to be taken into account when designing and interpreting self-report measures.

When you want to know something about a person, the most natural thing is to ask. Research methods that take the approach of asking the person directly are known as self-report methods, and mainly take the form of interviews, questionnaires, and rating scales. They are the most commonly used type of measure in the social sciences in general and in clinical psychology in particular.

For example, suppose that you have set up a new counseling service for adolescents and want to evaluate its effectiveness. You ask the users to rate the severity of their problems before and after counseling, using two standardized instruments. You also devise a semi-structured interview to assess the adolescents' overall satisfaction with the service and any specific criticisms they had of it. *Consumer satisfaction studies* like this have become important, with the increased emphasis on accountability to the consumer.

Instead of asking the person directly, you may instead, or in addition, ask someone who knows the person, such as a friend, family member, or therapist. This is often called using an *informant* (a term which has unfortunate connotations of sneakiness). It allows you to get the views of someone who knows the person well and who has greater opportunity than you to observe him or her in a natural setting. It is also useful when the respondent cannot give you reliable information. For example, in research with children, it is often useful to have the parents' and the teacher's views of the relevant behavior. This is why, as we discussed in the previous chapter, a more accurate term would be "verbal-report" rather than "self-report." However, the term "self-report" is commonly used to cover reports from both the person of interest and from other respondents, and we will retain that usage here.

Advantages and Disadvantages

The great advantage of self-report is that it gives you the respondents' own views directly. It gives access to phenomenological data, i.e., respondents' perceptions of themselves and their world, which are unobtainable in any other way. Many psychologists, e.g., Harré (1974) and Kelly (1955), argue that researchers should ask participants for their own views unless there are compelling reasons not to do so. An important principle in Kelly's development of Personal Construct Theory was "If you do not know what is wrong with a person, ask him, he may tell you" (quoted in Fransella, 1981: 166). Furthermore, self-report methods can be used to obtain information in situations where observational data are not normally available, e.g., for studying life histories, or behavior during a major disaster.

The main disadvantage of self-report is that there are a number of potential validity problems associated with it. The data are personal and idiosyncratic and thus may bear little relationship to "reality," as seen by you or others. More importantly, people are not always truthful. They may deceive themselves, such as when an alcoholic cannot admit his dependency to himself, or they may deceive the researcher, such as when a young offender does not want to reveal his socially undesirable thoughts or behavior. Furthermore, research participants may not be able to provide the level of detail, or use the concepts, that the researcher is interested in.

Arguments arising in two separate fields, psychoanalysis and social psychology, cast doubt upon the validity of self-reports. Psychoanalysts emphasize the limits to the person's conscious self-knowledge. They argue that many important feelings and experiences are unconscious, and prevented by defenses such as repression or denial from becoming conscious. Thus, a person's accounts cannot be taken at face value. Some psychoanalytically oriented researchers prefer projective measures, principally the Thematic Apperception Test (TAT), the Rorschach inkblot test, and sentence completion methods, which are designed to assess the person's unconscious thoughts and feelings, although the validity of these measures can also be hard to establish (Westen et al., 1999).

From the social psychological perspective of attribution theory, Nisbett and his colleagues (e.g., Nisbett & Ross, 1980; Nisbett & Wilson, 1977) have argued that people often do not know what influences their behavior, and that there are pervasive biases in the way that we account for our own and others' behavior. One common source of bias, known as the actor–observer effect, is the tendency for people to say that their own behavior is caused by situational factors and that other people's behavior is caused by dispositional factors (Fiske & Taylor, 1991; Jones & Nisbett, 1971). For example, a student might say that she failed an exam because she did not sleep well the night before, whereas she might say that her room mate failed the exam because she was too lazy to study for it. Another related type of bias, known as self-serving bias, is the tendency to take credit for success and deny responsibility for failure (Fiske & Taylor, 1991).

These strictures about the limits of self-report methods are important to bear in mind. However, this does not mean that all self-report data are invalid, only that they cannot be trusted in all cases (Ericsson & Simon, 1993). All measurement methods have limits, and the potential limitations of the data must be considered at the analysis and interpretation stage. Thus, we should not abandon this method of data collection, although it is often advisable to supplement self-report data with observational data (or at least self-report data from other perspectives). In addition, it is a good idea to be sensitive to the possibilities for self-deception in verbal protocols (see Churchill, 2000, for an example of "seeing through" self-deceptive self-reports).

Constructing an interview or questionnaire may appear to be straightforward, but the apparent simplicity is deceptive. Most people have been on the receiving end of an irritating, poorly designed questionnaire or interview, often in the context of market research. Designing good self-report measures is an art and a craft. For this reason, it is preferable, where possible, to use established measures rather than attempting to design your own from scratch. There is a huge literature on research interviews and questionnaires, including several entire books (e.g., Brenner et al., 1985; Kvale, 1996; Moser & Kalton, 1971; Oppenheim, 1992; Patton, 2002; Payne, 1951; Rossi et al., 1983; Sudman & Bradburn, 1982).

Terminology

An *interview* is a special type of conversation aimed at gathering information, although the interviewer usually has a written guide, known as an *interview protocol* or *schedule*. (Note that the interview protocol is not the same thing as the research protocol, which refers to the plan for the study as a whole, including, for example, the research design and the sampling procedure.) Interviews are usually conducted face to face, although occasionally they may be done over the telephone.

A *questionnaire*, on the other hand, refers to a structured series of written questions, which usually generate written responses. *Checklists* and *inventories* (the terms are used almost interchangeably) are a type of questionnaire which present a list of items in a similar format and ask respondents to rate all that apply to them. Two widely used examples of inventories are the Beck Depression Inventory (Beck et al., 1988)—a 21-item scale assessing the severity of depression—and the Symptom Checklist-90 (SCL-90-R: Derogatis, 1994), a 90-item checklist measuring the number and severity of psychological symptoms. The questionnaire may be composed of several *subscales*, each of which measures an internally consistent construct (such as the Somatization, Depression, and Hostility subscales of the SCL-90-R).

The term "survey" is widely used but imprecisely defined. It usually denotes a systematic study of a medium to large sample done either by interview or postal ("mail-out") questionnaire. A *census* means a survey of the whole population (as opposed to a sample from that population: see Chapter 10); the best known example is the government population census.

Mode of Administration

Since self-report data may be gathered either by written questionnaires or by interview, researchers need to consider which mode of administration would better suit their purposes. The advantages of written questionnaires are that:

- they are standardized (i.e., the wording is exactly the same each time);
- they allow respondents to fill them out privately, in their own time;
- they can be used to ensure confidentiality, via a code numbering system, and so they can potentially cover embarrassing, socially undesirable, or illegal topics (e.g., sexual behavior or drug use); and
- they are cheaper to administer.

The advantages of interviews are that they can use the rapport and flexibility of the relationship between the interviewer and the respondent to enable the interviewer to:

- ask follow-up questions, in order to clarify the respondent's meaning, probe for material that the respondent does not mention spontaneously, and get beyond superficial responses;
- ensure that the respondent answers all the questions;
- give more complicated instructions and check that they are understood;
- vary the order of the questions;
- allow the respondents to ask their own questions of the interviewer; and
- allow researchers to gather enough information to make judgments about the validity of the respondent's self-report.

Interviews are additionally appealing to clinical psychologists because their clinical skills can be used. However, clinicians also have some unlearning to do, as conducting a research interview is quite different from conducting a therapeutic or assessment interview (we will elaborate on this point later).

Open-ended and Closed-ended Questions

Self-report methods can yield either qualitative or quantitative data, depending largely on whether open-ended or closed-ended questions are used.

Open-ended questions are those that do not restrict the answer, which is usually recorded verbatim. For example, the question "How are you feeling right now?" might yield the responses "Fine, thanks," "Like death warmed up" or "Better than yesterday, at least." However, content analysis may be used at a later stage to classify the responses (e.g., into positive, negative, or neutral). Also, some open-ended questions may yield quantitative data (e.g., "How old are you?").

The advantages of open-ended questions are that they enable the researcher to study complex experiences: respondents are able to qualify or explain their answers, and also have the opportunity to express ambivalent or contradictory feelings. Furthermore, their initial responses are potentially less influenced by the researcher's framework. Respondents are free to answer as they wish, using their own spontaneous language.

The main disadvantage of open-ended questions, from the researcher's point of view, is that it is more difficult to evaluate the reliability and validity of verbal data. It is hard to ascertain the extent of such potential problems as interviewer bias and variability, and respondent deception, exaggeration, fabrication, and forgetting. It is not that the reliability and validity of qualitative self-report measures are inherently worse, they are just harder to evaluate, so that both the researchers and the readers are more likely to feel on shaky ground. (On the other hand, careful examination of the respondent's manner and word choice can provide important hints about the credibility of verbal data.)

A second issue is that open-ended questions typically generate large amounts of data (the "data overload" problem; Miles & Huberman, 1994), which are usually time consuming to analyze. For a start, most qualitative interviews need to be transcribed, which often takes considerable effort (this is where having sufficient funding to pay for transcription can save the researcher time and frustration). Furthermore, the analysis itself requires considerable effort and skill. This will be considered further in Chapter 12, where we cover the analysis and interpretation of qualitative data.

A final issue is that open-ended questions tend to produce a great variability in the amount of data across respondents. Verbally fluent respondents may provide very full answers, while less fluent respondents may find open-ended questions demanding to answer. In particular, open-ended questions in written questionnaires are often left blank, because they require more effort to complete.

Closed-ended questions constrain the answer in some way. Answers are usually recorded in an abbreviated form using a numerical code. For instance, the possible responses to the closed question "Are you feeling happy, sad, or neither, at the moment?" might be coded as 1 = "Happy," 2 = "Sad," and 3 = "Neither/Don't know." Responses can be made in the form of a dichotomous choice (i.e., when there are two possible responses, such as Yes/No), a multiple choice (i.e., where the respondent has to choose one response from several possibilities), a rank ordering (i.e., where a number of alternatives have to be put in order of preference or strength of opinion), or ticking one or more applicable items on a checklist.

The advantages of closed-ended questions are that the responses are easier to analyze, quantify, and compare across respondents. They also help to prompt respondents about the possible range of responses.

The major disadvantages of closed-ended questions are succinctly summarized by Sheatsley: "People understand the questions differently; respondents are forced into what may seem to them an unnatural reply; they have no opportunity to qualify their answers or to explain their opinions more precisely" (Sheatsley, 1983: 197). For example, in research on stressful life events, information from a checklist measure simply tells you whether an event has occurred, but you have no information about the meaning of the event for the individual. "The death of a pet" might mean that the goldfish passed away, or that an elderly person's sole companion has died. A semi-structured life events interview (e.g., that of Brown & Harris, 1978) allows the interviewer to probe further in order to establish the meaning and significance of each reported event. Furthermore, interview or questionnaire studies that consist entirely of closed questions can be an annoying experience for respondents, as they may feel that they are not getting a chance to put their views across, and may resent being controlled by the format.

The following sections examine qualitative and quantitative methods in turn. This structure is mainly for didactic purposes: we do not wish to artificially polarize the two types of methods. In practice, there is a continuum, ranging from unstructured, open-ended methods, through semi-structured interviews or questionnaires, to structured quantitative methods. As we will state repeatedly, it is possible, and often desirable, to combine both qualitative and quantitative procedures within the same study.

QUALITATIVE SELF-REPORT METHODS

For illustrative purposes, we will discuss qualitative self-report methods mostly in the context of the qualitative interview, since the interview is the most frequently used method within the qualitative tradition. However, there are various other qualitative self-report methods, such as: (1) open-ended questionnaires, e.g., the Helpful Aspects of Therapy form (Llewelyn, 1988); (2) personal documents approaches, which use pre-existing written records, such as personal journals (Taylor & Bogdan, 1998); and (3) structured qualitative questionnaires, e.g., the repertory grid (Kelly, 1955), although repertory grids are often analyzed quantitatively (see Winter, 1992).

- The semi-structured qualitative interview is the most common qualitative self-report method.

- It is usually based on an interview schedule, which lists the major questions to be asked and some possible probes to follow up with.

- The interview style is mostly based on open-ended questions, but can use other active listening responses, such as reflections.

- The interviewer should have an interested stance with a kind of free-floating attention, and attempt not to put words into the respondent's mouth.

The Qualitative Interview

In addition to using open-ended questions, qualitative interviews are usually loosely structured, and aim to get an in-depth account of the topic (Kvale, 1996; Patton, 2002; Taylor & Bogdan, 1998). They have similarities to psychological assessment and to journalistic interviews (but also important differences, which we will discuss below).

There are several different forms of qualitative interview (Patton, 2002). The most common is the semi-structured interview. Such interviews vary widely in length, from a few minutes to many hours, and take place on one occasion or across many occasions. Most qualitative interviews are one to two hours in length. At the upper end, intensive life story interviewing, described by Taylor and Bogdan (1998), may involve many interviews totaling up to 50 or 120 hours of conversation.

Alternatives to the semi-structured interview include: (1) the informal or unstructured conversational interview, which is most common as an element of participant observation; (2) the standardized open-ended interview, which consists of a uniform set of questions that are always administered in the same order, often with fixed follow-up questions; and (3) the questionnaire-with-follow-up-interview method favored by phenomenological researchers of the Duquesne school (e.g., Giorgi, 1975; Wertz, 1983). In the last, open-ended questionnaires are used to identify promising or representative respondents who are then interviewed in detail.

One other option is to conduct *focus group* interviews (e.g., Kitzinger, 1995; Krueger, 1994). This method, which originated in market research and public opinion polling, involves assembling a small group of respondents. The interviewer interacts with the whole group, following the same kind of semi-structured protocol as in an individual interview. The group format has the advantage of enabling respondents to react to each other's contributions, and thus possibly to explore the topic more deeply. The disadvantages are that the interview is subject to the usual group dynamics, such as conformity pressures, and giving more weight to the opinions of more vocal or prestigious members, which may affect its validity.

A note on terminology: we will tend to use the terms "respondent" or "interviewee" to refer to the person on the receiving end of the interview. Other possibilities are "informant" or "participant." We avoid the term "subject" because of its connotations of powerlessness (see Chapter 10). Likewise, there are a number of models of the relationship between the interviewer and interviewee. These range from traditional "subject" models, in which the interviewee is seen as a passive information provider responding to the researcher's questions, to "co-researcher" models, as in feminist (Oakley, 1981; Wilkinson, 1986) or New Paradigm (Reason & Rowan, 1981) research, in which the respondent is seen as an equal partner in the inquiry.

The Interview as a Narrative Process

Qualitative interviewing has increasingly been viewed as a key method for helping respondents "tell their stories." Indeed, narrative psychology has been one of the more important developments in psychology during the last two decades of the 20th century, with many writers proposing narrative as central to human communication and experience (e.g., McLeod, 1997; Murray, in press; Polkinghorne, 1988; Sarbin, 1986). There are many kinds of culturally defined narratives, including narratives of illness, victimization, recovery, faith journey, identity, etc. The urge to tell stories is so strong that qualitative researchers proceed at their peril if they try to ignore the power of narrative.

Many different formulations of narrative structure have been proposed (for a review, see McLeod, 1997), but the most basic narrative structure consists of three things. First, there is a beginning, in which the setting is described (e.g., "When I was 18, still living at home . . ."), the main character is introduced ("I had a friend Angel who I used to visit . . ."), and a situation or problem is introduced (". . . and Angel got cancer"). Second, a series of actions, obstacles, conflicts, reactions, and attempted solutions is described, often leading to a climax or turning point. Third, there is an ending or resolution to the story, often with some attempt to state the point or the person's current perspective ("Anyway, I still think about her; 29 is too young to die!").

Thus, in a narrative approach to interviewing, the researcher's main job is to help the respondent to tell their story, perhaps beginning with something like, "I wonder if you could tell me the story of [e.g., when you had your abortion] in as much detail as you feel comfortable giving me." Then, the researcher's job is to encourage the respondent to keep going, or to back up and provide missing information if they skip over something. (Narrative also has important therapeutic functions, especially in the treatment of traumatic or other difficult life situations; e.g., McLeod, 1997.)

Sample Interview

The following excerpt from a semi-structured interview comes from a British study of how adults with intellectual disabilities ("mental retardation" in the US terminology) and their keyworkers (caseworkers) experience the ending of their relationships, for example when staff move away. (The full transcript of the interview is given in Mattison & Pistrang, 2000: 202–217. Reproduced by permission of Free Association Books Ltd, London, England.) The interviewer (I) was a female graduate student in clinical psychology. The respondent (R) was Gill, a female staff member in a community residential setting; she is describing the ending of her relationship with her client Margaret (both names are pseudonyms). This excerpt starts about half way through the interview.

I: So, I wanted to ask you a bit about the guidance or support that you had around that process of preparing to leave.

R: A lot. Well, very good, yeah. The manager was very good. I was lucky, he was a very good manager and he supported me through it. I mean you could say it's like a bereavement in a way. For Margaret it was a bereavement and for myself as well, really. I mean you've lost a good friend, haven't you?

I: Yes, yes, and that sounds really hard.

R: Well you haven't lost them, but you're not having so much contact with them.

I: Yes, and bereavement seems to be a very helpful way of describing some aspects of this process.

R: Yes, I think it is a bereavement, yes. Because it is the loss of a friend. You haven't lost them, but then again. You know, when I first saw her at the club afterwards, I was really sort of choked up, and you sort of want to know all about her. Is she going on holiday? Is she doing this? Is she doing that? And you sort of feel, "Well I could be organizing that". You know, you do feel very (laughs)—as you say, it's a bereavement.

I: Yes, and on both sides as well, it sounds like—as much about how you felt as it was about how she felt.

R: Yes, yes, and of course Margaret had to find somebody else really. Because, as I say, she has since attached herself to another member of staff, and she's now in the process of moving, so then again, it will be new staff and a new place to live, and also for Tony [another of Gill's clients].

I: Aha.

R: Because you see this was an old institutional building, and they are all being moved out, in the community, into small housing. So she'll be in a new setting, new staff, new people, you know, new people altogether. So that's going to be hard, yeah.

I: Yes. I just wondered, you mentioned that she had attached herself to another member of staff. I wonder how that made you feel?

R: A little bit jealous, yes, a little bit jealous. But then again relief, because then you knew she was OK, because she did need that support and somebody to talk to really. Because as I say, she would sit on her bed and just think for hours, and you knew that it was all going round her head, and then she would suddenly wreck her room, for no apparent reason. And we really surmised that it was just the thoughts that were going through her head, and then suddenly she would just go mad—totally wreck everything.

I: This was around the time you were leaving, or in general?

R: This was in general, so as I say, we knew that she was a very sensitive, thinking lady. And she picked up a lot on atmospheres and things around her, so you've got to be more careful with her then—it sounds terrible—but you've got to be more careful with her than, say, Tony or any of the other clients, because, as I say, she felt things a lot more.

This excerpt illustrates the richness of the data that can come from a qualitative interview, and also gives a foretaste of the "qualitative overload" problem that is involved in analyzing the material (see Chapter 12). It also gives a picture of how the interviewer carries out her aim—to understand the participant's experience—by using questions to clarify and explore, and reflections to confirm understanding and encourage elaboration. In the following sections, we will look in more detail at the procedures used in conducting qualitative interviews.

The Interview Schedule

The first step is to prepare an interview schedule that lists the important areas to be addressed; it may have some standard questions to be asked. It is usually a good idea to structure the interview around some sort of framework, which could be, for example, conceptual or chronological. The interview typically starts with general questions, as a warm-up. The standard questions need not be covered in a fixed order, but the interview schedule serves as an aide-mémoire, to remind you what needs to be asked. It is vital to pilot test the interview schedule on a few respondents and revise it accordingly.

Young and Willmott (1957), in their classic study, *Family and Kinship in East London*, describe the use of their interview schedule:

> We used a schedule of questions, but the interviews were much more informal and less standardized than those in the general survey. Answers had to be obtained to all the set questions listed (though not necessarily in the same order), but this did not exhaust the interview. Each couple being in some way different from every other, we endeavored to find out as much as we could about the peculiarities of each couple's experiences and family relationships, using the set questions as leads and following up anything of interest which emerged in the answers to them as the basis for yet further questions. (Young & Willmott, 1957: 207)

For illustration, here is part of an interview schedule, from the Mattison & Pistrang (2000) study on the ending of keyworker (caseworker) relationships, described above. The excerpt includes three central sections of the interview schedule used with staff respondents. However, as Young and Willmott mention, there is not an exact correspondence between the questions in the schedule and those asked by the interviewer: the schedule is a vehicle for enabling the respondent to talk about the important issues.

Excerpt from an interview schedule (Mattison & Pistrang, 2000: 186–187). Reproduced by permission of Free Association Books Ltd, London, England.

Saying goodbye

This section focused on the process of ending the keyworker (caseworker) relationship. It asked about how the client was told and how/whether the client was prepared for the ending.

Can you tell me what happened when you left the post?

What actually happened on the day that you left?

How did the client find out that you were leaving?

What went into your thinking process about deciding to tell (or not to tell)? How did you decide when to tell him/her?

What, if any, preparation do you think the client needed? Did you get any guidance about this from a supervisor or manager?

Looking back on it now, do you think you would do anything differently?

The impact of ending on the client

The aim here was to elicit the participant's view of how his/her departure might have affected the client.

What do you think might have been the impact of your departure on the client?

Did you see him/her at all after you left?

If you had/had not told your client that you were leaving, how do you think s/he would have responded?

The impact of ending on the keyworker

The aim here was to elicit the participant's own feelings about the ending of the keyworking relationship.

What were your own feelings around this time?

What kind of support, if any, did you need around leaving? What support did you get?

Have you had any experiences in the past where important relationships have ended?

Interviewing Style

The interviewer's general stance should be one of empathic and non-judgmental attention, giving the respondent plenty of space to think and talk, and avoiding leading questions. If you are unclear about anything, probe further, although legal-style interrogation is obviously to be avoided.

In order to be an effective qualitative interviewer, you must start with an attitude of genuine interest in learning from others, in hearing their story, and you must be able to listen to them with tolerance and acceptance. The schizophrenia researcher, John Strauss, realized after 30 years of quantitative research that he had learned very little about the nature of schizophrenia; he felt that he had only really begun to learn when he started to listen to what the patients had to say when he asked them about their experiences (Strauss et al., 1987).

Your therapeutic skills, such as empathy and clinical intuition, come very much to the fore here. However, there must be a clear distinction between research and therapy (or assessment) interviews, as all therapeutic orientations involve interventions which are inappropriate for qualitative interviewing. For instance, it would be wrong to conduct a qualitative interview in cognitive-behavioral style, as this approach, like most therapies, is ultimately aimed at changing the client's thoughts and experiences rather than finding out about them. Even client-centered therapists may engage in too much paraphrasing, which can easily end up putting words in the respondent's mouth. Perhaps a better clinical analogy is the enquiry phase of projective testing (e.g., "What was it about the card that made you think of a flying pig?"), although this style of questioning does tend to fall into the traditional model of the detached interviewer. In general, clinical assessment interviews are also quite different from research interviews, as the former tend to be aimed at assembling the information into a coherent clinical formulation.

It is important, for two reasons, to tape record the interview. First, notes or memory are prone to inaccuracies and incompleteness. Second, extensive note taking runs the risk of distracting the respondent and interrupting the flow of the interview. Notes may suffice for interviews which are brief and highly structured; in such situations, note taking may also be acceptable to the respondent. However, if you have to interview without a tape recorder, your notes need to clearly identify which parts are the respondent's verbatim statements and which are your own summary. Written notes can also be used as a reminder during the interview, e.g., jotting down a particular phrase used by the respondent that you want to return to later on. In this case, note taking is brief and should be limited to those essential reminders needed to help you conduct the interview. Finally, as we suggested in Chapter 3, it is worth keeping a research journal to record your general impressions of each interview.

Specific Qualitative Interviewing Skills

If one is genuinely motivated to understand and learn about people by interviewing, then a number of technical skills in information gathering and listening become useful. One useful way to describe these skills is in terms of what are called "response modes" (Goodman & Dooley, 1976), that is, basic types of interviewer speech acts or responses. These can be divided into three groups: responses which are essential for qualitative interviewing; supplemental responses which are sometimes useful; and responses which should generally be avoided.

Essential response modes lean heavily on the "active listening" responses such as those made famous by client-centered therapy. Thus, two key responses are open questions—to gather information and to encourage the respondent to elaborate— and reflections—to communicate understanding and to encourage further exploration of content. Suggestions to guide the discussion ("Could you tell me about...") are also essential for beginning and structuring the interview, while brief acknowledgments (e.g., "I see" or "Uh-huh") build rapport and help the respondent keep talking. If a more active, paraphrasing style is used, you are more likely to need to account for the interviewer's possible influence on the data when you do your analysis.

Supplemental response modes. In addition, several other types of response are also sometimes useful, although they should not be overused. These include the following: closed questions, which can be used to test out ideas near the end of the interview; self-disclosures, which allow the interviewer to explain his or her goals for the interview and to build rapport by answering questions about him or her self; and reassurances or sympathizing responses ("It's hard"), to encourage openness in the respondent.

Responses to be avoided include problem-solving advisements, which give respondents suggestions about how to solve their problems; interpretations, which try to tell the respondent why they did something or what they actually felt; disagreements or confrontations, which cut off communication by criticizing or putting the respondent down (e.g., do not try to "catch out" respondents in contradictions); and giving respondents information (other than information about the structure and purpose of the interview itself).

Useful types of questions. Because questions are so important for organizing and structuring qualitative interviews, it is worth describing some of the most important types, in the order in which they typically occur in a qualitative interview.

- *Entry questions* set the interview up and help the respondent find a useful focus for describing his or her experiences (e.g., "Can you think of a particular time when you felt that way?" "Can you give me a flavor of what it was like for you to go through that?").

- *Unfolding questions* request information that will help the respondent unfold his or her story for the researcher (cf., Rice & Sapiera, 1984), including questions about activities ("What were you doing at that moment?"), intentions ("What did you want to accomplish?"), feelings ("What did that feel like, when you were standing there, listening to them talk?"), or sensory perceptions ("What were you noticing as you sat there?").

- *Follow-up probes* are questions that seek further information or clarification about something which the respondent has said. They may be standardized requests for elaboration. If the interviewer listens carefully to what the respondent says, he or she can probe more selectively when the respondent fails to answer a question clearly or says something which is ambiguous ("What do you mean when you say 'the doctor is like a friend'?").

- *Construal questions* are usually saved for later in the interview, because they ask the respondent for explanations and evaluations and thus move away from the predominant emphasis on description ("How do you make sense of that?").

- *Hypothesis-testing questions* are best saved for the end of the interview, in order not to "lead the witness." They can be useful for following up hunches or confirming the interviewer's understandings ("Are you saying that not knowing your diagnosis is what frightened you the most?").

Qualitative interviewers are sometimes confronted with apparently contradictory information from respondents. This should not necessarily be regarded as evidence of unreliability or invalidity. People will often have multiple, sometimes contradictory, feelings and views. It is a good idea to listen for such contradictions, because they may reflect ambivalent feelings or avoidance of painful experiences. During the interview, you may become aware of possible inconsistencies, which could be: (1) internal, between different parts of the story; (2) external, with another source, e.g., a document or another respondent; or (3) between manifest and latent content, e.g., between the words and the tone of voice. Rather than pouncing on them, it is a good idea to gently and tactfully inquire about them ("That's interesting, it sounds like you have several different kinds of feelings about your clients. Can you tell me more about that?").

Finally, as Kvale (1996) cautions, it is important for the researcher to track the relevance of the respondent's answers during the interview, in order to make sure that the research questions are being answered and the meaning of the respondent's statements is clear. Once the interview is transcribed and you sit down to analyze your data, it is generally too late to go back to your respondents in order to ask them to clarify what they meant! It is also important to scrutinize the data from your first interview before embarking on further interviews. This will make you aware of problems with superficial, vague, or ambiguous answers, so that you can modify your interview schedule and technique.

QUANTITATIVE SELF-REPORT METHODS

The literature on quantitative self-report methods is enormous, and we can only hope to skim the surface here. More extensive treatments can be found in Butcher (1999), Dawis (1987); Moser and Kalton (1971), Oppenheim (1992), Rossi et al. (1983) and Sudman and Bradburn (1982). For convenience, we will focus on written questionnaires with rating scales; however, everything that we have to say applies equally well to interviews and internet questionnaires designed to yield quantitative data.

- The central quantitative self-report method is the written questionnaire or rating scale.

- Questionnaire design may seem simple, but it is not. There is no shortage of badly designed questionnaires in circulation. The central maxim is "take care of the respondent."

- Most questionnaires use a Likert scale.

- Good items are clear, simple, and brief.

- There are a number of issues in designing the response scale, e.g., the number of points, the type of anchors, unipolar or bipolar scales.

- Response sets, such as acquiescence and social desirability, refer to tendencies to respond to items independently of their content. They need to be taken into account when designing and interpreting self-report measures.

As in other places in this book, we will describe the process from the viewpoint of constructing a measure, in order to give readers a better feel for the difficulties that are involved. The central point is that it is not just reliability and validity considerations that need to be taken into account when appraising a measure; it is worth looking closely at the fine detail of how the measure is put together.

Steps in Measure Development

If you are doing research involving a variable that no existing self-report instrument seems to measure satisfactorily, you may need to construct your own measure. This is not a step to be undertaken lightly, as it is time consuming and requires skill to do well. However, because many areas are either under-measured or are poorly measured, this is a common type of research. One often approaches a new research area only to find that no good measures exist, and then ends up by reformulating the research toward developing such a measure. (A common experience of researchers is to discover that such studies are often widely cited and more influential than their other research.)

If you need to construct a measure, the steps are roughly as follows:

- Having done a literature search to make sure that no existing instrument is suitable, develop a first draft of the scale based on theory, pilot qualitative interviews, or analysis of existing questionnaires.

- Progressively pilot the scale on respondents nearer and nearer to the intended target population (known as *pretesting*), modifying it accordingly. Expect to take it through several drafts, e.g., first to colleagues, second to friends or support staff (ask them to point out jargon or awkward phrasings), third and fourth to potential respondents. It is often worthwhile running small informal reliability and possibly factor analyses on a pilot sample of 20 or 30 respondents to see whether any items should be dropped or added before doing the larger, formal study.

• Once a satisfactory version of the scale has been developed, do a formal reliability study by giving the measure to a large sample (e.g., over 120 respondents) drawn from a population which approximates the population you are interested in. You can then examine its item characteristics (e.g., means and standard deviations), internal consistency, and factor structure. It is also typical to administer the measure twice to some of the participants, in order to assess its test-retest reliability.

• If the reliability and factor structure are satisfactory, you can conduct appropriate validity studies (see Chapter 4), which examine the measure's correlations with other criteria or constructs. (These studies may also be combined with the previous step.) The new measure is administered, along with a set of similar and different measures, such as a social desirability measure and measures that should not correlate with the new measure (to establish discriminant validity). It is also a good idea to use measures of more than one type or perspective, in order to reduce the problem of method variance (e.g., to use self-report measures plus observer ratings). The goal is to see whether the measure fits in with the pattern of correlations that would be predicted by the theoretical framework from which it was derived.

Questionnaire Design

Designing a questionnaire involves deciding on the topics to be covered and their sequence, writing the questions or items, and selecting an appropriate response scale. We will deal with each of these in turn.

In all aspects of questionnaire design, the golden rule is "take care of the respondents." Put yourself in their shoes and ask what the experience of being on the receiving end of the questionnaire is like. Make it as easy and free of frustration as possible. As part of the pilot testing, it is a good idea to fill out your questionnaire yourself (often a salutary experience) and give it to a few friends who will be able to give you constructive criticism.

The goal is to not get in the way of respondents' being able to communicate their thoughts and experiences. Trying not to alienate your respondents makes sense not only from a general human relations point of view, but it also makes good scientific sense. Irritated people will not give you good data (or even any data at all—they may just throw away your questionnaire).

Topic Coverage and Sequence

The questionnaire is often broken into subsections representing different topics or variables. The primary consideration is that, as a whole, it should adequately capture all of the concepts needed to answer the research questions. In other words, the data set should yield an answer to each of the research questions, or enable each of the hypotheses to be tested. Once this coverage has been achieved, the issue is then how to order the topic areas within the questionnaire.

It is usually better to start off with easy, non-threatening questions that all respondents can answer (Dillman, 2000). This engages the respondents and helps to establish rapport with them: even a written questionnaire is a form of interpersonal relationship. Demographic questions (i.e., about the respondent's age, sex, etc.) should usually be placed at the end of the questionnaire, as it is better to start with questions relevant to the topic of the interview.

Structured interviews often adopt the so-called *funnel approach*, i.e., they start out broadly and then progressively narrow down. This reduces the risk of suggesting ideas to the respondents or influencing their answers. The interview typically begins with open-ended questions, then moves in the direction of increasing specificity. The veteran pollster George Gallup (see Sheatsley, 1983) recommends the following ordering for public opinion research (e.g., to study opinions about sexual harassment): (1) test the respondents' awareness of, or knowledge about, the issue; then (2) ask about their level of interest or concern; then (3) about their attitudes; then (4) about the reasons for these attitudes; and finally (5) about the strength of their opinions.

Item Wording

Having established the coverage of topics, the next step is to write the individual questions or items. The wording of an item is of crucial importance, as the way that a question is phrased can determine the kind of response that is given (Sudman & Bradburn, 1982). It is worth heeding some key principles of item construction:

Neutrality. The language of the item should not influence the respondent, i.e., it should not suggest an answer. Possible errors take the form of *leading questions* (questions which are not neutral, which suggest an answer), questions with *implicit premises* (built-in assumptions that indicate the questioner's viewpoint) and *loaded words or phrases* (ones that are emotionally colored and suggest an automatic feeling of approval or disapproval). Some examples of such problematic questions follow, with commentary after each:

"Do you think that . . . ?" and "Don't you think that . . . ?"

These are leading questions that pull for a "yes" response.

"When did you stop beating your wife?"

This has become the clichéd example of an implicit assumption; it assumes the respondent has been beating his wife (Payne, 1951). Such questions are usually to be avoided. However, there are times when implicit premises are useful for normalizing behavior, by giving the respondent permission to talk honestly. For example, studies of sexual behavior may sometimes use questions such as: "How old were you the first time you . . . ?", rather than saying "Did you ever . . . ?"

"How often do you refer to a counselor?"

This question is a subtler variant of the implicit premise; it assumes that the respondent does refer to a counselor. It would be better to include "if at all," or, even better, to have two separate questions, e.g. "Do you refer . . . ?" and "If yes, how often . . . ?"

"Why don't you refer to a counselor more often?"

This question assumes that referring more often is desirable. A better question would be: "What factors influence your referral decisions?"

"How often did you break down and cry?"

"Break down" is a loaded phrase which gives crying a negative connotation. In this case, it could simply be omitted.

Clarity and simplicity. It is better to use simple, clear, everyday language, adopting a conversational tone. Make sure that the item does not demand a reading level or vocabulary that is too advanced for your respondents. In particular, try to avoid psychological jargon (it is helpful to ask a non-psychologist to read your questionnaire to detect it). Psychologists often become so used to their own technical language that they often forget that members of the public do not understand it or find it strange. This is another reason why it is vital to pilot the questionnaire on ordinary people.

Specificity. Lack of specificity gives rise to *ambiguities*, e.g.:

"Do you ever suffer from emotional problems?"

The phrase "emotional problems" means different things to different people. Therefore, it is better to define it or use alternatives. On the other hand, you could leave the phrase as it is, if you want to leave it open to people's own interpretations.

"Do you suffer from back pain?"

It is better to give a time frame, e.g., "in the last four weeks," and also to specify the anatomical area, perhaps with the aid of a diagram (since, for example, respondents may not know if shoulder or neck pain should be included).

"Do you like Kipling?" ("Yes, I kipple all the time.")

People will often respond to a question that they do not understand, rather than saying explicitly that they do not understand it.

Single questions. It is better to ask one thing at a time. Problems arise with *double-barreled questions*, i.e., ones with two independent parts:

> "Were you satisfied with the supervision and range of experience at your last clinical placement?"

The respondent could be satisfied with the supervision, but not the range of experience.

> "Were you satisfied with your placement or were there some problems with it?"

The two parts are not mutually exclusive: the respondent could be satisfied with a placement even though there were problems with it.

> "In order to ensure patients take their medication, should psychiatrists be given more powers of compulsory treatment?"

The respondent could disagree with the implications of the initial premise, but agree with the main statement.

Brevity. Short items are preferable. Sentences with multiple clauses can be difficult to process. As a final example of what to avoid, here is a classic of its kind, from no less a figure than the behaviorist John Watson, which violates this and most other principles of item writing:

> Has early home, school, or religious training implanted fixed modes of reacting which are not in line with his present environment—that is, is he easily shocked, for example, at seeing a woman smoke, drink a cocktail or flirt with a man; at card playing; at the fact that many of his associates do not go to church? (Watson, 1919, quoted by Gynther & Green, 1982: 356)

Constructing the Response Scale

With a *rating scale*, the respondent gives a numerical value to some type of judgement. There is a wide variety of scale types: Guttman scales, Thurstone scales, rankings, etc. (Nunnally & Bernstein, 1994). Here we will examine by far the most commonly used one, the Likert scale (see Figure 6.1 for some examples).

Just as the form of the question can influence the response, so can the form of the response scale (Schwarz, 1999). The major considerations in constructing response scales are:

How many scale points? The number of scale points can range from two upwards. (Scales with two choices are known as *binary* or *dichotomous*, with three or more, *multiple choice*.) There may be logical reasons for using a certain number of responses: e.g., some questions clearly demand a yes/no answer. However, it is

Agreement

How much do you agree or disagree with each of the following statements?

1	2	3	4	5	6	7
Disagree strongly	Disagree moderately	Disagree mildly	Neither agree nor disagree	Agree mildly	Agree moderately	Agree strongly

Frequency

How often do you . . . ?

0	1	2	3	4
Never	Seldom	Sometimes	Often	Very often

Quantity/proportion	**Degree/strength**
How many . . . ?	How (much) . . . ?
0 None	0 Not at all
1 Very few	1 Slightly
2 Some	2 Moderately
3 Very many	3 Very (much)
4 All	

Figure 6.1 Examples of anchor words for Likert scales

more frequently the case that the response scale must be decided by the researcher. The main issues are:

- The reliability increases with more scale points (Nunnally & Bernstein, 1994), although there seem to be diminishing returns beyond five points (Lissitz & Green, 1975). In addition, most people find it difficult to discriminate more than about seven points.

- People tend to avoid the extreme ends of scales, a phenomenon known as the *central tendency*. This means that it is usually better to have at least five scale points, because if you have three or four you tend to get a lot of responses in the middle.

- Instead of using discrete scale points, another approach is to ask respondents to put a mark on a 10 centimeter line (a *visual-analog scale*), and then use a ruler to make the measurement (McCormack et al., 1988). This is used, for example, in pain research, to assess the intensity of the respondent's pain experience.

Unipolar or bipolar. Response scales can either be unipolar or bipolar. A *unipolar* scale has only one construct, which varies in degree. For example, a scale measuring intensity of pain might range from "No pain at all" to "Unbearable pain." A *bipolar* scale has opposite descriptors at each end of the scale (e.g., "Active" at one end and "Passive" at the other). In Figure 6.1, the Agreement scale is bipolar; the others are unipolar.

Mid-point. Bipolar scales may or may not have a mid-point, representing such options as "Don't know," "Neutral," or "Neither one way or the other." In other words, they may have either an odd or an even number of steps.

The argument against having a mid-point is that people usually hold an opinion, one way or the other, which they will express if you push a little. This procedure is known as *forced choice*: e.g., "Do you agree or disagree with the following statements?" Forced choice makes data analysis easier, because respondents can be divided into those expressing a positive and those expressing a negative opinion. However, if a question is worded well you should not get a lot of middle responses in the first place.

The argument for having a mid-point is that neutrality represents a genuine alternative judgment and so it is coercive not to allow respondents to express their opinions in the way that they want to.

Anchoring. Anchoring refers to labeling the points of the scale in words as well as numbers. You usually want to define the steps explicitly, so that people are rating to the same criteria. However, this does make two measurement assumptions: (1) that the scale has interval properties (see Chapter 4), i.e., that its steps are all equal (for example, that the distance between "not at all" and "slightly" is the same as between "very" and "extremely"); and (2) that people understand the same thing by all the adjectives. Try to avoid modifiers with imprecise meanings, e.g., "quite" can sometimes intensify (equivalent to "very") and sometimes diminish (equivalent to "somewhat").

Sometimes researchers just anchor the end-points of the scales, as in visual-analog scales and *semantic differentials* (which use pairs of bipolar adjectives, such as good–bad, hard–soft, heavy–light). It is also possible to anchor alternate scale points as a compromise between anchoring every point and only anchoring the extremes.

Response Sets

Response sets refer to the tendency of individuals to respond to items in ways not specifically related to their content (Bradburn, 1983; Nunnally & Bernstein, 1994). They may be conceptualized as personality variables in their own right. The most commonly encountered response sets are acquiescence and social desirability.

Acquiescence ("yea-saying") refers to a tendency to agree rather than disagree. The classic example of acquiescence problems is with the California F-scale (Adorno et al., 1950), which was developed to measure authoritarian tendencies (the F stands for fascist). Early *item-reversal studies*, in which some of the items were replaced by their inverse, seemed to show that this scale was mostly measuring acquiescence rather than authoritarianism (although there is some dispute about this conclusion, see Rorer, 1965).

The way to get around acquiescence problems is to have an equal number of positively and negatively scored items in the scale. For example, in an assertiveness scale, the item "If someone jumps to the head of the queue, I would speak up" would be scored in the positive direction, while "I tend to go along with other people's views" would be scored in the negative direction. Thus, when the items are reversed and averaged, any tendencies to acquiesce would cancel themselves out.

Acquiescence has been noted as a particular problem when working with people with mental retardation ("intellectual disabilities" in the UK terminology). The title of Sigelman et al.'s (1981) paper, "When in doubt, say yes," is often quoted in this context. Sigelman et al. recommend some guidelines for good practice, for example, that researchers avoid "yes/no" questions and instead use open-ended questions with this population. However, Rapley and Antaki (1996) argue, from a conversation analysis point of view, that the assumption of an acquiescence bias in people with mental retardation is not fully substantiated by the evidence.

Social desirability refers to a tendency to answer in a socially acceptable way ("faking good"), either consciously or unconsciously (Crowne & Marlowe, 1960, 1964). This is especially a problem in occupational testing, as the following humorous advice for aspiring businessmen illustrates (it also embodies an old-fashioned assumption that business executives are always men):

> When an individual is commanded by an organization to reveal his innermost feelings, he has a duty to himself to give answers that serve his self interest rather than that of The Organization. In a word, he should cheat . . . Most people cheat anyway on such tests. Why then, do it ineptly? . . . When in doubt about the most beneficial answer, repeat to yourself: I loved my father and my mother, but my father a little bit more. I like things pretty much the way they are. I never worry about anything. (Whyte, 1959: 450, quoted in Crowne & Marlowe, 1964)

In clinical research, it is also important to consider the opposite tendency, i.e., where respondents may attempt to "fake bad." This may occur in forensic contexts, when offenders may be trying to obtain a lighter sentence or a softer prison regime; in the case of insurance claims for psychological trauma, where people may be attempting to get a larger settlement; or in the context of being on a waiting list for psychological therapy, where clients may be trying to get help sooner.

Possible ways to get around social desirability problems are:

- Embed a social desirability scale within the main instrument, such as the Marlowe-Crowne (1960) Social Desirability Scale, the L (Lie) scale on the Eysenck Personality Questionnaire (EPQ: Eysenck & Eysenck, 1975) and the Minnesota Multiphasic Personality Inventory (MMPI: Hathaway & McKinley, 1951), and the K (Defensiveness) scale on the MMPI. These provide a direct measure of the extent of socially desirable responding. Factor-analytic studies have found these scales to have two separate components, self-deception and impression management (Paulhus, 1984).

- Use a forced choice format, where the respondent chooses between alternatives of equal social desirability. For example, the Edwards Personal Preference Scale (Edwards, 1953), which measures personality dimensions such as achievement and affiliation, has paired items balanced for social desirability. However, some respondents may object to the constraining nature of such instruments.

- Use "subtle items," on which the acceptability of the response is not apparent, e.g., on the MMPI (Weiner, 1948). However, this practice raises questions about the face validity of the scale, and is not without controversy (Hollrah et al., 1995).

Assembling the Questionnaire and Looking Ahead

Having designed the questions and response scales, the final task is to assemble them into a coherent questionnaire. Once again, the maxim "take care of the respondent" should be primary. Try to make the experience of completing the questionnaire as engaging as possible, and minimize anything which might exhaust or irritate respondents.

Make the questionnaire look attractive by giving it a pleasing layout with readable typefaces, and use language which is easily understandable and welcoming. It also helps respondents work through the questionnaire if the topics are ordered in a logical sequence, and the transitions between different topic areas are made as smooth as possible. Simple things, such as introducing each section with phrases like "This section asks about . . .," can make the respondent's task easier.

Think about data analysis before the final draft, as you may want to print data entry instructions on to the questionnaire. If possible, try some quick analyses to examine your main research questions on the pilot sample.

We will deal with sampling in general in Chapter 10, but there are some issues specific to mail surveys. Dillman (2000) suggests aiming for a response rate of over 60%, and sending out reminder letters to increase the initial response. Bear in mind that people who return questionnaires are not usually representative of the whole target population: they tend to be higher on literacy, general education, and motivation. In order to conceptualize what would lead to sample bias, ask yourself why someone would not fill out the questionnaire. It is sometimes possible to estimate bias by comparing respondents with non-respondents on key variables. For instance, in a client satisfaction survey, it may be possible to see if the clients who filled out the survey questionnaire differed from those who did not, in terms of severity of problems or length of time in therapy.

A recent development in questionnaire research is the internet-based questionnaire (Dillman, 2000). Using HTML and database technology, web-savvy researchers can set up their questionnaires as forms to be completed on-line. For the less technically inclined, prospective participants can be identified and approached via the internet; people who agree to complete the questionnaire can then have it delivered by email (as an attached file); respondents can return their forms in the same way. The internet has the advantage of providing access to a wider potential sample of respondents, particularly important with difficult-to-access populations. For example, Barry et al. (2000) found that Arab respondents were more willing to respond when approached in this way than face to face, although respondents recruited via the internet did not appear to differ from those obtained in the usual way.

Integrating Qualitative and Quantitative Self-report Methods

It is worth re-emphasizing that our separation of interview and questionnaire, and qualitative and quantitative methods was for didactic, not practical, purposes. Our view is that all combinations of self-report/observational, qualitative/quantitative data collection methods have their uses. It is possible to use written questionnaires within observational protocols and to combine open-ended and closed-ended questions in the same questionnaire or interview. For example, it is often a good idea to begin and end structured quantitative interviews with general open-ended questions. Questions at the beginning give the respondents a chance to talk before they have been influenced by the researcher's framework, and questions at the end give them a chance to add anything that may not have been addressed within that framework.

CHAPTER SUMMARY

This chapter has covered the procedures for constructing self-report methods, such as interviews and questionnaires. The advantages of self-report are that it gives the person's own perspective, and that there is no other way to access the person's own experience. Its disadvantage is that there are potential validity problems: people's reports may contain errors due to deception, inaccurate recall, or the unavailability of the information to conscious processing.

There are both qualitative and quantitative approaches to self-report. The main qualitative self-report approach is the semi-structured interview. This allows a flexible interview style, with probes where necessary, and helps respondents describe their own experience in their own words. Qualitative interviewing is a distinct skill, different from clinical interviewing, including interviewing for psychological assessment.

The main quantitative self-report approach is the written questionnaire, using a Likert scale. There are a number of principles to follow in constructing quantitative self-report instruments, both concerning the wording of the items and the form of the response scale. Response sets, such as acquiescence and social desirability, refer to tendencies to respond to items independently of their content. They need to be taken into account when designing and interpreting self-report measures.

Although we have discussed qualitative and quantitative approaches separately, they can easily and fruitfully be combined within a single interview or questionnaire, or within a study as a whole.

FURTHER READING

Smith (1995) gives a brief overview of the qualitative semi-structured interview, and Kvale (1996) has a book-length account. Qualitative self-report procedures, and some illustrative studies, are described in the relevant chapters of Patton (2002) and Taylor and Bogdan (1998). Moser and Kalton (1971) is a classic text on the social survey approach to questionnaires. Rossi et al. (1983) provide a useful collection of chapters by eminent authorities; the chapters by Bradburn on response effects, Sheatsley on questionnaire construction, and Dillman on self-administered questionnaires are well worth consulting (Dillman's material can also be found in his 2000 book). Dawis (1987) reviews scale construction methods in the counseling psychology context.

CHAPTER 7

OBSERVATION

KEY POINTS IN THIS CHAPTER

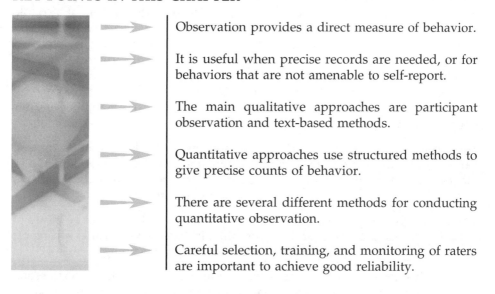

Observation provides a direct measure of behavior.

It is useful when precise records are needed, or for behaviors that are not amenable to self-report.

The main qualitative approaches are participant observation and text-based methods.

Quantitative approaches use structured methods to give precise counts of behavior.

There are several different methods for conducting quantitative observation.

Careful selection, training, and monitoring of raters are important to achieve good reliability.

In the physical and biological sciences, various forms of observation are the only possible data collection method, since the objects of study are animals and inanimate objects. In clinical psychology, however, researchers have a choice: whether to use observation, self-report, or a combination of the two.

Observation can take many forms. You may observe the person in their own natural setting, such as at home or at school. The ecological psychology studies of Roger Barker and his colleagues (Barker et al., 1978), which provide extensive accounts of behavior in community settings, are classic examples of this type. Or you may observe under standardized conditions in the clinic or laboratory. The Strange Situations Test (Ainsworth et al., 1978), which assesses a child's reactions to being separated briefly from his or her parent under standardized conditions, is a widely used example in attachment research.

Observation is a special activity, which does not come naturally to most people (Bakeman & Gottman, 1986; Patton, 2002). It is different from evaluation (of whether something is good or bad), explanation (of why something happened), or summary report. Observational methods thus require special training.

We are referring here to observation as a measurement method, not as a research design. Correlational research designs are sometimes called passive observation studies (see Chapter 8); this is something of a misnomer, as they may not use observation at all. Observational data may be used in descriptive, correlational, or experimental designs: there is no logical link between the measurement method and the design.

Advantages and Disadvantages

The advantage of observation is that it is a direct measure of behavior, and thus can provide concrete evidence of the phenomenon under investigation. For example, if you are studying couples' communication, the members of a couple may say in an interview that they "can't communicate and always end up getting nowhere." However, if you actually observe them interacting, you usually get a clearer indication of the nature of their problems: for example, one member of the couple may be critical and the other may withdraw. Another example is in studying children referred for behavior problems, where a father might say "my daughter is disobedient." Observing the interaction between the father and his daughter allows you to see for yourself what actually goes on between them.

Furthermore, observation enables you to assess the behavior within its context. Observing children within their family setting and also in the classroom allows the researcher to identify and measure situational variables (e.g., critical remarks from siblings or peers) that might contribute to problem behaviors.

Observation is also good for studying behavior that people may not be aware of (e.g., nonverbal behavior) or behavior that is inaccessible using self-report methods (e.g., because of denial, distortion, or simply forgetting).

The disadvantage of observation is that it can only be used to answer certain research questions, principally where you are interested in overt behaviors. Often research questions are more complex than this, and the overt behavior is only one aspect. Observational methods can however be used to study internal processes, in two ways. One is that the research participant can be the observer (i.e., engage in self-monitoring, see below). The other is that observations of behavior can be used to make inferences about cognitive processes or emotional states, for example using the emotional Stroop test (Williams et al., 1996), or using projective tests such as the Rorschach or the TAT (Westen et al., 1999).

Another disadvantage is that observational studies often have problems with reactivity of measurement: people may behave quite differently if they know they are being observed. A potential solution to the reactivity problem is to observe covertly, but this clearly raises ethical issues about deception (which we address below).

Qualitative and Quantitative Observation

Like self-report methods, observational data collection methods have been developed independently within the qualitative and the quantitative traditions.

Although the distinction between the two approaches is not always clear, since qualitative material can be analyzed in a quantitative way using content analysis, this chapter will look at each of these traditions in turn.

QUALITATIVE OBSERVATION

In qualitative observation, the observer attempts to record a narrative account, which, like a literary description, brings the scene to life. However, unlike a literary description, the account attempts to be explicit and systematic rather than metaphorical and intuitive.

As we discussed in Chapter 5, the historical roots of qualitative methods lie in ancient Greek and medieval histories and travelogues. Systematic qualitative observation as a research method was developed as part of the ethnographic approach in anthropology, e.g., the early work of Malinowski (1929) in the South Pacific (see Emerson, 2001). It also was found in medical case studies, Freud (1905/1977) being the outstanding example within psychological medicine. The data in such case studies are often not purely observational, as the clinician will also draw upon self-report data (to a major extent in the case of psychoanalytic case studies).

A number of different approaches fall under the qualitative observation umbrella (Good & Watts, 1996). This section examines two major ones: participant observation and text-based methods. (The analysis of data obtained from such methods is covered in Chapter 12.)

Participant Observation

Features of participant observation:

- Its roots lie in the ethnographic approach in anthropology.

- It involves the researcher becoming "immersed" in the setting, and taking extensive field notes.

- Methodological problems include reactivity and observer bias.

- Covert observation raises ethical issues.

Participant observation refers to a procedure in which the observer enters an organization or social group (such as a psychiatric hospital or a youth gang) in order to gain first-hand experience of its workings. It is characterized by a period of intense social interaction between the researcher and the people being observed, in their own setting, during which the data are collected unobtrusively and systematically (Taylor & Bogdan, 1998). Thus, participant observation involves: (1) the observer's immersion in the situation; (2) systematic, but unstructured observation; and (3) detailed recording of observations, generally from memory. (Note that the term "participant" is somewhat ambiguous in this context, as it can refer both to the researcher—the participant observer—and also to the people being observed—the research participants.)

The observer's role in the setting can be anywhere on the continuum from a complete participant, such as when Goffman worked as a mental hospital aide to make the observations in *Asylums* (1961), to a complete observer, such as when traditional ethnographers lived in cultures which they were not a part of. Taylor and Bogdan (1998) warn about the dangers of observing a setting with which one is overly familiar (due either to friendship or to expertise), as the study may be compromised by the researcher's inability to take multiple perspectives and by the temptation to censor reports or data which may offend colleagues or friends.

As the object of study is more often an organization or social group, rather than an individual, participant observation is more compatible with the framework of sociology and anthropology than psychology. It is particularly associated with the Chicago School of sociology and with the sociology of deviance (Emerson, 2001). Whyte's (1943) *Street corner society*, a study of Italian-American youth gangs, is a classic example of the genre. Whyte, who was a researcher at Harvard University, spent several years living in the Boston community that he was studying and talking to key informants (mostly members of the gang) in order to understand the structure of their organization. His observations involved joining in with their everyday activities, e.g., gambling, bowling, etc. After each period of observation, he wrote extensive field notes, which he later analyzed with the help of one of the informants in his study.

The narrative case study (see Chapter 9) also can be considered a form of participant observation, at least where the focus is on describing the therapeutic process, rather than on giving an account of the client's history. Studies of individual therapy represent the psychologically interesting situation where one member of a dyad is observing the development of that dyad. There are many such accounts from the perspective of both the therapist and the client, and Yalom and Elkin (1974) interestingly combine their parallel accounts of the same therapy in one volume.

Research Questions

In line with the phenomenological approach, most participant observation researchers try to start with no preconceptions about the phenomena under study. They will often go through a process of bracketing, that is, an attempt to identify their preconceptions and set them to one side (see Chapter 5). Anthropologists, in particular, will attempt to set aside their ethnocentric biases when observing other cultures. However, as we have discussed in Chapter 2, disinterested, theory-free observation is an unattainable ideal, since researchers are always observing from within a theory or world view that says what is important and what is trivial. The issue is being aware of and minimizing, rather than eliminating, the extent of one's biases. In any case, the participant observer usually attempts to start the observation unconstrained by prior hypotheses or specific variables of interest.

In practice, participant observation research usually has a clear focus (e.g., to study the social structure of a psychiatric in-patient ward). The research questions are usually discovery oriented. Participant observation is often conducted within the grounded theory approach (Rennie et al., 1988; Strauss & Corbin, 1998), in which the theory evolves as the study progresses.

Pragmatics

As we described in Chapter 3, you often gain access to the research setting via a gatekeeper, for example an administrator or senior doctor who decides whether to allow you into the organization. It is worth starting field notes at this point, since the process of negotiating entry says much about the workings of the organization that you are entering. Organizations that are conflict-ridden, suspicious, or highly bureaucratic will each have their characteristic ways of admitting (or excluding) outsiders.

Once in the setting, you may develop a set of *key informants* who provide in-depth accounts. However, be wary of over-reliance on any one informant, or of implicitly selecting informants whose views agree with your own; try to obtain stories from a variety of perspectives.

In the participant observation tradition, the period of observation is fairly extensive, usually lasting several months. The researcher is initially passive and works at establishing rapport, and attempts to avoid being forced into roles (e.g., "volunteer"). Some guidelines (e.g., Taylor & Bogdan, 1998) suggest that the researcher limit observation sessions (in order to avoid data overload) and observe at different days and times (e.g., nights, weekends).

It is useful to pay special attention to any unusual use of language in the setting, as this can often be a clue to important aspects of its structure (Taylor & Bogdan, 1998). The vocabulary used by staff to refer to clients may give important clues to their underlying feelings towards them. For example, do staff in a drug dependency unit refer to their clients as "patients," "junkies," or "addicts," or is there some local terminology by which they distinguish between different types of clients?

Field Notes

The observations are recorded in the form of field notes, which describe the setting and the people in it (possibly including a diagram), as well as their verbal and nonverbal behavior (Emerson, 2001; Taylor & Bogdan, 1998). Good field notes bring the scene to life. In addition, things that do not make sense should be recorded for later clarification, and your own actions should also be noted, in order to help to judge your effect. Finally, it is important to differentiate the behavior you are observing from your own reactions and interpretations; the latter should be noted and labeled as, for example, "Observer's Comments." As in all research, try to separate description from evaluation and be aware of how your preconceptions may be influencing your observations.

The researcher does not usually take notes or make tape recordings during the observation period, as this often distracts those being observed and is more likely to influence their behavior. Part of the skill of being a participant observer lies in developing your memory. In order to prevent memory overload, limit your time in the setting to an hour or two and write the notes immediately after leaving the field. Remembering key words and drawing a diagram of the setting are useful strategies. The guiding principle (which applies to other areas of life too!) is: "If it's not written down, it never happened."

To illustrate, here is an excerpt from field notes taken during Taylor and Bogdan's (1998) study of institutions for the mentally retarded (UK: people with intellectual disabilities). The field notes include detailed description as well as the observer's comments (labeled as O.C.):

As I get to the dayroom door, I see that all the residents are in the room. I can only see two attendants: Vince and another younger man. (O.C. It's interesting how I automatically assume that this other man is an attendant as opposed to a resident. Several hints: long hair, moustache, and glasses; cotton shirt and jeans, brown leather boots. He's also smoking a cigarette, and a resident, Bobby Bart, is buffing his shoes with a rag. Thus this attendant's dress and appearance differ from that of the residents.) Vince, who is 21, is wearing jeans, brown leather boots, and a jersey that has "LOVE" printed on it. He has long hair, sideburns, and a moustache.

I wave to Vince. He half-heartedly waves back. (O.C. I don't think that Vince has quite gotten used to me coming.) The other attendant doesn't pay any attention to me.

Several residents wave or call to me. I wave back.

Kelly is smiling at me. (O.C. He's obviously happy to see me.) I say to Kelly, "Hi, Bill, how are you?" He says, "Hi, Steve. How's school?" "OK." He says, "School's a pain in the ass. I missed you." (O.C. According to the attendants, Kelly attended school at the institution several years ago.) I say, "I missed you too."

I walk over to Vince and the other attendant. I sit down on a hard plastic rocker between Vince and the other atten., but slightly behind them. The other atten. still doesn't pay attention to me. Vince doesn't introduce me to him.

The smell of feces and urine is quite noticeable to me, but not as pungent as usual.

I, along with the attendants and perhaps five or six residents, am sitting in front of the TV, which is attached to the wall about eight feet off the floor and out of the residents' reach.

Many of the 70 or so residents are sitting on the wooden benches which are in a U-shape in the middle of the dayroom floor. A few are rocking. A couple of others are holding onto each other. In particular, Deier is holding onto the resident the attendants call "Bunny Rabbit." (O.C. Deier is assigned to "Bunny Rabbit"—to keep a hold of him to stop him from smearing feces over himself.)

A lot of residents are sitting on the floor of the room, some of these are leaning against the wall. A few others, maybe 10, just seem to be wandering around the room. (Taylor & Bogdan, 1998: 266)

This extract illustrates the richness and vividness of observational data, but also its wide-ranging and unfocused nature. It is difficult at first reading to know how to make sense of it all.

Ethical Issues

Two major ethical issues arise with participant observation: whether the observation should be overt or covert, and what to do when you observe illegal or immoral acts. These issues also may occur in quantitative observation, but have been more salient in the participant observation literature. (We discuss ethical issues in general in Chapter 10.)

There are many examples in the literature where the observers concealed the fact that they were conducting research. This was usually done in settings where reactivity of measurement would have been a major problem. Two well-known examples are Humphries' (1970) study of homosexual activity in men's public lavatories, which generated an enormous debate over its ethics, and Rosenhan's (1973) pseudopatient study. Researchers conducting covert observations argue that the nature of their research precludes their asking the consent of those being observed and that their findings bring benefits that justify the deception. However, such deception is contrary to the ethical principle of informed consent and lays the researcher open to charges of being a spy or a voyeur. Proposed research involving covert observation should be subjected to thorough consultation on its ethical status.

A related issue is what to do in cases where you observe illegal or immoral acts. For example, in the above study of state institutions for the mentally retarded, Taylor and Bogdan (1998) observed attendants beating and abusing residents. They argue that stepping out of the observer role could have had some short-term benefits, in that they may have been able to stop the specific instance of abuse. On the other hand, it would have effectively terminated their project, which had the potential to end the abuse by documenting it, and possibly leading to permanent changes in the institutional structure to prevent future abuse. In cases like this, researchers face complex dilemmas to which there are no clear-cut answers. In such situations, it is always important to seek out research colleagues or supervisors to help you explore the ethical issues.

Quality of the Data

Finally, participant observation raises some specific issues of reliability and validity:

- *Reliability*. It is hard to check observer accuracy in participant observation. Although it is theoretically possible to have two or more simultaneous observers in the setting, this is rarely done in practice. It is, however, quite possible to replicate an observation in several settings at once, as was done in Rosenhan's (1973) pseudopatient study. Reliability in participant observation can also be examined by considering the consistency of behavior across time.

- *Observer bias.* As we have discussed above, all observation is to some extent biased, in the sense of being governed by previous understandings and expectations, whether consciously by theory, or unconsciously by ethnocentricity or general world view. These biases affect how observers see things; reports from informants may also be biased because of their own particular perspectives and special interests (Kurz, 1983).

- *Reactivity.* The presence of an observer may alter the behavior of those being studied. This reactivity problem is not unique to qualitative approaches; it occurs with all types of observation. Participant observers may be able to mitigate it by allowing time for the people in the setting to become accustomed to them. Some researchers try to get around this problem by conducting covert observations, but this of course raises ethical problems (see above).

Text-based Research

The second area of qualitative observation, which we will look at briefly, is text-based research. Texts, of written or spoken forms of communication, provide the basis for a loosely organized set of research approaches referred to as *discourse analysis*. These texts include transcripts of conversations, official documents, television broadcasts, and newspaper articles.

Such methods are not new. There is a long tradition of discourse analysis within sociology, heavily influenced by linguistics (Labov and Fanshel, 1977; Potter & Wetherell, 1987; Sudnow, 1972). In the middle of the 20th century, some psychologists (e.g., Allport, 1942) advocated "personal documents" research, although this did not become a mainstream avenue for research at the time.

Text-based approaches involve a close study of the text under examination: the focus is on its structure, or its underlying assumptions and meanings, rather than on what it is supposed to be describing. This differs from self-report in that the intention is to analyze the text as a sample of communication, rather than to understand what the speaker or author is thinking or feeling.

Sources of Texts

Studies using these approaches can draw on a wide range of possible sources:

- *Personal documents.* The classic personal documents approach collected letters, diaries (e.g., of language acquisition), or other personal accounts (e.g., William James's, 1902, *Varieties of religious experience*).

- *Administrative records or archives* can be used, e.g., court records, and also, within the limits of confidentiality and consent, clinical case records including intake reports and contact notes (e.g., Todd et al., 1994).

- *Cultural texts* include widely disseminated published records. These could be self-help books, political speeches, entertainment media (e.g., TV, movies, computer games), or educational texts.

- *Visual representations* may include photographs, advertisements, and home videos.

- *Naturally occurring interactions.* Researchers may be interested in ordinary, everyday conversations (e.g., children's talk in a school playground) or specialized ones (e.g., psychotherapy interactions or telephone helplines).

- *Collected or "found" examples of language usage* include slang and metaphor, for example, to examine how people talk about mental illness. Researchers can also collect examples of a phenomenon of theoretical or practical interest. This is a heritage from natural history and linguistics in which research was done by collecting examples (e.g., Freud's collection of "slips of the tongue").

- *Invited or constructed texts* are set up or solicited by the researcher. For example, the researcher might ask participants to write personal accounts of difficult experiences, or might set up a family interaction task (e.g., to generate parent–teenager conversations). Qualitative interview transcripts can also be approached from a discourse rather than a self-report point of view (i.e., with a focus on how things are talked about, rather than on the content per se).

Examples

Historical research is the prototypical example of text-based research. From the point of view of psychology, historical research can be valuable for bringing the past alive, in order to help us understand the historical context of important ideas in psychology (e.g., the origin of psychoanalysis, Schwartz, 1999), for exemplifying important psychological processes in the lives of individuals (e.g., Erikson's, 1969, psychobiography of Gandhi), and for showing the psychological influence of the past on people's current experiences (Zeldin, 1994). Historical research generally makes use of multiple sources (e.g., the range of types of texts mentioned above), and in some cases, qualitative interviews (as in oral history). The power of careful historical analysis is illustrated by Runyan (1982), in his analysis of the large number of explanations for why the Dutch painter Vincent van Gogh cut off his ear. By careful analysis of historical records, Runyan was able to rule out all but a few explanations as being inconsistent with what is known about van Gogh's life.

Three other examples illustrate the wide variety of discourse analytic studies, particularly in relation to clinical psychology. The first is Madill and Barkham's (1997) study of a successful case of psychodynamic psychotherapy, which we outlined in Chapter 5. The second is Labov and Fanshel's (1977) classic study: a book-length report which analyzed a single 15-minute segment of a psychotherapeutic interview. They used microanalytic methods to examine both the content of the speech and also its paralinguistic features, such as voice spectrogram patterns. They revealed how much rich meaning is carried in subtle, barely noticeable, variations in speech, and demonstrated the complex nature of the mutual responsiveness between client and therapist.

The third example is Harper's (1994) study of how five mental health professionals used the term "paranoia." His analysis identified a number of discourses, or systematic ways of talking, about paranoia. For example, these included the "empiricist" account, where lists of characteristics and symptoms were the focus, and the "contingent" account, where personal and social values were acknowledged in interviewees' discussions. These discourses, and the ways in which professionals moved between them, seemed to serve particular functions, such as the assertion of professional legitimacy.

QUANTITATIVE OBSERVATION

- Quantitative observation involves systematic counting or timing of specified behaviors.

- A clear operational definition of the behaviors is essential (but not always easy).

- Lower levels of inference usually lead to better reliability.

- There are several different methods of conducting observations, e.g., interval recording and time sampling.

- The observers (also known as raters or judges) need to receive careful training and monitoring throughout the study.

The essence of quantitative observation (aside, of course, from its using numbers) is that the variables being observed and the methods for observing them are explicitly defined. It is characterized by the use of predefined behavior codes by trained observers (also called *raters* or *judges*) of demonstrated reliability. Quantitative observations are usually targeted at a small number of pre-specified behaviors, although they sometimes can be more wide ranging.

For instance, researchers observing aggression on a children's playground must specify precisely what constitutes and what does not constitute an aggressive act, e.g., when does a touch become a push or a punch? They must also specify which aspects of such acts will be recorded, e.g., type, frequency, or intensity. Thus, compared to qualitative observation, quantitative methods represent a gain in precision at the expense of a narrowing of scope and context.

Quantitative observations can be used to address several different types of research question. For example, they can be used for questions of description (e.g., Which types of verbal response modes are used in child psychotherapy?), for sequential analysis (e.g., Which types of client response are most likely to follow a therapist interpretation?), and for questions of covariation (e.g., Does observer-rated empathy correlate with treatment outcome?).

Background

Historically, quantitative observation methods developed in three different applied areas: behavioral observation, psychotherapy process research, and content analysis in communication. However, despite differences in language and underlying philosophy, many of the same methodological issues apply in all three areas. We will mostly draw on examples from behavioral observation, as that is where the method is most systematically articulated.

Behavioral observation has its conceptual roots in methodological behaviorism, which argues that psychology should restrict itself to observable behavior (see Chapter 4). Also, Mischel's (1968) argument, that the validity of traditional, trait-based assessment procedures was unacceptably low, gave an impetus to the development of practical methods for behavioral assessment in the clinical context. These methods attempt to eliminate inferences to internal constructs (Goldfried & Kent, 1972). There is now a substantial practical literature on behavioral observation in clinical work (e.g., Bellack & Hersen, 1988; Ciminero et al., 1986; Hayes et al., 1999; Haynes & O'Brien, 2000). Since, for the behaviorists, research and practice are closely related, many of the procedures can equally well be applied in research.

Psychotherapy process research began with the work of Carl Rogers and the client-centered group in the 1940s and 1950s. These were the first researchers to study recordings of actual therapeutic interactions, and the first to quantify aspects of the therapeutic relationship, such as therapist empathy (Kirschenbaum, 1979). Subsequent investigators have examined an enormous number of different process variables, ranging from global constructs, such as the quality of the therapeutic alliance, to specific types of responses used by the therapist and client (Greenberg & Pinsof, 1986).

Content analysis arose out of mass media communication research, which uses such material as newspapers or transcriptions of broadcasts as its subject matter (Krippendorff, 1980; Smith, 2000). For example, newspaper stories about mental illness might be content analyzed according to the underlying etiological model they espoused. However, the raw material need not be restricted to the mass media. Content analysis can be used with self-report data, transcriptions of meetings, etc. For example, Fewtrell and Toms (1985) used content analysis to classify the discussion in psychiatric ward rounds into categories such as medical treatment, mental state, and social adjustment. Content analysis provides a useful means of bridging quantitative and qualitative approaches, in that it applies quantitative analysis to verbal (qualitative) descriptions.

Procedures for Conducting Observations

As we discussed in Chapter 6 in the context of self-report measures, it is usually better to use an existing measure than to attempt to develop your own. Measure development is time consuming and difficult, and it is hard to publish work with unfamiliar measures. This is equally true in the context of quantitative observation; if at all possible, it is better to use an existing coding manual and rating scheme with established inter-rater reliability. We discuss observational measures here from the viewpoint of the researcher developing a measure; this viewpoint is taken partly in order to clarify the process involved in measure development, and partly to provide guidelines for measure development research.

Developing the Measures

The first step in quantitative observation is to operationally define the behavior to be observed. The goal is to specify the behavior sufficiently well, so that it can be observed with high inter-rater reliability. Often this means that the behavior should be defined so that it can be rated without the raters having to make large inferences, but for some variables this may not be possible. Giving clear definitions is harder than it seems, as even apparently simple behaviors such as head nods or eye contact, or giving advice in therapy, pose difficulties in delineation. More inferential constructs, such as the level of empathy offered by a therapist, are much more difficult to define.

Developing a good definition is an incremental process. It is often useful to start with informal qualitative observation, supplemented by a review of the literature on the variable of interest and similar observational measures. The researcher then develops an initial version of the codes and tries them out on some data. This leads to revision of the codes and an iterative cycle of testing and revision. When the researcher has a coding system that he or she can use, the next step is to attempt to teach the codes to raters, who then test them out on data. This leads to a further cycle of testing and revision, which improves the likelihood that others besides the researcher will be able to use the measure (a form of inter-observer generalizability referred to as *portability*). Finally, the researcher utilizes the measure in a study, the results of which may suggest yet more revisions, and so on.

Since many different dimensions of behavior can be examined, it is useful to have a framework to help guide one's choices. Table 7.1 gives one such framework, adapted from research on psychotherapy process (Elliott, 1991). Similar schemes could easily be constructed for other content areas of observation, e.g., children's behavior in the classroom or family interaction. Which aspects of which dimensions are important depends partly on the variables being observed and partly on the research questions.

Methods of Observation

Having specified the dimensions of the behavior to be observed, the next step is to choose an observational method. There are several choices (Altman, 1974; Cone, 1999; Hayes et al., 1999; Haynes & O'Brien, 2000).

Table 7.1   Five dimensions of observed behavioral process

1. *Perspective of Observation*: What is the point of view of the person doing the observation? (varies with involvement and role in setting, expertise)
   a. Researcher (trained observer)
   b. Expert participant (e.g., therapist, teacher)
   c. Index participant (e.g., client, student)
   d. Secondary participants (in supportive roles, e.g., family member)
2. *Person/Focus*: Which element of the behavioral process is studied?
   a. Index participant (client or client system; i.e., individual, family)
   b. Expert participant/system (clinician/clinical agency; e.g., therapist, teacher, clinic)
   c. Interaction of index and expert participant (e.g., quality of relationship, "fit")
3. *Aspect of behavior*: What kind of behavior or process variable is studied?
   a. Content: *What* is said, meant or expressed? (type of content: ideas, themes)
   b. Action/intention: What is *done* by what is said? Actions or behaviors carried out by participants, including intentions, tasks, response modes
   c. Style: *How* it is done, said or expressed (e.g., duration, frequency, intensity, paralinguistic and nonverbal behavior, vocal quality, apparent mood, interpersonal manner).
   d. Quality: How *well* it is done, said or expressed? (e.g., accuracy, appropriateness, acceptability, skillfulness).
4. *Unit Level*: At what level or "resolution" is the process studied? (Selected useful units)
   a. Sentence (idea unit): A single expressed or implied idea.
   b. Action/speaking turn (interaction unit): A response by one person, preceded and followed by actions by another person or different actions by the same person.
   c. Episode (topic/task unit): A series of action/speaking turns organized by a common task or topic, within an occasion.
   d. Occasion ("scene" unit): A time-limited situation in which two or more people meet to do something (e.g., session)
   e. Relationship (interpersonal unit): The entire course of a relation between two people.
   f. Organization (institution unit): A system of relationships organized toward a specific set of goals and located in a setting (e.g., a clinic)
   g. Person (self unit): Includes a person's system of relatively stable beliefs and characteristics and history of self-, other-, and organizational involvement.
5. *Sequential Phase*: What is the temporal or functional orientation taken toward a unit of process (i.e., towards what happened before, during and after the unit)?
   a. Context ("antecedents"): What has lead up to a unit of process? (e.g., previous speaking turn, earlier relationships).
   b. Process ("behaviors"): The process that is targeted for study at a given level (unit).
   c. Effects ("consequences"): The sequelae of a unit of process (e.g., reinforcement, treatment outcome).

(Adapted from Elliott, 1991, by permission of the Guildford Press.)

- *Narrative recording*, that is, writing an account of what happens, is equivalent to qualitative observation. It is used in the behavioral observation and ecological psychology traditions (e.g., Bakeman & Gottman, 1986; Barker et al., 1978). It is useful for hypothesis generation, measure development, and for arriving at ideas about causal relationships (in behavioral terms, the antecedents, behaviors and consequences). It is also good for low-frequency behaviors. However, it is difficult to assess the reliability of such observations. Narrative recording is often a preliminary step to developing more structured methods of observation.

- *Event recording* yields the simplest form of frequency data. The observer counts every occurrence of the behavior within the entire observation period. For example, if the observation is focusing on therapist response modes used during a 50-minute session, the final frequency count might be 35 questions, 32 reflections, five advisements, four interpretations and one self-disclosure. The advantages of event recording are that it is simple and that it can be done alongside other activities; the disadvantages are that you cannot analyze sequences or other complexities and that it is hard to keep observer attention or assess observer reliability at the event level.

- *Interval recording* divides the observation period into equal intervals (e.g., a 50-minute therapy session might be divided into 10 five-minute intervals) and the number of behaviors is recorded during each one. In *whole interval sampling*, the behavior is only recorded if it is present for the whole of the interval, as opposed to *partial interval sampling*, when it can be present for any part of the interval. The advantages of interval recording are that it allows you to analyze sequences and that it gives a rudimentary estimate of both the frequency and the duration of a behavior. It may be adapted to record several behaviors concurrently. Having timed intervals also helps keep the observers alert. The disadvantages are that it requires more observer effort, as you have to attend to timing as well as to the behavior.

- *Time sampling*. Observations are made only at specific moments of time, e.g., every five minutes or every half-hour. When observing large groups, *scan sampling* can be used, where each member of the group is observed sequentially. For example, Hinshaw et al. (1989) used scan sampling to observe the social interaction of hyperactive boys. The advantages of time sampling are that it yields a direct measure of the prevalence of a behavior in a group and that it is good for high rate, continuous behaviors; it also means that raters do not have to maintain continuous attention. The disadvantage is that low-frequency behaviors may be missed, as they might only occur between the observation times.

- *Sequential act coding* records events in the order in which they occur. In contrast to event recording, it usually requires a comprehensive coding system to cover all possible events. (Event recording may just focus on one or two events, e.g., specific aggressive acts in a school classroom.) To take a simplified example, researchers may classify events in a therapeutic interaction into client speech (C), therapist speech (T), and silence (S). Then a sequential act coding record might look like this: C,T,S,C,S,C.... This strategy is ideal for sequential analysis, because it relies on natural units (such as talking turns), not artificial units (such as time segments). However, disagreements on where the units begin and end can complicate reliability, and the method is inefficient if you are not interested in sequences.

- *Duration recording* is similar to sequential act coding, except that the focus is on timing the occurrence of a single behavior rather than categorizing events into codes. You can measure both *duration*, the interval between the start and the end of each behavior, and *latency*, the interval between behaviors. For example, Brock and Barker (1990) used this method to study the amount of "air time" taken up by each staff member during team meetings in a psychiatric day hospital.

- *Global rating scales*, in which the observer makes an overall judgement, often of the quality of the behavior, are usually based on a long period of observation. Clinical examples include the Brief Psychiatric Rating Scale (BPRS: Overall & Gorham, 1962), which rates several dimensions of psychiatric symptomatology, and the Global Assessment Scale (GAS: Endicott et al., 1976; used as Axis V in the DSM-IV diagnostic system) which rates overall psychiatric impairment. Global ratings, e.g., of empathy or transference, are frequently used in therapy process research (Greenberg & Pinsof, 1986). These are less precise than the behavioral observation methods, in that the observer is being asked to quantify an impression or judgement. On the other hand, global ratings are useful for complex or inferred constructs and can provide useful summaries of events. Many global rating scales have acceptable reliability.

- *Environmental measures*. Finally, an interesting category of observation focuses on the psychological environment as a whole, rather than specific individuals within it. Procedures include *behavioral mapping*, where the observers record the pattern of activity in a given environment. For example, Kennedy et al. (1988) used behavioral mapping to study the patterns of patient and staff activity in a spinal cord injury unit over the course of a single day. Environmental observation may also involve the use of *unobtrusive measures* (Webb et al., 1966), in which features of the physical environment are used to yield data on patterns of activity. Classic examples of unobtrusive measures are using the wear and tear on a carpet as an index of the popularity of museum exhibits, and using the accretion of graffiti as an index of youth gang activity.

Mechanics

The mechanics of recording the observations need to be as simple as possible, so that the recording does not interfere with making the observations themselves. Possible aids include coding sheets, stopwatches, counters, and electromechanical devices. The observations may be conducted in real time, or the interactions may be recorded on audio or video tape for subsequent observation and analysis.

It is not always necessary or possible for the researchers to do the observations. An alternative is to use *self-monitoring* methods (Bornstein et al., 1986). In self-monitoring, participants are taught to carry out the observations themselves. For example, an evaluation of couples' therapy might include the participants keeping written records of the number and type of arguments that they have over the course of several weeks. Self-monitoring can also be done by proxy, e.g., parents could keep records of their child's sleep problems. The advantage of self-monitoring is that it allows the researcher to obtain observational data over long time periods and also from private settings. It can also be adapted to monitor cognitions. For example, in a study of obsessive-compulsive disorder, participants might be asked to keep a record of their intrusive thoughts.

If you have sequential data from your observations, e.g., if you use interval or time-sampling methods, you can do more complex analyses of how the behaviors develop over time. This is a technical topic involving special statistics; Gottman and Roy (1990) describe some of the options.

Reliability and Validity Issues

An advantage of quantitative observation methods is that they facilitate the calculation of reliability (see Chapter 4 for a discussion of the statistical aspects of assessing inter-rater reliability). One practical problem is *observer drift*, where observers start out with high reliability, but then tend to develop idiosyncratic rules or become careless as the observation proceeds. To prevent this occurring, it is important to continually monitor the observers' reliability.

The main validity issue, aside from problems with the operational definition of the variables, is the *reactivity of observation*. As we discussed above, in the context of qualitative observation, the act of observing may alter the behavior being observed. The only solution is to make the observations as unobtrusive as possible, and to allow time for the people being observed to become habituated to the observers' presence. This may be easier with qualitative observation, which is usually done to a more leisurely timetable.

Practical Suggestions for Working with Raters

Researchers have various strategies available for maximizing the reliability and validity of observer ratings. These include:

- design or selection of measures with clear, well-defined variables and good examples of categories;
- careful selection of an adequate number of raters; and
- thorough training and management of raters.

Here we summarize some suggestions from Elliott (1989b; see also Cone, 1999; Moras & Hill, 1991) on how best to work with raters. Many of these considerations also apply to the use of multiple analysts in qualitative research (Hill et al., 1997).

Rater selection.   It is usually better to work with motivated volunteers, such as top students in advanced undergraduate seminars, who are interested in a career in clinical psychology. Occasionally you may have to drop a rater's data later due to consistent unreliability, so it is best to start out with at least three and preferably four raters.

Training.   It is a good idea to begin with a didactic presentation and modeling of the rating process, followed by group rating. This is followed by extensive practice, including weekly feedback on progress and problems. The SPSS Reliability procedure offers useful analyses for this, providing solid evidence both of progress and of problems, which can be shared with the group. For example, reliability checks will tell:

- which categories or dimensions show reliability problems;
- whether a reliability problem is general (spread across all raters) or specific (restricted to one or two raters);
- if a rater has misunderstood a category;
- if two raters have formed a clique which sets them apart from everyone else; and
- if particular raters differ greatly in their base rates for a category.

Training should continue until ratings on all variables reach an acceptable standard of reliability (see Chapter 4).

Management. The management and nurturing of raters is at least as important as their selection and training. To foster the "research alliance," communicate to the raters that their views will be taken seriously and encourage them to contribute to the refinement of the rating system. Regular meetings and feedback during the rating process help prevent alienation and produce more reliable and valid data. As far as practicable, raters should feel part of the whole research process, including the conceptual framework and the research questions (where it is not necessary to keep them blind), and analyses and interpretation; this may occasionally also include co-authorship, if important contributions are made to the study.

CHAPTER SUMMARY

This chapter has examined when and how observational methods of measurement might be used. The advantage of observation is that it provides a direct measure of behavior, thereby overcoming some of the validity problems of self-report that were discussed in the previous chapter. It is useful when precise records of behavior are needed, or for studying behaviors that are not amenable to self-report (e.g., nonverbal behavior, or physiological responses).

As in self-report, there are both qualitative and quantitative approaches to observation. The main qualitative approach is participant observation, which derives from ethnographic approaches in anthropology. Text-based methods can also be considered as observational in nature.

Quantitative approaches use structured methods to give precise counts of behavior. They have been developed in three disparate areas—behavioral observation, therapy process research, and content analysis—but the methodological issues are similar in all applications. There are a number of different methods for conducting quantitative observation, e.g., interval recording and time sampling. The choice between them depends on the nature of the research questions and the effort needed to make the observations. For all types of observation, careful selection, training, and monitoring of raters is important to achieve good reliability.

FURTHER READING

There is a good treatment of participant observation in many texts (e.g., Friedrich & Lüdke, 1975; Emerson, 2001; Taylor & Bogdan, 1998). We recommend perusing some of the classic studies using this method, as they are mostly stimulating and readable, e.g., Goffman (1961) and Whyte (1943). The classic text on personal documents methods is Allport (1942); for more contemporary views of text-based methods, see coverage in Taylor and Bogdan (1998), Berg (1995), Potter and Wetherell (1987) and van Dijk (1997a, 1997b). Quantitative observational methods are reviewed by Cone (1999), Haynes and O'Brien (2000), and Weick (1985). Greenberg and Pinsof (1986) review measures for use in psychotherapy process research, while Hill (1991) gives an introduction to therapy and counseling process research in general.

CHAPTER 8

FOUNDATIONS OF DESIGN

KEY POINTS IN THIS CHAPTER

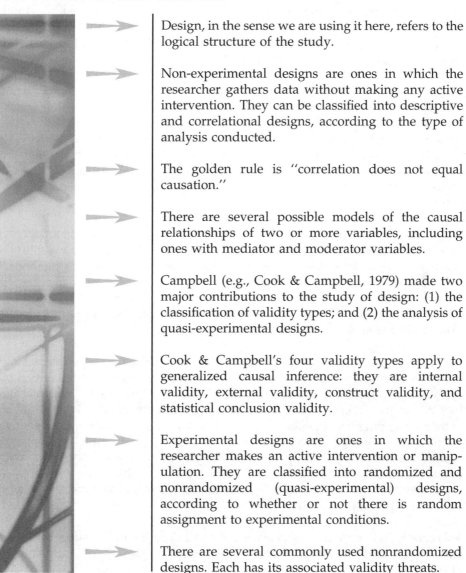

Design, in the sense we are using it here, refers to the logical structure of the study.

Non-experimental designs are ones in which the researcher gathers data without making any active intervention. They can be classified into descriptive and correlational designs, according to the type of analysis conducted.

The golden rule is "correlation does not equal causation."

There are several possible models of the causal relationships of two or more variables, including ones with mediator and moderator variables.

Campbell (e.g., Cook & Campbell, 1979) made two major contributions to the study of design: (1) the classification of validity types; and (2) the analysis of quasi-experimental designs.

Cook & Campbell's four validity types apply to generalized causal inference: they are internal validity, external validity, construct validity, and statistical conclusion validity.

Experimental designs are ones in which the researcher makes an active intervention or manipulation. They are classified into randomized and nonrandomized (quasi-experimental) designs, according to whether or not there is random assignment to experimental conditions.

There are several commonly used nonrandomized designs. Each has its associated validity threats.

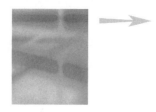

Randomized designs facilitate inferences about causality. They are central to the discussion of evidence-based practice and empirically supported therapies. However, they also have limitations and validity threats, and cannot be regarded as a scientific panacea.

The previous chapters have covered the groundwork and measurement phases of the research process; the present one begins our examination of the design phase. This order, first measurement then design, roughly corresponds to how you go about planning an actual research project: you usually begin by thinking about which variables interest you and how to measure them; next you think about design. From now on, we will put measurement behind us, working, for didactic purposes, on the assumption that it is unproblematic, even though we recognize that this is often not the case.

To clarify what we mean by the term "design," think of the questions "what, when, where and who?" about a research project. Measurement is the "what" aspect: what is being studied, what measurements are made. *Design*, in the sense we are using it here, denotes "when, where, and on whom" the measurements are taken: the logical structure that guides the data collection of the study. It covers such topics as the relative merits of large sample versus single-case studies, what type of control group, if any, is required, and who the participants will be.

The terms "research design" and "experimental design" are also sometimes used in a broader sense to denote everything to do with planning and executing a research project, synonymously with our use of the term "research methods." The more restricted sense of the term "design" that we are using here is consistent with its use in the statistical literature (e.g., Keppel, 1991; Kirk, 1995; Winer et al., 1991). Whether the broader or narrower meaning is intended is usually clear from the context.

Research designs can be classified into two fundamental types: experimental and nonexperimental designs. *Experimental designs* involve an active intervention by the researcher, such as giving one type of therapy to some clients and a second type to others, whereas *nonexperimental designs* simply involve measurement, without changing the phenomenon or situation to be measured. These two approaches to design reflect "the two disciplines of scientific psychology" (Cronbach, 1957, 1975). Experimentalists are often more concerned with examining the causal influence of external factors, which are amenable to experimental manipulation; nonexperimentalists are often more concerned with variation between people.

This chapter will examine nonexperimental and experimental designs, and their various subtypes, and also look at some general principles for assessing validity in research designs.

NONEXPERIMENTAL DESIGNS

Nonexperimental designs can be classified, according to their aims, into descriptive and correlational designs. As is obvious from their names, descriptive designs usually aim simply to describe, whereas correlational designs aim to examine associations in order to make predictions or explore causal linkages.

Descriptive Designs

Examples of descriptive studies frequently appear in the mass media: public opinion surveys, in which respondents are asked which political party they intend to vote for; the national census, which reports, for instance, the percentage of people living in various types of accommodation; and national unemployment statistics. However, the importance of systematic descriptive research is generally overlooked by clinical psychologists, even though such research is often valuable as a preliminary step in understanding a phenomenon of interest. Some examples of descriptive studies are:

- Descriptive epidemiological research, which aims to document the incidence and prevalence of specified psychological problems.

- Consumer satisfaction research, which assesses clients' satisfaction with a psychological service.

- Phenomenological research, which aims to understand the nature and defining features of a given type of experience.

Quantitative descriptive studies report their results using *descriptive statistics*, naturally enough. This is a technical term covering such statistics as percentage, mean, median, incidence, and prevalence. However, it is rare to have a purely descriptive study, as researchers often want to examine the associations between two or more variables of interest. For example, in a consumer satisfaction study you may want to see whether there is an association between client satisfaction and various client demographic characteristics, such as gender or ethnicity. This leads on to the next type of study, the correlational design.

Correlational Designs

Correlational studies aim to examine the relationship between two or more variables: in technical language, to see whether they covary, correlate, or are associated with each other. Such studies are also called *passive observation* or *naturalistic* studies, in contrast to studies employing active methods of experimental manipulation. (Passive observation, as a research design, should not be confused with participant observation, which is a data-gathering method.) In correlational studies, researchers measure a number of variables for each participant, with the aim of studying the associations among these variables. However, the term "correlational design" is slightly misleading, as it suggests that the associations between the variables will be assessed using a correlation coefficient. The drawback of correlation coefficients is that they measure only one type of association between variables, that is, a linear association. Nonlinear associations between variables also come under this heading (although they are infrequently addressed by most researchers, who tend to restrict their attention to linear models), and thus the term relational designs is perhaps more appropriate (Elliott, 1993). However, we are retaining the term "correlational designs" for consistency with the established literature.

A well-known example of a correlational design is Brown and Harris's (1978) study of the social origins of depression, which looked at the association between women's depression, their experience of stressful life events, and vulnerability factors (such as low intimacy with the husband and loss of the mother before the age of 11). Correlational designs are often also used to examine individual differences, for example in predicting which clients respond best to a psychological intervention. Examining such correlations is a common step in attempts to construct causal explanations. That is, one typically tries to predict what happens to whom (e.g., in therapy) in order to understand why it happens (e.g., what are the effective ingredients) or in order to improve an application (e.g., to learn how to enhance its outcome).

Measure development research, which aims to develop, evaluate or improve measures, uses both descriptive and correlational designs. As we discussed in Chapter 6, developing a new measure involves extensive testing of reliability and validity, using a correlational framework; it also involves providing normative data for the measure, using descriptive methods.

Correlational designs may be *cross-sectional*, in which all observations are made at the same point in time, or they may be *longitudinal*, in which measurements are made at two or more different time points. Correlational studies may use simple statistical measures of association, e.g., chi-square and correlation coefficients, or multivariate methods, such as multiple regression, factor analysis, and log-linear procedures. They may also use more advanced methods, which aim to map the underlying structure of complex data sets. These go under various names—path analysis, latent structure analysis, causal modeling, or structural equation modeling (e.g., Fassinger, 1987; Hoyle & Smith, 1994; Tabachnik & Fidell, 2001)—but the underlying logic is the same. They are used for evaluating how well conceptual models generated from previous research or theory fit the data.

Path analysis is both a method of conceptual analysis and a procedure for testing causal models. Its framework is a useful tool for planning out research, even if you never actually carry out a formal path analysis, in that it forces you to spell out your theoretical model. It is also useful for trying to conceptualize the results of correlational studies. The essence of path analysis is to tell a story in diagrammatic or flowchart form, showing which variables influence which others: the examples of different kinds of causal linkages that are given in the next section are depicted in the form of elementary path diagrams.

Correlation and Causation

The major drawback of correlational studies is that they cannot be used to make unequivocal causal inferences. The golden rule of research design is: *correlation does not equal causation*. Correlations may strongly suggest causal influences, but they cannot firmly establish them (although the absence of a correlation generally does rule out a causal relationship). You will see this rule frequently ignored in popular journalism and sometimes in the professional literature too.

The existence and nature of causal relationships involves some difficult philosophical problems (Cook & Campbell, 1979; White, 1990). First, it is not clear exactly what psychologists mean when they talk about "causes." In the natural and biological sciences, causes are understood as mechanical or biochemical physical processes. In the 20th century, starting with Freud, psychologists extended the idea of causation to include mental mechanisms (Slife & Williams, 1995). Over the years, psychologists have used a wide variety of explanations to understand people, including intentions, developmental precedents, situational cues and opportunities, trait or diagnostic categories, unconscious meanings, and biochemical processes.

Second, in psychology and epidemiology we are often dealing with probabilistic rather than deterministic causes. Thus, when we say that smoking causes lung cancer or that poverty causes ill-health, we are not talking about certain causation (there are always exceptions) but about increased risk. Similarly, in clinical psychology, when we say that an intervention causes change, we mean that the intervention sets the conditions for likely client change, but that change is not certain.

Third, going back to Bacon, Hume, and J.S. Mill (see Cook & Campbell, 1979; Haynes & O'Brien, 2000), philosophers and scientists have struggled with defining a set of conditions for inferring a causal relationship. Four generally agreed conditions are:

- *Covariation*: the two variables must occur together.
- *Precedence*: the hypothesized causal variable must reliably precede the effect variable.
- *Exclusion of alternative explanations*: other explanations for the observed covariation must be reasonably excluded.
- *Logical mechanism*: there must be a plausible account for the hypothesized causal relation.

Correlational studies can establish the first condition, that two variables, A and B, covary. Information relevant to the second condition, how they are ordered in time, may also be known. The third condition, that of eliminating alternative explanations, can be addressed to some extent with a correlational framework, while the fourth condition, providing a plausible account, can be derived from previous theory and research. (It is worth noting that this fourth condition has frequently been overlooked, and that many experimental designs are "causally empty"; see Haynes & O'Brien, 2000.)

Let us take a simplified example, derived from early formulations of client-centered theory (Rogers, 1957). Suppose that variable A represents therapist empathy and variable B represents the client's outcome at the end of therapy, and that research has established a significant positive correlation between therapist empathy and client outcome. Then a number of inferences about their causal relationships are possible, some of which are depicted in the following simple path diagrams (in which an arrow indicates the direction of a causal relationship):

1. A ⟶ B

First it may be that A causes B: higher therapist empathy brings about better client outcomes.

2. B ⟶ A

On the other hand, it is also possible that B causes A: clients who are improving in therapy may tend to generate more empathic responses from their therapists.

3. A   B
   ↖ ↗
    C

A very common problem is that A and B may both be caused by a third variable, C, e.g., client psychological mindedness. It is plausible that clients who are more psychologically minded could have better outcomes and also generate more empathy in their therapists. Thus the apparent causal relationship between A and B might be spurious: that is, entirely explained by the influence of the third variable, C. The presence of such third variables which provide competing causal explanations prevents the researcher from drawing accurate causal inferences and thus reduces the study's validity.

4. A → D → B

Yet another possibility is that A does not influence B directly, but only indirectly via D. Variables such as D are known as *mediator variables* (Baron & Kenny, 1986): they mediate (come in the middle of) the relationship between two other variables. For example, higher therapist empathy could lead specifically to increased client self-exploration, which could then lead to better client outcome. We would then say that the causal relationship between empathy and outcome was mediated by client self-exploration.

5. A ⟶ B
   ↑
   E

Here the relationship between A and B differs according to the values of E. Variables such as E are known as *moderator variables* (Baron & Kenny, 1986): they moderate the relationship between two other variables, acting like a gate or valve. E could represent the type of client presenting problem, e.g., anxiety or depression, or a demographic variable such as age or gender. If, for example, therapist empathy led to better client outcomes in men but not in women, we would say that the causal relationship between empathy and outcome was moderated by client gender.

The five possible relationships we have reviewed all assume that the obtained correlation reflects some kind of causal relationship. There is, however, a sixth possibility, which is often overlooked but which is essential to consider. The correlation may reflect a *conceptual confound*, between A and B: it may be due to overlapping meaning between the two variables. Thus, therapist empathy (particularly when rated by the client) may actually be a kind of outcome, which means that the correlation may simply reflect a correlation of one kind of outcome with another kind of outcome. This is one other reason why correlation does not equal causation.

It follows from this that the art of research design is to collect data in such a way as to examine the influence of third variables and of mediator and moderator variables, and to evaluate for conceptual confounding, in order to be able to draw clear inferences about the relationships between the variables under study. Experimental designs can help to do this by systematically manipulating one or more variables at a time.

EXPERIMENTAL DESIGNS

The word "experiment" has the same root as the word "experience": both derive from the Latin for try or test. Psychologists today usually think of an experiment as a study involving random assignment to two or more groups or conditions. However, this view is a recent development (within the past 50 years or so) and represents a methodological narrowing under the influence of positivism and biomedical research. Before that time, and today in its ordinary usage, an experiment referred to "the action of trying anything, or putting it to proof; a test, trial" (Oxford English Dictionary).

An experimenter interferes with the natural course of events, in order to construct a situation in which competing theories can be tested. These theories often concern causal influences between variables. In physics, formal experimentation began with Galileo, who attempted to test his theories of dynamics by rolling balls down inclined planes (Chalmers, 1990), initiating what we now call the hypothetico-deductive method. Before Galileo, science had relied on drawing generalizations from passive observations and from informal trial and error experimentation.

Experimental designs are of particular interest to clinical psychologists because therapeutic work itself can be thought of as an experimental intervention. The therapist considers a problematic situation in the client's life, forms a hypothesis about what is causing it and what might be done to improve it, attempts to change something about it, and then observes the results. Here the tentative connotation of experiment is apt: if the intervention does not work, the therapist then repeats the cycle by reformulating the problem, trying something else and once more observing the results. This experimental approach to therapeutic work lies at the core of the applied scientist model (see Chapter 2).

Most psychotherapy outcome studies use an experimental design. For example, Sloane et al.'s (1975) classic comparative outcome study randomly allocated clients into three conditions. Those in the first two received either psychodynamic therapy or behavior therapy from experts in each orientation; the third condition was a wait-list control group. (The results showed that both groups of therapy clients improved more than the controls, and that behavior therapy showed a marginal superiority over psychodynamic therapy on some of the outcome measures.)

Terminology

There is a considerable amount of terminology in the experimental design area. The treatment that is varied by the experimenter is known as the *independent* or *experimental variable*; the measure of the experimental variable's effect is known as the *dependent* or *outcome variable*. In the Sloane et al. (1975) study, the independent variable, or experimental condition, was the type of therapy (psychodynamic therapy, behavior therapy, or control group) and the dependent variables were measures of psychological symptoms, severity of distress, social functioning, etc., used to assess client improvement. (Note that the term "group" is often used to denote one of the experimental conditions. It is potentially confusing in clinical applications, as it wrongly suggests that group rather than individual therapy was used.)

Frequently, one or more of the groups in the design is subjected to an *experimental intervention* or *manipulation*, while another group provides a *control group*, because it is used to rule out or *control* for the influence of one or more third variables. For example, the wait-list group in the Sloane et al. (1975) study was used to control for the potential therapeutic benefits of the assessment interviews and also for the instillation of hope of successful outcome. It is important to keep in mind that some experiments ("quasi-experiments," see below) may use only one treatment condition. In the treatment literature, such one-group experiments are referred to as *open clinical trials*, often used to provide an initial test of a promising treatment, prior to pitting it against a control group or other treatment (a *randomized clinical trial*).

Many types of experimental designs are covered in the specialist statistical literature (e.g., Keppel, 1991; Kirk, 1995; Winer et al., 1991), such as factorial designs, repeated-measures designs and Latin squares. Here we will look at some of the simpler ones. The statistical method used in experimental studies is usually the analysis of variance (ANOVA), or related methods such as the t-test, multivariate analysis of variance (MANOVA), or the analysis of covariance (ANCOVA). However, before examining some specific types of designs, it is helpful to consider some general principles of validity, in order to provide a framework for thinking about the strengths and weaknesses of any given design.

Cook and Campbell's Validity Analysis

The work of Campbell and his collaborators (Campbell & Stanley, 1966; Cook & Campbell, 1979; Shadish et al., 2001) has been enormously influential: Cook and Campbell's (1979) book or its successor, Shadish et al. (2001), is required (though sometimes difficult) reading for all applied psychology researchers. Campbell's ideas were developed specifically in the context of designs that attempt to infer causality, which is why we are addressing them here under the heading of experimental designs. However, the concepts can be applied to all designs, descriptive and correlational as well as experimental. They are invaluable both for planning one's own research and for evaluating other people's.

The central thrust is an analysis of different types of design validity for generalized causal inference. We are now using the concept of validity in a broader sense than in Chapter 4, when we discussed the reliability and validity of measures; we will be talking here about the validity of the conclusions you can draw from the study as a whole. Campbell and Stanley (1966) introduced the fundamental distinction between internal and external validity. *Internal validity* refers to the degree to which causality can be inferred from a study: i.e., in the language of experimentation, is the independent variable producing the changes in the dependent variable? *External validity* refers to the degree to which the results of the study may be generalized over time, settings or persons to other situations, e.g., whether the patients studied in a clinical trial are representative of the patients seen in other settings. A related concept is *ecological validity*, which assesses how artificial the measures and procedures of the study are, compared to the world outside of the research setting.

Cook and Campbell's (1979) expanded treatment considered *statistical conclusion validity* in addition to internal validity (both of which concern interpreting covariation) and *construct validity* in addition to external validity (both of which concern the generalizability of the study—construct validity can be seen as assessing generalizability to the underlying construct which the different measures attempt to tap). In this chapter, we shall just look at internal validity. Construct validity, which derives from the work of Cronbach and Meehl (1955), is covered in Chapter 4. External validity is covered in Chapters 10 and 12, and statistical conclusion validity, which concerns the appropriateness of the statistical methods, is also covered in Chapter 12.

Four validity types (Cook & Campbell, 1979):

- Internal validity
- External validity
- Construct validity
- Statistical conclusion validity

The central dilemma is that there is often a trade-off between internal and external validity. It is possible to achieve high internal validity in a laboratory, where the researcher can exert considerable control. A common criticism of social psychology experiments of the 1960s and 1970s was that, although they had achieved high internal validity by being conducted in a controlled laboratory setting with a homogeneous population (often male US undergraduates), they had in so doing sacrificed their external validity, i.e., their generalizability or real-world relevance (Sears, 1986). In a nutshell, the designs were clever but artificial (Armistead, 1974; McGuire, 1973). The same criticism also applies to early analog studies of behavior therapy, which were conducted in artificial laboratory conditions with volunteer clients on specific phobias such as spider or public-speaking fears (Shapiro & Shapiro, 1983). Conversely, field research, which is conducted in natural settings with clinical populations, usually has high external validity. Unfortunately, this is often at the expense of lower internal validity, since experimental control is much more difficult to obtain in field settings, for a variety of reasons which we discuss below.

The thrust of Cook and Campbell's work is that all designs are imperfect, but that it is possible to analyze systematically the potential nature and consequences of their imperfections, which are known as *threats to validity*. The researcher's task is to try to achieve an optimal design given the aims and constraints of the research. To quote one prominent psychotherapy researcher: ". . . it is therefore impossible to design the perfect study. The art of outcome research design thus becomes one of creative compromise based upon explicit understanding of the implications of the choices made" (Shapiro, 1996: 202). Cook and Campbell's framework is an indispensable tool for thinking about the consequences of such compromises.

Cook and Campbell's Classification of Research Designs

In addition to analyzing validity issues, Campbell and his collaborators (Campbell & Stanley, 1966; Cook & Campbell, 1979) also proposed a taxonomy of designs. They introduced the fundamental distinction between *quasi-experimental* and *experimental* designs. Quasi-experiments are defined as "experiments that have treatments, outcome measures, and experimental units, but do not use random assignment to create the comparisons from which treatment-caused change is inferred" (Cook & Campbell, 1979: 6). However, in the light of our earlier discussion about the term "experiment" being too narrowly defined within psychology, it seems preferable to use the more precise terms nonrandomized and randomized designs instead of quasi-experiment and experiment. Cook and Campbell give an extensive listing of possible nonrandomized and randomized experimental designs. Here we will consider the most commonly used ones as illustrative examples.

Nonrandomized Designs

One-group Posttest-only Design

This rudimentary design can be depicted in the following diagram:

X O

In Cook and Campbell's notation, X stands for an experimental treatment, that is, something done to the participants, such as a clinical intervention. (The notation can also be extended to cases where X is not an experimental treatment, but rather some other event that occurs to the participants, such as a disease or a disaster.) O stands for an observation or measurement, of one or of several variables.

The one-group posttest-only design, originally labeled the one-shot case study by Campbell and Stanley (1966), is the simplest possible design. It is characterized as a quasi-experimental design because of the experimental intervention, X, although it can also be conceptualized as a type of descriptive study. One common application is in consumer satisfaction studies, in which clients are surveyed during or after a psychological intervention to find out how they felt about it. This design is useful for generating hypotheses about causation, but it is almost always insufficient for making causal inferences, because doing so invites the logical fallacy referred to as "*post hoc ergo propter hoc*" (because B happens after A, B must result from A).

However, as Cook and Campbell (1979) note, this design should not be dismissed out of hand in research aimed at testing causal explanations. It can be rescued if enough contextual information is available, and especially if one takes a detective work approach, looking for signs or clues about causality—what Cook and Campbell (1979) call "signed causes." In the clinical context, such signs might include post-treatment ratings of perceived change or retrospectively completed estimates of pre-treatment levels of functioning. (The detective metaphor is appropriate here, since Sherlock Holmes and his successors based their causal inferences—concerning whodunnit—upon post-hoc data.) Shadish et al. (2001) note that the interpretability of this design is enhanced when the effect is clear and measured in multiple ways; this allows for a pattern-matching approach that compares effects to potential causes, as an epidemiologist works backwards from a disease outbreak to possible causes.

One-group Pretest–Posttest Design

$O_1 \ X \ O_2$

This design extends the previous one by adding a pre-measure, which then allows a direct estimate of change over time. For example, this design may be used in evaluating the outcome of a clinical service. The psychologist might administer a measure of problem severity, such as the Beck Depression Inventory (Beck et al., 1988), to all clients before and after therapy.

However, it is not immediately possible to attribute change in the outcome variables to the experimental treatment, X. This is because, as in the previous design, it is risky to infer *post hoc ergo propter hoc*. For example, a newspaper headline in a feature on mental health stated: "Despite being the target of suspicion, the evidence that antidepressants work is indisputable: more than two-thirds of people taking them recover" (London *Observer*, 12 January 1992).

The inference appears to be that since taking antidepressants is associated with a good chance of recovery, therefore they must cause that recovery. (To see the logical fallacy more clearly, try substituting taking antidepressants with some less obviously psychotherapeutic activity, such as watching television.) In addition, the implication that the antidepressants cause recovery is further called into question since the recovery rate of depressed people who did not take antidepressants is not supplied—perhaps two-thirds of them recover also. The availability of such data would result in a nonequivalent groups pretest–posttest design, described below.

Cook and Campbell (1979) provide a checklist of possible *threats to internal validity* in this design. For researching the effects of psychological interventions, the most important ones are:

- *Endogenous change*, which refers to any kind of change within the person. The most important instance is *spontaneous recovery*, also called *spontaneous remission*, which means recovery occurring with no apparent external reason.

- *Maturational trends* refer to the growth or maturation of the person. This is a special case of endogenous change. It is, of course, especially relevant to research with children, who may often "grow out" of their psychological problems.

- *Reactivity of measurement*, where the act of making a measurement changes the thing being measured. For example, there may be practice effects on a psychological test, where participants perform better on a second administration of a test because they have learned how to respond. As a second example, clients in the wait-list control group in the Sloane et al. (1975) study were extensively interviewed as part of their initial assessment, which may well have had clinical benefits.

- *Secular drift*, that is, long-term social trends, such as a general reduction in smoking over the years.

- *Interfering events*, that is significant events other than the experimental intervention that occur between the pretest and the posttest. For example, fiscal changes such as increases in tobacco or alcohol taxes may reduce consumption; or an international crisis may increase general anxiety.

- *Regression to the mean*. Participants in clinical studies are often selected on the basis of their extreme scores on a measure of psychological distress, e.g., clients for a therapy outcome study might be selected (or select themselves) on the basis of high scores on an anxiety scale. The regression to the mean phenomenon is due to unreliability of measurement, which means that scores on the posttest will tend to show that clients have improved, even if the therapy was ineffective. This is because the extreme scores at the pretest will have partly reflected measurement error, which will tend not to be as extreme at the posttest.

One further problem in interpreting the findings from this and other experimental designs has to do with the *construct validity of the experimental intervention* (Cook & Campbell, 1979). The distinction between internal validity and the construct validity of the experimental intervention is sometimes hard to grasp. The question of internal validity asks whether change can be attributed to the intervention, X, or to something else; whereas the question of the construct validity of the experimental intervention accepts that X is producing the change and asks what about it (what construct) actually accounts for the change? Some possible construct validity problems are:

- *Confounding variables.* "Confounding" means occurring at the same time as, and thus inextricably bound up with. In the Sloane et al. (1975) study discussed above, the type of therapy was confounded with the person of the therapist, since each of the two interventions (behavior therapy and psychodynamic therapy) was delivered by two different sets of therapists. It is possible that the differences between the therapies could simply have reflected differences in the personality or skill of the therapists who delivered each of them.

- *Expectancy effects.* Clients may benefit from a service simply because they expect to, rather than as a direct result of what the service actually delivers. This expectancy effect is related to the *placebo effect* in drug studies, where patients may benefit from pharmacologically inert treatments.

- *Hawthorne effect*, in which the research itself produces beneficial change. This effect takes its name from a famous study in occupational psychology, in which decreasing the level of illumination in a factory was found to increase industrial output, but so also was increasing the level of illumination (Roethlisberger & Dickson, 1939).

The difference between O_2 and O_1 (i.e., the total pre-post change) is sometimes called the *gross effect* of the intervention (Rossi et al., 1999). The *net effect* is defined as the effect that can reasonably be attributed to the intervention itself, that is the gross effect minus the effect due to confounding variables and error. In clinical research it is often a good first step to use a simple design such as the one-group pretest–posttest (referred to as an *open clinical trial*) to demonstrate that a gross effect exists at all. Subsequent studies can then use more sophisticated designs with control or comparison groups to estimate the net effects, rule out the effects of possible confounding variables and examine which components of the intervention are actually responsible for client improvement.

Hunter and Schmidt (1990) argue that Cook and Campbell's (1979) list of validity threats has been widely misinterpreted as indicating that one-group pretest–posttest designs are automatically fatally flawed. Rather, researchers should be aware of, and attempt to mitigate the effect of, potential validity threats. If this is done, such designs will frequently allow causal inference of treatment efficacy.

Nonequivalent Groups Posttest-only Design

NR   X   O
NR   O

In the notation, NR stands for a nonrandomized assignment to experimental groups.

This is like the one-group posttest-only design, except that the group receiving the experimental treatment is compared to another similar group that did not receive the treatment. For example, an intervention could be instituted on one hospital ward and another ward be used as a comparison group. Another variation is to use the design to compare several different active treatments, for example, three different treatment regimes on three hospital wards.

Unlike the previous and the following design, this one provides no direct estimate of pre-post change. It can be used for retrospective studies, where there is no pre-measure, and post-measures are all that one can manage in the circumstances. (This design can also be regarded as correlational, since what is being studied is the association between the group membership variable and the outcome variable.)

In clinical applications, X usually represents an intervention. However, the conceptual framework of the design can also be used for comparing groups who differ in having experienced some life stressor, a kind of negative experiment. The effects of this stressor or experience (e.g., childhood sexual abuse, adoption, parental divorce) can then be evaluated and causal hypotheses generated. Similarly, some epidemiological case-control studies can also be considered under this category, where X would represent having some illness or predisposition to illness, e.g., being HIV positive.

The major threat to internal validity in this design (and equally in the following design) is *uncontrolled selection*. That is, since the assignment to groups is not random, one cannot assume that the two groups were the same before the treatment, X. Participants in the different groups may differ systematically on, for example, motivation, problem severity, or demographic characteristics. Even if the researcher is able to compare the groups on these variables, there still may be other important systematic differences that are not tested for. Beyond this, Shadish et al. (2001) provide an extensive list of threats to the validity of such case-control designs.

Example of a nonequivalent groups posttest-only design: the *Consumer Reports* study:

Seligman (1995) reported on the results of a large survey, conducted by the US consumer magazine, *Consumer Reports*, of people who had received psychological therapy. Respondents were asked about the kind of help they had received and their evaluation of it. The large sample made it possible to compare different groups within the design, for example, those that had been treated in different modalities of therapy, or by different types of professionals. It can therefore be regarded in part as a nonequivalent groups posttest-only design. Generally patients reported substantial improvement, and there were no differences between modalities or types of therapist, but there was a positive effect for length of therapy.

Nonequivalent Groups Pretest–Posttest Design

NR   O   X   O
NR   O (Y) O

This commonly used design combines the features of the previous two, and helps to rule out some of the associated internal validity threats. The group in the lower part of the diagram that does not receive the experimental intervention is called a *control group*. Several different types of control groups are possible, ranging from an alternative comparison treatment (Y in the diagram) to no treatment at all (in which case no letter is used in the diagram). The type of control group depends on the research question: whether you are trying to show that the experimental treatment is as good as or better than an established treatment, or simply better than nothing at all. We will discuss these issues more fully below under the heading of the randomized groups pretest–posttest design.

Humphreys and Moos (2001) used this design to investigate the value of self-help groups as an adjunct to the treatment of substance abuse. Using a large all-male sample drawn from in-patients in US Veterans' Administration hospitals, they compared in-patient programs that encouraged patients to participate in self-help groups with those that did not. They found that patients in the programs that emphasized self-help groups had lower demand for health-care, and lower health-care costs, in the year following discharge. (In addition to being a good example of a quasi-experimental design, this is also an example of a cost-offset study: see Chapter 11.)

The design can easily be extended to encompass two or more experimental or control groups. An example is the Stanford Three Community study (Farquhar et al., 1977), which studied the effects of the mass media and community interventions on the prevention of heart disease. It was conducted in three small towns in California. One town received only the pre-post measurement, another a sustained mass-media campaign, and a third mass-media plus community intervention in the form of face-to-face instruction. The results showed encouraging effects for the mass-media condition, which were augmented in the community support condition.

Eysenck's (1952) review of early psychodynamic psychotherapy outcome studies can also be considered within the framework of this design. Eysenck compared studies of patients treated with psychoanalysis or psychodynamic psychotherapy with other studies of the spontaneous remission rates of broadly comparable groups of untreated patients. The outcome variable was the patient's rated improvement at the end of therapy, or about two years after diagnosis in the case of the comparison groups. Eysenck famously concluded that no effect for psycho-therapy could be demonstrated, since the two-thirds improvement rate of therapy patients was much the same as the two-year spontaneous remission rate of people who were untreated. This quasi-experimental design, as Eysenck acknowledged at the time, has many weaknesses: his conclusions were subsequently much argued over (Bergin & Lambert, 1978), and led to the refinement in research designs that culminated in the Sloane et al. (1975) study and other more recent studies.

Prospective case-control studies, where a cohort of individuals is studied longitudinally to evaluate the impact of a disease or of stressful life events, can also be considered under this category. Because participants are being studied prospectively, then measures are obtained before the event of interest. For example, a cohort of elderly people might be studied at one-year intervals to examine the psychological impact of bereavement by comparing the individuals who become bereaved with those who do not.

As in the previous design, the major threat to internal validity is uncontrolled selection: that the two groups may differ systematically in ways other than the presence or absence of the experimental treatment or event of interest. Sometimes experimenters try to compensate for differences in the two groups by statistical methods, e.g., analysis of covariance or multiple regression (Cook & Campbell, 1979; Shadish et al., 2001). For example, if the experimental group turns out to be younger than the control group, age might be used as a covariate in the analysis (often described as *partialling out* the effects of the covariate, in this case age). This can be misleading when the nonequivalent groups are drawn from two different populations: it is like trying to equate an elephant and a mouse by adjusting for their relative weights. However, such analyses may be performed in randomized designs, when the groups are drawn from the same population. Another approach, which Rossi et al. (1999) refer to as *constructed controls*, is to try to match participants in each group on key variables, such as age, gender, and problem severity. However, this is difficult to accomplish and again can be misleading if the groups represent two different populations.

The interpretability of this and other nonrandomized experimental designs can be enhanced by adding pretests and later assessments to examine the process of change more closely and also by adding specific control groups to deal with specific internal validity threats.

Interrupted Time-Series Design

$$O_1 \quad O_2 \ldots \ldots O_{20} \quad X \quad O_{21} \ldots \ldots O_{40}$$

This design extends the one-group pretest–posttest design to cover multiple measures over time. It has a different rationale to the previous designs, in that it attempts to pinpoint causal influences by looking at discontinuities between a series of baseline measures and a series of follow-up measures (we have arbitrarily depicted 20 baseline and 20 follow-up points; in practice there may be considerably more). It is good for studying naturally occurring chronological data and can be used to analyze existing data from large samples, e.g., to look at changes in national alcohol or tobacco consumption following taxation changes, or reductions in injuries following legislation on car seat belts legislation (Guerin & MacKinnon, 1985). It can also be used in single case designs, in which participants serve as their own controls (see Chapter 9). The major threat to internal validity is the presence of interfering events: that something else occurring at the same time as the treatment, X, will affect the outcome variable, but this can be dealt with by careful monitoring for such events.

Randomized Designs

Randomized experimental designs (as opposed to nonrandomized or quasi-experimental designs) are characterized by the random assignment of participants to experimental conditions. The great advantages of randomization are that it reduces the likelihood of selection bias as a threat to internal validity and it allows the use of the statistical theory of error. Randomized experimental designs enable the experimenter to manipulate a single variable at a time, and thus any relationships established between the independent and dependent variables are more likely to fulfill the first three conditions for inferring causality discussed earlier in this chapter.

Randomized designs are the standard design used in medicine to evaluate new drugs or other medical or surgical treatments. They are known as randomized controlled (or sometimes clinical) trials, abbreviated to RCT in either case. In clinical psychology, RCTs are often known as *efficacy studies*, as opposed to *effectiveness studies*, which are uncontrolled studies conducted in field settings. There is considerable debate about the relative place of each type of research (see, e.g., Seligman, 1995), which essentially boils down to how much weight one gives to internal validity at the expense of other validity types, especially external validity. (We will address these issues further below, and also in Chapter 11.)

The theory of experimental design was developed by Fisher in the 1920s. The early work was mostly done in agriculture, looking at how crop yields were affected by different fertilizers or different varieties of grain. This agricultural origin accounts for some or the terminology which is still used to describe different experiments (e.g., split plots or randomized blocks refer to parts of fields); it also provides another area of application in which to picture specific designs. Here we will tend to focus on designs in therapy outcome research; it is one in which a lot of work has been done, and it is central to discussion of evidence-based practice and empirically supported therapies. The statistical textbooks (e.g., Keppel, 1991; Kirk, 1995; Winer et al., 1991) cover many different experimental designs. We will illustrate the issues in the context of the paradigmatic design in clinical research, the *randomized groups pretest–posttest design*:

R   O   X   O
R   O   (Y)   O

In the notation, R denotes a randomized assignment of participants to experimental conditions. Such assignment needs to be done without bias, in order to ensure that each participant has an equal chance of being in each condition. This may be done in several ways, e.g., by using random number tables, by flipping a coin, or by drawing lots. On the other hand, nonrandom methods of allocation, e.g., by assigning the first 10 participants to the experimental group and the next 10 participants to the control group, may introduce systematic error (Cook & Campbell, 1979). This design, or its close relatives, is the standard design for randomized controlled trials in medicine, in which a new therapy or drug is tested against a pill placebo or a no-treatment control.

The independent variable, i.e., whether or not the participants receive the experimental intervention, is known as a *between-groups factor* (since it divides the participants into groups). The design depicted above is said to have a between-groups factor with two levels (i.e., the experimental group and the control group). This basic design may be extended in several ways. Some examples are described below.

More than two levels. There can be more than two levels of the between-groups factor, i.e., there may be more than one experimental group or more than one control group. For example, the type of intervention factor in the Sloane et al. (1975) study had three levels: psychodynamic therapy, behavior therapy, and a wait-list control group.

Multi-factorial designs, in which there is more than one between-groups factor. For example, the second Sheffield Psychotherapy Project (Shapiro et al., 1994) had two between-groups factors: a two-level therapeutic orientation factor (cognitive-behavioral therapy versus psychodynamic-interpersonal therapy) and a two-level length of intervention factor (eight sessions versus 16 sessions).

The pretest–posttest design is an example of a *repeated-measures design*, i.e., one in which the same individuals are assessed at two or more points in time. Additional levels of the repeated-measures factor may be introduced, e.g., there may be a follow-up assessment six months or a year after the intervention has ended.

Blocking factors are ones that represent participant individual difference variables (e.g., type of presenting problem) within the overall research design (this is also referred to as *stratification*). Such factors are included in order to examine their effect as potential moderator variables or in order to ensure that the experimental groups are balanced on crucial variables. The procedure is that participants are grouped into the relevant categories before the randomization to experimental treatments takes place. For example, the Sloane et al. (1975) study had two blocking factors: client gender and the client's initial level of distress. The researchers first allocated potential clients to the appropriate cell in a two-by-two table (men/women by high/low distress). Then they randomly assigned people from the same cell to the therapists within each of the two experimental treatment conditions (behavior therapy or psychodynamic therapy) or to the wait-list control group.

In the educational context, analyses addressing the question of which interventions work best for which students are referred to as *aptitude-treatment interaction* studies (Snow, 1991), and this terminology has been adopted in studies of psychological therapies (Shoham-Salomon & Hannah, 1991). Designs that incorporate many treatment and client factors can attempt to analyze what treatment works best in what circumstances, or as Paul's (1967) famous question states: *"What* treatment, by *whom*, is most effective for *this* individual with *that* specific problem, and under *which* set of circumstances" (p. 111). However, such large-scale designs, within what has been called the matrix paradigm (Stiles et al., 1986), have serious practical limitations, not least because of the large number of participants required.

Analysis of covariance designs are similar to blocked designs, but are used when it is known that the individual difference variable being investigated, e.g., psychological-mindedness or severity of symptoms, has a linear relationship with the outcome variable. Analysis of covariance is a more powerful procedure than blocking, but the statistical assumptions that must be met before it can be employed are more restrictive. Keppel (1991) gives a useful discussion of the relative merits of the blocking versus the analysis of covariance approach.

Control and Comparison Groups

The terms *control* and *comparison* group are rather loosely defined. The implication of the term "control group" is that some active ingredient in the experimental group is missing (as in agricultural experiments, where the experimental groups might be given various fertilizers and the control group none), whereas the term "comparison group" implies that a viable alternative treatment is given. We will use the term "control group" as a shorthand for control or comparison groups. As we discussed above in the section on the nonequivalent groups pretest–posttest design, several types of controls are possible, depending on the research questions, although the selection of suitable control groups for psychotherapy research (and other applications) raises ethical, scientific, and practical problems.

No-treatment controls, in which the control group receives no treatment at all, are used to provide a maximum contrast with the therapy under investigation. However, there are serious ethical issues in withholding treatment from clinically distressed clients. Researchers must balance the possible harm resulting from an untested treatment with the denial of benefit resulting from a potentially effective one. This problem may not arise in a nonrandomized design, since a group of clients who might be unable (for geographical or other reasons) to receive the experimental treatment could be used as a control group. Furthermore, given that the effectiveness of established psychological therapies has been demonstrated, no-treatment controls have become scientifically uninteresting (Parloff, 1986): they are only useful in the early stages of research on a clinical problem area or diagnosis.

Wait-list controls often provide a workable compromise, particularly with short-term treatments or with mildly distressed clients. Clients who are randomly assigned to the wait-list group are given the same initial assessment, and then placed on a waiting list to receive the intervention once the experimental group has completed it (e.g., Sloane et al., 1975). Thus they control for the reactivity of the initial assessment, the instillation of hope, and spontaneous recovery.

Expectancy and relationship control groups control for expectancies of benefit, or instillation of hope, and also for the effects of contact with the therapist. In drug trials, where patients are given a sugar pill or other pharmacologically inert substance, they are known as *placebo control groups*. However, this terminology is too imprecise for the psychological context: it is better to be specific about what the control group is intended to control for. In pharmacology, clinical trials are ideally done in a *double-blind* study, where neither patients nor doctors know which experimental condition each patient is in, or *triple-blind studies*, where in addition the experimenters do not know. However, even in drug trials, this is not always practicable because patients and their physicians may be able to distinguish between active drugs and placebos, e.g., by their side effects. In psychological applications, any control treatment should appear as credible to clients as the experimental one. Expectancy or relationship controls generally work well for clinical trials in drug research, but are questionable for psychotherapy research, where relationship factors or aspects of the therapeutic alliance (so-called "non-specific factors" or "common factors") are generally the best predictors of outcome (Hubble et al., 1999).

Comparative treatment groups use an established comparison treatment, rather than a placebo, that might be expected to have a benefit equal to that of the experimental treatment (Parloff, 1986). They provide an ethical way of doing research. Given the broad equivalence of most major forms of therapy, they are unlikely to produce statistically significant effects unless the sample is quite large (over 60 clients per group; Kazdin & Bass, 1989). In these situations, the researchers' concern is often to show comparability rather than differences, but this requires performing statistical equivalence testing (see Chapter 12), something that is rarely done.

Dismantling studies aim to see what the effective components of a treatment are. The full treatment is compared to a comparison group, which receives that treatment minus one component. For example, a cognitive-behavioral treatment for fear of heights which includes relaxation training might be compared to a treatment that is exactly the same except for the relaxation component. The reverse strategy is also possible: *constructive* (or *additive*) designs examine the effects of adding additional components intended to enhance the effectiveness of a therapy.

Practical Limitations of Randomization

Although randomized experiments are scientifically valuable, they may be hard to carry out in practice, for several reasons (Cook & Campbell, 1979; Haaga & Stiles, 2000; Rossi et al., 1999):

- Random assignment to experimental groups does not ensure that the groups will be equivalent or that they will stay equivalent. Randomization is by definition a chance process, and will thus occasionally produce some unusual distributions. Problems of nonequivalence become more acute if the sample sizes are small or if there are a large number of "nuisance variables" on which the researcher is trying to equate the groups (Hsu, 1989).

- Many experiments suffer from *attrition*, that is, some participants may drop out of the study before the treatment is completed and the post-measures are collected. Attrition reduces the equivalence of the experimental and control groups (Flick, 1988; Howard et al., 1986). One potential way to deal with this is to conduct *intent-to-treat analyses*, in which all participants who enter the study are included in the analysis, and the latest available data is used from those who drop out before the end (Kendall, Flannery-Schroeder et al., 1999b). However, such analyses are likely to be too conservative.

- There may be *leakage* between the conditions. For example, if half of the patients on a hospital ward are taught a useful skill, e.g., relaxation, they may then teach it to other patients in the control condition. In drug trials, there is anecdotal evidence that patients in the experimental group may sometimes share their medication with patients in the control group who have been deprived of it.

- Other staff may not understand the need for randomization, seeing it as antithetical to the principle of giving individualized care to each client, and thus it may be hard to obtain the necessary cooperation for the study.

- Randomized experiments are costly and time consuming, and should therefore only be used where there is prior evidence that the experimental treatment is beneficial.

- Randomization cannot be used ethically to study the impact of negative experiences, e.g., smoking, drug use, disasters, or psychological trauma. In these cases, nonrandomized experimental designs or correlational designs must be used (which is why there is more scope for interested parties, such as tobacco companies, to dispute the results).

- Randomized trials do not take account of patient choice (Brewin & Bradley, 1989). Outside of research studies, clients will select a treatment based on their individual preferences: randomized trials may thus give clients a treatment that they do not want and which they may consequently fare less well with. King et al. (2000) carried out an interesting example of a "preference trial" in which depressed clients were allowed to choose the treatment they received, and were subsequently compared to clients who were assigned to treatment (there were no differences).

A realization of these problems with randomized experimental designs, which for a long while were regarded as a scientific panacea, has shaped the growing interest in nonrandomized experimental designs and in correlational designs, especially in naturalistic clinical settings ("effectiveness studies").

Evaluating RCTs

It is easy to feel bewildered by all the complexities of randomized designs. Few readers are likely to be involved in conducting treatment trials, but all practicing psychologists need to be aware of the results from such trials in order to keep up with and evaluate the state of the evidence. What are some of the features of RCTs that lend credibility to their findings? Recent writings on evidence-based practice or empirically supported treatments (e.g., Chambless & Hollon, 1998; Roth & Fonagy, 1996; Sackett et al., 1997; Seligman, 1995) have attempted to specify features of good practice in experimental design. The following list summarizes their main criteria:

- The study uses *randomized assignments* to conditions, in order to rule out selection effects, together with an analysis to demonstrate that the groups actually were *similar after randomization*.

- *Specific interventions*. The intervention is specified, so that it is clear what therapy is being delivered, it is constant across therapists, and it can be repeated by other investigators if necessary. This requirement has led, in contemporary RCTs (e.g., the NIMH depression study, Elkin, 1994, or the second Sheffield Psychotherapy Project, Shapiro et al., 1994), to the *manualization* of therapy and the inclusion of checks that these treatment protocols are faithfully adhered to.

- *Appropriate control groups* are used, so that it is clear what the therapy is being compared with (e.g., wait-list controls, treatment as usual, or other comparative treatment groups).

- The *groups were treated equivalently* apart from the experimental variable in question (e.g., they had the same length of treatment, equivalent therapists, the same assessments, etc.).

- The raters and assessment interviewers were *blind* to the experimental condition the patient was in. However, it is usually not possible to conduct double-blind, or triple-blind studies in psychology, as it is in medicine, since the therapists know what they are giving, and the clients usually know what they are getting (Seligman, 1995).

- The patients form a *specific, homogeneous group*. This usually means that they meet criteria for a single DSM diagnosis: patients with comorbidities are often excluded.

- There was a *low attrition rate* in the study.

- The patients are *followed-up* after the termination of therapy (e.g., at six months or a year).

- Demonstrations of the efficacy of a treatment are replicated by independent teams of researchers, thus demonstrating the portability of treatments across research settings.

Some authors (e.g., Chambless & Hollon, 1998) have attempted to use criteria such as these in order to conclude that certain therapies can be considered as *empirically supported treatments* and others not. However, these attempts have been highly controversial (see Elliott, 1998, for a survey of the arguments on both sides). Key issues include the use of criteria that favor some treatments over others and the dismissal of all non-RCT research. While we regard RCTs as potentially powerful research designs, we believe that nonrandomized designs also have a place, particularly when they use naturalistic client populations or clinical settings. It seems unproductive to force all treatment research into the same mold, as different research designs have complementary strengths and weaknesses—no single design provides a "royal road" for evaluating therapy outcomes.

Conclusion: Choosing a Research Design

The central issue for researchers is to choose a design appropriate to the research questions and to the stage of the research program and research area. In the early stages of investigating the treatment of a problem, or where there has been little previous research, you are probably unsure of the nature of the phenomena you are looking at. Furthermore, a newly established clinical service may not be stable: its operational policies and modus operandi may be constantly changing (Rossi et al., 1999). In these cases, a simple descriptive or correlational design is usually better. Later on, when you are clearer about what the important variables are and how they interrelate, and are more able to specify the nature of the treatment, you can proceed to the next stage by using a one-group pretest–posttest design or systematic case study designs (see Chapter 9). Then, if the treatment appears effective and resources and circumstances allow, you can move on to more sophisticated randomized experimental designs to test efficacy, perhaps adding correlational components in order to pin down the effects of crucial variables and to test competing theoretical models. Also, several studies taken together can often help eliminate specific competing theoretical explanations.

We have drawn heavily on Cook and Campbell's (1979) analysis of threats to validity (see also Shadish et al., 2001). Their central theme is that no research design is perfect: the important thing is to be aware of the strengths and weaknesses of whatever design you decide to adopt. It is important not to read Cook and Campbell as saying that research designs must have no validity problems at all, or that certain designs are automatically flawed (Hunter & Schmidt, 1990). Their message is to do the best that you can in the circumstances, but to be aware of potential problems that may arise later on in interpreting the findings. Thus, research designs require careful planning and analysis in order to anticipate the potential results and competing explanations.

CHAPTER SUMMARY

Design, in the restricted sense in which we are using it here, refers to the logical structure of the study. It encompasses such issues as whether there is a control group and whether the data are collected at one time point or several. The central classification is into experimental and nonexperimental designs, which depends on whether or not the researcher is making an active intervention (also known as an experimental manipulation).

Nonexperimental designs can be classified into descriptive and correlational designs, according to the type of analysis conducted. The golden rule when interpreting the results from nonexperimental designs is that "correlation does not equal causation": if two variables are correlated there is not necessarily a causal relationship between them. There are several possible models of the causal relationships of two or more variables, including mediator and moderator variable models, as well as conceptual confounding between cause and effect variables.

The work of Campbell and colleagues (e.g., Cook & Campbell, 1979) has made two major contributions to the study of research design: (1) the classification of validity types; and (2) the analysis of quasi-experimental designs. Cook and Campbell (1979) analyze several nonrandomized (quasi-experimental) designs, examining the validity threats associated with each one.

Cook and Campbell's four validity types are internal validity (which assesses the evidence for the existence of causal relationships), external validity (which assess the study's generalizability), construct validity (the meaning of the measurement operations, including the experimental manipulation), and statistical conclusion validity (the appropriateness of the statistical methods).

Experimental designs are classified into randomized and nonrandomized (quasi-experimental) designs, according to whether or not there is random assignment to experimental conditions. There are several commonly used nonrandomized designs. Each has its associated validity threats.

Randomized experimental designs have the potential to address many of the validity problems associated with nonrandomized designs and thus to facilitate inferences about causality. They are central to the discussion of evidence-based practice and empirically supported therapies. However, they do have some practical, scientific, and ethical limitations, and should not be regarded as a scientific panacea.

FURTHER READING

Cook and Campbell's (1979) ideas on causation, validity, and on the different experimental and correlational designs are essential reading for all serious researchers; their classic book has recently been updated by Shadish et al. (2001), but the original is still worth reading. Christensen (2001) and Kerlinger (1986) give an overview of design from the standpoint of experimental psychology. A statistical treatment of randomized designs is given in the standard texts, such as Keppel (1991), Kirk (1995), and Winer et al. (1991). Shapiro (1996) and Kendall, Flannery-Schroeder et al. (1999) illustrate the issues as applied to therapy outcome research. Seligman's (1995) paper on the *Consumer Reports* effectiveness study, together with subsequent commentary in the October 1996 issue of *American Psychologist* (volume 51, issue 10), airs the central issues in the efficacy versus effectiveness debate. The Summer 1998 special issue of *Psychotherapy Research* (volume 8, issue 2) and the February 1998 issue of *Journal of Consulting and Clinical Psychology* (volume 66, number 1) both debate the research issues raised by the empirically supported therapies movement.

As in other areas of research, it is worth reading some classic studies. The two that we have looked at in this chapter provide a good starting point: Brown and Harris (1978) for a descriptive, correlational design, and Sloane et al. (1975) for a randomized experimental design in therapy outcome research. Influential contemporary examples of RCTs are the NIMH study (Elkin, 1994) and the second Sheffield Psychotherapy Project (Shapiro et al., 1994).

CHAPTER 9

SMALL-N DESIGNS

KEY POINTS IN THIS CHAPTER

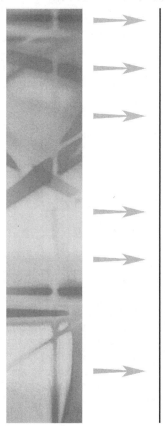

Small-N designs follow the idiographic approach of looking in depth at the individual.

They are often appealing to clinicians, as a way of combining research and practice.

They derive from several different traditions: narrative case studies in neuropsychology and medicine, operant behaviorism, Shapiro's single case approach, and idiographic research in personality theory.

There are two main types of design: single case experiments and naturalistic case studies.

Single case experiments are characterized by frequently administered measurements and the experimental manipulation of an intervention, in which participants serve as their own controls. They are most often used within operant behavioral approaches to therapy.

Naturalistic case studies range from narrative approaches, such as Freud's, to more structured studies using systematic measurement of process and outcome.

Small-N designs, such as systematic case studies and single case experiments, are a potentially appealing way of blending science and practice, since they enable clinicians to integrate formal research methods into their everyday work (Hayes et al., 1999). From the practitioner's point of view, the advantages of small-N research are that it is usually inexpensive, not very time consuming and, more importantly, that its underlying philosophy is often congenial to practitioners, since it addresses individual uniqueness and complexity.

Recall the nomothetic versus idiographic distinction that we introduced in Chapter 4. Nomothetic methods compare across individuals, looking for general patterns or laws; idiographic methods look intensively within a single individual, to gain greater understanding of that person's unique personality or psychological responses. Nomothetic approaches, particularly the large group experimental and quasi-experimental designs that we examined in the previous chapter, have long been criticized on the grounds that individual variation and uniqueness get submerged by the act of averaging across a larger group (Bergin & Strupp, 1972; Dukes, 1965).

For example, in psychotherapy research, Kiesler (1966) has drawn attention to the existence of "uniformity myths": i.e., the implicit assumption by researchers that clients are all similar, that different therapists each deliver an identical intervention, and so on. For instance, in an outcome study, the overall difference between the mean pre-therapy score and the mean post-therapy score on a depression measure may indicate that the therapy is beneficial. However, this positive mean change may conceal the fact that, although most clients have improved, a significant minority of clients have deteriorated (Bergin, 1971). Such differential responses would not be discovered without challenging the uniformity myth and paying attention to each individual client's unique pattern of change.

As a second example, in neuropsychological case-control research, client heterogeneity may obscure important effects (Shallice, 1979). Clients may vary in their responses to neurological lesions according to such factors as age, premorbid functioning, or the size of the lesion, and this variation will only become apparent if one looks in detail at each single case.

Small-N designs can therefore make up for some of the drawbacks of nomothetic, group comparison designs. The idiographic approaches described in this chapter provide ways of rigorously examining individuals' responses, particularly in the context of evaluating psychological interventions.

Historical Background

Small-N studies were the dominant paradigm in medicine and in psychology until the beginning of the 20th century. Before then, statistical theory barely existed. Then, in the early decades of the century, Pearson and Fisher developed methods such as correlation and the analysis of variance. These methods were originally developed within the agricultural context, in order to systematically assess the yields of different fertilizers or strains of wheat, but they were rapidly adopted in medicine and psychology. In agricultural research, large samples and group comparison designs work very well; and examining the response of individual plants is less relevant. However, the agricultural metaphor does not translate easily to clinical psychology, where individual differences are often of major importance. In recognition of this, there has been a resurgence of small-N methods in the past 30 years, deriving its impetus from several different traditions.

Traditions of small-N research:

- Single case studies in medicine and neuropsychology
- Operant behaviorism
- Shapiro's single case approach
- Idiographic personality research

First, there is the narrative case study, which is a continuation of the long tradition of descriptive case studies in medicine. The first published studies of psychological therapy were case studies, those of Sigmund Freud being the outstanding example. Often case studies are reported to illustrate the development of new theoretical approaches. For example, both Rogers' (1951) *Client-centered therapy* and Beck's (1976) *Cognitive therapy and the emotional disorders* exemplify their theoretical ideas by presenting case illustrations, including excerpts of verbatim transcripts from therapy sessions.

Arising out of the same medical tradition is the single case study in neuropsychological research. Luria (1973) dates the birth of scientific neuropsychology to 1861, when Broca described a case of speech impairment that was associated with a localized lesion of the brain. Since that time, case studies have continued to play an important role in the development of the area, and currently seem to be enjoying a resurgence of popularity (Shallice, 1979; Wilson, 1987). Methodologically, examples range from qualitative narrative case studies (e.g., Sacks, 1985) to small-N studies using intensive quantitative neuropsychological test data (e.g., Shallice et al., 1991).

Second, there is the tradition of applied behavior analysis (i.e., operant behaviorism), guided by Skinner's view that the goal of behavioral science is "to predict and control the behavior of the individual organism" (Skinner, 1953, p.35). Single case experimental designs, aimed at demonstrating such prediction and control, were first developed in the 1950s and 1960s (Davidson & Costello, 1969), and studies using these designs proliferated in the 1970s. *The Journal of Applied Behavior Analysis* is devoted to publishing examples of this kind of work.

Third, innovative measurement methods for single case designs were pioneered by Monte Shapiro, who developed a measurement technique known as the Shapiro Personal Questionnaire, which enables each patient's problems to be quantified and monitored on a day-by-day or week-by-week basis (Phillips, 1986; Shapiro, 1961a, 1961b). In contrast to the operant work, Shapiro's approach takes a more phenomenological stance, being tailored to the individual client's view of his or her problems, and it is less concerned with the experimental manipulation of treatments.

Fourth, there is the idiographic tradition in personality research. Allport (1962) passionately criticized psychology's almost exclusive reliance on nomothetic methods: "Instead of growing impatient with the single case and hastening on to generalization, why should we not grow impatient with our generalizations and hasten to the internal pattern?" (Allport, 1962, p.407). Murray (1938) developed an approach to studying personality based on intensive investigation. Proposition one of his theory, which captures the key idea of this chapter, is "The objects of study are individual organisms, not aggregates of organisms" (Murray, 1938, p.38).

The terminology of the area partly reflects these different traditions. *Single case designs* (also referred to as *N = 1 designs*) are characterized by repeated measures on a single case. They usually involve an experimental manipulation of a treatment, although there are quasi-experimental versions, e.g., time series designs. Studies that do not use intensive repeated measures and do not have an experimental manipulation, for example, the classic case history approach, are referred to as *case studies* (Bromley, 1986; Dukes, 1965), although the boundary between the two approaches is not always clear. This chapter will focus first on single case experimental designs and then on case studies. Although the focus is on design, we also include some suggestions about measurement, because small-N designs call for some specific measurement approaches.

SINGLE CASE EXPERIMENTAL DESIGNS

Single case experimental designs are used to test an experimental intervention on a single individual. The essence of the design is that each individual participant serves as their own control. Single case experiments also involve repeated measurements, which allow the process of change to be closely monitored. A key assumption of these designs is that they are based on an adequate functional analysis of the problem, providing an understanding of the situational variables (cues and reinforcers) which appear to be controlling the problem behavior (Haynes & O'Brien, 2000; Morgan & Morgan, 2001). Such a behavioral case formulation is established during a preliminary behavioral assessment period. The experimental design then serves as a test of the functional analysis.

Procedure

As with group comparison designs, the first step is to select the measure, or measures, to be used. In single case experimental designs, the measures need to be capable of frequently repeated administration (Nelson, 1981): that is, they must be brief and minimally reactive. The two most common types are observer ratings (e.g., staff ratings of a patient's self-injurious behavior on an in-patient ward) and the client's own ratings from self-monitoring (e.g., of their obsessional thoughts). Having chosen the measure, the next step is to select an appropriate frequency of measurement: usually it is daily, but it may also be, say, hourly or weekly, depending on the nature of the behavior being monitored.

All designs start with a series of *baseline* measures, i.e., measures taken to establish the level of the target variable before the clinical intervention is introduced. These continue until the measurements are stable, preferably for 10 to 20 observations. After that, the first experimental treatment phase begins. These designs have their own special notation, based on the first few letters of the alphabet: A stands for the baseline, or no-treatment phase; B, C, D, etc. stand for the various treatments or interventions. There are many possible single case designs, each of which raises practical and sometimes ethical issues. We will look at four commonly used ones here; more elaborate designs are given in specialist textbooks (e.g., Hayes et al., 1999; Barlow & Hersen, 1984; Kazdin, 1982).

Common single case designs:

- AB design
- Reversal (ABAB) design
- Multiple baseline design
- Changing-criterion design

AB Design

The AB design (see Figure 9.1), in which the baseline is followed by an intervention, is the simplest form of single case experiment. For example, the effectiveness of a positive parenting approach to manage a six-year-old girl's tantrums might be investigated. The parents would be asked to observe the number and severity of their daughter's tantrums (suitably operationalized) every day for two weeks (this constitutes the baseline, or A, phase of the design). Then, in the intervention, or B, phase of the design, they would be taught a new way of responding to their daughter, such as time-outs for the tantrums and

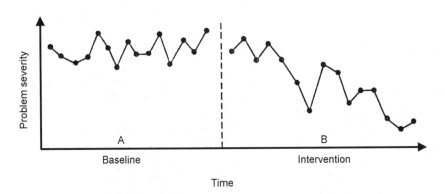

Figure 9.1   The AB design

praise for good behavior. If the intervention is effective, there will be a reduction in the target problem behavior's severity and frequency.

The drawback of the AB design is that, in the absence of other information, it only gives weak evidence for the causal influence of the experimental treatment. It suffers from many of the same threats to internal validity as the one-group pretest–posttest design (Cook & Campbell, 1979; see also Chapter 8), for example, that an interfering event may occur at the same time as the treatment is introduced (e.g., the girl could make a new friend at school, and so be happier, which reduces her need to tantrum). More elaborate designs have therefore been developed to try to overcome this problem, and, in particular, to build in opportunities to replicate the treatment effect, thus increasing its credibility.

The Reversal (or ABAB) Design

The reversal (or ABAB) design is an AB design immediately followed by its own replication (see Figure 9.2). It is the classic operant behavior modification design. For instance, in the child's tantrum example above, once the intervention had been shown to be effective, the baseline, no-treatment, phase would be re-instituted, followed finally by the intervention again. The rationale is that changes in frequency of the target behavior after these reversals demonstrate the experimental control of the intervention.

There are also more complicated variants of this design, e.g., the ABACAB design in which a second intervention, C, is introduced after the second baseline phase. For example, a token economy on an in-patient ward might have its contingencies modified in the second phase.

The ABAB design suffers from three major problems. First, the effects of many interventions are not reversible. In other words, clients do not automatically relapse when treatment ends: permanent learning or personality change may occur, or the problem may not recur once it has been dealt with. Thus, this design

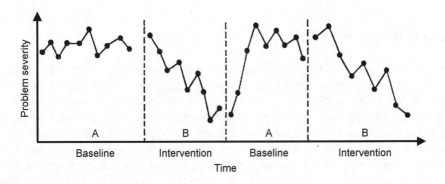

Figure 9.2   The ABAB design

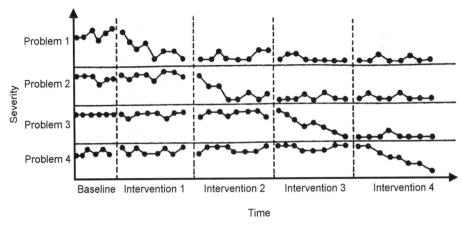

Figure 9.3   The multiple baseline design

could not be used to study the impact of psychodynamic or cognitive therapy, for example, because these therapies, if successful, effect irreversible changes in the way that clients think and feel about themselves. The design's expectation of reversibility is based on the assumption that external processes control behavior. Second, even if the intervention is reversible, there are serious ethical problems with the withdrawal of treatment in the second and subsequent baseline phases. This problem is similar to the ethical dilemma faced in having no-treatment control groups in group comparison designs, but it is more acute because in this case treatment is withdrawn rather than withheld. For example, when the intervention is withheld, the design is "successful" if the child reverts to having tantrums, or if psychiatric in-patients recommence self-injurious behaviors. Thus, the design creates a conflict of interest between clinical and scientific goals. Third, switching the intervention on and off may have undesirable psychological consequences. For example, it may lead to the client's losing trust in the therapist, or may even lead to the problem behavior being harder to extinguish because it is maintained on a partial reinforcement schedule.

Multiple Baseline Design

With several (presumed independent) target behaviors (e.g., a child who suffers from tantrums, nocturnal enuresis, and dog phobia) or one target behavior in several independent settings (e.g., aggression at home, in the classroom, and on the playground), you can use a multiple baseline design. Similar interventions targeted at each behavior, or in each setting, are introduced sequentially and their impact on all the target behaviors is measured (see Figure 9.3). The idea is to replicate the effect of the intervention on each particular problem or setting. For example, Chadwick and Trower (1996) used this design to investigate the effects of cognitive therapy for paranoid delusions. The intervention was

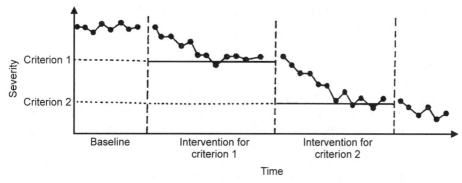

Figure 9.4   The changing-criterion design

targeted sequentially at the client's negative self-evaluation and two separate delusional ideas, and each of these problems was reduced in severity in the predicted order.

Barlow and Hersen (1984) interestingly fit the famous early psychoanalytic case of Anna O (Breuer & Freud, 1895/1955) into this schema, since Breuer targeted various separate interventions, such as hypnosis and interpretation, at each of Anna O's symptoms in turn. However, this design assumes that changes will not generalize from one problem or setting to other problems or settings—that is, it is based on the behaviorist assumption that behavior is situationally specific. Thus, although the within-participant version of this design is theoretically amenable to non-behavioral therapies, it is not really applicable to therapies which aim for general change, in spite of claims to the contrary (Morgan & Morgan, 2001).

An extension of this design involves replication across multiple cases, which is a special case of a *clinical replication series* (Hayes et al., 1999). For example, Bennun and Lucas (1990) used a version of this design to investigate the impact of a two-component intervention with couples in which one partner had a long-standing diagnosis of schizophrenia. Using a "multiple single case design" with a sample of six couples, they showed that the first component of the intervention—education—had an impact on the well spouse's perception of their ability to cope, but had no effect on presenting symptoms. The second component of the intervention—problem solving and communication training—had an impact on positive symptoms of schizophrenia.

Changing-Criterion Design

This design is used to demonstrate experimental control over a single problem behavior that may be progressively reduced in severity (see Figure 9.4). It is particularly useful in working with clients who are dependent on drugs or alcohol. For example, it may be used in a smoking-cessation program, in which the client progressively cuts down to more stringent targets (e.g., Criterion 1 would be 20 cigarettes a day, Criterion 2 would be 15 a day, and so on down). Or it could be used with a positive behavior that is being shaped, e.g., appropriate social interaction in autistic children.

Data Analysis

Data from single case designs are normally displayed on a graph, similar to those in Figures 9.1 to 9.4. Part of the appeal of these designs is that the success or failure of the intervention is usually immediately obvious from the graph (Morley & Adams, 1991). It can often be helpful to show such graphs to the clients, to enable them to monitor their progress and to demonstrate clearly that the intervention is working. An emerging use, discussed in Chapter 11, is to provide feedback to therapists, especially when the treatment is not going well (Lambert et al., 2001).

However, in some cases, the changes may be less clear cut, or a measure of their magnitude may be required. This has led some researchers to call for the use of statistical methods in single case designs. The topic of which, if any, statistical tests to use is too technical to cover here: Morley and Adams (1989) describe some possibilities.

Generalization

Although single case studies are essentially idiographic, the investigator often wishes to generalize beyond the specific individuals studied in order to make broader claims about the effectiveness of the treatment tested. This can be done by conducting a *clinical replication series* (Hayes et al., 1999), that is, by replicating the same study on several individuals. In this way the external validity of the findings are strengthened. (See Chapter 10 for further discussion of generalization issues.) The notion of a clinical replication series is derived from Cronbach's (1975) concept of *locally intensive observation*. As a finding is tested in other settings, varying conditions will test the limits of its external validity and lead to richer theory:

> As [the researcher] goes from situation to situation, his first task is to describe and interpret the effect anew in each locale, perhaps taking into account factors unique to that locale . . . As results accumulate, a person who seeks understanding will do his best to trace how the uncontrolled factors could have caused local departures from the modal effect. That is, generalization comes late and the exception is taken as seriously as the rule. (Cronbach, 1975, p.125)

Such an approach can be applied equally well in experimental and naturalistic, non-experimental, approaches.

NATURALISTIC CASE STUDY DESIGNS

As we have noted, although behaviorally oriented researchers (e.g., Hayes, 1981; Morgan & Morgan, 2001) often claim that experimental single case designs can readily be adapted to non-behavioral treatments, the emphasis on observable events and experimental manipulation makes most of these designs problematic for studying psychodynamic, experiential, and cognitive therapies. Naturalistic case study designs—the narrative case study, the systematic case study, and time-series designs—are usually more appropriate to these types of therapy.

Narrative Case Studies

The narrative case study is the traditional description of a client or treatment, based on the clinician's case notes and memory. Freud's case histories, e.g., "Little Hans" (Freud, 1909/1955) or "Dora" (Freud, 1905/1953) are classic examples of this genre. Case studies have played an important role in the development of the psychological therapies. They can serve a number of purposes (Dukes, 1965; Lazarus & Davison, 1971). These include documenting the existence of a clinical phenomenon, often a rare one (e.g., early case studies of multiple personality disorder), disproving a universal proposition by demonstrating a counter-example (e.g., the proposition that only women suffer from hysteria could be disproved by documenting the case of a man with hysteria), demonstrating a new intervention, and generating hypotheses about causes. Valuable information can be gathered from case studies, as long as their nature and limitations are understood. In general, case studies can tell us what is possible, but not what is typical. Similarly, they can suggest a possible connection or cause, but cannot provide strong confirmatory evidence for it.

Uses of narrative case studies:

- Documenting the existence of a phenomenon

- Disproving a universal proposition

- Demonstrating a new intervention

- Generating causal hypotheses

However, Spence (1986) and others have argued that narrative case studies such as Freud's contain too much "narrative smoothing": that is, they are too selective and have often been altered (either deliberately or unconsciously) to tell a better story. Narrative distortions can be investigated by a self-experiment on one's own clinical work (see box overleaf).

Like the one-group posttest-only design that we discussed in Chapter 8, narrative case studies can be used to infer possible causal explanations if sufficient additional information is available. In psychohistorical case studies (see Chapter 6), for example, Runyan (1982) points out that careful consideration of the known facts often allows the researcher to rule out most of the possible competing explanations for an event.

Self-experiment on narrative distortion

Tape-record a therapy session. A day later (or even an hour later!), write down from memory a brief chronological account of what happened during the session. Then, listen to the tape of the session while taking detailed notes and noting any inaccuracies. In addition to large amounts of missing material, you will also find that you have collapsed things that happened at different times, got some things out of order and may have attributed statements to the wrong speaker or even completely fabricated things.

Systematic Case Studies

Given the problems with narrative case studies (reliance on memory, anecdotal data collection, narrative smoothing), it is worth considering how to improve the quality of information from case studies, in order to strengthen the conclusions which may be drawn from them. Methodologists such as Kazdin (1981) and Hayes et al. (1999) have considered more systematic approaches to single case research, and have proposed the following features for improving their credibility:

- systematic, quantitative (versus anecdotal) data;

- multiple assessments of change over time;

- multiple cases;

- change in previously chronic or stable problems; and

- immediate or marked effects following the intervention.

The combination of these features substantially improves the researcher's ability to infer that a treatment caused an effect (i.e., it increases the internal validity of the study). Note that the first three features are design strategies over which the researcher has some control, while the last two (previous stability and discontinuous change) are outcomes specific to the particular case.

Several writers have recently proposed adding further features to this list (see Elliott, 2002), advocating expanded single case designs which take an interpretive approach to examining client change and its causes. These designs aim to: (1) demonstrate that change occurred; (2) examine the evidence for concluding that therapy was responsible for the change; (3) examine alternative explanations for the change; and (4) examine which processes in therapy might have been responsible for change. They emphasize the use of a *rich case record* of comprehensive information on therapy outcome and process (e.g., using multiple perspectives, sources, and types of data), and *critical reflection* by the researcher, who systematically evaluates the evidence.

A number of procedures, involving varying degrees of time and effort, may be used. We will address each of the above four areas, giving suggestions for how systematic case studies could be carried out by practising clinicians. A good example of a systematic case study which illustrates many of the design features described here is Parry et al.'s (1986) study of "the anxious executive" (see box).

Example of a systematic case study: "The anxious executive" (Parry et al., 1986)

Parry et al. (1986) present a systematic case study of a senior manager who sought help for anxiety and depression related to stress at work and in his marriage. The case was drawn from a large research project examining psychotherapy outcome. Using multiple quantitative measures, including the Shapiro Personal Questionnaire, as well as therapist and client session-by-session accounts, the study examined in detail the changes that occurred over the course of therapy. It was able to identify the characteristics of sessions that had particular short-term outcomes, both positive and negative. It offers a good example of the potential strength of systematic case studies for providing a rich description of process and outcome.

Demonstrating that Change Occurred

The task here is to improve upon anecdotal impressions of client improvement or deterioration. There are several options, which we have roughly ordered from least to most time consuming, so that clinicians may begin with a minimum requirement and work up to more elaborate procedures.

- Administer a *simple standardized measure*, tailored to the particular client's problem, before and after therapy. For example, give the Beck Depression Inventory (Beck et al., 1988) to a depressed client.

- Add an *individualized measure*, before and after therapy (Mintz & Kiesler, 1982). These ask clients to identify the major problem areas that they want to change, and to rate the severity of these problems. For example: the target complaints procedure (Battle et al., 1966) or the Shapiro Personal Questionnaire (Elliott, Mack, & Shapiro, 1999; Phillips, 1986; Shapiro, 1961a).

- Use *additional standardized measures*, covering a broader range of variables. These may include measures of clinical or interpersonal distress, e.g., CORE Outcome Measure (Barkham et al., 2001), the Inventory of Interpersonal Problems (Horowitz et al., 1988), or a global symptom inventory such as the SCL-90-R (Derogatis, 1994).

- Add *more assessment points*, for example at mid-treatment (or every 5 to 10 sessions) or at follow-up (e.g., six months after treatment). A session-by-session measure can also be extremely useful, if only because it ensures some measure of outcome is collected if the client drops out of treatment. Any brief, easy-to-complete client or therapist-rated measure can be used for this purpose, including many of the measures mentioned above.

- Use a *qualitative approach*. As McLeod (2001) has argued, outcome has both qualitative as well as quantitative elements, and qualitative interviews may be more sensitive to negative or unexpected effects as well as allowing researchers to evaluate the plausibility of clients' claims to have changed. The Change Interview (Elliott, 1999; Elliott et al., 2001) is one example of a semi-structured qualitative outcome interview that can be given every 5 to 10 sessions, and at the end of therapy.

- Add further cases, creating a *clinical replication series* (Hayes et al., 1999).

Linking Change to the Therapy

Here the task is to provide evidence to support a causal link between therapy and client outcome. As in single case experimental designs, your conclusions are more credible if data suggesting causal links can be replicated within the case. Such evidence may also help to identify the effective ingredients of the intervention. Forms of potential evidence may include:

- *Client self-report* about therapeutic effectiveness. This may include general client satisfaction measures (e.g., the Client Satisfaction Questionnaire; Larsen et al., 1979) or measures that identify specific helpful aspects of therapy (e.g., the Helpful Aspects of Therapy form; Llewelyn, 1988).

- Significant *within-case correlations* between theoretically relevant within-session processes (e.g., therapeutic alliance) and session outcomes.

- Qualitative evidence of important *within-therapy events* immediately preceding client improvements (e.g., particular themes addressed within a therapy session are followed by changes related to those themes).

- Evidence of reliable *change in stable or chronic problems*.

Evaluating Alternative Explanations

In addition to evaluating evidence that links client change to therapy, it is also important to search systematically for evidence that nontherapy processes may account for change. Cook and Campbell's (1979) list of internal validity threats (see Chapter 8) can be used; in addition, Elliott (2002) highlights validity threats that are specific to single case studies. For example, Elliott proposed eight nontherapy explanations for apparent client change. The first four involve the possibility that the client has not really improved:

- *Nonimprovement.* Apparent changes are trivial or even negative.

- *Statistical artefacts.* Apparent changes reflect statistical artefacts, such as measurement error or regression to the mean.

- *Relational artifacts*. Apparent changes reflect attempts to please the therapist or researcher.

- *Client expectations*. Apparent changes reflect client expectations or wishful thinking.

The next four explanations assume that client improvements are real, but that nontherapy factors account for them:

- *Self-correction*. Changes are due to client self-help efforts independent of therapy, or the self-limiting nature of short-term or temporary problems.

- *Extra-therapy factors*. Changes result from life events outside of therapy, such as changes in relationships or work, or from help obtained from friends or family.

- *Psychobiological factors*. Changes are caused by medication or other remedies, or by recovery from physical illness.

- *Reactive effects of research*. Changes can be attributed to taking part in research, including interactions with research staff, altruism, and increased self-monitoring.

The researcher's task is to systematically evaluate both positive evidence (in favor of therapy as the cause of change and against nontherapy factors) and negative evidence (against therapy as the cause of change and in favor of nontherapy explanations). This weighing of both sides is analogous to political debate or legal proceedings, and it can be carried out by the researchers themselves or by independent judges.

Examining Therapy Process

There are a variety of systematic ways to assess therapeutic process, that is, what happens in a session and the client's reactions to that session (see Greenberg and Pinsof, 1986). Such information helps to elucidate the nature of therapeutic relationships and has the potential for generating theory about the mechanisms of change. Process data can therefore also be used to support inferences about linking client change to the therapy (see section above). Some ways of examining therapy processes include:

- *Records of therapy sessions*. Audiotapes, videotapes, or detailed process notes are an excellent source of information about what actually happens in sessions. (They can also be used to corroborate or clarify self-report data.)

- *Therapeutic relationship measures* can be administered every session, or less frequently (e.g., each three to five sessions). The most widely used such measure is the short form of the Working Alliance Inventory (Tracey & Kokotovic, 1989).

- *Self-report session measures* can be completed by the client or the therapist. The Helpful Aspects of Therapy form (Llewelyn, 1988) is a qualitative measure of client perceptions of significant therapy events. The Session Evaluation

Questionnaire (Stiles, 1980) and the Session Impacts Scale (Elliott, 1993; Elliott & Wexler, 1994) are quantitative measures of clients' immediate reactions to sessions.

- *Orientation-specific measures*, completed by the therapist or the supervisor after each session, can be used to assess the therapist's adherence to the treatment model (e.g., the Cognitive Therapy Scale: Beck et al., 1979).

Time-Series Designs

The final example of naturalistic case study designs is the time-series design. The aim of this design is to evaluate causal processes using correlational methods. Two or more variables are monitored over time and their interrelationship is examined statistically; a large number of observations is needed in order to meet the statistical assumptions behind the analysis. These designs originated in econometrics, where, for example, the effect of one year's interest rates on the following year's economic activity may be analyzed using monthly data over 25 years, which yields 300 data points.

Gottman and his co-workers have promoted these methods within clinical psychology in general and in the study of psychological therapies in particular (e.g., Gottman, 1981; Gottman & Roy, 1990). Complex statistical methods are needed to assess the evolving relationships within and between variables (Gottman, 1981; Skinner, 1991). An interesting application was Moran and Fonagy's (1987) use of time-series methods to study the process and impact of child psychoanalysis on an adolescent girl with diabetes. They demonstrated an association between certain psychoanalytic content themes, e.g., the girl's anger with her father, and the study's principal outcome variable, variations in her blood glucose level.

CONCLUSION

Small-N designs thus represent both a way to look at individual uniqueness and complexity, and also a viable research method for practicing clinicians. Like all research methods, they have their strengths and weaknesses. They are good for looking at phenomena in depth, demonstrating that certain phenomena exist, or disconfirming theories by providing counterexamples. They are poor at establishing typicalities or general laws.

In line with our methodological pluralism stance, we would argue that a thorough investigation of any topic area needs to combine both large-N and small-N approaches. It is possible, even desirable, to examine single cases within the context of a larger group comparison study. Rogers' (1967) classic case of "A silent young man" is taken from a larger experimental study, as is Parry et al.'s (1986) case of "The anxious executive." These two examples both give a human dimension that is lacking in the predominantly statistical reports from the larger projects.

CHAPTER SUMMARY

There is a central distinction between nomothetic and idiographic approaches to research. Nomothetic designs look at groups of individuals (see Chapter 8); idiographic designs look at separate individuals in depth. Idiographic designs, often called small-N, single case, or N = 1 designs, can be appealing to clinicians as a way of combining research and practice. They derive from several different traditions: narrative case studies in neuropsychology and medicine, operant behaviorism, Shapiro's single case approach, and idiographic research in personality theory. There are two main types of design: single case experiments and naturalistic case studies.

Single case experiments are most often used within operant behavioral approaches to therapy, to demonstrate the intervention's control over a problem behavior. They are characterized by frequently administered measurements and the experimental manipulation of an intervention. They have a baseline phase before the intervention is introduced; the participant thereby serves as their own control.

Naturalistic case studies range from narrative approaches, such as Freud's, to more structured studies using systematic measurement of process and outcome. Several authors have articulated criteria for increasing the credibility of case studies. A number of procedures can be used to demonstrate that client change occurred and that it was linked to the therapy.

FURTHER READING

Most of the references on single case experimental designs cover similar ground. Barlow and Hersen (1984) and Kazdin (1982) are the two standard textbooks; there are good chapter-length treatments by Gaynor et al. (1999), Morley (1996) and Peck (1985). Hayes et al. (1999) and Morgan and Morgan (2001) set these designs against a background of scientist-practitioner professional issues.

Bromley (1986) and Yin (1989) discuss case studies as a general research method. It is a good idea to read some of the classic narrative case studies, both from a research and a clinical point of view. Any of Freud's are worthwhile: "Little Hans" (Freud, 1909/1955) or "Dora" (Freud, 1905/1953) provide a good starting point. On the behavioral side, there is Watson and Rayner's (1920) famous (and ethically dubious) case of Little Albert. Carl Rogers pioneered the application of audiotape to client–therapist interaction in single cases: his case of "A silent young man" (Rogers, 1967) is an excellent example of a process-oriented narrative case study. Parry et al. (1986) and Moran and Fonagy (1987) are interesting examples of case studies using more intensive quantitative methods.

More information on the measures mentioned in this chapter can be obtained from the references cited; several can be obtained from the website of the Network for Research on Experiential Therapies (http://experiential-researchers.org).

CHAPTER 10

THE PARTICIPANTS: SAMPLING AND ETHICS

KEY POINTS IN THIS CHAPTER

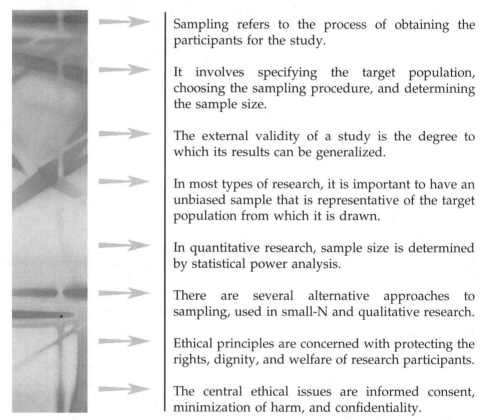

Sampling refers to the process of obtaining the participants for the study.

It involves specifying the target population, choosing the sampling procedure, and determining the sample size.

The external validity of a study is the degree to which its results can be generalized.

In most types of research, it is important to have an unbiased sample that is representative of the target population from which it is drawn.

In quantitative research, sample size is determined by statistical power analysis.

There are several alternative approaches to sampling, used in small-N and qualitative research.

Ethical principles are concerned with protecting the rights, dignity, and welfare of research participants.

The central ethical issues are informed consent, minimization of harm, and confidentiality.

The final aspect of design concerns the participants in the research. It addresses the "who?" question that we posed in Chapter 8: who will you be studying, and to whom do you intend to apply the findings of the study. We will also consider ethical issues here, since they concern the researcher's relationship with the participants.

We usually prefer the term "participants" to the old-fashioned, but still current, term "subjects." The latter term, with its monarchic connotations, has undesirable implications of powerlessness and passivity. The stock phrase "running the subjects" is especially to be avoided: one of our students once wrote something like "the subjects were run in their own homes", which conjures up an image of indoor jogging. For interviews and questionnaires, you can speak of "respondents" or "interviewees." (For observational research, the term "observees" does not yet exist!) In ethnography, the term "informants" is typically used, although this has unfortunate connotations of surreptitiousness. New paradigm researchers (e.g., Reason & Rowan, 1981) may use the term "co-researchers," to emphasize the idea of the participant as an equal partner in the research enterprise.

This chapter has two separate sections: sampling and ethics. We have placed this material here, after the chapters on measurement and the first two chapters on design, because some of the issues to be considered depend on knowledge of those topics. Furthermore, beginning researchers often focus on the population and how it will be sampled before they have formulated what they will be studying. However, it is worth thinking about some of the issues covered here during the groundwork phase of the project, after choosing the area to be investigated and developing the research questions (see Chapter 3). Problems of access to populations are bound up in some of the organizational and political issues which we discussed in that chapter. At an extreme, if there is no sample available, there is no study.

SAMPLING

Sampling refers to the process of specifying and obtaining the participants for the study. In chronological order, the practical steps involved are: (1) specifying the target population; (2) choosing the sampling procedure; and (3) determining the sample size. We will deal with each of these in turn, and then consider some alternative approaches. Although we will mainly be using language associated with the quantitative research tradition, we intend our discussion to have a general application. Qualitative researchers may sometimes be less concerned about representativeness, but we contend that all researchers must decide, implicitly or explicitly, how to respond to these sampling issues.

It helps to think in terms of three nested sets (see Figure 10.1):

- The *universe* is the broad population to which eventual generalization of the findings is desired.

- The *target population* is the defined group from which the participants in the study are to be selected.

- The *sample* is the subset of the target population consisting of those participants who actually take part in the study. There may be a gap between the ideal and the actual sample: the terms *intended* versus *achieved* sample can be used to denote this.

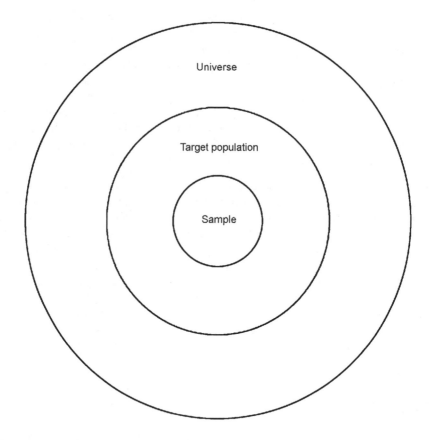

Figure 10.1 The universe, the target population, and the sample

For example, you may be interested in the incidence of depression in British women who consult their general practitioners (family doctors). In this case, the universe may be all British women who visit their general practitioners, the target population all women who consult 10 specific doctors in September 2002, and the intended sample one in 20 of those women. The achieved sample will be the subset of women actually interviewed. In the case of a census, the universe, the target population, and the intended sample are one and the same (e.g., in a national census they consist of all members of that country's population), although the achieved sample will fall short of this, as some people are inevitably missed out.

A quantitative measurement made in a sample is called a *statistic*; it is usually done to estimate a population *parameter*. For instance, the prevalence of depression in a sample of women visiting their general practitioners is a statistic; this may be used to estimate the overall prevalence of depression in the target population of women users of those practices, which is a parameter.

Generalizability

Usually researchers are not just interested in the specific sample itself; rather they want to generalize the findings to other groups. The extent to which this is possible is referred to as the *external validity* of the study (Cook & Campbell, 1979). External validity is captured by the question, "To what extent do the results of my study apply beyond the specific people, situations or incidents in the sample, to others like them?" Of course, generalizability is not just a matter of sampling, since it also involves consideration of the setting, the time, the measures, and so on. We consider these aspects of external validity later on, when we discuss analysis and interpretation in Chapter 12.

From a purely sampling point of view, there are two types of generalization, corresponding to the transitions from one subset to the next in Figure 10.1. The first type is generalizing from the sample to the target population. In quantitative research this is known as statistical inference, and there is a well-established set of procedures to accomplish it. However, these procedures make certain assumptions, such as unbiased sampling from the target population, which we will examine below. The second type is generalizing from the target population to another population or to a larger universe. This is done on the grounds of general plausibility, rather than any statistical argument. For example, can the results of a study of socially anxious patients seen at hospital X in Los Angeles be generalized to hospital Y in New York? To people with social anxiety who do not seek help? To other countries or cultures? If these groups of people are plausibly similar enough, then the results can be generalized across them; if not, then the findings must be considered as specific to the original target population until replications in other populations are conducted.

In the case of qualitative and small-N research, the argument for generalizability always depends upon plausibility, in a similar way to the second step of generalization in quantitative methods.

The importance of external validity depends on the type of research. Basic research on general human processes places a high value on external validity, since it seeks universal generalizability. Applied research may also seek to generalize, though often less widely, for example to a particular client group. For evaluation and action research, external validity is often less important, since the research seeks an understanding of, and solutions to, a particular problem in a particular setting, and seeks generalizability only to the immediate future.

The Target Population

The first step in sampling is to specify the target population. It can be defined in terms of, for instance, gender, social class, problem type, or problem severity. The definitions are usually phrased in terms of specific *inclusion* or *exclusion criteria*. The sample may be defined narrowly (e.g., married women aged 35–45 living within the Liverpool city boundaries with no significant medical or psychiatric history) or broadly (e.g., all British women aged 18 and over). Narrowly defined populations are called *homogeneous*, broadly defined ones *heterogeneous*.

Researchers must make a trade-off when deciding upon the breadth of the target population. A homogeneous sample has the advantage of reducing the degree of extraneous variability (i.e., statistical noise) in the sample, which gives more power to detect effects that you are interested in and more precision in estimating the magnitude of those effects. In analysis of variance terms, homogeneity reduces the proportion of error variance to total variance. For example, if you are researching the influence of life events on depression, any relationship will be harder to detect in a more heterogeneous sample, since depression is a function of many variables other than life events.

On the other hand, the increase in precision from a narrow definition of the target population is bought at the expense of the following:

1. There will be reduced generalizability to a larger universe (e.g., if you are studying women in their thirties, the findings will not necessarily apply to women of all age groups).

2. Practical difficulties will result, including the problem that the more stringent are the inclusion criteria, the harder it is to find participants, since more people have to be screened or you have to get referrals from more specialized services. Mintz (1981) called this Waskow's Law: "As soon as you completely specify a population, it will disappear."

3. Having a homogeneous sample precludes examining individual differences, e.g., if there is little variability in age within your sample, you cannot look at age as an individual difference variable.

Bias and Representativeness

In order to make inferences from the sample to the target population from which it is drawn, the sample should ideally be an *unbiased* sample of that population. This means that every member of the target population should have an equal chance of being selected for the sample. A number of different sampling techniques may be used to generate a representative sample (Cochran, 1977; Robson, 1993; Sudman, 1976). For example, in probability sampling every member of the target population has a given chance, say one in 10, of being included in the study; whereas in stratified sampling, the target population is first subdivided into groups, e.g., according to social class or diagnostic variables, before making the allocation to the study.

Psychologists are typically careless about sampling methods: they tend to rely on *convenience sampling* (i.e., whoever they can get) and hope that their results will generalize, if the sample is large enough. However, it is wrong to assume that a sample large enough to have sufficient statistical power is large enough to ensure generalizability. No matter how large the sample is, you can only generalize safely if the sample is representative of the target population. A sample of 5000 male college students still does not allow you to generalize your findings to a population of female factory workers.

However, eliminating bias is not always feasible. Even with a well-designed sampling plan, there is usually a gap between the intended and the achieved sample. For example, research using postal questionnaires often has around a one-third nonresponse rate (Dillman, 2000). Nonresponders usually differ considerably from responders, e.g., in terms of interest, motivation, and educational level. Similarly, studies which recruit volunteers via advertisements or the internet may get an unrepresentative sample.

Sometimes, it is possible to estimate the nature of the sampling bias and partially control for it statistically when you analyze the data. For example, if respondents are older on average than nonrespondents, you can look at the association of age with whatever variable you are studying, and possibly use partial correlations to remove its influence. However, as we discussed under the nonequivalent groups pretest–posttest design in Chapter 8, posthoc statistical adjustments can only partially compensate for a biased sample, because of unreliability of measurement and because you can never fully compensate for all possible variables on which bias may occur. Such posthoc analyses are often worth doing, but must be treated with caution.

Another serious drawback of the convenience sampling approach is that certain populations may be under-represented. For example, Graham (1992) analysed the participants used in studies published in the major American Psychological Association journals. She concluded that all too often papers reported that "most of the subjects were white and middle class" and that psychological research has ignored black and ethnic participants.

Sample Size

From the point of view of inferential statistics, the obvious rule of thumb is that the larger the sample is, the better, since you are then more able to separate out the variance associated with the effects you are interested in from the variance due to errors of sampling and measurement. In other words, with a large sample you are more able to separate the signal from the noise. However, as Cohen (1990) has pointed out, a sample can be too large, in the sense that it exceeds the requirements for statistical power (see below), thus involving a waste of research effort, and it is also likely to identify trivially small effects. If you are fortunate enough to be well funded, a better strategy may be to carry out several smaller studies on different populations, rather than one large one.

The attainable sample size may also depend on practical issues, such as recruitment difficulties, time constraints, money, and the rarity of the condition studied.

Statistical Power Analysis

The main way of estimating the appropriate sample size is known as statistical power analysis (Cohen, 1988, 1990, 1992; Kraemer & Thiemann, 1987). In a nutshell, the statistical power of a study is the likelihood that it will detect an effect that is actually present, for example, a difference in effectiveness between two treatments. It is analogous to the power of a microscope in laboratory research. Just as a study using a low-magnification microscope will miss out fine details, so a low-power study in psychology will have a low chance of detecting subtle effects; conversely a high-power study will have a good chance. Many studies in clinical psychology have simply not been powerful enough and thus may have overlooked the presence of important effects (Cohen, 1990; Kazdin & Bass, 1989).

In any study, there are four related parameters. For any given statistical test, if you know any three of them, you can find the other.

- The *sample size* (N) is usually what you want to determine, but, if you know it in advance, it facilitates the calculation of the other parameters.

- *Alpha* (α) is the probability of detecting an effect when in fact none exists (this is called a *Type I error* or *false positive*). In most psychological research, alpha is set by arbitrary convention at <0.05, but a more lenient value of <0.10 is sometimes used for exploratory research or defining nonsignificant trends. On the other hand, more stringent values (e.g., 0.01 or 0.001) may be used to increase the confidence in one's findings or to control for the effects of conducting multiple tests of statistical significance.

- *Beta* (β) is the probability of missing an effect which is in fact present (this is called a *Type II error* or *false negative*). *Statistical power* is defined as 1 minus beta $(1 - \beta)$: it is the probability of detecting an effect that is really there. Cohen (1988, 1992) recommends 0.80 as the standard level for power. If you were interested in rejecting a false null hypothesis with a high degree of certainty, a power of 0.95 would be recommended (equivalent in stringency to the alpha <0.05 standard). Conversely, it would be inadvisable to design a study whose power was less than 0.50; you are wasting your time and that of your participants if you design a study that has less than a 50–50 chance of finding an effect that is present.

- *Effect size* is the key concept in power analysis. It is a measure of the strength of the underlying relationship that you are interested in. Effect sizes are usually talked about in terms of small, medium, and large effects. A large effect can be thought of as one which is large enough to see with the naked eye—that is, without statistical analysis. The way the effect size is calculated depends on the type of statistical methods used in the study (e.g., chi-square, t-test, correlation or analysis of variance). This is reviewed by Cohen (1988, 1992), who presents rough standards for what amounts to a small, a medium, and a large effect with each type of statistical test. For example, in correlational studies, a Pearson correlation coefficient of 0.10 is considered to be a small effect, 0.30 a medium effect, and 0.50 a large effect. Clinical psychology researchers usually deal with medium effect sizes, though small effects may be of interest in epidemiological research. Note that effect size is not the same as clinical significance (see Chapter 12); an effect may be large but trivial, if the variable which shows the effect is trivial.

In order to estimate the required sample size for your study, you need to carry out a statistical power calculation. For this, you first need to select your alpha and beta levels and establish your effect size. As discussed above, the most commonly adopted values are an alpha of 0.05 and a power of 0.80. A rough estimate of the effect size can be obtained from previous research or theoretical knowledge of the topic area. It is usually worth trying out the calculation for a range of effect size estimates.

Power analysis tables are provided in various sources. Cohen (1988) and Kraemer and Thiemann (1987) give detailed treatments, and Cohen's (1992) "power primer" presents a clear summary of the central concepts and a useful table to calculate sample sizes for common designs. There are also commercially available computer programs to do the calculations. Tables 10.1 and 10.2 summarize the sample size estimates for two common statistics, t-tests and correlations. For example, in a design which compares two groups using a t-test, with medium effect sizes and an alpha of 0.05, a sample of 64 per group is needed to attain a power of 0.80; with a larger effect, the required sample size decreases. Studies with many variables (e.g., factor analytic studies of long inventories) or many subgroups (e.g., norming a psychological test on different subpopulations) require larger samples. In fact, the sample size requirements for certain types of research, e.g., comparative therapy outcome research, are so large that we recommend that you only conduct such studies if you have the adequate funding and staffing to do so.

Alternative Approaches to Sampling and Generalizability

Qualitative research typically uses smaller samples than traditional quantitative research, as does, obviously, small-N research. Unsurprisingly, the most common criticism of such research is that you cannot generalize the results. In this section, we will describe some alternatives to the traditional approach to sampling and generalizability.

Table 10.1 Estimated sample sizes for t-tests

Effect size (Cohen's d)	n per group	total n
medium ($d = 0.5$)	64	128
large ($d = 0.8$)	26	52

Note: alpha = 0.05; power = 0.80

Table 10.2 Estimated sample sizes for correlations

Effect size (Pearson's r)	total n
medium ($r = 0.3$)	84
large ($r = 0.5$)	28

Note: alpha = 0.05; power = 0.80

Generalizability through Replication

A rational (as opposed to a statistical) approach to generalizability and sampling can be found in the behavioral N = 1 tradition (see Chapter 9), in which research is carried out one case at a time, varying the conditions and relevant client characteristics and measuring the effects until you achieve an understanding of the causal relationships involved. The relevant characteristics of the case, including any background and situational variables which appear to be important, are carefully described.

In this approach, you then attempt to replicate the first case study by finding a case as similar as possible to the first case (this is referred to as *direct replication*: see Sidman, 1960). If you obtain different results (i.e., there is a failure to replicate), you try to understand what made this case different from the first, and then try to find a case which matches the first (or second) on this variable. If the same results are obtained, you next begin to vary apparently relevant features of the case in order to establish the limits of generalizability in a rational manner (this is referred to as *systematic replication*). Replications establish the breadth or range of generalizability, while failures to replicate establish the limits of generality, just as a control group would in traditional research; the two complement each other. Thus, as Cook and Campbell (1979) note, external validity is better served by a number of small studies with specified samples than by a single large study. Cronbach (1975) refers to this approach as *locally intensive observation*; Hayes et al. (1999) call it a *clinical replication series*.

Falsificationist Approach

From a falsificationist framework (cf. Popper, 1963; see Chapter 2), researchers are not concerned with representativeness or generalizability, but with looking for counterexamples to existing theory. These could consist of a single case (Dukes, 1965; Eysenck, 1975; Meehl, 1978). For example, in physics, if a theory of gravitation implies that unsupported apples will fall to the ground, then a single levitating apple will falsify it. Similarly within clinical neuropsychology, a single example of a patient with a certain pattern of abilities may invalidate a proposed model of mental structure (Shallice, 1988). In these instances, qualitative or quantitative descriptive research which establishes the existence of the counter-example can be of crucial importance.

Networking or Snowballing

When the size and composition of the target group is unknown at the outset, it is possible to use a sampling procedure known as *networking* or *snowballing* (Patton, 2002; Rossi et al., 1999), which operates by asking each respondent to name one or two other people who fit the research criteria. Sampling continues up to the point where additional respondents provide little or no extra information. For example, Pistrang (1990) used this method to study the mental health needs of London's Chinese community. She wanted to interview community and health workers who were involved with the Chinese population in London's West End. Before the project started, it was not known precisely how many such workers there were or where they were to be found, but increasing numbers of interviewees were located via networking as the project progressed, up to a final total of 20. However, a potential problem with the snowballing procedure is that the initial respondents might direct you to other like-minded people who share their viewpoint, and thus the researcher needs to be aware of possible biases in the achieved sample.

Purposive Sampling

In qualitative and case study research, the term *purposive sampling* is often used to denote a systematic strategy of selecting the participants according to criteria that are important to the research questions. It is similar to specifying the target population in quantitative research, in that the researcher attempts to select participants fitting specific criteria, but it is a less rigid process, being guided by the researcher's judgement (Robson, 1993).

Theoretical Sampling

In grounded theory, the sampling approach is referred to as *theoretical sampling* (Strauss & Corbin, 1998). It is a type of purposive sampling, in which the researcher's emerging theory determines the sampling strategy as the study develops. It resembles the replication sampling approach of the behavioral single case researchers. The difference is that the behaviorists are trying to establish control over behaviors, while the grounded theorists are trying to develop a rich description and test emerging theory.

The procedure is that the researcher analyzes the data as they are collected, and develops tentative theoretical concepts from early on in the study. As ideas form about what are the important dimensions or conditions, the sampling strategy is modified to take these into account. For example, in a study of postpartum depression, the researcher may theorize, after interviewing several women, that an important aspect is the degree of control that the women experienced over their childbirth. She may then sample women who had different types of childbirth procedures, in order to examine variations in perceived control and its consequences.

In grounded theory, sampling stops when little new information emerges and a rich set of categories has been developed. This is referred to as *saturation*.

Conclusion

The essential point is that researchers need to think carefully about whom the conclusions of their study can apply to and how they are going to support the strength of those conclusions. All too often, clinical psychology researchers seem to neglect sampling and generalizability issues. Unfortunately, there is a long tradition of clinicians making over-confident generalizations based on observations of the biased sample of clients who have appeared in their consulting rooms. Freud's case histories were partly responsible for this, as modesty in drawing inferences was not one of Freud's characteristics. Neurotic Victorian women seeking psychoanalysis are not a good foundation on which to base general theories about the human condition; or, more precisely, it is possible to form one's theories with such a population, but they must be replicated in other ways if they are to have credibility. Clinicians often seem unaware that people who seek professional help for their psychological problems are in a minority (e.g., Kessler et al., 1994). Thus clinical researchers need to develop more humility about the limits of application of their findings.

True random sampling, in the sense of drawing participants randomly from a large population of potential participants, is rarely performed in clinical psychology research. Usually, convenience sampling is used—that is, whomever can be obtained at the time of the study (e.g., all the participants who can be recruited in a given time period). Researchers need to take this into account when analyzing the data and making generalizations.

Having dealt with sampling issues, we will now examine the other major topic area that is raised by working with the participants, that is, ethics.

ETHICAL ISSUES

The major ethical principles in clinical psychology research are:

- *Informed consent.* The researcher gives full information about the study and participants freely choose whether to enter it.

- *Avoidance of harm.* Harm may be direct (such as stress or humiliation) or consist of deprivation of benefit (such as in control groups in clinical trials). There may be a difficult trade-off between the potential harm to individual participants and the potential benefits of knowledge to humanity.

- *Privacy* is the right not to provide information; *confidentiality* is the right to have any personal information kept securely.

- All clinical psychology research should be reviewed by experienced researchers external to the project, including ethics committees or Institutional Review Boards.

Ethical principles are concerned with protecting the rights, dignity, and welfare of research participants. Interest in the ethics of psychological research grew out of outrage at earlier abuses, including medical research in Nazi concentration camps during World War II and early stress induction research by psychologists

(Bersoff & Bersoff, 1999; Koocher & Keith-Spiegel, 1998). These concerns were further fuelled by the widespread use of deception in the social-psychological research of the 1950s and early 1960s which shaped the public attitude of psychologists as scientific deceivers. The civil rights movement and populism of the 1960s and 1970s resulted in a greater sensitivity to ethics on the part of psychologists (Imber et al., 1986; Korchin & Cowan, 1982). Finally, especially in the United States, concerns about litigation and the general trend toward increased bureaucratization and governmental control of research led in the 1970s and 1980s to government-mandated practices for the review of research involving human participants.

Previous chapters have touched on some ethical issues associated with particular research methods or designs, such as covert observation or no-treatment control groups. Here we will examine some central principles common to all psychological research. Following Korchin and Cowan (1982), we group them under the headings of: (1) informed consent; (2) minimization of potential harm/deprivation of benefit; and (3) confidentiality and protection of privacy.

However, before examining these principles, some general points need to be made. First, the researcher is under an obligation to explore and seek others' advice and judgments about the specific ethical issues involved in his or her study. Second, as Korchin and Cowan (1982) noted, validity and ethics should not be seen as separate issues. Instead, unethical practice reduces the external validity of the research, because it results in research procedures that cannot be translated into practice. Conversely, poorly designed research reduces the ethical standing of the research, because in such situations, there are usually only minimal scientific or social benefits possible to counterbalance the possible risks of participation in the research. Finally, it is worth noting that we are operating in the domain of value judgments, in which one needs to balance negative effects (usually accruing to the participant) with positive effects (usually accruing to society in general). Sometimes there are conflicting ethical considerations, and difficult choices need to be made for which there are no clear-cut answers.

Informed Consent

Informed consent refers to disclosure by the researcher, before the study, of what will happen during the study and of any other information that might affect the person's decision to participate. This enables prospective participants to make a free and informed decision about whether or not to enter the study. Thus informed consent involves both full information and freedom of choice.

Full Information

Full information refers to the principle of telling prospective participants everything that they need to know in order to make a rational decision about whether to take part in the study. An important corollary is that the participant be able to understand the information provided (i.e., that it is not written in overly technical or bureaucratic prose or in a language in which the participant is not fluent).

Problems arise when the person's understanding of the issues is limited. Informed consent becomes difficult with children or with adults who are not fully competent to make their own decisions (Bersoff & Bersoff, 1999; Koocher & Keith-Spiegel, 1998), or even with well-informed and educated adults in complicated clinical trials in medicine (Thornton, 1992). For example, if the child is less than seven, parental permission plus the child's verbal agreement is usually required. If the child is between seven and 17, then his or her written assent is usually required in addition to parental permission. Similarly, with adults with severe dysfunctions (e.g., people with severe mental retardation—intellectual disabilities in the UK usage— or people who are psychotic), then sensitivity and clinical skills are required, and the level of readability and comprehensibility of the description is important.

A second issue is the role of deception in psychological research. Although it is more common in social than in clinical psychology, there are some well-known examples of deception, e.g., Rosenhan's (1973) "pseudopatient" study, in which participant observers faked a psychotic symptom in order to gain admission to a mental hospital as a patient. There is also the less dramatic issue of deception by omission: good scientific practice dictates that participants should not be aware of the hypotheses under investigation, since this knowledge may cause them to alter their behavior. Thus deception is a matter of degree, ranging from relatively trivial instances of withholding information about specific hypotheses or naturalistic observation of public behavior, to more serious cases of lying to the participants. Deception is an especially serious problem when the study uses fictional environments or contrived situations (e.g., in Good Samaritan studies when a serious crime or accident is feigned), or when double deception (i.e., false debriefing) is used.

At a minimum, a full debriefing is needed at the end of any study in which deception is used, in order to provide complete information, including the rationale for the deception, and to answer all questions about the study. However, debriefing cannot always be relied upon to undo the effects of the deception, because this may cause greater pain when the participants learn that they have been deceived. For this reason, Korchin and Cowan (1982) recommend that alternative methods should be used wherever possible, including obtaining the person's consent to be uninformed, seeking feedback from surrogate participants who are similar to proposed participants, role playing and simulation research, and naturalistic, descriptive research.

Freedom of Choice

Freedom of choice requires that the participant's consent be voluntary, without direct or indirect pressures to take part. There should be no coercion, explicit or implicit. Thus, the researcher must foster the possible participant's autonomy and self-determination and should evaluate implicit situational or personal factors which may limit freedom.

There is often a considerable power imbalance between the researcher and the potential participant. In this case, the problem of making sure that there is no implicit coercion becomes acute. This is often an issue in clinical settings, where a therapist or doctor wishes to conduct research with his or her patients, who may fear that refusal will prejudice their treatment. It is also an issue with captive populations, e.g., psychiatric in-patients, prisoners, or students. Such power imbalances inevitably limit freedom. It is a matter for concern that these populations tend to be overused by psychologists.

Informed Consent Form

In practice, the study is described and the participant's consent is recorded by means of an information sheet and informed consent form. Although specific requirements vary (depending on the particular study and the setting in which it is conducted), at a minimum these should contain:

- a description of the study's procedures;

- an explanation of its risks and potential benefits;

- an offer by the researchers to answer questions at any time;

- the statement that participants may withdraw their consent at any time during the study without prejudice, especially without prejudice to their present or future treatment; and

- a space at the end of the form for the potential participant to sign in acknowledgement that they understand what the study involves.

The informed consent form is given to participants to read and sign after the study is fully described to them and after they have had a chance to ask any questions about it, but before the study proper begins. It is good practice to give participants a duplicate copy of the information sheet to retain for their records.

Harms and Benefits

In general, research should not harm the participants. However, some people may freely consent to suffer harm for the greater good of humanity, e.g., in testing new medical procedures. There is a trade-off between any harm caused to the participants versus the potential gain to humanity from the knowledge acquired.

In psychological research, harm is most likely to come from such things as stirring up painful feelings or memories, threats to one's self-image, and humiliation. Two extreme examples are Milgram's (1964) obedience studies, in which participants believed themselves to be giving dangerous electric shocks to other participants, and Zimbardo's (1973) prison simulation, in which college students, role playing prison guards, brutalized other participants who were role playing prisoners. In addition to psychological risk to the individual, there is also the possibility of social risk, e.g., to members of ethnic or cultural groups who may be harmed by the findings of studies examining group differences (Scarr, 1988).

As part of debriefing the participants after the data collection, you should ask whether they experienced any distress or had any concerns during the study. Furthermore, if the respondent becomes upset during the study itself, you may need to terminate, or at least suspend, data collection. Your clinical skills become useful here, both in detecting the presence of distress and also in being able to respond to it appropriately. However, in some cases participants may need to be referred to sources of help outside of the study, for example, if an interview about psychological trauma stirs up painful memories, or if a study of marital interaction produces considerable conflict in the couple. Occasionally, people may volunteer for psychological studies in order to find a way of getting help for their difficulties.

Withholding of Benefit in Clinical Trials

Randomized controlled trials (RCTs) highlight a number of ethical issues (Imber et al., 1986). Although participants are unlikely to be harmed, there are several dilemmas about *withholding of benefit*. In other words, there are tensions between the clinical perspective, which emphasizes doing the best for each individual patient, and the scientific perspective, which emphasizes having a well-designed study. The researcher must therefore balance the need for useful knowledge about a treatment's efficacy against the likely consequences for individual participants, who may receive less than optimal treatment in the study. These tensions appear in the following areas:

- *Control groups.* No-treatment or placebo controls mean that some patients are deprived of a potentially valuable treatment, being instead given an inferior treatment or none at all (see Chapter 8). Wait-list controls pose a less serious problem, but they still mean that, for some patients, treatment is delayed.

- *Specified treatments versus clinical judgement.* Patients in RCTs receive specified, unvarying treatments, often manualized ones, thereby diminishing the capacity of the clinician to make informed judgements about how the patient is responding, and to vary the therapy accordingly.

- *Randomization.* As we discussed in Chapter 8, Brewin and Bradley (1989) argue that most patients have preferences about which treatments they want, and that the act of random assignment to experimental conditions deprives them of choice. Being in a less preferred treatment (even though they have consented to the lack of choice) may result in a less than optimal outcome.

- *Narrow inclusion criteria.* Since clinical trials usually have specific inclusion criteria, often based on a single DSM diagnosis, people with significant clinical concerns not may be admitted into the treatment program, on the grounds that their problems are too complicated.

- *Referrals at termination.* In normal clinical practice, a therapist can refer a patient for further help at the end of therapy. However, in an RCT which has a follow-up assessment, this is not possible or may be discouraged, as the researchers need to see how the patients fare without any additional therapy. Again, patients are deprived of optimal treatment as a result.

Privacy and Confidentiality

Invasion of privacy and loss of confidentiality are special cases of harm. *Privacy* refers to the person's right not to provide information to the researcher, while *confidentiality* refers to the person's right (and the researcher's corresponding obligation) to withhold information from third parties.

In a trivial sense, all psychological research invades privacy, since otherwise it would not be finding out anything new. However, the ethical issue of privacy is concerned with the intrusiveness of research. Different people have different personal boundaries: some do not mind disclosing intimate information about themselves, while others want to maintain a tight control on what is known about them. The researcher needs to be aware of each participant's limits on disclosing information and respect their right to withhold certain information.

Types of confidentiality protection include anonymity, in which no identification is possible, and the more usual situation of protecting the participant's identity through secure research codes which are separated from the data itself. Participants are likely to be more open and to provide better data if they feel assured of confidentiality safeguards. Finally, it is important to keep in mind that no confidentiality guarantee is absolute, in that research records are always vulnerable to theft or legal subpoena.

Ideally, the information sheet or informed consent form should specify who will have access to the data and the findings. (As an aside, the adjective "strict," which often precedes "confidentiality" is superfluous, since something is either confidential or it is not.) When audiotapes or videotapes are made, it should be clear who will hold them, for what purposes, and for how long; it is good practice to have a separate informed consent form to cover consent to make, retain, and possibly publish extracts from recordings. When case material is written up, the participants' personal details should be altered so that they are unrecognizable (this sometimes requires creativity).

The issue of confidentiality becomes increasingly critical as the information becomes more sensitive or potentially damaging, should it become known to others. The kinds of danger from potential breaches of confidentiality include embarrassment, loss of employment, legal action, labeling, and social stigma. In these situations, the researcher should give details on the information sheet or informed consent form about the kinds of information that the participants will be asked to provide.

Ethics Self-study Exercise

We recommend that the researcher review his or her study in order to appraise its risks and benefits (Davison & Stuart, 1975). This self-appraisal begins by asking "What risks are possible? How serious are they? How likely are they?"

The risk estimates typically increase when new procedures (i.e., new measurement or intervention methods) are employed, as opposed to established, tested procedures. Another important situational factor is the degree of coercion. The researcher should ask "What obvious or implicit pressures are operating on prospective participants, which may prevent them from refusing to take part?" These may include the need for psychological or medical treatment, in order to impress legal authorities or to be released from prisoner or patient status.

Having evaluated the study's risks, the researcher should then ask "What benefits are likely? For whom? How realistic are they?" Some benefits may accrue directly to the participant, including help with problems, self-knowledge or growth, general education, and increased self-esteem or altruism; other benefits are more general, such as the knowledge gained and the increased potential for helping others.

In general, greater potential risks, lesser benefits, unknown procedures, and coercive situations call for stronger safeguards for informed consent and participant safety. These safeguards include greater disclosure of risks; careful screening and exclusion of at-risk participants (e.g., borderline personality disorder in short-term expressive therapy); supervision and monitoring of the participant's condition during the course of the study; and the use of contingency plans for removing participants from the study and finding appropriate treatment for research-induced problems. Finally, Davison and Stuart (1975) argue that there are some situations in which it is impossible to conduct ethical research, e.g., prisons can be said to be inherently coercive to such an extent that no valid consent can obtained.

In evaluating the risk–benefit ratio, be aware of the dangers of self-deception: there is a tendency for researchers to rationalize and underestimate research risks while overestimating benefits, under implicit assumptions such as "The ends justify the means" and "What is good for me must be good for psychology." You will ultimately have an easier conscience if you follow the precept that "People are more important than data."

Ethics Committees

You cannot do psychological research without coming into contact with the committee delegated by your university, hospital, or other agency to review the ethical treatment of human participants in research (Bersoff & Bersoff, 1999; Bruce, 1990; Ceci et al., 1985). These committees are known as Institutional Review Boards (IRBs) in the USA and ethics committees in the UK. The purposes of this review process are to protect the participants in the research, and also to protect the institution from legal reprisals for ethical lapses and harm done to research participants. Another purpose is to comply with the regulations of grant-giving institutions.

Ethics committees are typically made up of academics, drawn from a range of disciplines, and medical doctors. Many committee members may be unfamiliar with psychological research. In the USA, their make-up is dictated federally, including a balance of gender and scientific discipline and the inclusion of physicians and lay persons from the community. This range of backgrounds usually provides a breadth of perspectives to evaluate the ethical appropriateness of the research. However, occasionally, ethics committees appear to exceed their brief, and to make decisions on political rather than ethical grounds (Ceci et al., 1985). For example, we knew of one project, which aimed to examine how much psychiatric patients knew about the side effects of their psychotropic medication, that was refused ethical permission. It seemed that this was not because the project was unethical, but rather because certain committee members felt threatened by what the results might say about the state of professional practice.

Committees can sometimes take months to process an application, so it is wise to apply early, especially if your research is being done to a tight deadline (this particularly applies to student projects). However, there is a dilemma here, since if you apply for ethical approval early in the planning stage, before your protocol is finalized, your application may look less polished and your study may also change somewhat after it has been approved. If your research is still in the planning stage, you can attach a cover letter saying that the study is being developed but you would like to apply for provisional approval of the draft protocol. Alternatively, if your protocol changes, e.g., as a result of pilot studies, you can file an amendment with the ethics committee or IRB.

There are often three levels of review: exempt, expedited, and full review.

Exempt status. A study may pose such minimal risks as to be exempt from regular review. Such research includes: (1) Surveys using interviews or questionnaires, where the participants are not identifiable or are not asked to reveal sensitive information of a personal or potentially damaging nature; (2) Research on established educational practices, where the participants are not at risk and are not identifiable; (3) Research using existing archival or public data, where the participants cannot be identified; and (4) Overt observation of public behavior, under the same conditions of confidentiality and unintrusiveness.

The catch with exempted review status is that you are not allowed to make this decision yourself (because of possibly vested interests). Thus, there is usually some form of screening required to determine whether a study should be exempted or not. A typical procedure for doing this is to consult with the ethics committee chair or one's departmental review committee.

Expedited review. The next level of review is expedited, a fast-track review process for only low-risk studies. Examples include the use of archival data where a particular use of the data has not previously been consented to; and non-stress-inducing behavioral research without manipulation of participants' behavior or emotions. In expedited review, the researcher still submits forms to the committee, which may subject the study to limited review by a sub-committee (e.g., the chair plus one other committee member).

Full review.   The third level is full review, which applies to everything that does not fit the exempt or expedited criteria, to all government grants, and to all research with people who are not competent to give informed consent, including children and mentally disabled adults. Sometimes, the researcher may be requested to meet with the committee to answer specific questions about the study.

Some research practices, such as deception and covert observation, raise red flags and are usually scrutinized carefully by ethics committees. These practices have a number of potential costs (Bersoff & Bersoff, 1999), including the fact that they tend to undermine trust in psychology; they may change people's behavior (e.g., decreasing bystander intervention in emergencies because people now think it might be an experiment); and their artificiality may yield distorted findings of low external validity. Finally, proposals for work in socially sensitive areas (Sieber & Stanley, 1988), such as child sexual abuse, are usually more thoroughly scrutinized.

CHAPTER SUMMARY

This chapter has covered issues concerning the researcher's relationship with the participants: how participants are obtained for the study and how they are treated once they are in it. The process of obtaining the participants is known as sampling. It involves specifying the target population from which the sample will be drawn, choosing the sampling procedure, and determining the sample size. It also involves thinking about the universe to which the results of the study are intended to be applied. The degree to which a study's results can be generalized is known as external validity: it is one of Cook & Campbell's (1979) four validity types.

In most types of research, it is desirable to have an unbiased sample, representative of the target population from which it is drawn. There are various sampling techniques available to achieve this. However, psychological research often tends to rely on convenience samples, which may introduce biases. In traditional quantitative research, the sample size is determined by statistical power analysis. There are alternative approaches to sampling, such as systematic replication in $N = 1$ research and purposive or theoretical sampling in qualitative studies.

Ethical principles are concerned with protecting the rights, dignity, and welfare of research participants. The central ethical issues are informed consent, minimization of harm, and confidentiality. Informed consent has two components: that the researcher gives full information about the study and that participants are able to freely choose whether to enter it. It is important to be aware of the subtle pressures on people to participate, particularly when the researcher is in a position of power or authority. In clinical psychology research, harm may be direct (such as stress or embarrassment) or it may consist of deprivation of benefit (such as when participants in control groups in clinical trials get an inferior treatment, or none at all). There may be a difficult trade-off between potential harm to individual participants and potential benefits of knowledge to humanity. Privacy and confidentiality are special cases of potential harm: privacy is the individual's right not to provide information; confidentiality is the right to have any information kept securely.

All clinical psychology research should be reviewed by peers, including ethics committees or Institutional Review Boards.

FURTHER READING

More detail on sampling is given in Sudman's (1976) book, *Applied Sampling*, which covers the issues in a non-technical way; Cochran (1977) provides the statistical background. There is an excellent summary available on the internet from the UK National Audit Office (http://www.nao.gov.uk/publications/ Samplingguide.pdf). Cohen (1990) gives a good overview of the issues in statistical power analysis and Cohen (1992) provides a "power primer" covering the most commonly used cases. Alternative views of sampling and generalization are covered in Patton (2002), Sidman (1960), Strauss and Corbin (1998), and Taylor and Bogdan (1998).

Researchers should familiarize themselves with the relevant set of ethical principles (e.g., American Psychological Association, 1992; British Psychological Society, 1990). Koocher and Keith-Spiegel (1998) give a general overview of ethics in psychology, with a focus on clinical practice, and include some useful case vignettes. The chapters by Korchin and Cowan (1982) and Bersoff and Bersoff (1999), in successive editions of Kendall, Butcher et al.'s *Handbook of Research Methods in Clinical Psychology* (1999), both give interesting discussions of ethics in clinical research; we have drawn on them heavily here.

CHAPTER 11

EVALUATION RESEARCH

KEY POINTS IN THE CHAPTER

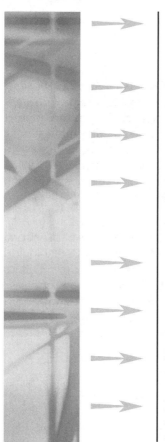

Evaluation is applied research that aims to assess the worth of a service, often judging it against specified goals.

It includes service audit, quality assurance, needs assessment, and outcomes evaluation.

Organizational and political issues are crucial in evaluation research.

The evaluator begins an evaluation by asking two basic questions:
"What is the service trying to do?"
"How will you know if it has done it?"

Evaluations can address the process or outcome of a service.

Process evaluation examines who is coming to the service and what service they are being given.

Outcome evaluation examines the impact of the service—whether users benefit or not.

In addition to examining clinical outcome, evaluators may look at client satisfaction, and at economic indicators of costs and benefits.

In everyday parlance, evaluation means judging the worth of something. Good applied psychologists do this informally: they build up a personal knowledge base of which interventions work best with whom. Clinical psychology training, in particular, emphasizes a reflective, self-critical attitude towards one's work, and encourages evaluation of one's own practice.

Here we will use the term "evaluation" in a more formal sense, to denote applied research into the implementation and effectiveness of clinical services.

Much of the early evaluation work was done in the US in an educational context, where it is known as *program evaluation*. It arose as a way of monitoring the federal money spent on large-scale social programs in the 1960s, such as Head Start, a pre-school educational intervention program (Rossi et al., 1999; Shadish et al., 1991).

This chapter departs from our chronological, research process framework. We have so far concentrated on fundamental issues in research methods, which can be applied across different content areas of psychological research. This chapter draws on ideas from the groundwork, measurement, and design chapters, and applies them to the task of studying specific services in specific settings. Evaluation is a messy area in which sociopolitical and organizational issues are often as prominent as scientific ones (Cowen, 1978; Weiss, 1972). The design compromises that we discussed in Chapter 8 become more acute here. Evaluation researchers often face a Hobson's choice: they can either collect inadequate data or no data at all.

We are devoting a separate chapter to evaluation both because it has its own distinct body of literature, and also because we anticipate that many readers will never conduct basic clinical research, but they may well become involved in evaluation research. We argue that evaluation should be a routine part of clinical psychology: much clinical work is based on custom and practice rather than any formal knowledge base, and evaluating it is a way of seeing whether or not it lives up to its claimed benefits.

Planning an evaluation begins with two questions: "What is the service trying to do?" and "How will you know if it has done it?" The procedures used in evaluation research aim to answer these basic questions. This chapter looks at the practical issues in incorporating evaluation into working clinical services. Before that, however, we will examine some of evaluation research's basic concepts and specialized vocabulary.

What is Evaluation?

We defined "evaluation" above as a form of applied research. However, as we discussed in Chapter 2, the distinction between pure and applied research is better regarded as a continuum rather than a dichotomy. Evaluation, at the applied end of the continuum, differs from pure research in several ways (Hayes et al., 1999; Milne, 1987; Watts, 1984; Weiss, 1972):

- Its primary aim is to assist decision making, rather than to add to an existing body of knowledge. Thus it tends to be less concerned with theory and more with solving a particular setting's operational problems.

- It is done on behalf of a decision-maker, often a manager, who may be distinct from the evaluator.

- It takes place in a complex "action setting" (Weiss, 1972), as opposed to a more controlled academic research environment.

- Its participants are usually users of the service, rather than research volunteers, and their interests as clients are paramount.

- It is intended for immediate use and is usually done under considerable time pressure.

- It is often written up for purely local consumption, rather than for wider dissemination in professional journals. This may be partly because it may not meet exacting scientific standards and partly because the time and effort needed to write up the findings for publication may be beyond the evaluator's resources. Sometimes, also, evaluators are unable to publish their findings because the people who commissioned the study do not want its results to be known by their commercial competitors.

There is a long-standing debate over whether evaluation is an art or a science. On the one hand, Campbell and his collaborators have argued for the use of rigorous research methods in evaluation (e.g., Cook & Campbell, 1979). On the other hand, Cronbach (1982), and more recently, Patton (1997) have argued that evaluation is an art, and that it should be tailored to the specific circumstances and interests of the program being evaluated. The issue is whether general principles of evaluation can be laid down, or whether the selection of methods must largely be left to the expertise of the specific practitioner in the specific setting. We stand in between these two positions, regarding evaluation as part of a broadly based local clinical science (Trierweiler & Stricker, 1998). In any case, we see evaluation as being as systematic an endeavor as one can manage within practical and organizational constraints.

Types of Evaluation

Evaluation has its fair share of jargon, and several terms are used to describe the type of evaluation being conducted.

Scriven (1972) classified evaluation into formative and summative approaches. A *formative* evaluation is typically used for internal program purposes, and feeds back its results to influence the service as it continues to develop (or form itself). A *summative* evaluation provides an overall summary, typically for administrative purposes; it is often done on a larger scale with its results delayed until after the end of the evaluation period. Formative evaluations thus lend themselves to evaluating new services; while summative evaluations lend themselves to well-established ones.

Donabedian (1980), a key figure in the quality assessment literature, distinguished three different foci of evaluation: (1) *structure* refers to the resources that are available for a service, such as staff, buildings, and equipment such as psychological tests; (2) *process* refers to the activities that constitute the service delivery—in psychology these are essentially a series of help-intended conversations or assessment procedures; (3) *outcome* is how the service affects the clients, e.g., how they change psychologically as a result. The parallel concepts of input, activities, and output, which originated in economics, are also sometimes used (Fenton Lewis & Modle, 1982). The present chapter mostly addresses process evaluation: evaluation of structure is psychologically uninteresting (except from an organizational development point of view), and outcome evaluation overlaps considerably with our earlier discussion of design (Chapter 8).

The variables to be examined in an evaluation can also be conceptualized using Maxwell's (1984) widely cited list of six criteria for quality assessment: access to services, relevance to need, effectiveness, equity, social acceptability, and efficiency/economy. For example, Parry (1992) used this framework to address how psychotherapy services might be evaluated.

Evaluation, Audit, and Quality Assurance

The term *clinical audit* (or *service audit*) is current in the UK (Cape & Barkham, in press; Crombie et al., 1993; Firth-Cozens, 1993; Parry, 1992). Its history in medicine stretches back to the beginning of the 20th century (Lembcke, 1967; Young, 1982). Audit is a loosely defined term that refers to an intensive examination of one or more aspects of a service. For example, an out-patient psychotherapy service might audit the ethnic background of its referrals. An audit can be specific, as in this example, or it can be more wide ranging. It may be described as medical audit, to indicate that it is being performed by doctors (the term "clinical audit" usually means that it is done by a multi-professional team).

Definitions of audit tend to emphasize comparison against an agreed standard (e.g., Crombie et al., 1993; Firth-Cozens, 1993). For example, an audit of waiting times in an out-patient service might involve the standard that all clients should receive an appointment within six weeks of referral. Under this definition, simply monitoring practice prior to a standard having been set, or developing a standard itself, are important precursors to audit, but not audit proper.

Audit is often depicted as a circular process—known as "the audit cycle" (Figure 11.1)—which emphasizes using audit to make changes, either in clinical practice or in the standards governing practice. Audit thus involves a continuous process of evaluating, feeding back, making changes, and evaluating again.

Both audit and evaluation are closely linked to *quality assurance*, which emphasizes setting-up procedures to ensure that the standard of a service's work remains consistently high (Cape, 1991; Green & Attkisson, 1984; Young, 1982). Quality assurance is related to various quality management methods originating from business and industry, such as total quality management, statistical process control, and continuous quality improvement (Cape & Barkham, in press). Methods for quality assurance in clinical psychology could include peer review or systematic involvement of service users in monitoring delivery.

Audit and evaluation are retrospective, looking at the service after it has happened (although the results will naturally be fed back to help improve the service). Quality assurance, on the other hand, is essentially prospective,

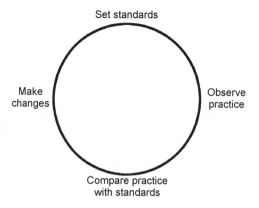

Figure 11.1   The audit cycle

ensuring that no future problems occur in the service (although it is also retrospective in the sense of identifying problems and making sure that they do not happen again). To take a hypothetical example from manufacturing (where much of this language originated), evaluation (or audit, or quality inspections) will count the number of flies in the baked beans; quality assurance procedures will try to stop them getting in there in the first place.

The Sociopolitical Context

It is vital never to underestimate the sense of threat that accompanies evaluation. Even people who feel largely positive about it will often be worried or irritated by it; other people may just pay lip service to enlightened attitudes about evaluation, but ultimately be defensive and obstructive. Some of the most important concerns are as follows:

- An oppressive sense of being continually scrutinized, that can feel like Orwell's "Big Brother is watching you."

- Resentment at having to take the time to provide the data for evaluation, since it leaves less time for client contact.

- Fear that the results of evaluation may provide ammunition for managers or other colleagues to attack the quality or quantity of work being done.

- Annoyance that the criteria used in evaluations do not capture the important aspects of a service's work. Evaluations may just focus on quantitative measures that are easy to collect, such as numbers of clients seen, rather than more valid but less tangible indicators of quality.

These are important objections. Even if you do not feel them strongly yourself, they will be undoubtedly felt, if not voiced, by a significant proportion of your colleagues. As we discussed in Chapter 3, this is an area where clinicians can use their skills to understand and possibly reduce the sense of threat. Clinical psychologists typically have had better training in this than other professionals involved in evaluation.

Internal versus External Evaluation

We have been tacitly assuming that you are evaluating a service which you yourself partly deliver: this is often called an in-house evaluation. An alternative possibility is that an external evaluation consultant be used. External consultants are usually less emotionally attached to the service and more able to weigh it dispassionately. On the other hand, external evaluators are usually more threatening, less knowledgeable about the service, and more expensive. For the rest of the chapter, we will assume that you are conducting an in-house evaluation, since that is the more common situation. However, psychologists are sometimes employed as external consultants to evaluate other services. External evaluations cover the same ground as in-house evaluations, but in addition they require the evaluator to possess specialized consultancy skills.

Our own view is that, despite its potential difficulties, evaluation of the services they deliver needs to become a routine component of psychologists' work, and that evaluation can be made more relevant if conducted by the psychologists themselves. The mental health field, in particular, is awash with programs and interventions that are very poorly monitored. No one knows what their effects are, and there is often at best a lack of interest in, and at worst a contempt for, the views of the clients. Furthermore, the current climate of managed care in the USA and clinical governance in the UK emphasizes evaluation, audit, and quality assurance (Cape & Barkham, in press; Crombie et al., 1993; Lyons et al., 1997). So the issue is not whether to evaluate, but how to. We believe that it is better to take control of evaluation yourself, than to have it imposed upon you.

What Stakeholders want from Evaluation

The various *stakeholders* (evaluation jargon for someone who has an interest) in the service will each have different reasons for wanting the evaluation done. These reasons are not necessarily mutually incompatible, but each stakeholder will attach their own weighting to each one. For example:

- People funding a service (e.g., managers or grant-giving bodies) may want to know whether it is doing what it is supposed to be doing, and whether it is using its resources effectively.

- Clinicians may want to test the effectiveness of an intervention or to compare it to other interventions. They may also want to know if their professional time is being used efficiently.

- Service planners may want to justify the development or continuation of a service, or to improve its delivery.

- Service users, or their parents, guardians, or carers, may be concerned about the accessibility, convenience, and effectiveness of the service.

- Community leaders may want to know if the service is reaching its intended target population.

Aside from these overtly expressed, rational reasons, there may also be some less legitimate, covert reasons for evaluating (Weiss, 1972). For example, evaluation may be used to delay making a decision, or as an empty public relations exercise, or as a way of generating information that can be used to justify closing down an awkward service. Evaluation is a complex political arena, in which some people do nasty things for nasty reasons, but rarely admit that they are doing so.

The next section examines the preparatory thinking that is needed to set up an evaluation. Then we will look at ways of monitoring the process of service delivery, and finally touch on evaluation of impact and effectiveness.

PREPARATION FOR EVALUATING A SERVICE

As we stated at the beginning of the chapter, the first question to address in evaluating a service is "What is the service trying to do?" This is usually followed by the subsidiary question "Why is the service trying to do that?" Before the evaluation proper can proceed, these preparatory questions must be addressed. We have adapted the framework that Rossi et al. (1999) set out in their influential evaluation textbook. The process of answering these two questions can be broken down into the six steps shown in the box below.

Six preparatory steps for evaluating a service:

1. setting down the aims and objectives;

2. specifying the impact model;

3. specifying the target population;

4. estimating the extent of the target problem in the target population;

5. assessing the need for the service; and

6. specifying the delivery system design.

These tasks are all easier to do when you are setting up a new service, as building in evaluation is much easier at the planning stage when there is some flexibility. Moreover, addressing evaluation issues at the outset can help to define the service's goals and procedures. Specifying how a new service will be evaluated usually helps clarify what it is trying to achieve, and vice versa. However, these preparatory steps are also useful if you are evaluating an existing service.

Aims and Objectives

Aims and objectives are the *sine qua non* of evaluation, especially for new services. They articulate what the service is for. Without knowing what the service is trying to do, the evaluator has no benchmarks against which to measure its operation. People often confuse aims and objectives, or speak about them as though they are the same. However, there is a useful distinction to be made between the two terms.

Aims are global statements of the desired outcomes of the service, expressed in a general, often rather idealized way. For example: "The service aims to reduce depression in mothers of young children." *Objectives* are specific goals, ideally occurring within a specific period of time, that detail what the service is actually going to do to achieve its aims and that give specific targets to indicate whether or not the aims have been met. The objectives should be clear, simple and, if possible, measurable, so that there will be no ambiguity about whether each one has been reached. For example, "The service plans to set up three support groups for mothers of children under two years of age in the London Borough of Camden by the end of the current financial year."

Aims and objectives:

Aims are global statements of desired outcomes.

Objectives are specific goals, which:

- ideally occur within a specific time period;

- detail what the service will do to achieve its aims;

- indicate whether or not the aims will have been met; and

- are clear, simple, and, if possible, measurable.

The exercise of specifying aims and objectives often helps to clarify the goals of a service. Carrying it out within a clinical team usually results in the team members having a better understanding of each other's values and assumptions. Furthermore, without aims and objectives, team members may not know what they are supposed to be doing or may even be pulling in different directions or undermining each other. For example, in a community alcohol service, some members may emphasize prevention, others counseling, some individual work, others work with couples or groups, yet others research. While there is clearly healthiness in this diversity, the team also needs a sense of direction so that its energies are not spread too thinly.

The Impact Model

The impact model specifies the theoretical or empirical basis for each of the activities that the service is undertaking (Rossi et al., 1999). It may never be formally specified, but thinking about each of its three components helps team members to plan an effective service. These components are:

- The *causal hypothesis*, which describes what causes or maintains the target problem(s) that the service is seeking to modify.

- The *intervention hypothesis*, which specifies how the proposed intervention will affect that causal determinant.

- The *action hypothesis*, which asserts that the proposed intervention will in fact reduce the target problem(s).

For instance, in our maternal depression example, the causal hypothesis is that depression in mothers of young children is partly caused by a lack of social support; the intervention hypothesis is that a support group will increase social support; and the action hypothesis is that the support group will decrease maternal depression. These three parts of the impact model are depicted in Figure 11.2.

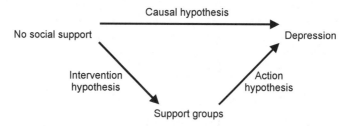

Figure 11.2 The impact model

Sometimes, however, it may not be possible or necessary to address the cause of the problem directly. For instance, with adult survivors of child sexual abuse we cannot alter the cause, because it occurred years ago. Furthermore, addressing the cause may not be the best strategy for alleviating the target problems: etiology does not necessarily determine treatment. The point of specifying the impact model is simply to make the rationale for the service's actions as explicit as possible.

The Target Population

Having specified the impact model, the next step is to identify the targets, direct and indirect, for the intervention. *Direct targets* are those people on whom the intervention is specifically focused, e.g., mothers of children under two. It is important to define the unit of analysis, which could be individuals, families or groups. *Indirect targets* are those people who may benefit indirectly from the service, e.g., the families of the above women. Including the indirect targets gives a full picture of the impact of the service. Ideally, the targets should be specified in the aims and objectives of the service.

Target boundaries should be clearly defined using both inclusion and exclusion criteria, e.g., a specified geographical catchment area, and demographic and clinical characteristics of the client group. It is important to strike a balance between criteria that are overinclusive and those that are too restrictive. The following model, taken from a local drop-in service for people with severe mental health problems, is a good example of a target description with both inclusion and exclusion criteria:

> To be in the Target Group, a person has to be: aged over 16 years; be living, staying or sleeping out in the South Camden sector of Bloomsbury Health District; have severe and enduring mental health problems; have positive or negative symptoms of psychotic illness; have had previous contact with mental health services; not be actively involved with other services; be experiencing severe social problems. People who meet these criteria but whose primary problem is due to the abuse of alcohol or drugs do not come into the Target Group. (Compass Project, 1989)

Estimating the Extent of the Target Problem in the Target Population

When planning a service, it is naturally important to estimate the extent of the target problem in the target population. Three epidemiological concepts are useful here. *Incidence* is the number of new cases during a specified time period, e.g., the one-year incidence of flu. *Prevalence* is the number of existing cases, either at a specified time ("point prevalence"), or during a time interval. For example, Pantelis et al.'s (1988) point prevalence study attempted a census of all individuals diagnosed as suffering from schizophrenia in the South Camden sector of London on a specific day.

Incidence and prevalence are related to each other by the duration of the illness: higher incidence or a longer duration will both increase the prevalence. Incidence is a more useful measure for illnesses of short duration, e.g., flu; prevalence is more useful for those of longer duration, e.g., Alzheimer's disease. With psychological problems, it is not always clear whether to measure the extent of the target problem in terms of incidence or prevalence. For example, in providing services for dealing with cases of child abuse, do you want to measure the number of new cases per month (incidence), or the total number of cases on the social services list (prevalence)? The issue is whether you are concerned with detecting and treating new cases as they appear or with knowing the number of existing cases in a population, whatever the time of origin.

The third concept, *population at risk*, is the subset of the general population that is more at risk of contracting a disease, e.g., intravenous drug users are a population at risk for HIV infection. It is particularly helpful to consider this target group for preventive projects.

There are several methods for estimating the extent of the target problem. There is a trade-off between their validity on the one hand and their complexity and cost on the other.

1. *Surveys* and *censuses* can be done in order to get the respondents' direct estimates of the size and severity of a problem. They generally yield the most valid data, especially if they include structured interview measures, but they

are time consuming and expensive to carry out. Two large national surveys of the prevalence of psychological disorders provide useful comparative data: the US National Comorbidity Study (Kessler et al., 1994), and the UK National Survey of Psychiatric Morbidity (Bebbington et al., 2000a).

2. *Rates under treatment*. The size of the target problem in the target population can sometimes be estimated by looking at the rates under treatment in similar communities (if they exist). The number of people who seek treatment is usually a small fraction of the actual number of cases, but there may be ways of estimating the size of the untreated population, based on previous studies. For example, in the National Comorbidity Study, only about a quarter of people suffering from a psychological disorder had ever in their lifetime received help from mental health specialty services (Kessler et al., 1994), and in the UK National Survey of Psychiatric Morbidity, fewer than 14% of people with a neurotic disorder were currently receiving any formal treatment (Bebbington et al., 2000a).

3. *Indicators*. This method uses statistical techniques, such as multiple regression, to predict the size of the target problem from nonclinical criteria. For example, one indicator of the number of heroin addicts in a community is the number of arrests for sale or possession of the drug (Hartnoll et al., 1985).

4. *Key informants*. The researcher can use "networking" or "snowballing" sampling methods (see Chapter 10) to find knowledgeable people who might be able to help estimate the extent of the target problem. This is a simple and inexpensive method. In our experience, 20 or 30 respondents are usually sufficient. The advantage is that it develops the support of influential workers in the community; the drawback is the possible bias of the individuals surveyed. Qualitative and/or quantitative interviewing methods can be used.

Needs Assessment

Assessing the extent of the target problem in the target population is the first step in planning a service, as it gives an indication of what the volume of demand is likely to be. However, it is easy to assume that everyone suffering from the target problem needs or desires the service, which is not necessarily true. Needs assessments collect data that are more relevant to the service's operation: they are the health-care equivalent of market research.

The concept of *need* is often used in a technical sense, defined as a problem for which there is a potentially effective intervention (Bebbington et al., 1997; McKillip, 1987; Stevens & Gabbay, 1991). Under this somewhat counter-intuitive definition, need is assessed by professionals, rather than by the users themselves. It is not determined by the severity of the problem, but by whether something effective can be done about it. In contrast, *demand* is defined as what people ask for and *supply* as what is provided.

Stevens and Gabbay (1991), in an article nicely entitled "Needs assessment needs assessment," discuss the relationship between need, demand, and supply.

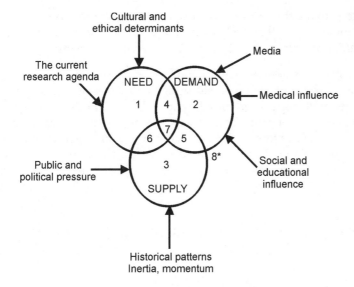

NEED   What people benefit from

DEMAND   What people ask for

SUPPLY   What is provided

*The external field where a potential service is not needed, demanded or supplied

Figure 11.3 Need, demand, and supply: influences and overlaps. Crown copyright. Reproduced from Stevens & Gabbay (1991) with the permission of the Controller of Her Majesty's Stationery Office

They depict the relationship of the three concepts using a Venn diagram (see Figure 11.3). The diagram helps conceptualize and label the areas where the concepts overlap, e.g., need that is supplied (areas 6 and 7) is called "met need" and need that is not supplied (areas 1 and 4) is called "unmet need."

Needs and demands can be assessed using the methods described above for assessing the extent of the target problem. However, such studies are not always popular with health-service managers and politicians, as they often imply spending further resources to satisfy whatever unmet needs are identified.

Delivery System Design

With new services, the foregoing are the preliminary steps in establishing the likely need and demand. The final step is to design the service itself. The delivery system design, which is ideally set out in the form of an *operational policy document*, specifies how the clinical team will go about delivering the service. It includes the organizational arrangements, such as procedures and activities, and structural aspects such as the physical setting, staff, and materials that are required to provide the service. The discussion needed to produce an operational policy document, and the existence of the document itself, may help anticipate some common problems in newly established clinical teams.

Once it has decided on its operational policy, the team can use role-plays or simulations to try to predict whether things will work smoothly in practice (e.g., what exactly will happen when a client walks in the door or when someone makes a telephone referral). Larger scale services may use operations research methods (a set of scientifically based procedures to aid decision making) to see if the services are planned in an optimal way, for example, whether the staffing levels at different sites are appropriate for the anticipated workloads.

MONITORING THE PROCESS OF SERVICE DELIVERY

Monitoring the process of service delivery:

- The central question is "Who does what to whom?"

- Monitoring service delivery can be divided into monitoring coverage and implementation.

- Monitoring coverage asks the question "Who is the service reaching?"

- A service is biased if it favors certain subgroups of its target population at the expense of others.

- Coverage can be assessed from service records, by surveys, and by examining dropouts.

- Monitoring implementation asks "What service is being given?"

- Implementation can be assessed by observation, service records or databases, and surveys.

Having gone through the above preparatory steps, the evaluation now focuses on what kind of service is being delivered: i.e., the process of the service, in Donabedian's (1980) terminology. Monitoring the process of service delivery means asking "Who does what to whom?" It also addresses such questions as "Is this service being delivered in the best possible way?" and "Is it accessible to its consumers?" (Maxwell, 1984). This differs from outcome evaluation, covered below, which assesses whether users benefit from the service.

Rossi et al. (1999) distinguish two main targets of monitoring delivery: coverage and implementation. Monitoring coverage asks the question "Who is the service reaching?", whereas monitoring implementation asks "What service is being given?" In addition, there is financial monitoring (to make sure that the funds are being properly used) and legal monitoring, to make sure that the service operates within the relevant laws (e.g., equal opportunities, health and safety). These latter areas are specialized activities, being the province of accountants and lawyers respectively, and we will not cover them here.

Coverage and Bias

Coverage is defined as the extent to which the service reaches its intended target population: is it reaching everyone it is supposed to, or just a certain subgroup of the target population, or even mainly people outside the target population? The related concept of *bias* is defined as the extent to which subgroups of the target population participate differentially, i.e., the degree to which some subgroups receive greater coverage than others. Bias may arise from several factors:

- Self-selection, e.g., if only the more motivated people come to a drop-in service.

- Program actions, e.g., if staff favor some service users at the expense of others. In particular, there may be *creaming*: that is, a bias towards the more advantaged subgroups of the target population. For instance, when Community Mental Health Centers were first set up in the USA, they tended to see a large proportion of better functioning people who were easier to work with, neglecting older people and people with severe and enduring difficulties (Orford, 1992). Other examples of program bias are where services do not adequately cater for the needs of physically disabled users or of users from certain ethnic groups (possibly because of unconscious racism).

- Unforeseen influences, such as where the service is located, e.g., if it is poorly served by transportation (strictly speaking, this is an aspect of structure rather than process). These factors may again reflect unconscious program bias.

Undercoverage occurs when some people in the target population have unmet needs. This is often a problem in face-to-face psychology services, as there are usually many people in the community who need the service but do not get it (Bebbington et al., 2000b; Kessler et al., 1994). *Overcoverage* occurs when some inappropriate targets are served. For example, in health promotion campaigns, e.g., to reduce smoking or to promote safer sex, material may inevitably be directed at some people outside the target population. This is usually not a great problem.

Assessing Coverage

Several methods can be used to assess coverage:

- *Service records* are the most obvious and commonly used method. Most psychology services keep records of basic client information, often in a computer database. These records can be analyzed according to demographic characteristics, e.g., client gender, age, or ethnicity, and possibly also according to clinical characteristics such as presenting problem or referral source.

- *Surveys* can be used when services are not targeted at defined groups of individuals, but at an entire community. They are more appropriate for preventive, health education or health promotion services. For instance, Barker et al. (1993) assessed the coverage of a BBC television series on preventive mental health. Although it was viewed by a national audience, the series was primarily aimed at certain subgroups of the population, that is, those people who were experiencing psychological problems themselves or who had a friend or relative who was. A national survey was used to estimate the nature of the viewing audience and their reactions to the series.

• *Analysis of dropouts* can be used to assess bias, by comparing people who participate fully in a service with those who drop out before the end. A high dropout rate clearly indicates that something is wrong with the service. It may reflect client dissatisfaction, or conditions in the community that prevent full participation (e.g., stigmatization of service users). Data on dropouts can come from service records or from surveys designed to find nonparticipants. Such data help identify subgroups of the target population who are not receiving the service. It may be possible to ask nonusers about their perceptions of the service and then to use their opinions to re-design the intervention to be more suited to their needs (an example of the formative use of evaluation).

An Index of Coverage Efficiency

If you need to specify precisely the accuracy of coverage, the following efficiency index can be used (Rossi et al., 1999):

$$\left(\frac{\text{number served in target population}}{\text{total number in target population}} - \frac{\text{number not in target population}}{\text{total number served}} \right) \times 100$$

This takes a value of $+100$ when the actual number served is equal to the designated target population, with no inappropriate targets. It takes a value of -100 if only inappropriate targets are served, and an intermediate value when there is a mixture of appropriate and inappropriate targets. For example, with a target population estimated at 2000, assume that you actually serve 1000, of which 800 are appropriate. Then the efficiency index would be: $(800/2000 - 200/1000) \times 100 = +20$.

The formula provides a means of estimating the trade-offs in a service including appropriate and inappropriate targets. A manager confronted with an index of -40 might impose additional selection criteria to eliminate some of the inappropriate targets, and extra recruitment to secure replacements. Another option would be to expand the program to include more appropriate targets, i.e., keep the same number of inappropriate targets but increase the total number served.

Service Implementation

Monitoring service coverage focuses on whom the service is reaching; monitoring service *implementation* or delivery focuses on what kind of service the users are getting. Is the service's delivery consistent with its design specifications, i.e., is it delivering what it is supposed to be delivering? You can look at both descriptive aspects, to label what components of the service are given, and quality aspects, to describe how well they are given. Implementation can be assessed by:

- *Observation* (qualitative or quantitative) in the clinical setting.

- *Service records*, e.g., in antenatal care, to ensure that the right number of visits were made and the correct things done at each one. Standard clinical records can be augmented by asking clinicians to complete a checklist of activities. They can be given a standard form to tick off each procedure as it is completed, e.g., in HIV pre- and post-test counseling, or an audit team can review the casenote files at regular intervals to make sure that they are complete and that proper procedures are being followed.

- *Management information systems* and computerized case registers can keep track of the type of service each client received at each visit.

- *Service user surveys* may be desirable when it is not possible to obtain user data routinely as part of service activities, or when the size of the target group is large and it is more efficient to do a sample survey than to obtain data on all participants. You can ask the clients about what kind of service they actually received. A natural step if you are doing this is also to ask them about their satisfaction with the service and what its impact was, which leads into the final area, outcome evaluation.

OUTCOME EVALUATION

- Outcome evaluation examines the impact of the service.

- One key area of impact is the extent of clinical benefit.

- Necessity often dictates simple one-group pretest–posttest designs.

- Outcome is assessed using measures linked to the objectives of the service.

- Studies often include measures of user satisfaction.

- It is important to address economic variables in addition to psychological ones.

Outcome evaluation examines the impact of the service. It asks the crucial question "Do users benefit from this service?" Benefits may be manifest in the form of an improvement in the target problem (sometimes known as "health gain") or in the form of changes in attitude about the problem, so that the client, or other stakeholders such as parents or carers, experience it as less problematic.

It is also important to bear in mind the possibility of negative outcomes. Many programs, especially in the political arena, are subject to the *"law of unintended effects."* In other words, policy changes that are intended to make matters better actually end up by making them worse. Or they make improvements in one area at the expense of deterioration in another. An example within clinical psychology is "psychological debriefing" for victims of traumatic incidents. Such programs were established with the plausible rationale that having counseling immediately after a trauma might prevent the development of post-traumatic stress disorder. However, research has shown that, far from helping many victims, psychological debriefing may often make them worse off than if they had had no intervention at all (Mayou et al., 2000).

Assessing outcome involves applying the research methods that we have discussed in previous chapters, in so far as it can be done within the constraints of the clinical setting. The first step is to choose outcome measures that capture the key objectives of the service (e.g., a service aimed at helping depressed adults might use the Beck Depression Inventory). The second step is to select a research design that will assess any changes in those measures and, if possible, enable such changes to be attributed to the service itself rather than to other variables (Cook & Campbell, 1979; see also Chapter 8). Of course, in many working services, this is a counsel of perfection, and the evaluator may have to be content with drawing inferences from less than adequate designs or measures.

Recall the efficacy versus effectiveness research distinction, which we examined in Chapter 8. (Efficacy research uses randomized designs, often in highly controlled research clinic settings; whereas effectiveness research uses non-randomized designs to study interventions as they actually happen in real-world settings.) Evaluation research is by definition effectiveness research, and will often use very simple designs, such as the one-group pretest–posttest design.

Naturalistic field research of this sort is clearly imperfect from the point of view of internal validity. The issue here, however, is whether it is good enough to draw plausible conclusions that can aid practical decisions (Seligman, 1995). Managers and policy makers are often more convinced by research conducted in their own service, even if it is scientifically flawed, than by a methodologically sound piece of research published in a reputable scientific journal, which was conducted in another setting by other investigators (Watts, 1984).

Client Satisfaction Surveys

One scientifically problematic, but professionally valuable, area of study is client satisfaction research (Lebow, 1982). Clients' views of the service they have received are usually assessed via standardized self-report instruments, e.g., the Client Satisfaction Questionnaire (CSQ: Larsen et al., 1979), which can be adapted to most clinical services.

Clients' views are often minimized or dismissed by professionals, usually on two grounds. First, that the clients' views are invalid, because of their psychological problems, or the transference aspects of the therapeutic relationship, or positive response sets generally. Second, client satisfaction surveys mainly use a one-group posttest-only design, which has many internal validity threats (Cook & Campbell, 1979; Seligman, 1995; see also Chapter 8).

Invalidity and design problems are hard to overcome in client satisfaction research, but it seems wrong to use these problems to dismiss the whole enterprise out of hand (Lebow, 1982). Professionals' views of the effectiveness of the services they deliver also suffer from validity problems; service evaluation ideally needs to take both perspectives into account, and ideally that of third parties (e.g., family members) as well. Positive response sets in clients' reports can be avoided to some extent by asking clients explicitly to list any problems with or complaints about the service (Parry, 1992), and threats to internal validity can be taken into account when interpreting the findings.

One published example of such research is the *Consumer Reports* study (Seligman, 1995), which we discussed in Chapter 8. It used a large, though unrepresentative, sample to gather post hoc consumer views from people who had had psychological therapy, looking, for example, at their satisfaction with different therapeutic modalities and orientations. Seligman (1995), while acknowledging the problems with this approach, highlighted its usefulness in terms of examining how people experience therapy as it is actually conducted in the real world.

Patient-focused Research and Outcomes Management

One distinctive approach to evaluation research in clinical services is patient-focused research (Lambert, 2001). This sets out to evaluate the outcome of individual patients, in contrast to the groupings of patients that are the usual focus of evaluation research. The basic procedure is to compare each patient's progress throughout the therapy against the trajectory that would be expected, given that patient's initial clinical status. (Such trajectories are established via normative research involving thousands of clients, but in practice it would be sufficient to note instances in which clients show statistically reliable deterioration.) Departures from the trajectory can be noted and acted upon. Feeding back to clinicians information on each patient's outcome as the therapy progresses, particularly if the patient is doing less well than would be expected, has been shown to enhance the final clinical outcome (Lambert et al., 2001). Furthermore, this information on the progress of individual patients can be used to initiate improvements in the service delivery system, an approach known as *outcomes management* (e.g., Lyons et al., 1997).

Cost-effectiveness

A final issue to consider is cost-effectiveness evaluation (Krupnik & Pincus, 1992; Mangen, 1988). This compares the service's costs with its outcomes, in order to ensure that its funds are being well used. In economic terms, it compares inputs to outputs. This kind of evaluation has become more prominent in both the US and the UK, as purchasers of health-care services (in the US health maintenance organizations or insurance companies, in the UK health authorities) must decide what to spend their limited resources on. Their decisions will be based on which services they think will give the greatest outcome per unit of resource employed.

There are clearly problems in measuring both input and output. At the input end, costing must take into account both direct costs, principally psychologists' contact time, and overheads, such as the cost of buildings, equipment, and support staff (Cape et al., 1993).

The output end of the calculation is even more problematic, since there is no universally agreed upon measure of effectiveness or of benefit. Different health-care services (e.g., heart surgery compared to psychiatric in-patient treatment) use different criteria to measure outcome. One possible solution, derived from health economics, is to combine quality of life and life expectancy into *quality adjusted life years,* or "QALYs." Thus an outcome of a treatment, say an operation for cancer, may give a person a high quality of life for a short time or a medium quality of life for a longer time. These outcomes would be considered equivalent in terms of QALYs. Such an approach, although it fulfils the economists' goal of giving a single index upon which to base resource allocation, clearly makes a number of problematic assumptions about how to weight quite different clinical outcomes (Cox et al., 1992) and is also difficult to apply to psychological interventions.

Another approach is to attempt to measure the economic burden of illness or psychological disorder in terms of lost productivity, increased social services expenditure, and increased use of medical services (e.g., general practitioner consultations, emergency room visits, or in-patient hospitalization). Then the outcome of a psychological intervention can be partly assessed by the savings made in terms of increased productivity and reduced social services and health-care expenditure—often referred to as "cost offset"—which may represent a substantial financial return in relation to the expenditure on the psychological intervention (Krupnik & Pincus, 1992).

An example of a cost-offset study is Humphreys and Moos's (2001) analysis of the consequences of encouraging substance abuse patients to participate in self-help groups. (We cited this study in Chapter 8 as an example of a quasi-experimental design, but it is noteworthy in the present context for its attention to economic variables.) The study compared in-patients in substance abuse programs that emphasized self-help groups with patients in programs that emphasized a traditional cognitive behavioral approach, in terms of their subsequent health-care costs in the year following discharge. Humphreys and Moos found that the patients who were in the cognitive-behaviorally oriented programs received post-discharge care costing an average of $12,100 per year, whereas patients in the self-help oriented programs received post-discharge care costing an average of $7,400 per year, thus demonstrating a significant cost offset for those programs that featured self-help groups as part of the therapy.

A simple form of cost-effectiveness analysis, and one with direct relevance to practitioners, is to compare practitioner input, measured in terms of number of sessions, with client output in terms of clinical improvement. All therapists must ask themselves, implicitly or explicitly, whether it is better to give one client 20 sessions or two clients 10 sessions (or 10 clients two sessions). Cost-effectiveness evaluation attempts to make the basis of such decisions explicit. Howard et al.'s (1986) analysis of dose-response relationships in psychotherapy falls under this heading. They used the statistical technique of probit analysis on a data set drawn from 15 published studies to estimate the improvement rate of clients after a given number of sessions. They estimated, for example, that 53% of clients had improved by eight sessions and that 74% of clients had improved by 26 sessions. However, to be a true cost-effectiveness analysis, the input must then be expressed in monetary terms: that it costs so many dollars to produce such and such an outcome.

CHAPTER SUMMARY

Evaluation is applied research that aims to assess the worth of a specific service. It includes the areas of clinical audit, quality assurance, needs assessment, and outcomes evaluation, although each of these areas has its own distinct literature. Evaluation studies are conducted for the benefit of the various stakeholders in the service, although different stakeholders often have different priorities for the evaluation. Organizational and political issues are crucial, both in deciding the priorities of the evaluation, and in addressing the sense of threat that often accompanies it. To start with, the evaluator asks two central questions: "What is the service trying to do?" and "How will you know if it has done it?" Answering these questions is simpler if the service has explicit, agreed-upon aims and objectives, and a well-thought out rationale for why it is doing what it does.

Evaluations can address the process or the outcome of a service. Process evaluation examines who is coming to the service and what services they are being given. It is important to ensure that the service delivery does not unfairly favor certain subgroups of the population at the expense of others. Outcome evaluation examines the impact of the service—whether users benefit or not. In addition to examining clinical outcome, evaluators may look at client satisfaction, and at economic indicators of costs and benefits.

FURTHER READING

Rossi et al.'s (1999) text, which we have drawn on extensively here, gives a comprehensive framework for conducting a program evaluation. Shadish et al. (1991) present the conceptual background, and discuss the ideas of the major figures in the modern American program evaluation movement. Weiss (1972), in one of the founding texts of this movement, gives an excellent discussion of the rational and irrational feelings about evaluation. Patton's (1997) *Utilization-focused evaluation* is also appealing for its broad, practical approach. Seligman's (1995) *Consumer Reports* study and the subsequent commentary on it (in the October 1996 special issue of *American Psychologist*) give an airing to many of the issues raised by using imperfect research designs to answer practical questions. The quality assurance and audit literature as applied to clinical psychology are reviewed by Cape and Barkham (in press) and Firth-Cozens (1993).

CHAPTER 12

ANALYSIS, INTERPRETATION, AND DISSEMINATION

KEY POINTS IN THIS CHAPTER

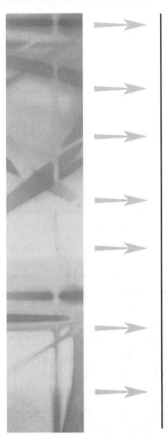

The final stage of the research process involves making sense of your data, first for yourself, then for a wider audience.

Analysis means establishing what the findings are and how they answer the research questions.

Qualitative analysis is an inductive process of developing a set of themes or a conceptual framework that captures the main ideas in the data.

Quantitative analysis can be exploratory or confirmatory, depending on the research questions.

The concepts of statistical conclusion validity, effect size, and clinical significance are used to evaluate the strength and significance of quantitative findings.

Interpretation involves understanding the psychological meaning of the results, and their scientific and professional implications.

Dissemination means communicating both the findings and your understanding of them to other people.

Having collected the data, the final stage of the research process consists of making sense of the findings, first for yourself, then for a wider audience. This stage can itself be broken down into three parts: analysis, interpretation, and dissemination. Analysis means establishing what the findings are and how they answer the research questions, interpretation means understanding the findings in terms of their broader implications, and dissemination means communicating them to other people. Analysis is typically reported in the Results section of a research paper; interpretation is reported in the Discussion section. As always, the components overlap and intermingle: an interpretation of the findings might suggest a further analysis of the data, or presenting the study at a conference might lead to new ideas about its interpretation. However, for simplicity, we will cover the three components as though they were distinct and sequential.

The goal of the analysis is simple: to use the data to answer the research questions. We will look at the steps undertaken in the qualitative and quantitative approaches. However, the specific techniques of data analysis, both qualitative and quantitative, involve specialized methods that are beyond our present scope. Here we will focus on the general strategies that researchers use when analyzing their data.

QUALITATIVE DATA ANALYSIS

- Qualitative analysis can take either a within-case (idiographic) or a cross-case approach.

- The first step is usually to transcribe the data (paying attention to confidentiality issues).

- It is important to become familiar with the data, by listening to tapes and rereading transcripts.

- Qualitative analysis is an inductive procedure, which involves three related processes: identifying meaning, categorizing, and integrating.

As described in Chapters 6 and 7, qualitative data come in various forms, such as transcripts from interviews, field notes from observations, or other kinds of texts. It is usually unstructured and often voluminous. Qualitative researchers are faced with finding ways of systematically analyzing these collections of words. This problem is compounded by the well-known issue of "qualitative overload": that qualitative investigations, even ones with a small sample size, usually generate vast quantities of data. This abundance of data needs to be analyzed and represented to the reader clearly and accurately.

Much has recently been written about qualitative data analysis. Key references include Strauss and Corbin's (1998) description of the grounded theory approach; Smith et al.'s (1999) presentation of interpretative phenomenological analysis; Potter and Wetherell's (1987) book on discourse analysis, as well as some more general approaches (e.g., Miles & Huberman, 1994; Patton, 2002; Taylor & Bogdan, 1998). There are also several computer programs now available to assist with qualitative analysis (e.g., Atlas-TI; EZ-Text; or QSR-Nud*ist). Some of these tend to favor a particular analytic approach (e.g., Nud*ist is based on grounded theory analysis).

Here we will attempt to sketch out some general principles in analyzing qualitative data. However, it is worth noting that different qualitative orientations use different methods of analysis, and they tend to use different vocabulary to describe similar procedures.

Different orientations, and the goals of particular studies, also vary in the depth of interpretation or inference. Some approaches keep to a fairly descriptive level, without much interpretation. Others go beyond description: they attempt to explain the meanings, causes, structures, or patterns in the phenomenon being examined. The degree of interpretation partly depends on the goal of the particular investigation.

Flexibility is required in all phases of qualitative research, including the analysis. It is important to adapt the analytic method to the data, to the research question, and to your own cognitive style and talents. However, it is also important to be explicit about your procedures. In other words, flexibility does not mean vagueness or sloppiness.

Within-case and Cross-case Analysis

Regardless of one's general approach to qualitative research, the data may be analyzed either within or across cases.

Within-case analysis is idiographic in nature, concentrating on understanding the features of a single case, or a small number of cases. The material may be presented with minimal interpretation, by organizing it chronologically into a narrative. In this descriptive, narrative approach, the researchers restrict themselves to arranging the material into a story, which is allowed to speak for itself. Such presentations can be an excellent way of demonstrating the existence of a phenomenon. A good example is Bogdan and Taylor's (1976) study of "Ed Murphy," which demonstrates the existence of perceptive self-awareness in a young man labeled as being "retarded."

However, even when qualitative researchers focus on individual cases, they are usually interested in going beyond the descriptive level. This approach is consistent with clinical psychologists' interest in understanding the meaning of individuals' situations. For example, Varvin and Stiles (1999) studied a political refugee's experience of therapy, using a particular theoretical framework (the "assimilation model") to interpret the data.

Cross-case analysis looks across individuals in order to identify common themes about the phenomenon being studied, aiming to see which aspects are shared across participants. Usually the researcher is also interested in describing variations within the phenomenon, that is, themes or patterns that characterize only some participants' accounts. For example, Knox et al. (1997) studied 13 clients' perceptions of self-disclosure from their therapists. They identified several categories of consequences, some of which were typical (e.g., "therapist seen as more real") and some variant (e.g., "client used therapist as model").

Preliminaries to Qualitative Data Analysis

Data Preparation

The first step in qualitative analysis is to prepare the data. In interview studies or studies using recorded interactions, this involves transcribing the recordings— usually a laborious and time-consuming process.

Transcription is in fact a form of analysis (Riessman, 1993), because of the many theory-guided decisions that must be made along the way. For example, decisions must be made about how to break the speech or interaction into units, and how to record nonverbal and paralinguistic elements of speech (e.g., speech rate, loudness, pausing). Even the seemingly straightforward task of writing down the spoken words turns out to be complicated by repetitions and irrelevancies, as well as our unconscious tendency to edit what we hear, ignoring things that don't make sense and hearing what we expect to hear. Clearly, there is no single correct method of transcription; rather, the transcription method should be chosen for the task at hand. Thus, for the careful analysis of moment-by-moment interaction, many researchers use Jefferson's system, e.g., presented in ten Have (1999), which measures pauses and the exact beginning and end of interruptions, among other things (see also Mergenthaler & Stinson, 1992, for widely used standards for transcribing therapy sessions). On the other hand, for transcribing a qualitative interview, the best approach is the simple method illustrated in the sample interview given in Chapter 6.

Before beginning the analysis, it is vital to check the transcripts for accuracy, and also to ensure that participants' anonymity is preserved by removing or disguising names and other identifying information. In research using multiple perspectives and sources of information (e.g., Comprehensive Process Analysis: Elliott, 1989a), the different types of data must also be collated. Patton (2002) refers to the compendium of data on a case as a case record.

Immersion

Before the formal analysis, it is important to immerse yourself in the data, by listening to the tape recordings and by reading the transcripts several times over. This gives you an overall feel for the data's scope and meanings, although you may not be able to articulate your understanding at this stage. Systematic understanding is a product of the formal analysis.

Processes in Qualitative Data Analysis

Qualitative data analysis can be thought of as involving three separate sets of processes, which we will call *identifying meaning*, *categorizing*, and *integrating*. Naturally, this division is a simplification: the processes represent related activities and the boundaries between them are to some extent arbitrary. Furthermore, the processes are not linear: researchers often cycle back and forth between them. Different approaches to qualitative analysis make use of different forms and mixes of these activities. However, they all describe an inductive process, which is common to all qualitative research, of going from the raw data to ideas about the data.

It is usually unwise to begin by analyzing the transcript as a whole: global analysis encourages ignoring data that do not fit one's expectations or emerging understanding. For this reason, most approaches adopt some type of microanalysis, involving close attention to words and phrases. Some approaches, notably grounded theory, suggest dividing the data into units before coding. The most common is the *meaning unit*, which consists of material on a single point in the participant's description, often approximating a verbal sentence. Its use is largely a practical strategy; its exact definition is not critical and may vary among researchers and among studies with different research objectives.

Identifying Meaning

The researcher begins the formal part of the analysis by going through the data and trying to identify the ideas that are being expressed. That is, before categories can be created, the data must be understood. However, texts can be understood in many different ways. Thus, it is not surprising that different approaches to qualitative data analysis take different systematic approaches to reading and translating the data in ways that help reveal their meaning. Many of the approaches to qualitative inquiry noted in Chapter 5 emphasize distinctive approaches:

- *Data summary*. Some approaches (empirical phenomenology, grounded theory analysis) include a step of condensing what is expressed by each meaning unit into a brief phrase (e.g., "felt numb at first"). This is most useful with large meaning units, and may involve some translation of what respondents have said into psychological language.

- *Explicating implicit meaning*. More interpretive or hermeneutic approaches, including some forms of empirical phenomenology and discourse analysis, may focus on bringing out what is said implicitly "between the lines." This is not unconscious meaning but rather what the speakers would have understood each other to have meant.

- *Interpreting unconscious meaning*. Other interpretive and critical approaches (including forms of discourse analysis) may read beyond the speaker's apparent awareness, based on some interpretive theory (e.g., psychoanalysis, Jungian archetypes, feminist theory). This approach is necessary when the analyst is dealing with apparent self-deception on the part of the respondent; however, it may not sit well with readers who don't share the interpretive framework of the analyst.

- *Process description*. Finally, discourse and narrative analysis approaches focus on characterizing the nature of the observable speech action (e.g., minimizing, playing up; summing up).

Although different brands of qualitative analysis emphasize different ways of reading data, in actual practice there is much overlap. In carrying out a qualitative analysis, you will want to consider making flexible use of a range of such activities, as appropriate to your data and research questions.

Categorizing

All forms of qualitative analysis engage in some form of category generation, in which the researcher groups together important concepts or ideas. The previous ("identifying meaning") phase usually results in a tentative set of labels corresponding to the set of ideas in the data; the task now is to organize them conceptually.

Sometimes, the data are first organized into large "domains" corresponding to major aspects of the phenomenon being studied. These domains do not provide answers to the research questions, rather they are ways of organizing the data in order to make it easier to analyze. Domains may be structured in different ways, for example, corresponding to topics addressed by the research questions, or following a broad narrative structure (e.g., "background," "event," and "aftermath").

The process of giving initial labels leads to the identification of key concepts, often referred to as "categories" or "themes." Such categories usually consist of a word or phrase that captures an essential meaning, often at a more abstract level. Categories are not necessarily mutually exclusive; that is, a particular unit of data may be assigned to a number of different categories. For example, consider one statement from a client with intellectual disabilities (mental retardation in the US usage) in Mattison and Pistrang's (2000) study of the ending of keyworker relationships: "It does worry me because it means having to make a fresh start with someone else that I don't know their philosophies." When first encountered, early in the analysis, this statement was tentatively assigned to several different categories: "worry," "starting again," and "uncertainty."

The category names may derive from numerous sources, including the respondent's own words, the research literature, or metaphor. The development of categories is an interpretive process that involves both close attention to the meanings expressed in the data and the researcher's own ideas.

Two methods are useful here: psychological reflection and the constant comparative method. Wertz (1985) has described *psychological reflection* in terms similar to therapeutic empathy. In particular, he describes a process of "entering and dwelling," in which the researcher attempts to immerse themself in the participant's world. The researcher tries to slow down the story and to dwell on its details and meanings, setting aside (bracketing) the assumption that he or she already understands what is being described. At the same time, the researcher tries to step back from the description, attending to meanings rather than matters of truth or falsity. Often, this process incorporates a dialogue with the data, in which the researcher asks such questions as, "What is really meant here?",

"What kind of thing is being described?", and "How does this relate to the phenomenon I'm trying to understand?" This method is both descriptive and interpretive in that it tries to stay close to the data while still generating a deeper understanding through drawing out the participant's implicit meanings and assumptions.

The *constant comparative method*, originally articulated by Glaser and Strauss (1967), essentially involves exploring similarities and differences between the emerging categories. As new categories are identified, they are compared to the other ones in the current set. If an idea is similar to an existing category, it is added to that category and may help to clarify or elaborate it. If it is judged to differ from existing categories, it is noted as a possible new category.

The process of categorization continues until *saturation* is reached; that is, until categories are no longer added or elaborated. As analysis proceeds, the researcher discovers that fewer and fewer categories are added, and the analytic process becomes more and more one of coding data into existing categories.

Integrating

As categories begin to emerge from the data, the researcher attempts to make connections between them. The aim is usually to create some sort of conceptual framework, rather than a list of unrelated categories. Often a hierarchical structure can be identified, with more descriptive, lower order categories functioning as properties or defining features of more abstract, higher order categories. The process is cyclical and interpretive, involving refining and linking concepts, going back to the original data to check for accuracy, and revising the categories and the framework.

For example, in a study of the benefits of mutual support groups for parents of children with disabilities (Solomon et al., 2001), three broad categories were identified: "control and agency in the world," "sense of belonging to a community," and "self-change." Each of these subsumed several lower order categories: e.g., "sense of belonging" included "being understood," "sharing emotions," and "friendships."

In the grounded theory approach, researchers attempt to identify a single, higher order, unifying category—often referred to as a "core category." It is intended to capture the essence of the phenomenon, the headline of the story. For example, in Solomon et al.'s (2001) study of mutual support groups, the core category of "identity change" captured the essence of the three broad categories listed above.

Finally, it is important for the researcher to find some way of summarizing the analysis in an integrative way. This takes different forms in different approaches. In empirical phenomenology, the researcher attempts to weave the analysis into evocative, condensed summaries of varying lengths, from a paragraph to a couple of pages. Grounded theorists, on the other hand, often prefer tree diagrams that depict hierarchical category structures with the core category at the top. Others provide flow charts that capture the unfolding of respondents' experiences through a series of stages, sometimes with alternative paths to depict variations. The aim is to provide the reader with a map of the main points of the analysis.

Good Practice in Qualitative Analysis

As we described in Chapter 5, much has been written recently about ways of evaluating qualitative research. Several of these criteria pertain specifically to analysis. For example, it has been widely recommended that researchers implement procedures for checking the credibility of their analysis: these include using several analysts, having another researcher audit the data trail, or checking back with the respondents or others like them (Elliott et al., 1999; Yardley, 2000).

It is important for the researcher to consider whether the research questions have been thoroughly and clearly answered. What remaining ambiguities are there? How could the analysis have been continued? Is the analysis coherent and integrated, without oversimplifying the data? Does the analysis illuminate the phenomenon? These questions, which are also suggested in guidelines for evaluating qualitative research (see Chapter 5), need to be addressed by researchers throughout the analysis.

QUANTITATIVE DATA ANALYSIS

Steps in quantitative analysis:
- data entry
- data checking
- data reduction
- exploratory analyses
- statistical significance testing for answering research questions
- analyzing the strength and clinical significance of effects.

Before formal analyses or hypothesis testing can be carried out, researchers need to prepare their data and explore its general properties.

Data Entry

The data are usually entered into a spreadsheet, such as the SPSS data editor, or Microsoft Excel. Prior to data entry, all of the variables must be named and defined, and any labels or codes for various values entered into the computer (e.g., the sex of the respondent might be coded as 1 = male, 2 = female).

In the common case of a multiple-item scale, it is usually better to enter the scores on all the items, rather than just the total scale score, in order to reduce scoring errors and to allow for the possibility of analyzing the scale's reliability or factor structure. Any reverse-scored items need to be recoded so that their values are consistent with the rest of the items in the scale. This can be done manually before the data are entered, but it is usually simpler and more reliable if the computer performs the recoding, creating new, reversed variables.

Data Checking

Data errors can arise either from typing mistakes at data entry or from incorrect computer commands. It is important to check for both possibilities. In order to ensure that the data have been entered correctly, it is a good idea to proof-read the entries by asking someone to read them aloud from a printout and checking them against the original source. Rosenthal (1978) estimated that, on average, about 1% of data points are wrongly entered. Sometimes computer scan sheets can be used in order to eliminate typing errors, but these also need to be checked to ensure that they have been properly filled in.

To check that the data are being processed correctly, some simple descriptive analyses can be performed (Tabachnik & Fidell, 2001). These also provide some basic statistics that you will probably need for the Results section of your research report. For nominal scale data, frequency analyses can be used; for interval scale data, summary descriptive statistics are useful, including the mean, the standard deviation, minimum and maximum values, and the number of valid observations. Such analyses help you to check that missing values are being handled properly and that there are no out-of-range values (e.g., "56" entered for a variable that is supposed to range from 1 to 7). Discrepancies in standard deviations (i.e., ones much smaller or larger than other variables of the same type) often indicate problems with unreliability or restricted ranges, which may suggest the elimination of items or measures before further analyses are carried out.

Data Reduction

Data reduction involves condensing the data, so that it is more manageable and easier to analyze. One obvious approach consists of simply dropping some of the variables from the data set. Researchers are often over-ambitious in the beginning stages of a project and then realize at the start of the analysis that they have more variables than they know what to do with. Such planning errors can often be corrected by eliminating variables from the analyses. It is usually better to focus your energy on thoroughly analyzing a few important variables, rather than struggling to analyze everything that you optimistically included because you thought it might be interesting to look at.

Once the basic variables have been decided upon, the data set can be reduced by summing or averaging the items of any multi-item scales to provide a total score or subscale scores (e.g., by using the SPSS Compute command). With a new scale, it is important first to conduct an item analysis (e.g., using the SPSS Reliability procedure), as the averaging process assumes that the items are parallel (see Chapters 4 and 6). Item analysis will identify bad items, that is, items which do not hang together with the rest of the scale, and will also show whether the scale as a whole has a high enough internal consistency to warrant its use as a homogeneous measure. Once these analyses are done, the item scores can be dropped from the data set or simply ignored.

A third method of data reduction is factor analysis (Floyd & Widaman, 1995; Tabachnik & Fidell, 2001), a multivariate statistical technique that is designed to determine the structure of a set of variables. It is often used as a step in measure development research (see Chapter 6), to investigate the number of underlying dimensions of a new measure or set of measures. Factor analysis can also be used for data reduction purposes, when the researcher wants to represent most of the information in a large number of variables by a small number of independent factors.

Item analyses tend to be regarded as preparatory analyses and are usually reported in the Method section of the research paper, whereas factor analyses tend to be regarded as proper analyses in their own right and are usually reported in the Results section.

Data Exploration

The final preparatory step is to get a feel for the patterns in your data. Even if you are working within a hypothesis-testing framework, it is still a good idea to look at the data from other angles to see what else they can teach you, if only to generate ideas for future studies. Scientific advances often come from unexpected findings, which purely confirmatory procedures may fail to pick up (Merbaum & Lowe, 1982). It is worth trying to develop a playful attitude to the analysis, looking at things from different angles, so that you end up feeling that you know the data inside out.

Several statistical techniques have been developed to assist this process. Tukey's (1977) *Exploratory data analysis* is the standard reference volume; briefer accounts are given by Jackson (1996) and Lovie and Lovie (1991). Exploratory data analysis (usually abbreviated to EDA) methods emphasize displaying the data graphically, and, in line with its spirit of taking a more playful stance towards one's data, they often have appealing names, such as "stem and leaf plots" or "box and whisker plots."

A first set of analyses involves looking at the frequency distributions of each of the variables. This will enable you to check, for example, whether or not the variables are approximately normally distributed, whether there is any systematic pattern to the missing data, and whether there are any outlying observations that will distort the subsequent analyses. For some descriptive studies, e.g., opinion surveys or consumer satisfaction research, knowledge of the frequency distributions may be all that is required to answer the research questions.

A second set of preliminary analyses involves exploratory correlations, particularly among all the independent variable measures and among all the dependent variable measures. Such analyses usually reveal patterns in the data that help you to understand subsequent results. For example, if one criterion measure performs differently from the others, it is useful to have studied its patterns of correlations with the other variables. Similarly, repeated confirmation of hypotheses is less impressive if the variables in question are strongly interrelated, suggesting that they are different measures of the same underlying construct.

There is a dilemma between, on the one hand, the desire to get the maximum mileage out of the data, by conducting many analyses, and, on the other hand, the need to avoid the common error of overanalyzing the data, of trying to relate everything to everything else (known as "fishing expeditions" or "data dredging") and thereby capitalizing on chance associations, leading to high rates of experimentwise error. As we discussed above, you need to be ruthless in deciding which are the most important variables that you want to focus on and then omitting the rest.

Statistical Significance Testing for Answering the Research Questions

For some discovery-oriented research, exploratory statistical analyses may be all that is required. Broad research questions are addressed with exploratory analyses, most of which may not be precisely planned in advance; instead, the researcher will follow up interesting leads as the analysis progresses. On the other hand, more focused research questions or hypotheses call for *confirmatory* analyses. These are aimed at testing pre-stated hypotheses, with specific planned tests corresponding to each one. In other words, exploratory data analysis is inductive, whereas confirmatory analysis is deductive (Tukey, 1977).

In either case, you need to select statistical tests that are appropriate to your research questions and design. The complexity of the design and the nature of the research questions will determine the complexity of the analysis. For some designs, simple descriptive or correlational statistics will suffice; others may require complex multivariate methods.

The choice of statistical methods lies outside the scope of this text. Detailed treatments can be found in the standard statistics texts (e.g., Howell, 2002; Siegel & Castellan, 1988; Tabachnik & Fidell, 2001; Winer et al., 1991). It is also worth seeking advice from psychologist colleagues or from statisticians: even experienced researchers need help for more complicated analyses (although statisticians prefer to be consulted before the data are collected, in order to have some input into the design).

Analyzing the Strength and Significance of Quantitative Effects

The final step in analyzing the findings of a study is to evaluate the strength and significance of the findings: are the results substantial or are they trivial? This might seem to be a matter of interpretation, but statistical methods for addressing these issues have continued to emerge, especially over the past 20 years. In addition to statistical significance (based on probability), these include effect size (based on amount of covariation), and clinical significance (based on practical impact).

It is helpful first to return to Cook and Campbell's (1979) four validity types (see Chapter 8). We have previously examined construct validity and internal validity. The other two validity types are statistical conclusion validity, which we examine next, and external validity, which we touched on in Chapter 10 but will address further in the Interpretation section of this chapter.

Statistical Conclusion Validity

As we discussed above, statistical analysis will often demonstrate that two variables covary, i.e., that they are associated with each other. For example, therapist empathy may be found to be associated with client improvement. The assessment of statistical conclusion validity asks whether positive or negative conclusions about covariation are sound. It is a preliminary step before making causal inferences (which are covered under internal validity). Three questions need to be addressed (Cook & Campbell, 1979).

First, was the study sensitive enough to permit reasonable inferences about covariation? Greater sensitivity is obtained either by larger sample sizes or by reducing the amount of error, both of which give greater statistical power (see Chapter 10). Error can be reduced both by selecting measures that are more reliable and by choosing a research design that controls for extraneous variation, for example, by using a repeated-measures design, by selecting a homogeneous sample (see Chapter 10), or by incorporating an individual difference variable as an extra factor in an experimental design (see Chapter 8).

Second, if the study was sensitive enough, do the variables in fact covary? Here the issue is whether the right statistical tests were performed. Did they meet the assumptions behind them (e.g., for a normal distribution)? Was an appropriate error rate (alpha level, i.e., the critical value of p) set? How likely is it that the results were due to chance variations? "Fishing expeditions," that is, conducting a lot of significance tests in a large data set until something interesting turns up, will produce spuriously significant results. For example, if you correlate 10 variables with 10 other variables, you will have 45 distinct significance tests. Suppose that 10 of the 45 correlations are statistically significant at a conventional alpha level of $p < 0.05$. In this case, your best guess is that two or three of these 10 correlations (i.e., 45 multiplied by 0.05) are significant by chance alone, but you will have a difficult time telling which correlations are probably genuine and which are most likely spurious!

Of course, if you have to conduct multiple statistical tests, the alpha level at which the tests are performed should be made more stringent (Howell, 2002). Unfortunately, this will reduce your power to detect any real effects, sometimes drastically, because in clinical research samples are generally small and difficult to obtain.

Third, if the variables do in fact covary, how meaningful is that covariation? This seemingly straightforward question opens up a number of difficult issues about how to measure the significance of the findings. There are three ways to do this, which we will examine in turn: statistical significance, effect sizes, and clinical significance.

Statistical Significance

Statistical significance defines the meaningfulness of an effect in terms of how improbable it is that it would occur by chance alone. However, many writers have argued that statistical significance in itself does not reveal much (e.g., D. Bakan, 1966; Cohen, 1990; Hayes et al., 1999; Lykken, 1968; Oakes, 1986). One issue is the arbitrariness of the conventional criterion of $p<0.05$, in other words that a result has to have a probability of less than 1 in 20 of occurring by chance in order to be counted as being statistically significant. A result with a p of 0.049 is barely stronger than one with a p of 0.051, yet the first will be reported and the second will not. There is no logical reason why 1 in 20 was settled on, the convention could just as well have been 1 in 25 or 1 in 18.

A more serious issue is that, given a large enough sample size, any effect will become statistically significant at whatever alpha level has been set, since no null hypothesis is ever exactly true (Meehl, 1978). Thus a result may be statistically significant but practically trivial. For example, in testing a new therapy for depression, a mean difference of two points on the Beck Depression Inventory between the experimental and control group may reach statistical significance with a large enough sample, but it would be clinically irrelevant, especially if both groups remained severely depressed.

A third and currently controversial issue is whether it is ever valid to conclude that two groups are equivalent. This issue has implications for hotly debated questions such as whether different therapies have equivalent outcomes. It is a truism in statistics that failing to show a difference between two groups does not mean that they are equivalent. In other words, "you can't prove the null hypothesis." However, Rogers et al. (1993) recently adapted procedures from biometric research on drug equivalence, to outline a method of *equivalence analysis*. This allows researchers to demonstrate the equality (within limits) of two or more groups (see Elliott et al., in press, for an application in psychotherapy research).

Effect Sizes

One potential solution to the problems of statistical significance is to also evaluate the meaningfulness of findings in terms of the amount of covariation, that is, the *effect size* (see our discussion of statistical power analysis in Chapter 10). There are a number of different effect size measures, depending on the statistical comparison being carried out. The basic principle is to create an index of the strength of the relationship between two variables that is independent of the sample size. In general, effect sizes should always be reported along with statistical significance tests, as they provide important information for interpreting findings.

The calculations involved are best illustrated by considering a simplified one-group pretest–posttest comparison. In this case, the most appropriate effect size measure is the difference between the pre- and the post-therapy mean scores, divided by the pooled standard deviation for pre- and post-therapy. For example, in a study of virtual reality exposure therapy for fear of flying (Rothbaum et al., 2000), the mean pre-treatment score on the Fear of Flying Inventory was 105.85, the mean post-treatment score was 86.14 and the pooled standard deviation can be calculated as 36.65. The effect size therefore is (105.85 − 86.14)/36.65, which comes to 0.54 (Cohen, 1988, classifies 0.50 as a medium effect). Thus, using effect size measures, we can say that these clients showed, on average, a moderate improvement in self-reported fear over the course of the therapy.

Meta-analysis.   Effect size measures have an important additional advantage: they make it possible to compare the strength of findings across different studies. Such comparisons are done using a method called *meta-analysis*: a study of studies. This is a sophisticated procedure, which was pioneered by Smith and Glass (1977) in a seminal paper analyzing psychotherapy outcome studies.

Meta-analysis is a form of research in its own right, which uses quantitative techniques to aggregate findings across studies and to look at what features of a study are associated with specific results. For example, in the psychotherapy outcome literature, you can examine whether studies that use a sample of volunteer, college-student clients have a different pattern of results from studies that use a sample drawn from a clinical population who were actively seeking help for their difficulties (Shapiro & Shapiro, 1983). Although its general principles are not difficult to understand, conducting a meta-analysis is a technical business whose mechanics lie beyond our present scope. Further details can be found in Durlak and Lipsey (1991) or Rosenthal and DiMatteo (2001).

The advantage of meta-analysis over traditional reviewing methods is that it is a more powerful way of aggregating the literature and of detecting trends across studies, although it has been criticized for giving too much weight to methodologically unsound studies. In recent years it has become the standard method for systematically reviewing large bodies of literature, throughout psychology and in many other disciplines.

Its relevance here is twofold. First, it is often useful to use meta-analytic methods to compare and combine results within a study: for example, when you have several different outcome measures, effect sizes can be used to characterize the largest or smallest areas of change, and also to provide an overall summary index for the study (mean effect size). Second, effect sizes can be used to compare the results of a single study with the findings from other similar studies in the literature. This involves calculating the effect sizes and comparing them with the corresponding effect sizes obtained in other similar studies or from meta-analyses, thus revealing how the findings fit in with the rest of the literature.

Clinical Significance

One problem with effect sizes is that they compare differences in mean scores against the standard deviations of the groups, rather than against any absolute standard. Although effect sizes are more meaningful than p-values, the presence of a large effect size still does not guarantee that a result is clinically significant. For example, in a two-group experimental design, a large effect could be due to small standard deviations in the experimental and control groups, rather than a substantial difference in the means themselves. A pre-post study of a psychological intervention could have a large effect size, but the clients may not feel much better after it.

The search for a way of capturing which findings are clinically important and which are trivial has led to the development of indices of clinical significance, most closely associated with the work of Jacobson and his colleagues (e.g., Jacobson et al., 1999; Jacobson & Truax, 1991). Such indices are now being routinely incorporated into studies where clinical change is being assessed.

These ideas are again best illustrated in the context of psychotherapy outcome research. The first thing is to ascertain whether there is *reliable change*, that is, whether the observed change is greater than the fluctuations that might be expected to arise from unreliability in the measuring instrument. Jacobson and Truax (1991) present a formula for a *Reliable Change Index (RCI)*, which involves calculating the value that any pre-post change has to exceed in order for it to be considered as reflecting more than random error of measurement. However, reliable change is clearly just an initial requirement: the more important issue is whether any change is clinically meaningful.

The concept of *clinical significance* attempts to encapsulate quantitatively what we usually mean when we say that an intervention with an individual client was successful, which is that the client's level of functioning (in terms, say, of a depression, anxiety, or self-esteem measure) has substantially improved after the intervention.

Substantial clinical improvement normally implies one of three things: (a) that the client is no longer in the abnormal range, (b) that they are back in the normal range (sometimes known as "high endstate functioning"), or (c) that they are at least half-way between the two. These different ways in which a successful outcome may be conceptualized can be expressed more formally (Jacobson & Truax, 1991):

a. That the client's post-intervention score no longer represents abnormal functioning, that is, that it has moved outside the range of the dysfunctional population. Outside the range is usually defined as more than two standard deviations away from the mean of the dysfunctional population.

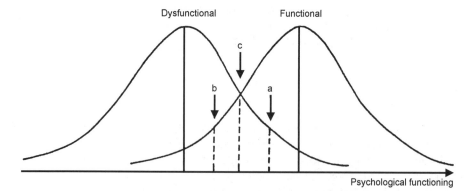

a. The area to the right of this line depicts the scores corresponding to criterion 1.

b. The area to the right of this line depicts the scores corresponding to criterion 2.

c. This line represents the mid-point between the means of the dysfunctional and the functional groups.

Figure 12.1 Three criteria for clinical significance. From Jacobson & Truax (1991). Copyright 1991 the American Psychological Association. Adapted by permission.

b. That the client's post-intervention score represents a return to normal functioning, that is, it has moved inside the range of the functional population. Inside the range is usually defined as being within two standard deviations of the mean of the functional population.

c. That the client's post-intervention score is more likely to be in the functional than the dysfunctional population. This is usually defined as being closer to the mean of the functional population than the dysfunctional population.

These three criteria are illustrated in Figure 12.1 (adapted from Jacobson & Truax, 1991), which locates the cut-off points for each of the three possible criteria on the distributions of the dysfunctional and functional groups. Which of the three criteria to adopt in any given study depends on which of the three ways best fits your conceptualization of a significant outcome of the intervention that you are researching. Criterion (c) represents a possible compromise, since it is defined in terms of where the "weight of the evidence" falls. In measures like the CORE Outcome Measure (Barkham et al., 2001), criterion (c) falls about one standard deviation above the mean for the normal population, where it provides a useful cut-off between "normal" and "moderately distressed."

INTERPRETATION

The analysis yields the basic findings of the study; the interpretation attempts to spell out their implications or broader meanings. Within the quantitative tradition, analysis is often a technical exercise, which follows set rules and requires expertise more than inspiration, whereas interpretation requires imagination and insight into the psychological meaning of the phenomena. It is a

---

Interpretation involves:

- understanding the meaning of the findings, in terms of previous research and theory

- assessing the strengths and limitations of the study

- considering the scientific and professional implications of the findings.

---

broader conceptual task, aimed at bringing the results of the study to bear on the issues that initially inspired it. In qualitative research, the distinction between analysis and interpretation is not so clearly drawn; nevertheless, there is still room for taking a broader view of one's findings or representations of the data.

Interpretation consists of three related parts. The first is to understand the meaning of the findings, in terms of previous research and theory. The second is to assess the strengths and limitations of the study, to see whether it can really support the interpretations that you bring to it. The third is to ask what are the scientific and professional implications of the findings: what do they suggest about future research, and how do they relate to clinical practice?

Understanding the Meaning of the Findings

Having examined the strength and significance of the findings, the next step is to understand what they mean. This task involves relating the findings back to the literature: the research, theory, or conceptual model that the study was based upon. How do the data answer the research questions? Do they support or contradict the theoretical model on which the study was based? How do you explain any discrepancies between your expectations and the findings?

You may also wish to speculate more imaginatively about what the findings mean. Speculation is quite acceptable if labeled as such: that is, if you warn your readers that you are not claiming that your speculations are securely grounded in the evidence.

"The facts are friendly"

Although it is much easier said than done, it is worth reminding yourself to approach this task with an open mind. Try not to be defensive or dogmatic about your theories, but allow the data to speak for themselves. Carl Rogers used to say "the facts are always friendly" (Kirschenbaum, 1979: 205); in other words, do not fight the results, even if they cause you discomfort. The opposite of the attitude of openness is to deny the validity of the results if they conflict with your preconceived ideas: rather than adjusting your theories, you adjust reality instead. Research may force us to rethink our ideas, which can be a painful process, but if we are unwilling to revise our views, what is the point of doing the research in the first place?

The old debate about the effectiveness of psychodynamic versus behavioral psychotherapy provides a classic example of arguing from preconceived positions rather than assimilating the data. Researchers and clinicians often uncritically accepted the validity of studies that supported their theoretical stance (either pro- or anti-behavioral approaches), while highlighting flaws in studies that contradicted them (Shapiro & Shapiro, 1977). Many similar examples can be found in other areas of the psychological and scientific literature. Much rarer are instances of researchers who have publicly changed their position as a result of their own or other people's findings.

Finally, researchers also need to consider the weaknesses of their chosen theoretical explanation. Could the findings be explained in other ways than in terms of your pet theory? Are they compatible with other frameworks than your own? How would a psychoanalyst or a biologically oriented psychiatrist view them? Often these questions lead on to developments or refinements in the original theoretical model, which then lead on to ideas for further research (much like the cycle of inquiry that we described in Chapter 2).

In practical terms, this attitude of openness to your data means that you should not give in to the temptation to skim through your results attending only to the findings that confirm your hypotheses. In fact, the results that deviate from your expectations are worth at least as much reflection and discussion as those that confirm them, because they are the key to revising your understandings of what you are studying, as well as improving your design, data collection, and analysis methods.

Strengths and Limitations of the Study

All studies have their strengths and limitations. The task for researchers (and readers) is to weigh up the relative merits and flaws of any study. Some weaknesses are trivial and can be mentioned in passing; others will be more serious but may—or may not—be offset by particular strengths.

The seriousness of a study's weaknesses determines how much credence can be given to its findings. Researchers need to ask whether there are any problems with their study that might have influenced the results: they owe it to themselves and their readers to make these explicit. (In qualitative research this process is sometimes called discounting.) The physicist Richard Feynman forcefully expressed his belief in this aspect of scientific honesty:

> It's a kind of scientific integrity, a principle of scientific thought that corresponds to a kind of utter honesty—a kind of leaning over backwards. For example, if you're doing an experiment, you should report everything that you think might make it invalid—not only what you think is right about it: other causes that could possibly explain your results . . . Details that could throw doubts upon your interpretation must be given, if you know them. You must do the best you can—if you know anything at all wrong, or possibly wrong—to explain it. (Feynman, 1985: 341)

It is useful here to return to Cook and Campbell's (1979) concept of internal validity (see Chapter 8). Are there any possible third variables that might account for your findings equally well? In what other ways could your findings be explained, in addition to the variables that your research has focused on?

External Validity

An important aspect of assessing the strengths and limitations of a study is to ask to what extent its findings can be generalized beyond its immediate context. This is the external validity question (Cook & Campbell, 1979). It examines the representativeness of the study: its range of application across persons, settings, and times. Any peculiarities of the sample, procedures, setting, or timing will reduce the external validity.

A dilemma for researchers is that the demands of external validity and those of statistical conclusion validity often conflict. For example, one way to reduce error, and therefore to increase the statistical conclusion validity of the study, is to draw the sample from a homogeneous target population. However, this will make the sample less representative and thus lower the study's external validity. As frequently happens with decisions in research, there is no clear-cut answer here.

The role of external validity in qualitative research is controversial (Bryman, 1988; Willig, 2001). Some qualitative researchers reject the whole notion of representativeness, arguing that they are attempting to develop particular contextualized understandings of particular cases, and that generalizability is not an issue. Others argue that the representativeness of their sample (referred to as "horizontal generalization") is not the issue, but what is important is whether the theoretical ideas that are generated are capable of broader application ("vertical generalization"). Yet others argue that external validity is important in qualitative research, and can be obtained by careful sampling in order to draw a qualitatively representative sample, that is, a sample that includes the important variations and aspects of the phenomenon being studied. In any case, possible sample limitations need to be considered when drawing conclusions from a qualitative study, if that study claims to be interested in developing general knowledge about a phenomenon.

Replication

The best way to increase external validity is via replication. The more that you can reproduce the initial findings under diverse conditions, the more convincing will they become. Lykken (1968), drawing from Sidman (1960), distinguished three types of replication: (1) *literal* replication is an exact duplication of the study conducted by the original researchers using identical procedures; (2) *operational* replication is carried out by other researchers, using the methods published by the authors of the original study; and (3) *constructive* replication replicates the basic idea of the study, but uses different methods, for example, a different population or alternative measures of the same constructs. If the results of a study hold up under several constructive replications, we can begin to develop an understanding of the range of situations and persons to which its results generalize.

Research programs often begin with laboratory studies which have low external validity, since it may be a good idea to start out by a simple test of one's theories in such a setting, rather than in an expensive and time-consuming field study. For example, early behavior therapy studies used college student volunteers who had spider phobias for which they had not sought help. However, if the first laboratory or analog studies prove to be successful, the researcher then needs to conduct more ecologically valid studies to give the findings credibility. On the other hand, a researcher with primarily applied interests might want to begin with small-scale field studies, thus avoiding the initial laboratory work.

Scientific and Professional Implications

Scientific Implications

As we discussed in Chapters 1 and 2, research is often a circular process, in that the data may only partially answer the research questions. Often the study reveals, with the benefits of hindsight, that the research questions could have been better formulated, that the theory on which it was based was inadequate, that there were measurement or design weaknesses, or perhaps that the approach shows promise and could be expanded or applied more broadly. All of these conclusions have scientific implications, in that they will lead naturally on to a plan for future research in the area.

Professional Implications

Finally, in clinical research it is important to consider what implications your findings have for professional practice. What would you suggest practitioners (e.g., therapists, teachers) do, or not do, differently on the basis of your study?

For example, Rennie's (1994) qualitative study of clients' deference in psychotherapy suggests that therapists be aware that clients frequently make unspoken, negative appraisals of their relationship with the therapist; Rennie discusses several ways in which therapists might deal with this. As a second example, the second Sheffield Psychotherapy Project (Shapiro et al., 1994) found that severely depressed clients showed substantially greater improvement after 16 sessions as opposed to eight sessions, which suggests that very brief therapy is not to be recommended for this client group.

Consideration of the professional implications of the study leads naturally on to the next section, dissemination, which considers how the findings and their implications will be made known to people who might use them.

DISSEMINATION

- Dissemination is the last step in the research process: it is often difficult but rewarding.

- Research may be disseminated through a variety of outlets, from academic journals and conferences through to more popular media.

- It is worth paying close attention to your writing, to tell your story as clearly and economically as possible.

- Research does not always translate directly into practice: several factors influence whether findings are ever acted upon.

Research is basically a public activity. On rare occasions, you may be doing it for yourself alone, but normally your goal is to communicate your findings to others. Usually this involves a written report or published article, but it may also involve presentation in the research setting, at conferences, or for policy-makers in government departments.

Writing up

Writing up the project can seem a mountainous task. It is easier if you start the process early on and think of the write-up as accumulating progressively by a series of successive approximations over the course of the project. It is worth starting to plan the report and write a first draft of the Introduction and Method sections while you are collecting your data.

Having said that, many people resist writing up, for various reasons. For some, putting pen to paper is the hardest step of all. It is arduous and intellectually demanding, since it forces you to present your ideas in a clear and watertight way. Fear of criticism—one's own or others'—can lead to procrastination. Also, the workload and the emotional stresses of many clinical jobs can make it hard to find the time for writing.

Good research reports are usually simple. They tell the story of the research project, sticking to the main themes without bogging the reader down in irrelevant detail. It is worth continually bearing in mind the one or two key questions that guided the investigation (or at least the part of it that you are writing up) and to structure your report around those themes. This is often hard to do at the end of a study, because you have often lost perspective on what is important, and cannot see the wood for the trees. Try to step back and distance yourself from your study (this is not easy if you have just spent months fretting over it), attempting to see it through the eyes of a general informed reader, as though it were done by someone else. Get criticism from trusted colleagues. Presentations at seminars or conferences are often a good way of shaping up your work and getting other people's reactions to it.

Writing Style

Not only should you try to tell a simple and clear story, but also try to tell it in simple and clear prose. Journal articles in psychology, and in the social sciences generally, are notorious for using incomprehensible jargon or over-elaborate sentence constructions. Much psychology writing is impenetrable or pretentious. An article we recently came across was entitled "Effects of informational valence and occupational favorability on vocational differentiation: A test of the disconfirmation hypothesis." While we are sympathetic to the authors' attempt to describe their study precisely, and often find ourselves writing in technical jargon, this sort of prose runs the risks of sounding pompous (by using specialized words like valence, favorability, or differentiation) and of lulling the readers to sleep (all those "ation" rhythms rock you like a cradle).

George Orwell's much quoted spoof rewrite of a Biblical passage is a paradigmatic example of the contrast between vigorous writing and psychological waffle:

> Here is a well-known verse from Ecclesiastes:

> I returned and saw under the sun, that the race is not to the swift, nor the battle to the strong, neither yet bread to the wise, nor yet riches to men of understanding, nor yet favor to men of skill; but time and chance happeneth to them all.

> Here it is in modern English:

> Objective consideration of contemporary phenomena compels the conclusion that success or failure in competitive activities exhibits no tendency to be commensurate with innate capacity, but that a considerable element of the unpredictable must be taken into account. (Orwell, 1946/1968: 156; reproduced by permission of the estate of the late S. M. B. Orwell.)

Many style guides are available to help combat the tendency to write like Orwell's second paragraph. We recommend Lanham's (1979) amusing and idiosyncratic *Revising prose*, which presents a 10-step method for editing one's own writing, and Strunk and White's (1959) miniature gem *The elements of style*.

Psychology journals have complicated stylistic requirements of their own, which can deter novice authors. The APA *Publication manual* (American Psychological Association, 2001a) is comprehensive and detailed, ranging from general issues about layout and style to minutiae about where to put commas in the reference list. It also includes a helpful section on how to avoid sexist language and ethnic bias. Sternberg (1988) and Kazdin (1995) summarize the stylistic guidelines and provide useful advice on how to write up a project.

Publication

It is always worth considering publishing your research, even though your primary aim may be to write it up for a course requirement or part of a local evaluation. The initial research report itself may not be very useful. Dissertations and theses are often long, formalized, and indigestible, and evaluation reports are usually geared to the interests of a local audience. On the other hand, research reports in professional journals at least aim for brevity and comprehensibility. If the study does not meet the exacting methodological standards of the APA or BPS flagship journals, consider less demanding outlets, often those attached to specific sections, divisions, or interest groups of a professional body. You may also want to present your work at conferences, which is often a good stepping stone to publication.

The process of submitting an article for publication is as follows:

1. Identify the journal that you are aiming for, as different journals have different requirements, both in terms of content and style. The anticipated readership of the journal will partly determine what material to include and how to present it.

2. The front or back cover of the journal will have a section describing the topics and the kinds of articles the journal publishes, and another headed something like "instructions for authors," which gives the journal's stylistic rules and instructions for submitting the typescripts to the editor.

3. Send the original typescript and as many copies as requested, with a short cover letter addressed to the editor. You should receive an acknowledgement of receipt within two or three weeks.

4. If your paper does not meet the broad requirements of the journal, the editor will send it straight back. Otherwise, it will be sent out to reviewers, who are ideally blind to the authors' identity. Reviewers are normally asked to return their reviews to the editor within a month, but they often take longer. On the basis of the reviews, the editor then makes one of the following decisions: accept the paper immediately, accept it subject to specified amendments, request revisions and resubmission, or reject it. Mainstream journals tend to have high rejection rates: for example, in 2000, the *Journal of Consulting and Clinical Psychology* had a 72% rejection rate (American Psychological Association, 2001b) and the *British Journal of Clinical Psychology* had an 80% rejection rate (British Psychological Society, 2001).

5. The editor will communicate their decision to you in a cover letter, enclosing copies of the reviews. You then have to decide how to proceed, based on your perception of the reviewers' and editor's comments on your work. Bad reviews, both in the sense of negative ones or sloppy ones, can be upsetting. The whole process can be somewhat arbitrary, in that different reviewers do not always agree (Fiske & Fogg, 1990). Even if you get unfavorable reviews, it is important not to give up. At least try a couple of other journals before concluding that your work is not worth publishing. The potential pleasure and professional recognition that comes from getting your work in print repays some investment of effort.

Authorship Issues

If the research has been done as part of a team (or if your supervisor has had a major input), the issue arises of who will be listed as authors and in what order.

Authorship issues can often arouse feelings of competition or resentment in the research team and so it is helpful to start discussing them early on in a research project (see Chapter 3). However, sometimes everyone's contributions can only be evaluated once the study is completed.

To be listed as an author, an investigator should have made a substantial scientific contribution to the paper, e.g., a major contribution to the formulation or design (American Psychological Association, 1992; Fine & Kurdek, 1993; Koocher & Keith-Spiegel, 1998). Minor contributions that do not merit authorship, e.g., help with interviewing or data analysis, or a senior doctor's permission to study patients under his or her care, should be mentioned in the acknowledgements section. The order of authorship should reflect each person's contribution.

Utilization

Ideally, research should serve a purpose, not just be an empty exercise. You can increase the likelihood of its having an impact if you actively promote your findings. Articles in academic journals are only read by a select few, so it is worth putting effort into disseminating your work more widely. This can be done informally, by discussing the research with people who might use it to make decisions (e.g., managers, policy-makers, government officials). Or it could be done by writing more accessible articles, e.g., in widely read magazines, such as *Psychology Today* (in the US) or *Nursing Times* (in the UK), or in the popular press. You may even want to write a press release in order to interest radio or television stations in your findings, or post a version of your findings on a website.

The process of how research findings get taken up, if at all, is not always clear. Academic research can feel narrow and inward looking, just feeding on itself, but sometimes findings do permeate through to influence practice. Weiss (1972, 1986) has developed models of research utilization, the thrust of her work being that the relationship between research and policy is nonlinear and complex (for further discussion, see also Robson, 1993; Patton, 1997; Shadish et al., 1991; Tizard, 1990). The naive idea that research has a direct influence upon policy is rarely borne out in practice. Often research is ignored, misapplied, or used to buttress only one side of an argument.

However, there are cases where, for better or worse, research findings appear to strike a chord and become incorporated into far-reaching policy decisions. The studies carried out in the 1950s and 1960s, demonstrating the dehumanizing effects of long-stay institutions, provide an example of research influencing practice. Although this research may have been used simplistically, and possibly only as a cover for cost cutting by conservative politicians, it also made forceful points that have an enduring resonance.

THE END

By the time you have finished writing up your study—particularly if it is a student project—you may be thoroughly fed up with it and painfully aware of its flaws. You may even be thinking of giving up research altogether. Although we understand that reaction, having felt it many times ourselves, we hope that you will give yourself a well-earned break and that after you have recovered you will return to do more research. Consider going back to the drawing board and using your hard-won wisdom to start the cycle again by designing a better study. The field of clinical psychology needs to strengthen its knowledge base through high-quality research. Psychologists who can draw on both research and clinical skills—whom we would call good scientist-practitioners—are central to this process.

CHAPTER SUMMARY

The final stage of the research process consists of three interrelated parts: analysis, interpretation, and dissemination. Analysis means establishing what the findings are, and in particular how the data answer the research questions.

Qualitative analysis is an inductive procedure. Although different qualitative orientations use different approaches to analysis, some general principles can be outlined. Analysis starts with preparing and organizing the data (usually involving transcribing interviews). The analysis itself involves three related processes: identifying meanings in the data, grouping ideas into categories, and integrating them into a set of themes or a conceptual framework. Qualitative analysis can be done using either a within-case (idiographic) or a cross-case approach.

Quantitative analysis may be either exploratory or confirmatory, depending on the type of research questions. It involves preparing the data, exploring its properties, conducting statistical tests to address the research questions, and evaluating statistical significance. The concepts of statistical conclusion validity, effect size, and clinical significance are typically used to evaluate the strength of the findings.

Interpretation and dissemination are the final stages of the research process. First, the researcher needs to evaluate the psychological meaning of the results, as well as their scientific and professional implications. The strengths and limitations of the study must also be assessed. Dissemination involves communicating both the findings and your understanding of them to other people. It is often a difficult but rewarding task, as it involves painstaking attention to the detail of what you are trying to communicate. Research may be disseminated through a variety of outlets, from academic journals and conferences through to more popular media. It does not always translate directly into practice: a complex set of factors influences whether research is ever acted upon.

FURTHER READING

Robson (1993) covers the fundamental steps in both quantitative and qualitative analysis, and also discusses the dissemination and impact of research. Statistical methods are covered in the standard texts, e.g., Howell (2002) for a general coverage, Siegel and Castellan (1988) for non-parametric methods, Winer et al. (1991) for analysis of variance, and Tabachnik and Fidell (2001) for multivariate analysis (and also a good account of the preliminary steps in data preparation).

There are a number of sources for qualitative analysis. Some present general approaches (e.g., Creswell, 1998; Miles & Huberman, 1994; Patton, 2002; Taylor & Bogdan, 1998) or give an overview of a range of specific approaches (e.g., Richardson, 1996; Willig, 2001); others present one theoretical approach in detail. Among the latter are Strauss and Corbin (1998) on grounded theory, Smith et al. (1999) on interpretative phenomenological analysis, Hill et al. (1997) on consensual qualitative research, and Potter and Wetherell (1987) on discourse analysis.

Cook and Campbell (1979) are, as always, a key source in thinking generally about interpreting findings. Clinical significance is covered in a June 1999 special section of the *Journal of Consulting and Clinical Psychology*. Meta-analysis is described in Rosenthal and DiMatteo (2001). It is also worth reading a meta-analysis in your own area of interest, to get a feel for what the final product looks like.

Rudestam and Newton (2000) cover the process of writing up, including a discussion of barriers to writing. Robson (1993) gives a good overview of models for understanding how research findings are taken up in practice.

CHAPTER 13

EPILOGUE

> Thus scientific methodology is seen for what it truly is—a way of preventing me from deceiving myself in regard to my creatively formed hunches which have developed out of the relationship between me and my material. (Rogers, 1955: 275)

We started this book by comparing a research project to telling a story. Our own narrative of how a research project progresses is now drawing to a close. The book has been structured around the four basic stages of the research process, that is, the steps that researchers go through when they are doing a project (although they do not usually go through them in the neatly ordered sequence that we have depicted). These stages are: (1) groundwork; (2) measurement; (3) design; and (4) analysis, interpretation, and dissemination. Separating out the important issues according to the stage in which they are prominent is helpful both when planning research and also when reading research.

This chapter brings together some central ideas that run through the book: methodological pluralism (matching the method to the problem), appraising research, and combining research with practice. Finally, we end with some images of research.

Methodological Pluralism

Our central theme has been methodological pluralism: that no single approach to research is best overall, rather, what is important is that the methods be appropriate for the questions under investigation. It can also be labeled appropriate methodology, by analogy with the catchphrase "appropriate technology" (although strictly speaking the word "methodology" should only be used in its precise meaning of the study of methods). No single research method is inherently superior to any other: all methods have their relative advantages and disadvantages.

However, we want to make it clear that methodological pluralism is not equivalent to methodological anarchy. Unlike Feyerabend (1975), we are not saying that "anything goes." Quite the reverse, in that we have tried to outline methodological rules and principles within the context of each method. Some of these principles are common to all approaches, some are relevant only to specific research approaches or genres.

Wherever they are applied, the central purpose of these methodological rules is, as Carl Rogers aptly said in the quotation forming the epigraph to this chapter, to prevent one's deceiving oneself and others by drawing conclusions that are not supported by the data. In terms of the simple model of research that we presented in Chapter 2, the essence of the research attitude is finding ways to test your ideas against your experience of the world.

This book has covered both traditional, quantitative methods and the more recent (at least within psychology), qualitative methods. Although the proponents of each approach have sometimes represented warring factions, we believe that the debate has often been too polarized and that it is possible, indeed desirable, to combine multiple methods within a single study or research program.

Our message is not that knowing about research methods enables you to produce the perfect piece of research. However, we do hope that, having read this book, you will be better able to make informed choices in your own research, or at least informed compromises. As we have said throughout, there are always compromises and trade-offs in research. However, although we are saying that there is no one right way to do research, there definitely are wrong ways. Consideration of how research might be done badly leads in to the next section, on appraising research.

Appraising Research

We have aimed to give readers the conceptual tools needed to become both better producers and better consumers of research. Throughout the book we have pointed to issues that need to be considered in evaluating studies, whether from the standpoint of the researcher or the reader. Here, we will focus on the consumer's perspective, and address how the concepts that we have raised in the context of planning and executing research can be applied when you are reading and evaluating research reports.

The more you know about research methods, the more you are able to recognize the problems in a piece of research. However, this does not mean that appraisal equals negative criticism. It is easy to criticize research. Psychology training often does a good job of teaching students how to pull studies apart; but it is usually less good at giving them a sense of perspective. Our own students are often quick to find numerous flaws (many of which we consider to be trivial) in research papers, but they are less able to take a broader view, and to see things in balance.

Thinking about the different stages of the research process helps you to conceptualize some of the important issues to consider when evaluating a piece of research. We have discussed general criteria that apply to all types of research as well as some that apply to specific approaches. We present these general criteria below, as they apply roughly to each of the stages in the research process.

Criteria for evaluating research

Groundwork. The first question to ask is "Who cares?" In other words, is the topic worth researching, has it been done before, does the study have the potential to add useful knowledge or to develop theory?

Is the literature review relevant and up to date? Does it cover empirical, methodological, and theoretical issues, and does it place the study in the context of scientific research in the area? Is the rationale for the study clearly articulated (possibly including an indication of the conceptual model linking the variables under investigation)? Are appropriate research questions or hypotheses clearly formulated?

Measurement. How are the main constructs defined and measured? Do the measurement methods (used in a broad sense to cover both quantitative and qualitative methods) adequately capture the constructs of interest? Are the methods appropriate to the research questions? If quantitative measures are used, do they have acceptable reliability and validity? If qualitative methods are used, have they been placed in the context of the researcher's theoretical orientation?

Design. Are the procedures described in sufficient detail to enable the reader to understand what was done and, if necessary, to be able to replicate the study? Is the design of the study appropriate to the research questions? Will it enable the desired inferences to be drawn?

Is the sampling procedure clearly specified? Are the size and composition of the sample appropriate to the research questions and data analysis? Does the study conform to the relevant professional and ethical standards?

Analysis. Do the analyses address each of the research questions? Are the data presented clearly and coherently? (Any tables and figures should be both understandable and informative.) In quantitative studies, are data reduction techniques and statistical tests used correctly? In qualitative studies, is the analysis grounded in examples, and have procedures been included to check the credibility of the analysis?

Interpretation. Are the findings interpreted in the context of the research questions and the wider theoretical context in which the work was carried out? Are interpretations supported by the data? (However, speculations are in order if labeled as such.) Are competing explanations for the findings considered? Is the generalizability of the findings assessed? Are weaknesses of the study addressed? Are the scientific and professional implications of the findings discussed?

Presentation. Is the paper readable? (Consider its general prose style, use of jargon and sexist or other offensive language.) Is the paper's length appropriate for its content?

Although we have tried to make them as generally applicable as possible, not all of the criteria will apply to all pieces of work, nor will each criterion have equal weight.

In arriving at an overall evaluation of a research paper, take into account that strengths in some areas may compensate for weaknesses in others. Rather than simply listing the flaws of a study, try to estimate how they distort the conclusions of the research. Some technical flaws in the procedure may have a negligible impact on the results. The more important or innovative the topic or methods, the more forgivable should be any shortcomings: it is relatively easy to do methodologically sound but trivial research; it is harder to do innovative research that makes a scientific or professional impact.

Combining Research with Practice

As we hope to have made clear throughout this book, we believe there are benefits to be gained from the scientist-practitioner approach in its various expressions. Research helps advance practice by developing and testing new procedures; practice helps advance research by providing a source of, and a testing ground for, new ideas and methods, and by giving a reminder of the complexity of human behavior that helps counterbalance the simplifying tendency of much research. Researchers and practitioners have not always seen eye to eye: they have different needs and live in different "worlds"—even when they are the same person! Despite these difficulties, we believe that the relationship between the two activities is ultimately mutually enriching.

However, although a scientist-practitioner approach is good for the field as a whole, it does not follow that combining the two activities is right for everyone. We recognize that actually carrying out research may not be everyone's cup of tea. As we discussed in Chapter 2, although there are many positive reasons for becoming involved in research, there are also several reasons why combining research and practice is problematic. Different individuals will weigh up each of these reasons differently, and decide to what extent, if at all, they want to be involved in doing research. We do maintain, however, that at a minimum, practitioners need to be sufficiently informed about research methods to be able to understand and appraise research, even if they are not actually doing it themselves.

In the past, the scientist-practitioner role has been identified with a narrow conception of research, which has put many psychologists off attempting to do their own research. It is certainly true that some types of research are prohibitively complicated, costly, and time consuming for the individual practitioner, randomized comparative therapy outcome research being the prime example. It is also unrealistic to expect that most practitioners would have the resources to conduct the kind of research that meets the exacting requirements of the major scientific journals. However, it is possible to work within a broader conceptualization of the scientist-practitioner model. We have tried to outline some possible methods that can be adopted by practitioners working on their own (especially the small-N approaches outlined in Chapter 9 and the evaluation methods in Chapter 11).

Another strategy to increase one's involvement in research is to make it a group endeavor. For us, one of the central pleasures of research is the process of working with other colleagues. Teamwork provides stimulation through discussing mutually interesting ideas and struggling to resolve disagreements or differences in perspectives. It also brings support to what can otherwise be a lonely enterprise. We would strongly echo Hodgson and Rollnick's (1996) advice to form a research team if at all possible.

We hope to have conveyed the message that research need not be as forbidding a process as is often imagined. Some of the old rigidities are now dissolving; it is widely recognized that there are many different approaches to research. It is possible to work in a genre of research that suits your own values, abilities, and ways of thinking. However, research is not to be undertaken lightly. It requires time and effort and it can be an intellectual struggle: rigorous thinking does not usually come easily. But we hope that ultimately the potential enjoyment and stimulation that research gives will encourage at least some of our readers to consider becoming involved in it themselves.

Some Images of Research

We began this book with the metaphor of research as a story. We will end with three additional images of the research process.

First, research can be understood as a *need*, a modern expression of the innate, universal human need to understand and master one's environment. This is how Cook and Campbell (1979) see research, with the framework of "evolutionary epistemology," that is, as part of what has made it possible for human beings to survive and prosper. This may be seen as an aspect of the growth tendency (Rogers, 1961), or as a biologically adaptive, inherited trait of curiosity, or simply as the "joy of knowing." In any case, research is one of the primary contemporary vehicles for living out this basic part of what it means to be human. We are not saying that research is always fun (much of it is drudgery!), but only that it is marked by moments of understanding and accomplishment which make it all worthwhile.

Second, research is a *journey*, a metaphorical going out on a voyage of exploration, like Odysseus (to use Kvale's, 1996, analogy), or Darwin's voyage of discovery on the *Beagle*. This voyage begins with optimism and excitement but often veers toward danger, risk, and disappointment, sometimes almost crashing on the rocks of rigid methodology or running the danger of being sucked down into a whirlpool of confusing alternatives (Kvale, 1996). Sometimes, we make it home with a research project, and sometimes it fails and is never heard from again, buried at the back of a filing cabinet. But generally, if we persist, we will return safely with a story or two to tell about the adventure.

Third, research is a cultural *tradition*, a means of developing and communicating important ideas between people and across time. The methods and concepts we use are part of the syntax and vocabulary of this tradition; we use them as a modern rhetoric, to establish ourselves and our work as credible and persuasive. But this also means that research is not complete until it is communicated to others. Viewing research as a cultural tradition also suggests that we can expect our field's research methods to continue to evolve and change, and to produce new forms and contents. This is simply what it means for something to be a living tradition: if it were set in stone, it would be dead!

Finally, being part of a tradition means that as you proceed, you first borrow (with credit!) some of the tradition's voices; then you master the techniques, which means that you make some of these voices your own; and then you allow the tradition to speak through you. In the end, perhaps the best goal for a researcher is this: to become part of the tradition of knowledge and method in your field, adding your voice to those who have gone before, speaking to and through those who come after you, even when they no longer even recognize that it is your voice, among many others, that speaks in them. In this book, we have tried to provide a basic foundation in the tradition of clinical research, and we have invited you to enter into it.

REFERENCES

Addison, R.B. (1989). Grounded interpretive research: An investigation of physician socialization. In M.J. Packer & R.B. Addison (eds), *Entering the circle: Hermeneutic investigation in psychology* (39–57). Albany, NY: SUNY Press.

Adorno, T.W., Frenkel-Brunswick, E., Levinson, D.J. & Sanford, R.N. (1950). *The authoritarian personality*. New York: Harper.

Ainsworth, M.D.S., Blehar, M.C., Waters, E. & Wall, S. (1978). *Patterns of attachment: A psychological study of the strange situation*. Hillsdale, NJ: Erlbaum.

Albury, D. & Schwartz, J. (1982). *Partial progress: The politics of science and technology*. London: Pluto Press.

Allport, G.W. (1942). *The use of personal documents in psychological science*. New York: Social Science Research Council.

Allport, G.W. (1962). The general and the unique in psychological science. *Journal of Personality, 30*, 405–422.

Altman, J. (1974). Observational study of behaviour: Sampling methods. *Behaviour, 49*, 227–267.

American Psychological Association (1947). Recommended graduate training in clinical psychology. *American Psychologist, 2*, 539–558.

American Psychological Association (1992). Ethical principles of psychologists and code of conduct. *American Psychologist, 47*, 1597–1611.

American Psychological Association (2001a). *Publication manual* (5th edn). Washington, DC: American Psychological Association.

American Psychological Association (2001b). Summary report of journal operations, 2000. *American Psychologist, 56*, 693.

Anderson, R.J., Hughes, J.A. & Sharrock, W.W. (1986). *Philosophy and the human sciences*. Totowa, NJ: Barnes & Noble.

Armistead, N. (ed.) (1974). *Reconstructing social psychology*. Harmondsworth: Penguin Books.

Bakan, D. (1966). The test of significance in psychological research. *Psychological Bulletin, 66*, 423–437.

Bakan, P. (1966). *The duality of existence*. Chicago: Rand McNally.

Bakeman, R. & Gottman, J.M. (1986). *Observing interaction: An introduction to sequential analysis*. New York: Cambridge University Press.

Barker, C., Pistrang, N., Davies, S., Shapiro, D.A. & Shaw, I. (1993). You in Mind: A preventive mental health television series. *British Journal of Clinical Psychology, 32*, 281–293.

Barker, R.G., Wright, H.F., Schoggen, M.F. & Barker, L.S. (1978). *Habitats, environments, and human behavior*. San Francisco: Jossey-Bass.

Barkham, M., Margison, F., Leach, C., Lucock, M., Mellor-Clark, J., Evans, C., Benson, L., Connell, J., Audin, K. & McGrath, G. (2001). Service profiling and outcomes benchmarking using the CORE-OM: Toward practice-based evidence in the psychological therapies. *Journal of Consulting and Clinical Psychology, 69*, 184–196.

Barlow, D.H. & Hersen, M. (1984). *Single case experimental designs: Strategies for studying behavior change* (2nd edn). Oxford: Pergamon.

Baron, R.M. & Kenny, D.A. (1986). The moderator-mediator variable distinction in social psychological research: Conceptual, strategic and statistical considerations. *Journal of Personality and Social Psychology, 51*, 1173–1182.

Barry, D., Elliott, R. & Evans, E.M. (2000). Foreigners in a strange land: Ethnic identity, self-construal, socialization practices, and self-esteem in male Arab immigrants. *Journal of Immigrant Health, 2*, 133–144.

Battle, C.C., Imber, S.D., Hoehn-Saric, R., Stohe, A.R., Nash, C. & Frank, J.D. (1966). Target complaints as criteria of improvement. *American Journal of Psychotherapy, 20*, 184–192.

Baum, A., Revenson, T.A. & Singer, J.E. (eds) (2001). *Handbook of health psychology.* Mahwah, NJ: Lawrence Erlbaum Associates.

Bebbington, P.E., Brugha, T.S., Meltzer, H., Jenkins, R., Ceresa, C., Farrell, M. & Lewis, G. (2000a). Neurotic disorders and the receipt of psychiatric treatment. *Psychological Medicine, 30*, 1369–1376.

Bebbington, P.E., Marsden, L. & Brewin, C.R. (1997). The need for psychiatric treatment in the general population; the Camberwell Needs for Care survey. *Psychological Medicine, 27*, 821–834.

Bebbington, P.E., Meltzer, H., Brugha, T.S., Farrell, M., Jenkins, R., Ceresa, C. & Lewis, G. (2000b). Unequal access and unmet need: Neurotic disorders and the use of primary care services. *Psychological Medicine, 30*, 1359–1367.

Beck, A.T. (1976). *Cognitive therapy and the emotional disorders.* New York: International Universities Press.

Beck, A.T., Rush, A.J., Shaw, B.F. & Emery, G. (1979). *Cognitive therapy of depression.* New York: Guilford.

Beck, A.T., Steer, R.A. & Garbin, M.G. (1988). Psychometric properties of the Beck Depression Inventory: Twenty-five years of evaluation. *Clinical Psychology Review, 8,* 77–100.

Belenky, M.F., Clinchy, B.M., Goldberger, N.R. & Tarule, J.M. (1986). *Women's ways of knowing: The development of self, voice, and mind.* New York: Basic Books.

Bellack, A.S. & Hersen, M. (1988). *Behavioral assessment: A practical handbook* (3rd edn). New York: Pergamon.

Bennun, I. & Lucas, R. (1990). Using the partner in the psychosocial treatment of schizophrenia: A multiple single case design. *British Journal of Clinical Psychology, 29*, 185–192.

Berg, B.L. (1995). *Qualitative research methods for the social sciences* (2nd edn). Boston, MA: Allyn & Bacon.

Berger, P.L. & Luckmann, T. (1966). *The social construction of reality: A treatise in the sociology of knowledge.* New York: Doubleday.

Bergin, A.E. (1971). The evaluation of therapeutic outcomes. In A.E. Bergin & S.L. Garfield (eds), *Handbook of psychotherapy and behavior change: An empirical analysis.* New York: Wiley.

Bergin, A.E. & Garfield, S.L. (eds) (1994). *Handbook of psychotherapy and behavior change* (4th edn). New York: Wiley.

Bergin, A.E. & Lambert, M.J. (1978). The evaluation of therapeutic outcomes. In S.L. Garfield & A.E. Bergin (eds), *Handbook of psychotherapy and behavior change: An empirical analysis* (2nd edn). New York: Wiley.

Bergin, A.E. & Strupp, H.H. (1972). *Changing frontiers in the science of psychotherapy.* Chicago: Aldine.

Bersoff, D.M. & Bersoff, D.N. (1999). Ethical perspectives in clinical research. In P.C. Kendall, J.N. Butcher & G.N. Holmbeck (eds), *Handbook of research methods in clinical psychology* (2nd edn). New York: Wiley.

Bhaskar, R. (1975). *A realist theory of science*. Leeds: Leeds Books.

Blythe, R. (1979). *The view in winter*. Harmondsworth: Penguin Books.

Bogdan, R. & Taylor, S. (1976). The judged, not the judges: An insider's view of mental retardation. *American Psychologist, 31*, 47–52.

Bolger, E.A. (1999). Grounded theory analysis of emotional pain. *Psychotherapy Research, 9*, 342–362.

Bornstein, P.H., Hamilton, S.B. & Bornstein, M.T. (1986). Self-monitoring procedures. In A.R. Ciminero, K.S. Calhoun & H.E. Adams (eds), *Handbook of behavioral assessment* (2nd edn). New York: Wiley.

Bradburn, N.M. (1983). Response effects. In P.H. Rossi, J.D. Wright & A.B. Anderson (eds), *Handbook of survey research*. London: Academic Press.

Bradburn, N.M. & Sudman, S. (1979). *Improving interview method and questionnaire design: Response effects to threatening questions in survey research*. San Francisco: Jossey-Bass.

Brenner, B., Brown, J. & Canter, D. (1985). *The research interview: Uses and approaches*. London: Academic Press.

Breuer, J. & Freud, S. (1895/1955). Case histories. In J. Strachey (ed. and trans.), *The standard edition of the complete works of Sigmund Freud* (Vol. 2). London, Hogarth Press.

Brewin, C.R. & Bradley, C. (1989). Patient preferences and randomised clinical trials. *British Medical Journal, 299*, 313–315.

British Psychological Society (1990). Ethical principles for conducting research with human participants. *The Psychologist, 3*, 269–272.

British Psychological Society (2001). Summary of journal operations 2000. *The Psychologist, 10*, 550.

British Psychological Society Division of Clinical Psychology (1995). *Professional practice guidelines*. Leicester: British Psychological Society.

Brock, D. & Barker, C. (1990). Group environment and group process in psychiatric assessment meetings. *International Journal of Social Psychiatry, 36*, 111–120.

Bromley, D.B. (1986). *The case-study method in psychology and related disciplines*. Chichester: Wiley.

Brooks, N. (1996). Writing a grant application. In G. Parry & F.N. Watts (eds), *Behavioural and mental health research: A handbook of skills and methods* (2nd edn), pp. 157–171. Hove: Lawrence Erlbaum.

Brown, G.W. & Harris, T. (1978). *Social origins of depression: A study of psychiatric disorder in women*. London: Tavistock.

Bruce, V. (1990). Ethics committees. *The Psychologist, 3*, 463–464.

Bryant, C.G.A. (1985). *Positivism in social theory and research*. London: Macmillan.

Bryman, A. (1988). *Quantity and quality in social research*. London: Unwin Hyman.

Butcher, J.N. (1999). Research design in objective personality assessment. In P.C. Kendall, J.N. Butcher & G.N. Holmbeck (eds), *Handbook of research methods in clinical psychology* (2nd edn). New York: Wiley.

Campbell, D.T. & Fiske, D.W. (1959). Convergent and discriminant validation by the multitrait-multimethod matrix. *Psychological Bulletin, 56*, 81–105.

Campbell, D.T. & Stanley, J.C. (1966). *Experimental and quasi-experimental designs for research*. Chicago: Rand-McNally.

Campbell, R. & Wasco, S.M. (2000). Feminist approaches to social science: Epistemological and methodological tenets. *American Journal of Community Psychology, 28*, 773–791.

Cape, J. (1991). Quality assurance methods for clinical psychology services. *The Psychologist, 4*, 499–503.

Cape, J. & Barkham, M. (in press). Practice improvement methods: Conceptual base, evidence-based research, and practice-based recommendations. *British Journal of Clinical Psychology*.

Cape, J., Pilling, S. & Barker, C. (1993). The measurement and costing of psychology services. *Clinical Psychology Forum, 60,* 16–21.

Carlson, R. (1972). Understanding women: Implications for personality theory and research. *Journal of Social Issues, 28,* 17–32.

Ceci, S.J., Peters, D. & Plotkin, J. (1985). Human subjects review, personal values, and the regulation of social science research. *American Psychologist, 40,* 994–1002.

Chadwick, P.D.J. & Trower, P. (1996). Cognitive therapy for punishment paranoia: A single case experiment. *Behaviour, Research and Therapy, 34,* 351–356.

Chalmers, A.F. (1982). *What is this thing called science?* (2nd edn). Milton Keynes: Open University Press.

Chalmers, A.F. (1990). *Science and its fabrication.* Milton Keynes: Open University Press.

Chambless, D.L. & Hollon, S.D. (1998). Defining empirically supported therapies. *Journal of Consulting and Clinical Psychology, 66,* 7–18.

Charmaz, K. (1991). *Good days, bad days: The self in chronic illness and time.* New Brunswick, NJ: Rutgers University Press.

Cherry, D.K., Messenger, L.C. & Jacoby, A.M. (2000). An examination of training model outcomes in clinical psychology programs. *Professional Psychology: Research & Practice, 31,* 562–568.

Christensen, L.B. (2001). *Experimental methodology* (8th edn). Boston: Allyn & Bacon.

Churchill, S.D. (2000). "Seeing through" self-deception in narrative reports: Finding psychological truth in problematic data. *Journal of Phenomenological Psychology, 31,* 44–62.

Ciminero, A.R., Calhoun, K.S. & Adams, H.E. (eds) (1986). *Handbook of behavioral assessment* (2nd edn). New York: Wiley.

Clinical Science Program, Indiana University (n.d.). Retrieved November 24, 2001, from http://www.indiana.edu/~clinpsy/

Cochran, W.G. (1977). *Sampling techniques* (3rd edn). New York: Wiley.

Cohen, J. (1960). A coefficient of agreement for nominal scales. *Educational and Psychological Measurement, 20,* 37–46.

Cohen, J. (1988). *Statistical power analysis for the behavioral sciences* (2nd edn). Hillsdale, NJ: Erlbaum.

Cohen, J. (1990). Things I have learned (so far). *American Psychologist, 45,* 1304–1312.

Cohen, J. (1992). A power primer. *Psychological Bulletin, 112,* 155–159.

Compass Project (1989). Annual report. London: Bloomsbury Health Authority (now renamed the Camden & Islington Health Authority).

Comte, A. (1830–1842). *Cours de philosophie positive* (6 vols). Paris: Bachelier.

Cone, J.D. (1999). Observational assessment: Measure development and research issues. In P.C. Kendall, J.N. Butcher & G.N. Holmbeck (eds), *Handbook of research methods in clinical psychology* (2nd edn). New York: Wiley.

Cook, T.D. & Campbell, D.T. (1979). *Quasi-experimentation: Design and analysis issues for field settings.* Chicago: Rand-McNally.

Corrie, S. & Callahan, M. (2000). A review of the scientist-practitioner model: Reflections on its potential contribution to counselling psychology within the context of current health care trends. *British Journal of Medical Psychology, 73,* 413–427.

Cowen, E.L. (1978). Some problems in community program evaluation research. *Journal of Consulting and Clinical Psychology, 46,* 792–805.

Cowen, E.L. & Gesten, E. (1980). Evaluating community programs. In M.S. Gibbs, J.R. Lachenmeyer & J. Sigal (eds), *Community psychology* (pp. 363–393). New York: Gardner.

Cox, D.R., Fitzpatrick, R., Fletcher, A.E., Gore, S.M., Spiegelhalter, D.J. & Jones, D.R. (1992). Quality of life assessment: Can we keep it simple? *Journal of the Royal Statistical Society (Series A), 155,* 353–393.

Creswell, J.W. (1998). *Qualitative inquiry and research design: Choosing among five traditions.* Thousand Oaks, CA: Sage.

Crombie, I.K., Davies, H.T.O., Abraham, S.C.S. & Florey, C. du V. (1993). *The audit handbook: Improving health care through clinical audit.* Chichester: Wiley.

Cronbach, L.J. (1957). The two disciplines of scientific psychology. *American Psychologist, 12,* 671–684.

Cronbach, L.J. (1975). Beyond the two disciplines of scientific psychology. *American Psychologist, 30,* 116–127.

Cronbach, L.J. (1982). *Designing evaluations of educational and social programs.* San Francisco: Jossey-Bass.

Cronbach, L.J., Gleser, G.C., Nanda, H. & Rajaratnam, N. (1972). *The dependability of behavioral measurements: Theory of generalizability of scores and profiles.* New York: Wiley.

Cronbach, L.J. & Meehl, P.E. (1955). Construct validity in psychological tests. *Psychological Bulletin, 52,* 281–302.

Crowne, D.P. & Marlowe, D. (1960). A new scale of social desirability independent of psychopathology. *Journal of Consulting Psychology, 24,* 349–354.

Crowne, D.P. & Marlowe, D. (1964). *The approval motive: Studies in evaluative dependency.* New York: Wiley.

Davidson, P.O. & Costello, C.G. (eds) (1969). *N=1: Experimental studies of single cases.* New York: Van Nostrand.

Davison, G.C. & Stuart, R.B. (1975). Behavior therapy and civil liberties. *American Psychologist, 30,* 755–763.

Dawis, R.V. (1987). Scale construction. *Journal of Counseling Psychology, 34,* 481–489.

Denzin, N.K. (1989). *Interpretive biography.* Newbury Park, CA: Sage.

Derogatis, L.R. (1994). *SCL-90-R administration, scoring, and procedures manual* (3rd edn). Minneapolis, MA: National Computer Systems.

Dilke, O.A.W. (1987). *Mathematics and measurement.* London: British Museum Press.

Dillman, D.A. (1983). Mail and other self-administered questionnaires. In P.H. Rossi, J.D. Wright & A.B. Anderson (eds), *Handbook of survey research.* London: Academic Press.

Dillman, D.A. (2000). *Mail and internet surveys: The tailored design method.* New York: Wiley.

Donabedian, A. (1980). *The definition of quality and approaches to its assessment.* Ann Arbor: Health Administration Press.

Dukes, W.F. (1965). "N=1". *Psychological Bulletin, 64,* 74–79.

Durlak, J.A. & Lipsey, M.W. (1991). A practitioner's guide to meta-analysis. *American Journal of Community Psychology, 19,* 291–332.

Eagleton, T. (1983). *Literary theory: An introduction.* Oxford: Basil Blackwell.

Edwards, A.L. (1953). *Edwards Personal Preference Schedule.* San Antonio, Texas: The Psychological Corporation.

Elkin, I. (1994). The NIMH Treatment of Depression Collaborative Research Program: Where we began and where we are. In A.E. Bergin & S.L. Garfield (eds), *Handbook of psychotherapy and behavior change* (pp. 114–139). New York: Wiley.

Elliott, R. (1983a). Fitting process research to the practising psychotherapist. *Psychotherapy: Theory, Research & Practice, 20,* 47–55.

Elliott, R. (1983b). "That in your hands": A comprehensive process analysis of a significant event in psychotherapy. *Psychiatry, 46,* 113–129.

Elliott, R. (1984). A discovery-oriented approach to significant change events in psychotherapy: Interpersonal Process Recall and Comprehensive Process Analysis. In L.N. Rice & L.S. Greenberg (eds), *Patterns of change: Intensive analysis of psychotherapy process.* New York: Guilford.

Elliott, R. (1989a). Comprehensive Process Analysis: Understanding the change process in significant therapy events. In M.J. Packer & R.B. Addison (eds), *Entering the circle: Hermeneutic investigation in psychology* (pp. 165–184). Albany, New York: SUNY Press.

Elliott, R. (1989b). Issues in the selection, training and management of raters. Presented at Society for Psychotherapy Research, Toronto, Canada.

Elliott, R. (1989c). Statistical considerations for sample size in qualitative research. Unpublished manuscript, Department of Psychology, University of Toledo.

Elliott, R. (1991). Five dimensions of therapy process. *Psychotherapy Research, 1,* 92–103.

Elliott, R. (1993). Therapy process research and clinical practice: Practical strategies. In M. Aveline & D.A. Shapiro (eds), *Research foundations for psychotherapy practice.* Chichester: Wiley.

Elliott, R. (1998). Editor's introduction: A guide to the empirically-supported treatments controversy. *Psychotherapy Research, 8,* 115–125.

Elliott, R. (1999). *Client Change Interview Protocol.* Network for Research on Experiential Psychotherapies website: http://experiential-researchers.org/instruments/elliott/changei.html

Elliott, R. (2000). *Rigor in psychotherapy research: The search for appropriate methodologies.* Unpublished manuscript, University of Toledo.

Elliott, R. (2002). Hermeneutic single-case efficacy design. *Psychotherapy Research, 12,* 1–21.

Elliott, R., Fischer, C.T. & Rennie, D.L. (1999). Evolving guidelines for publication of qualitative research studies in psychology and related fields. *British Journal of Clinical Psychology, 38,* 215–229.

Elliott, R., Greenberg, L.S. & Lietaer, G. (in press). Research on experiential psychotherapies. In M.J. Lambert, A.E. Bergin & S.L. Garfield (eds), *Handbook of psychotherapy and behavior change* (5th edn). New York: Wiley.

Elliott, R., Mack, C. & Shapiro, D.A. (1999). *Simplified Personal Questionnaire Procedure.* Network for Research on Experiential Psychotherapies website: http://experiential-researchers.org/instruments/elliott/pqprocedure.html

Elliott, R., Slatick, E. & Urman, M. (2001). Qualitative Change Process Research on Psychotherapy: Alternative Strategies. In J. Frommer and D.L. Rennie (eds), *Qualitative psychotherapy research: Methods and methodology* (pp. 69–111). Lengerich, Germany: Pabst Science Publishers.

Elliott, R. & Wexler, M.M. (1994). Measuring the impact of sessions in process-experiential therapy of depression: The Session Impacts Scale. *Journal of Counseling Psychology, 41,* 166–174.

Embretson, S.E. & Prenovost, L.K. (1999). Item response theory in assessment research. In P.C. Kendall, J.N. Butcher & G.N. Holmbeck (eds), *Handbook of research methods in clinical psychology* (2nd edn). New York: Wiley.

Emerson, R.M. (2001). *Contemporary field research: Perspectives and formulations* (2nd edn). Boston, MA: Little, Brown & Co.

Endicott, J., Spitzer, R.L., Fleiss, J.L. & Cohen, J. (1976). The Global Assessment Scale: A procedure for measuring overall severity of psychiatric disturbance. *Archives of General Psychiatry, 33,* 766–771.

Ericsson, K.A. & Simon, H.S. (1993). *Protocol analysis: Verbal reports as data* (revised edn). Cambridge, MA: MIT Press.

Erikson, E. (1969). *Gandhi's truth.* New York: Norton.

Eysenck, H.J. (1952). The effects of psychotherapy: An evaluation. *Journal of Consulting Psychology, 16,* 319–324.

Eysenck, H.J. (1975). Who needs a random sample? *Bulletin of the British Psychology Society, 28,* 195–198.

Eysenck, H.J. & Eysenck, S.B.G. (1975). The Eysenck Personality Questionnaire (Adult). Sevenoaks: Hodder & Stoughton, Ltd.

Farquhar, J.W., Maccoby, N., Wood, P.D. & Alexander, J.K., Brietrose, H., Brown, B.W., Haskell, W.L., McAlister, A.L., Meyer, A.J., Nash, J.D. & Stern, M.P. (1977). Community education for cardiovascular health. *Lancet, 1977*(1), 1192–1195.

Farr, R.M. & Moscovici, S. (eds) (1984). *Social representations*. Cambridge: Cambridge University Press.

Fassinger, R.E. (1987). Use of structural equation modeling in counseling psychology research. *Journal of Counseling Psychology, 34*, 425–436.

Fenton Lewis, A. & Modle, W.J. (1982). Health indicators: what are they? An approach to efficacy in health care. *Health Trends, 14*, 3–7.

Fetterman, D.M. (1989). *Ethnography: Step by step*. Newbury Park, Sage.

Fewtrell, W.D. & Toms, D.A. (1985). Pattern of discussion in traditional and novel ward round procedures. *British Journal of Medical Psychology, 58*, 57–62.

Feyerabend, P. (1975). *Against method*. London: Verso.

Feynman, R.P. (1985). *"Surely you're joking, Mr. Feynman!"*. London: Vintage Books.

Fine, M.A. & Kurdek, L.A. (1993). Reflections on determining authorship credit and authorship order on faculty–student collaborations. *American Psychologist, 48*, 1141–1171.

Firth-Cozens, J. (1993). *Audit in mental health services*. Hove: Lawrence Erlbaum Associates.

Fiske, D.W. & Fogg, L. (1990). But the reviewers are making different criticisms of my paper! Diversity and uniqueness in reviewer comments. *American Psychologist, 45*, 591–598.

Fiske, S.T. & Taylor, S.E. (1991). *Social cognition* (2nd edn). New York: McGraw-Hill.

Flick, S.N. (1988). Managing attrition in clinical research. *Clinical Psychology Review, 8*, 499–515.

Floyd, F.A. & Widaman, K.F. (1995). Factor analysis in the development and refinement of clinical assessment instruments. *Psychological Assessment, 7*, 286–299.

Fonagy, P. (1982). Integration of psychoanalysis and empirical science: A review. *International Review of Psycho-Analysis, 9*, 125–145.

Fonagy, P. & Moran, G. (1993). Advances in the systematic study of the individual case. In N.E. Miller, L. Luborsky, J. Barber & J. Docherty (eds), *A guide to psychotherapy research and practice*. New York: Basic Books.

Fox, C.M. & Jones, J.A. (1998). Use of Rasch modeling in counseling psychology research. *Journal of Counseling Psychology, 45*, 30–45.

Fransella, F. (1981). Repertory grid technique. In F. Fransella (ed.), *Personality: Theory, measurement and research*. London: Methuen.

Freud, S. (1905/1953). Fragments of an analysis of a case of hysteria ("Dora"). In J. Strachey (ed. and trans.), *The standard edition of the complete works of Sigmund Freud* (Vol. 7). London: Hogarth Press.

Freud, S. (1909/1955). Analysis of a phobia in a five year old boy ("Little Hans"). In J. Strachey (ed. and trans.), *The standard edition of the complete works of Sigmund Freud* (Vol. 10). London: Hogarth Press.

Freud, S. (1905/1977). *Case histories* (2 vols). Harmondsworth: Pelican.

Friedrich, J. & Lüdke, H. (1975). *Participant observation: theory and practice*. Farnborough: Saxon House.

Garfield, S.L. & Bergin, A.E. (eds) (1986). *Handbook of psychotherapy and behavior change* (3rd edn). New York: Wiley.

Garfinkel, H. (1967). *Studies in ethnomethodology*. Englewood Cliffs, New Jersey: Prentice Hall.

Gaynor, S.T., Baird, S.C. & Nelson-Grey, R.O. (1999). Application of time-series (single-subject) designs in clinical psychology. In P.C. Kendall, J.N. Butcher & G.N. Holmbeck (eds), *Handbook of research methods in clinical psychology* (2nd edn). New York: Wiley.

Geertz, C. (1973). *The interpretation of cultures*. New York: Basic Books.

Georgaca, E. (2000). Reality and discourse: A critical study of the category of "delusions". *British Journal of Medical Psychology, 73,* 227–242.

Gergen, K.J. (1985). The social constructionist movement in modern psychology. *American Psychologist, 40,* 266–275.

Gergen, K.J. (1994). *Realities and relationships: Soundings in social construction.* Cambridge, MA: Harvard University Press.

Gergen, K.J. (2001). Psychological science in a postmodern context. *American Psychologist, 56,* 803–813.

Giorgi, A. (1975). An application of phenomenological method in psychology. In A. Giorgi, C. Fischer & E. Murray (eds), *Duquesne studies in phenomenological psychology* (Vol. 2). Pittsburgh, PA: Duquesne University Press.

Giorgi, A. (1985). Sketch of a psychological phenomenological method. In A. Giorgi (ed.), *Phenomenology and psychological research.* Pittsburgh: Duquesne University Press.

Glaser, B. G. (1978). *Theoretical sensitivity.* Mill Valley, CA: Sociology Press.

Glaser, B.G. & Strauss, A.L. (1967). *The discovery of grounded theory: Strategies for qualitative research.* Chicago: Aldine.

Goffman, E. (1961). *Asylums: Essays on the social situation of mental patients and other inmates.* Garden City, New York: Doubleday.

Goldfried, M.R. (1980). Toward delineation of therapeutic change principles. *American Psychologist, 35,* 991–999.

Goldfried, M.R. & Kent, R.N. (1972). Traditional versus behavioral personality assessment: A comparison of methodological and theoretical assumptions. *Psychological Bulletin, 77,* 409–420.

Good, D.A. & Watts, F.N. (1996). Qualitative research. In G. Parry & F.N. Watts (eds), *Behavioural and mental health research: A handbook of skills and methods* (2nd edn). Hove: Lawrence Erlbaum Associates.

Goodman, G. (1972). *Companionship therapy: Studies in structured intimacy.* San Francisco: Jossey-Bass.

Goodman, G. & Dooley, D. (1976) A framework for help-intended communication. *Psychotherapy: Theory, Research and Practice, 13,* 106–117.

Gottman, J.M. (1981). *Time-series analysis: A comprehensive introduction for social scientists.* New York: Cambridge University Press.

Gottman, J.M. & Roy, A.K. (1990). *Sequential analysis: A guide for behavioral researchers.* New York: Cambridge University Press.

Gould, S.J. (1981). *The mismeasure of man.* New York: Norton.

Grace, R.C. (2001). On the failure of operationism. *Theory & Psychology, 11,* 5–33.

Graham, S. (1992). "Most of the subjects were white and middle class": Trends in published research on African Americans in selected APA journals, 1970–1989. *American Psychologist, 47,* 629–639.

Green, R.S. & Attkisson, C.C. (1984). Quality assurance and program evaluation: similarities and differences. *American Behavioral Scientist, 27,* 552–582.

Greenberg, L.S., Rice, L.N. & Elliott, R. (1993). *Facilitating emotional change: The moment-by-moment process.* New York: Guilford Press.

Greenberg, L.S. & Pinsof, W. (eds) (1986). *The psychotherapeutic process: A research handbook.* New York: Guilford.

Greenson, R.R. (1967). *The technique of psychoanalysis* (Vol. 1). New York: International Universities Press.

Guba, E.G. & Lincoln, Y.S. (1989). *Fourth generation evaluation.* Newbury Park, CA: Sage.

Guerin, D. & MacKinnon, D.P. (1985). An assessment of the California child passenger restraint requirement. *American Journal of Public Health, 75,* 142–144.

Gynther, M.D. & Green, S.B. (1982). Methodological problems in research with self-report inventories. In P.C. Kendall & J.N. Butcher (eds), *Handbook of research methods in clinical psychology*. New York: Wiley.

Haaga, D.A.F. & Stiles, W.B. (2000). Randomized clinical trials in psychotherapy research: Methodology, design, and evaluation. In C.R. Snyder & R.E. Ingram, *Handbook of psychological change* (pp. 14–39). New York: Wiley.

Hamlyn, D.W. (1970). *The theory of knowledge*. Garden City, NY: Doubleday Anchor.

Hammen, C. (1992). Life events and depression: The plot thickens. *American Journal of Community Psychology, 20*, 179–193.

Hardy, G.E. (1993). Organisational issues: Making research happen. In M. Aveline & D.A. Shapiro (eds), *Research foundations for psychotherapy practice*. Chichester: Wiley.

Harper, D.J. (1994). The professional construction of "paranoia" and the discursive use of diagnostic criteria. *British Journal of Medical Psychology, 67*, 131–143.

Harré, R. (1974). Blueprint for a new science. In N. Armistead (ed.), *Reconstructing social psychology*. Harmondsworth: Penguin Education.

Hartnoll, R., Daviaud, E., Lewis, R. & Mitcheson, M. (1985). *Drug problems: Assessing local needs—A practical manual for assessing the nature and extent of problematic drug use in a community*. Drug Indicators Project, Department of Politics and Sociology, Birkbeck College, London University.

Hathaway, S.R. & McKinley, J.C. (1951). *Minnesota Multiphasic Personality Inventory manual*. New York: Psychological Corporation.

Hayes, S.C. (1981). Single case experimental design and empirical clinical practice. *Journal of Consulting and Clinical Psychology, 49*, 193–211.

Hayes, S.C., Barlow, D.H. & Nelson-Gray, R.O. (1999). *The scientist practitioner: Research and accountability in the age of managed care* (2nd edn). Needham Heights, MA: Allyn & Bacon.

Haynes, S.N. & O'Brien, W.O. (2000). *Principles of behavioral assessment: A functional approach to psychological assessment*. New York: Plenum.

Helman, C.G. (1990). *Culture, health and illness: An introduction for health professionals* (2nd edn). London: Wright.

Henwood, K.L. & Pidgeon, N. (1992). Qualitative research and psychological theorising. *British Journal of Psychology, 83*, 97–111.

Herbert, J.D., Lilienfeld, S.O., Lohr, J.M., Montgomery, R.W., O'Donohue, W.T., Rosen, G.M. & Tolin, D.F. (2000). Science and pseudoscience in the development of Eye Movement Desensitization and Reprocessing: Implications for clinical psychology. *Clinical Psychology Review, 20*, 945–971.

Hess, A.K. & Weiner, I.B. (eds) (1999). *The handbook of forensic therapy*. New York: Wiley.

Hill, C.E. (1991). Almost everything you ever wanted to know about how to do process research on counseling and psychotherapy but didn't know who to ask. In C.E. Watkins & L.J. Schneider (eds), *Research in counseling* (pp. 85–118). Hillsdale, NJ: Erlbaum.

Hill, C.E., Thompson, B.J. & Williams, E.N. (1997). A guide to conducting consensual qualitative research. *The Counseling Psychologist, 25*, 517–572.

Hinshaw, S.P., Henker, B., Whalen, C.K., Erhart, D. & Dunnington, R.E. (1989). Aggressive, prosocial, and nonsocial behavior in hyperactive boys: Dose effects of methylphenidate in naturalistic settings. *Journal of Consulting and Clinical Psychology, 57*, 636–643.

Hodgson, R. & Rollnick, S. (1996). More fun, less stress: How to survive in research. In G. Parry & F.N. Watts (eds), *Behavioural and mental health research: A handbook of skills and methods* (2nd edn). Hove: Lawrence Erlbaum Associates.

Hollrah, J.L., Schlottmann, R.S., Scott, A.B. & Brunetti, D.G. (1995). Validity of the MMPI subtle items. *Journal of Personality Assessment, 65*, 278–299.

Honderich, T. (ed.) (1995). *The Oxford companion to philosophy*. Oxford: Oxford University Press.

Horowitz, L.M., Rosenberg, S.E., Baer, B.A., Ureño, G. & Villaseñor, V.S. (1988). Inventory of interpersonal problems: Psychometric properties and clinical applications. *Journal of Consulting and Clinical Psychology*, 56, 885–892.

Horowitz, M.J. (1982). Strategic dilemmas and the socialization of psychotherapy researchers. *British Journal of Clinical Psychology*, 21, 119–127.

Hoshmand, L.T. & Polkinghorne, D.E. (1992). Redefining the science–practice relationship and professional training. *American Psychologist*, 47, 55–66.

Howard, K.I., Kopta, M., Krause, M.S. & Orlinsky, D.E. (1986). The dose-effect relationship in psychotherapy. *American Psychologist*, 41, 159–164.

Howard, K.I., Krause, M.S. & Orlinsky, D.E. (1986). The attrition dilemma: Towards a new strategy for psychotherapy research. *Journal of Consulting and Clinical Psychology*, 54, 106–110.

Howell, D.C. (2002). *Statistical methods for psychology* (5th edn). Pacific Grove, CA: Duxbury Press.

Hoyle, R.H. & Smith, G.T. (1994). Formulating clinical research hypotheses as structural equation models: a conceptual overview. *Journal of Consulting and Clinical Psychology*, 62, 429–440.

Hsu, L.M. (1989). Random sampling, randomization, and equivalence of contrasted groups in psychotherapy outcome research. *Journal of Consulting and Clinical Psychology*, 57, 131–137.

Hubble, M.A., Duncan, B.L. & Miller, S.D. (1999). *The heart and soul of change: What works in therapy*. Washington, DC: American Psychological Association.

Humphreys, K. & Moos, R. (2001). Can encouraging substance abuse patients to participate in self-help groups reduce demand for health care? A quasi-experimental study. *Alcoholism: Clinical and Experimental Research*, 25, 711–716.

Humphries, L. (1970). *Tearoom trade*. Chicago: Aldine.

Hunter, J.E. & Schmidt, F.L. (1990). *Methods of meta-analysis*. Newbury Park, CA: Sage.

Husserl, E. (1931). *Ideas: General introduction to pure phenomenology*. London: George Allen & Unwin. (Original German edition, 1913.)

Imber, S.D., Glanz, L.M., Elkin, I., Sotsky, S.M., Boyer, J.L. & Leber, W.R. (1986). Ethical issues in psychotherapy research: Problems in a collaborative clinical trials study. *American Psychologist*, 41, 137–146.

Jackson, P.R. (1996). Analysing data. In G. Parry & F.N. Watts (eds), *Behavioural and mental health research: A handbook of skills and methods* (2nd edn). Hove: Lawrence Erlbaum Associates.

Jacobson, N.S. & Truax, P. (1991). Clinical significance: A statistical approach to defining meaningful change in psychotherapy research. *Journal of Consulting and Clinical Psychology*, 59, 12–19.

Jacobson, N.S., Roberts, L.J., Burns, S.B. & McGlinchey, J.B. (1999). Methods for defining and determining the clinical significance of treatment effects: Description application, and alternatives. *Journal of Consulting and Clinical Psychology*, 67, 300–307.

Jahoda, M. (1958). *Current concepts of positive mental health*. New York: Basic Books.

James, W. (1902). *Varieties of religious experience: A study in human nature*. New York: Longmans.

James, W. (1907/1981). *Pragmatism*. Indianapolis: Hackett.

Jennings, J.L. (1986). Husserl revisited: The forgotten distinction between psychology and phenomenology. *American Psychologist*, 41, 1231–1240.

Joffe, H. (1996). AIDS research and prevention: A social representational approach. *British Journal of Medical Psychology*, 69, 169–190.

Joffe, J.M. & Albee, G.W. (eds) (1981). *Prevention through political action and social change*. Hanover: University Press of New England.

Jones, E.E., Ghannam, J., Nigg, J.R. & Dyer, J.F.P. (1993). A paradigm for single-case research: The time series study of a long-term psychotherapy for depression. *Journal of Consulting and Clinical Psychology*, 61, 381–394.

Jones, E.E. & Nisbett, R.E. (1971). The actor and the observer: Divergent perceptions of the causes of behavior. In E.E. Jones, D.E. Kanouse, H.H. Kelley, R.E. Nisbett, S. Valins & B. Weiner (eds), *Attribution: Perceiving the causes of behavior*. Morristown, NJ: General Learning Press.

Kazdin, A.E. (1981). Drawing valid inferences from case studies. *Journal of Consulting and Clinical Psychology*, 49, 183–192.

Kazdin, A.E. (1982). *Single case research designs: Methods for clinical and applied settings*. Oxford: Oxford University Press.

Kazdin, A.E. (1995). Preparing and evaluating research reports. *Psychological Assessment*, 7, 228–237.

Kazdin, A.E. & Bass, D. (1989). Power to detect differences between alternative treatments in comparative psychotherapy outcome research. *Journal of Consulting and Clinical Psychology*, 57, 138–147.

Kelly, G.A. (1955). *The psychology of personal constructs*. New York: Norton.

Kendall, P.C., Butcher, J.N. & Holmbeck, G.N. (eds) (1999). *Handbook of research methods in clinical psychology* (2nd edn). New York: Wiley.

Kendall, P.C., Flannery-Schroeder, E.C. & Ford, J.D. (1999). Therapy outcome research methods. In P.C. Kendall, J.N. Butcher & G.N. Holmbeck (eds), *Handbook of research methods in clinical psychology* (2nd edn). New York: Wiley.

Kennedy, P., Fisher, K. & Pearson, E. (1988). Ecological evaluation of a Rehabilitative Environment for spinal cord injured people: Behavioural mapping and feedback. *British Journal of Clinical Psychology*, 27, 239–246.

Kenny, D.A. (1979). *Correlation and causality*. Chichester: Wiley.

Keppel, G. (1991). *Design and analysis: A researcher's handbook* (3rd edn). Englewood Cliffs, New Jersey: Prentice Hall.

Kerlinger, F.N. (1986). *Foundations of behavioral research* (3rd edn). New York: Holt, Rinehart & Winston.

Kessler, R.C., McGonagle, K.A., Zhao, S., Nelson, C.B., Hughes, M., Eshleman, S., Wittchen, H.-U. & Kendler, K.S. (1994). Lifetime and 12-month prevalence of DSM-III-R psychiatric disorders in the United States. *Archives of General Psychiatry*, 51, 8–19.

Kiesler, D.J. (1966). Some myths of psychotherapy research and the search for a paradigm. *Psychological Bulletin*, 65, 110–136.

Kimble, G.A. (1984). Psychology's two cultures. *American Psychologist*, 39, 833–839.

King, M., Sibbald, B., Ward, E., Bower, P., Lloyd, M., Gabbay, M. & Byford, S. (2000). Randomised controlled trial of non-directive counselling, cognitive-behavior therapy and usual general practitioner care in the management of depression as well as mixed anxiety and depression in primary care. *Health Technology Assessment*, 4 (19).

Kirk, R.E. (1995). *Experimental design: Procedures for the behavioral sciences* (3rd edn). Belmont, CA: Brooks/Cole.

Kirschenbaum, H. (1979). *On becoming Carl Rogers*. New York: Delta.

Kitzinger, J. (1995). Introducing focus groups. *British Medical Journal*, 311, 299–302.

Knox, S., Hess, S.A., Petersen, D.A. & Hill, C.E. (1997). A qualitative analysis of client perceptions of the effects of helpful therapist self-disclosure in long-term therapy. *Journal of Counseling Psychology*, 44, 274–283.

Koch, S. (1964). Psychology and emerging conceptions of knowledge as unitary. In T.W. Wann (ed.), *Behaviorism and phenomenology* (pp. 1–45). Chicago: University of Chicago Press.

Koocher, G.P. & Keith-Spiegel, P. (1998). *Ethics in psychology: Professional standards and cases*. New York: Oxford University Press.

Korchin, S.J. (1976). *Modern clinical psychology: Principles of intervention in the clinic and community*. New York: Basic Books.

Korchin, S.J. & Cowan, P. (1982). Ethical perspectives in clinical research. In P.C. Kendall & J.N. Butcher (eds), *Handbook of research methods in clinical psychology*. New York: Wiley.

Kraemer, H.C. (1981). Coping strategies in psychiatric clinical research. *Journal of Consulting and Clinical Psychology*, 49, 309–319.

Kraemer, H.C. & Thiemann, S. (1987). *How many subjects? Statistical power analysis in research*. Newbury Park, CA: Sage.

Krippendorff, K. (1980). *Content analysis: An introduction to its methodology*. London: Sage.

Krueger, R.A. (1994). *Focus groups: A practical guide for applied research* (2nd edn). Thousand Oaks, California: Sage.

Krupnik, J.L. & Pincus, H.A. (1992). The cost-effectiveness of psychotherapy: A plan for research. *American Journal of Psychiatry*, 149, 1295–1305.

Kuhn, T.S. (1970). *The structure of scientific revolutions* (2nd edn). Chicago: University of Chicago Press.

Kurz, D.E. (1983). The use of participant observation in evaluation research. *Evaluation and Program Planning*, 6, 93–102.

Kvale, S. (1996). *Interviews: An introduction to qualitative research interviewing*. Thousand Oaks, CA: Sage.

Labov, W. & Fanshel, D. (1977). *Therapeutic discourse*. New York: Academic Press.

Laing, R.D. (1959). *The divided self: An existential study in sanity and madness*. London: Tavistock Publications.

Lakatos, I. (1970). Falsification and the methodology of scientific research programmes. In I. Lakatos & A. Musgrave (eds), *Criticism and the growth of knowledge*. Cambridge: Cambridge University Press.

Lakatos, I. & Musgrave, A. (eds) (1970). *Criticism and the growth of knowledge*. Cambridge: Cambridge University Press.

Lambert, M.J. (2001). Psychotherapy outcome and quality improvement: Introduction to the special section on patient-focused research. *Journal of Consulting and Clinical Psychology*, 69, 147–149.

Lambert, M.J. & Bergin, A.E. (1994). The effectiveness of psychotherapy. In A.E. Bergin & S.L. Garfield (eds), *Handbook of psychotherapy and behavior change* (4th edn). New York: Wiley.

Lambert, M.J., Hansen, N.B. & Finch, A.E. (2001). Patient-focused research: Using patient outcome data to enhance treatment effects. *Journal of Consulting and Clinical Psychology*, 69, 159–172.

Lambie, J. (1991). The misuse of Kuhn in psychology. *The Psychologist*, 4, 6–11.

Lanham, R. (1979). *Revising prose*. New York: Scribners.

Larsen, D.L., Attkisson, C.C., Hargreaves, W.A. & Nguyen, T.D. (1979). Assessment of client/patient satisfaction: Development of a general scale. *Evaluation and Program Planning*, 2, 197–207.

Lather, P. (1991). *Getting smart: Feminist research and pedagogy with/in the postmodern*. New York: Routledge.

Lazarus, A.A. & Davison, G.C. (1971). Clinical innovation in research and practice. In A.E. Bergin & S.L. Garfield (eds), *Handbook of psychotherapy and behavior change*. New York: Wiley.

Lebow, J. (1982). Consumer satisfaction with mental health treatment. *Psychological Bulletin*, 91, 244–259.

Lembcke, P.A. (1967). Evolution of the medical audit. *Journal of the American Medical Association*, *199*, 543–550.

Levi-Strauss, C. (1958/1963). *Structural anthropology*. Garden City, NY: Doubleday Anchor.

Lincoln, Y. & Guba, E.G. (1985). *Naturalistic inquiry*. Beverly Hills, CA: Sage.

Linehan, M.M. (1993). *Cognitive behavioral treatment of borderline personality disorder: The dialectics of effective treatment*. New York: Guilford Press.

Lissitz, R.W. & Green, S.B. (1975). Effect of the number of scale points on reliability: A Monte Carlo approach. *Journal of Applied Psychology*, *60*, 10–13.

Llewelyn, S.P. (1988). Psychological therapy as viewed by clients and therapists. *British Journal of Clinical Psychology*, *27*, 223–237.

Lovie, A.D. & Lovie, P. (1991). Graphical methods for exploring data. In A.D. Lovie & P. Lovie (eds), *New developments in statistics for psychology and the social sciences*. Leicester: BPS Books and Routledge.

Luria, A.R. (1973). *The working brain: An introduction to neuropsychology*. New York: Basic Books.

Lykken, D.T. (1968). Statistical significance in psychological research. *Psychological Bulletin*, *70*, 151–159.

Lyons, J. S., Howard, K. I., O'Mahoney, M. T. & Lish, J. D. (1997). *The measurement and management of clinical outcomes in mental health*. New York: Wiley.

Lyotard, J.-F. (1979). *La condition postmoderne: Rapport sur le savoir* (trans. 1984 as *The postmodern condition: A report on knowledge*). Manchester: Manchester University Press.

McCormack, H.M, Horne, D.J. de L. & Sheather, S. (1988). Clinical applications of visual analogue scales: A critical review. *Psychological Medicine*, *18*, 1007–1019.

McGuire, W.J. (1973). The yin and yang of progress in social psychology: Seven Koan. *Journal of Personality and Social Psychology*, *26*, 446–456.

McKillip, J. (1987). *Need analysis: Tools for the human services and education*. Newbury Park: Sage.

McLeod, J. (1997). *Narrative and psychotherapy*. London: Sage.

McLeod, J. (2001). *Qualitative research in counselling and psychotherapy*. London: Sage.

Macran, S., Stiles, W. B. & Smith, J. A. (1999). How does personal therapy affect therapists' practice? *Journal of Counseling Psychology*, *46*, 419–431.

Madill, A. & Barkham, M. (1997). Discourse analysis of a theme in one successful case of psychodynamic-interpersonal psychotherapy. *Journal of Counseling Psychology*, *44*, 232–244.

Madill, A., Jordan, A. & Shirley, C. (2000). Objectivity and reliability in qualitative analysis: Realist, contextualist and radical constructionist epistemologies. *British Journal of Psychology*, *91*, 1–20.

Mahoney, M.J. (1976). *Scientist as subject: The psychological imperative*. Cambridge, MA: Ballinger.

Mahrer, A.R. (1988). Discovery-oriented psychotherapy research: Rationale, aims, and methods. *American Psychologist*, *43*, 694–702.

Malinowski, B. (1929). *The sexual life of savages in North Western Melanesia*. London: Routledge & Kegan Paul.

Mangen, S. (1988). Assessing cost-effectiveness. In F.N. Watts (ed.), *New developments in clinical psychology* (Vol. 2). Chichester: Wiley.

Marrow, A.J. (1969). *The practical theorist: The life and work of Kurt Lewin*. New York: Basic Books.

Mattison, V. & Pistrang, N. (2000). *Saying goodbye: When keyworker relationships end*. London: Free Association Books.

Maxwell, R.J. (1984). Quality assessment in health. *British Medical Journal*, *288*, 1470–1472.

May, R., Angel, E. & Ellenberger, H.F. (1958). *Existence: A new dimension in psychiatry and psychology*. New York: Basic Books.

Mayou, R.A., Ehlers, A. & Hobbs, M. (2000). Psychological debriefing for road traffic accident victims. *British Journal of Psychiatry*, *174*, 589–593.

Meehl, P. (1978). Theoretical risks and tabular asterisks: Sir Karl, Sir Ronald, and the slow progress of soft psychology. *Journal of Consulting and Clinical Psychology*, *46*, 806–834.

Meltzoff, J. (1998). *Critical thinking about research*. Washington, DC: American Psychological Association.

Merbaum, M. & Lowe, M.R. (1982). Serendipity in research in clinical psychology. In P.C. Kendall & J.N. Butcher (eds) *Handbook of research methods in clinical psychology*. New York: Wiley.

Merganthaler, E. & Stinson, C.H. (1992). Psychotherapy transcription standards. *Psychotherapy Research*, *2*, 125–142.

Miles, M.B. & Huberman, A.M. (1994). *Qualitative data analysis: An expanded sourcebook* (2nd edn). Thousand Oaks, CA: Sage.

Milgram, S. (1964). Issues in the study of obedience: A reply to Baumrind. *American Psychologist*, *19*, 848–852.

Milne, D. (1987). *Evaluating mental health practice: Methods and applications*. Beckenham: Croom Helm.

Milne, D., Britton, P. & Wilkinson, I. (1990). The scientist-practitioner in practice. *Clinical Psychology Forum*, *30*, 27–30.

Mintz, J. (1981). Tactical problems in research design. Paper presented to the Society for Psychotherapy Research, Aspen Colorado, June, 1981.

Mintz, J. & Kiesler, D.J. (1982). Individualized measures of psychotherapy outcome. In P.C. Kendall & J.N. Butcher (eds), *Handbook of research methods in clinical psychology*. New York: Wiley.

Mischel, W. (1968). *Personality and assessment*. New York: Wiley.

Mondada, L. (1998). Therapy interactions: Specific genre or "blown up" version of ordinary conversational practices? *Pragmatics*, *8*, 155–166.

Moondog (1991). Quoted on BBC Radio 4, 24 May 1991.

Moran, G.S. & Fonagy, P. (1987). Psychoanalysis and diabetic control: A single case study. *British Journal of Medical Psychology*, *60*, 357–372.

Moras, K. & Hill, C.E. (1991). Rater selection for psychotherapy process research: An evaluation of the state of the art. *Psychotherapy Research*, *1*, 113–123.

Morgan, D.L. & Morgan, R.K. (2001). Single-participant research design. *American Psychologist*, *56*, 119–127.

Morley, S. (1996). Single case research. In G. Parry & F.N. Watts (eds), *Behavioural and mental health research: A handbook of skills and methods* (2nd edn). London: Lawrence Erlbaum Associates.

Morley, S. & Adams, M. (1989). Some simple statistical tests for exploring single-case time-series data. *British Journal of Clinical Psychology*, *28*, 1–18.

Morley, S. & Adams, M. (1991). Graphical analysis of single-case time-series data. *British Journal of Clinical Psychology*, *30*, 97–115.

Morrow-Bradley, C. & Elliott, R. (1986). Utilization of psychotherapy research by practising psychotherapists. *American Psychologist*, *41*, 188–197.

Moser, C.A. & Kalton, G. (1971). *Survey methods in social investigation*. London: Heinemann.

Murray, H.A. (1938). *Explorations in personality*. New York: Oxford University Press.

Murray, M. (in press). Narrative psychology. In J. Smith (ed.), *Qualitative psychology: A practical guide to methods*. London: Sage.

Neimeyer, R.A. (1993). An appraisal of constructivist psychotherapies. *Journal of Consulting and Clinical Psychology*, *61*, 221–234.

Nelson, R.O. (1981). Realistic dependent measures for clinical use. *Journal of Consulting and Clinical Psychology*, *49*, 168–182.

Nisbett, R.E. & Ross, L. (1980). *Human inference: Strategies and shortcomings of social judgement*. Englewood Cliffs, NJ: Prentice-Hall.

Nisbett, R.E. & Wilson, T.D. (1977). Telling more than we know: Verbal reports on mental processes. *Psychological Review, 84*, 231–239.

Nunnally, J.C. & Bernstein, I.H. (1994). *Psychometric theory* (3rd edn). New York: McGraw-Hill.

O'Sullivan, K.R. & Dryden, W. (1990). A survey of clinical psychologists in the South East Thames Health Region: Activities, role and theoretical orientation. *Clinical Psychology Forum, 29*, 21–26.

Oakes, M. (1986). *Statistical inference: A commentary for the social and behavioural sciences*. Chichester: Wiley.

Oakley, A. (1981). Interviewing women: A contradiction in terms. In H. Roberts (ed.), *Doing feminist research*. London: Routledge & Kegan Paul.

Oppenheim, A.N. (1992). *Questionnaire design, interviewing and attitude measurement* (new edn). London: Pinter.

Orford, J. (1992). *Community psychology: Theory and practice*. Chichester: Wiley.

Orwell, G. (1946/1968). Politics and the English language. Originally published in *Horizon*, reprinted in *The collected essays and letters of George Orwell (Vol. 4): In front of your nose 1945–1950*. Harmondsworth, Middlesex: Penguin Books.

Overall, J.E. & Gorham, D.R. (1962). The brief psychiatric rating scale. *Psychological Reports, 10*, 799–812.

Packer, M.J. & Addison, R.B. (eds) (1989). *Entering the circle: Hermeneutic investigation in psychology*. Albany, NY: SUNY Press.

Pantelis, C., Taylor, J. & Campbell, P. (1988). The South Camden schizophrenia survey: An experience of community-based research. *Bulletin of the Royal College of Psychiatrists, 12*, 98–101.

Parloff, M.B. (1986). Placebo controls in psychotherapy research: A sine qua non or a placebo for research problems? *Journal of Consulting and Clinical Psychology, 54*, 79–87.

Parry, G. (1992). Improving psychotherapy services: Applications of research, audit and evaluation. *British Journal of Clinical Psychology, 31*, 3–19.

Parry, G. & Gowler, D. (1983). Career stresses on psychological therapists. In D. Pilgrim (ed.), *Psychology and psychotherapy: Current trends and issues*. London: Routledge.

Parry, G., Shapiro, D.A. & Firth, J. (1986). The case of the anxious executive: A study from the research clinic. *British Journal of Medical Psychology, 59*, 221–233.

Patton, M.Q. (1997). *Utilization-focused evaluation* (3rd edn). Thousand Oaks, CA: Sage.

Patton, M.Q. (2002). *Qualitative research and evaluation methods* (3rd edn). Thousand Oaks, CA: Sage.

Paul, G.L. (1967). Strategies of outcome research in psychotherapy. *Journal of Consulting Psychology, 31*, 109–118.

Paulhus, D.L. (1984). Two-component models of socially desirable responding. *Journal of Personality and Social Psychology, 46*, 598–609.

Payne, S.L.B. (1951). *The art of asking questions* (Studies in Public Opinion number 3). Princeton: Princeton University Press.

Peplau, L.A. & Conrad, E. (1989). Feminist methods in psychology. *Psychology of Women Quarterly, 13*, 379–400.

Peterson, D.R. (1991). Connection and disconnection of research and practice in the education of professional psychologists. *American Psychologist, 46*, 422–429.

Phillips, J.P.N. (1986). Shapiro personal questionnaire and generalized personal questionnaire techniques: A repeated measures individualized outcome measurement. In L.S. Greenberg & W.M. Pinsof (eds). *The psychotherapeutic process: A research handbook* (pp. 557–590). New York: Guilford.

Pidgeon, N. & Henwood, K. (1996). Grounded theory: Practical implementation. In J.T.E. Richardson (ed.), *Handbook of qualitative research methods for psychology and the social sciences*. Leicester: British Psychological Society.

Pilgrim, D. & Treacher, A. (1992). *Clinical psychology observed*. London: Routledge.

Pistrang, N. (1990). Leaping the culture gap. *The Health Service Journal, 100(5204)*, 878–879.

Polkinghorne, D. (1983). *Methodology for the human sciences*. Albany, NY: Human Sciences Press.

Polkinghorne, D. (1988). *Narrative knowing and the human sciences*. Albany, NY: State University of New York Press.

Polkinghorne, D. (1989). Phenomenological research methods. In R.S. Valle & S. Halling, *Existential-phenomenological perspectives in psychology: Exploring the breadth of human experience* (pp. 41–60). New York: Plenum.

Pollio, H.R. (1982). *Behavior and existence*. Monterey, CA: Brooks/Cole.

Pollner, M. (1987). *Mundane reason: Reality in everyday and sociological discourse*. Cambridge: Cambridge University Press.

Popper, K.R. (1959). *The logic of scientific discovery*. New York: Basic Books. (Original German edition, 1934).

Popper, K.R. (1963). *Conjectures and refutations: The growth of scientific knowledge*. London: Routledge & Kegan Paul.

Potter, J. & Wetherell, M. (1987). *Discourse and social psychology*. London: Sage.

Prilleltensky, I. (1997). Values, assumptions, and practices: Assessing the moral implications of psychological discourse and action. *American Psychologist, 52*, 517–535.

Rapley, M. & Antaki, C. (1996). A conversation analysis of the "acquiescence" of people with learning disabilities. *Journal of Community and Applied Social Psychology, 6*, 207–227.

Reason, P. & Rowan, J. (eds) (1981). *Human enquiry: A sourcebook of new paradigm research*. Chichester: Wiley.

Reichenbach, H. (1938). *Experience and prediction: An analysis of the foundations and the structure of knowledge*. Chicago: University of Chicago Press.

Reicher, S. (2000). Against methodolatry: Some comments on Elliott, Fischer, and Rennie. *British Journal of Clinical Psychology, 39*, 1–6.

Rennie, D.L. (1990). Toward a representation of the client's experience of the psychotherapy hour. In G. Lietaer, J. Rombauts & R. Van Balen (eds), *Client-centered and experiential psychotherapy towards the nineties* (pp. 155–172). Leuven, Belgium: Leuven University Press.

Rennie, D.L. (1994). Clients' deference in psychotherapy. *Journal of Counseling Psychology, 41*, 427–437.

Rennie, D.L. & Brewer, L. (1987). A grounded theory of thesis blocking. *Teaching of Psychology, 14*, 10–16.

Rennie, D.L., Phillips, J.R. & Quartaro, G.K. (1988). Grounded theory: A promising approach to conceptualization in psychology. *Canadian Psychology, 29*, 139–150.

Rice, L.N. & Greenberg, L.S. (eds) (1984). *Patterns of change*. New York: Guilford Press.

Rice, L.N. & Sapiera, E.P. (1984). Task analysis and the resolution of problematic reactions. In L.N. Rice & L.S. Greenberg (eds), *Patterns of change*. New York: Guilford Press.

Richardson, J.T.E. (ed.) (1996). *Handbook of qualitative research methods for psychology and the social sciences*. Leicester: British Psychological Society.

Riessman, C.K. (1993). *Narrative analysis*. Newbury Park, CA: Sage.

Riger, S. (1992). Epistemological debates, feminist voices: Science, social values, and the study of women. *American Psychologist, 47*, 730–740.

Robson, C. (1993). *Real world research: A resource for social scientists and practitioner-researchers*. Oxford: Blackwell.

Roethlisberger, F.S. & Dickson, W.J. (1939). *Management and the worker*. Cambridge, MA: Harvard University Press.

Rogers, C.R. (1951). *Client-centered therapy: Its current practice, implications, and theory*. Boston, MA: Houghton Mifflin.

Rogers, C.R. (1955). Persons or science? A philosophical question. *American Psychologist, 10*, 267–278.

Rogers, C.R. (1957). The necessary and sufficient conditions of therapeutic personality change. *Journal of Consulting Psychology, 21*, 95–103.

Rogers, C.R. (1961). *On becoming a person: A therapist's view of psychotherapy*. Boston, MA: Houghton Mifflin.

Rogers, C.R. (1967). A silent young man. In C.R. Rogers, E.T. Gendlin, D.J. Kiesler & C. Truax, *The therapeutic relationship and its impact: A study of psychotherapy with schizophrenics*. University of Wisconsin Press.

Rogers, C.R. (1975). Empathic: An unappreciated way of being. *Counseling Psychologist, 5*, 2–10.

Rogers, C.R. (1985). Towards a more human science of the person. *Journal of Humanistic Psychology, 25*, 7–24.

Rogers, J.L., Howard, K.I. & Vessey, J.T. (1993). Using significance tests to evaluate equivalence between two experimental groups. *Psychological Bulletin, 113*, 553–565.

Rorer, L. (1965). The great response style myth. *Psychological Bulletin, 63*, 129–156.

Rose, S., Kamin, S.J. & Lewontin, R.C. (1984). *Not in our genes: Biology, ideology and human nature*. Harmondsworth, Penguin Books.

Rosenhan, D.L. (1973). On being sane in insane places. *Science, 179*, 250–258.

Rosenthal, R. (1978). How often are our numbers wrong? *American Psychologist, 33*, 1005–1008.

Rosenthal, R. & DiMatteo, M.R. (2001). Meta-analysis: Recent developments in quantitative methods for literature reviews. *Annual Review of Psychology, 52*, 59–82.

Rossi, P.H., Freeman, H.E. & Lipsey, M.W. (1999). *Evaluation: A systematic approach* (6th edn). Thousand Oaks, CA: Sage.

Rossi, P.H., Wright, J.D. & Andersen, A.B. (eds) (1983). *Handbook of survey research*. London: Academic Press.

Roth, A. & Fonagy, P. (1996). *What works for whom? A critical review of psychotherapy research*. New York: Guilford.

Roth, A., Fonagy, P. & Parry, G. (1996). Psychotherapy research, funding, and evidence-based practice. In A. Roth & P. Fonagy, *What works for whom? A critical review of psychotherapy research*. New York: Guilford.

Rothbaum, B.O., Hodges, L., Smith, S., Lee, J.H. & Price, L. (2000). A controlled study of virtual reality exposure therapy for the fear of flying. *Journal of Consulting and Clinical Psychology, 68*, 1020–1026.

Rudestam, K.E. & Newton, R.R. (2000). *Surviving your dissertation: A comprehensive guide to content and process* (2nd edn). Newbury Park: Sage.

Runyan, W.M. (1982). *Life histories and psychobiography: Explorations in theory and method*. New York: Oxford University Press.

Russell, B. (1961). *History of Western philosophy*. London: George Allen & Unwin.

Rust, J. & Golombok, S. (1999). *Modern psychometrics: The science of psychological assessment* (2nd edn). London: Routledge.

Sackett, D.L., Richardson, W.S., Rosenberg, W. & Haynes, R.B. (1997). *Evidence-based medicine: How to practice and teach EBM*. New York: Churchill Livingstone.

Sacks, H. (1995). *Lectures on conversation*. Malden, MA: Blackwell.

Sacks, H., Schegloff, E.A. & Jefferson, G. (1974). The simplest systematics for the organization of turn-taking in conversation. *Language, 50*, 696–735.

Sacks, O. (1985). *The man who mistook his wife for a hat*. London: Duckworth.

Santor, D.A., Ramsay, J.O. & Zuroff, D.C. (1994). Nonparametric item analyses of the Beck Depression Inventory: Evaluating gender item bias and response option weights. *Psychological Assessment, 6*, 255–270.

Sarbin, T.R. (ed.) (1986). *Narrative psychology: The storied nature of human conduct*. New York: Praeger.

Scarr, S. (1988). Race and gender as psychological variables: Social and ethical issues. *American Psychologist, 43*, 56–59.

Schegloff, E.A. (1999). Discourse, pragmatics, conversation, analysis. *Discourse Studies, 1*, 405–435.

Schwartz, J. (1992). *The creative moment: How science made itself alien to modern culture*. London: Jonathan Cape.

Schwartz, J. (1999). *Cassandra's daughter: A history of psychoanalysis in Europe and America*. London: Allen Lane: The Penguin Press.

Schwartz, N. (1999). Self-reports: How the questions shape the answers. *American Psychologist, 54*, 93–105.

Scriven, M. (1972). The methodology of evaluation. In C.H. Weiss (ed.), *Evaluating action programs*. Boston, MA: Allyn & Bacon.

Sears, D.O. (1986). College sophomores in the laboratory: Influences of a narrow data base on social psychology's view of human nature. *Journal of Personality and Social Psychology, 51*, 515–530.

Seligman, M.E.P. (1995). The effectiveness of psychotherapy: The *Consumer Reports* study. *American Psychologist, 50*, 965–974.

Shadish, W.R., Cook, T.D. & Campbell, D.T. (2001). *Experimental and quasi-experimental designs for generalized causal inference*. Boston, MA: Houghton Mifflin.

Shadish, W.R., Cook, T.D. & Leviton, L.C. (1991). *Foundations of program evaluation: Theories of practice*. Newbury Park: Sage.

Shallice, T. (1979). Case study approach in neuropsychological research. *Journal of Clinical Neuropsychology, 1*, 183–211.

Shallice, T. (1988). *From neuropsychology to mental structure*. Cambridge University Press.

Shallice, T., Burgess, P.W. & Frith, C.D. (1991). Can the neuropsychological case-study approach be applied to schizophrenia? *Psychological Medicine, 21*, 661–673.

Shapiro, D.A. (1996). Outcome research. In G. Parry & F.N. Watts (eds), *Behavioural and mental health research: A handbook of skills and methods* (2nd edn). Hove: Lawrence Erlbaum Associates.

Shapiro, D.A., Barkham, M., Rees, A. Hardy, G.E., Reynolds, S. & Startup, M. (1994). Effects of treatment duration and severity of depression on the effectiveness of cognitive-behavioral and psychodynamic-interpersonal psychotherapy. *Journal of Consulting and Clinical Psychology, 62*, 522–534.

Shapiro, D.A. & Shapiro, D. (1977). The "double standard" in the evaluation of psychotherapies. *Bulletin of the British Psychological Society, 30*, 209–210.

Shapiro, D.A. & Shapiro, D. (1983). Comparative therapy outcome research: Methodological implications of meta-analysis. *Journal of Consulting and Clinical Psychology, 51*, 42–53.

Shapiro, F. (1999). Eye Movement Desensitization and Reprocessing (EMDR) and the anxiety disorders. Clinical and research implications of an integrated psychotherapy treatment. *Journal of Anxiety Disorders, 13*, 35–67.

Shapiro, M.B. (1961a). A method of measuring psychological changes specific to the individual psychiatric patient. *British Journal of Medical Psychology, 34*, 151–155.

Shapiro, M.B. (1961b). The single case in fundamental clinical psychological research. *British Journal of Medical Psychology, 34*, 255–262.

Shapiro, M.B. (1967). Clinical psychology as an applied science. *British Journal of Psychiatry, 113*, 1039–1042.

Shapiro, M.B. (1985). A reassessment of clinical psychology as an applied science. *British Journal of Clinical Psychology, 24*, 1–11.

Shavelson, R.J., Webb, N.M. & Rowley, G.L. (1989). Generalizability theory. *American Psychologist, 44*, 922–932.

Sheatsley, P.B. (1983). Questionnaire construction and item writing. In P.H. Rossi, J.D. Wright & A.B. Anderson (eds), *Handbook of survey research*. London: Academic Press.

Shlien, J. (1970). Phenomenology and personality. In J.T. Hart & T.M. Tomlinson (eds), *New directions in client-centered therapy*. Boston: Houghton Mifflin.

Shoham-Salomon, V. & Hannah, M.T. (1991). Client-treatment interaction in the study of differential change processes. *Journal of Consulting and Clinical Psychology, 59*, 217–225.

Shrout, P.E. & Fliess, J.L. (1979). Intraclass correlations: Uses in assessing rater reliability. *Psychological Bulletin, 86*, 420–428.

Sidman, M. (1960). *Tactics of scientific research: Evaluating experimental data in psychology*. New York: Basic Books.

Sieber, J.E. & Stanley, B. (1988). Ethical and professional dimensions of socially sensitive research. *American Psychologist, 43*, 49–55.

Siegel, S. & Castellan, N.J. (1988). *Nonparametric statistics for the behavioral sciences* (2nd edn). New York: McGraw-Hill.

Sigelman, C.K., Budd, E.C., Spanhel, C.L. & Schoenrock, C.J. (1981). When in doubt, say yes: Acquiescence in interviews with mentally retarded persons. *Mental Retardation, 19*, 53–58.

Skinner, B.F. (1953). *Science and human behavior*. New York: Macmillan.

Skinner, B.F. (1974). *About behaviorism*. London: Jonathan Cape.

Skinner, C.J. (1991). Time series. In P. Lovie & A.D. Lovie (eds), *New developments in statistics for psychology and the social sciences* (Vol. 2). Leicester: British Psychological Society.

Slife, B.D. & Williams, R.N. (1995). *What's behind the research? Discovering hidden assumptions in the behavioral sciences*. London: Sage.

Sloane, R.B., Staples, F.R., Cristol, A.H., Yorkston, N.J. & Whipple, K. (1975). *Psychotherapy versus behavior therapy*. Cambridge, MA: Harvard University Press.

Smith, C.P. (2000). Content analysis and narrative analysis. In H.T. Reis & C.M. Judd (eds), *Handbook of research methods in social and personality psychology*. New York: Cambridge University Press.

Smith, J.A. (1995). Semi-structured interviewing and qualitative analysis. In J.A. Smith, R. Harré & L. Van Langenhove (eds), *Rethinking methods in psychology*. London: Sage.

Smith, J.A. (ed.) (in press). *Qualitative psychology: A practical guide to methods*. London: Sage.

Smith, J.A., Harré, R. & Van Langenhove, L. (eds) (1995). *Rethinking methods in psychology*. London: Sage.

Smith, J.A., Jarman, M. & Osborn, M. (1999). Doing interpretative phenomenological analysis. In M. Murray & K. Chamberlain (eds), *Qualitative health psychology* (pp. 218–240). London: Sage.

Smith, M.L. & Glass, D.V. (1977). Meta-analysis of psychotherapy outcome studies. *American Psychologist, 32*, 752–760.

Snow, R.E. (1991). Aptitude-treatment interaction as a framework for research on individual differences in psychotherapy. *Journal of Consulting and Clinical Psychology, 59*, 205–216.

Sokal, A. & Bricmont, J. (1999). *Intellectual impostures: Postmodern philosophers' abuse of science* (2nd edn). London: Profile Books.

Solomon, M., Pistrang, N. & Barker, C. (2001). The benefits of mutual support groups for parents of children with disabilities. *American Journal of Community Psychology, 29*, 113–132.

Spence, D.P. (1986). Narrative smoothing and clinical wisdom. In T.R. Sarbin (ed.), *Narrative psychology: The storied nature of human conduct* (pp. 211–232). New York: Praeger.

Spinelli, E. (1989). *The interpreted world: An introduction to phenomenological psychology.* London: Sage.

Sternberg, J.C. (1988). *The psychologist's companion: A guide to scientific writing for students and researchers.* Cambridge: Cambridge University Press.

Stevens, A. & Gabbay, J. (1991). Needs assessment needs assessment. *Health Trends, 23,* 20–23.

Stevens, S.S. (1935). The operational definition of psychological concepts. *Psychological Review, 42,* 517–527.

Stevens, S.S. (1946). On the theory of scales of measurement. *Science, 103,* 677–680.

Stewart, I. (1989). *Does God play dice? The new mathematics of chaos.* London: Penguin Books.

Stiles, W.B. (1980). Measurement of the impact of psychotherapy sessions. *Journal of Consulting and Clinical Psychology, 48,* 176–185.

Stiles, W.B. (1992). Producers and consumers of psychotherapy research ideas. *Journal of Psychotherapy Practice & Research, 1,* 305–307.

Stiles, W.B. (1993). Quality control in qualitative research. *Clinical Psychology Review, 13,* 593–618.

Stiles, W.B., Shapiro, D.A. & Elliott, R. (1986). "Are all psychotherapies equivalent?" *American Psychologist, 41,* 165–180.

Strauss, A. & Corbin, J. (1998). *Basics of qualitative research: Techniques and procedures for developing grounded theory* (2nd edn). Newbury Park, CA: Sage.

Strauss, J.S., Harding, C.M., Hafez, H. & Lieberman, P. (1987). The role of the patient in recovery from psychosis. In J.S. Strauss, W. Boker & H. Brenner (eds), *Psychosocial treatment of schizophrenia* (pp. 160–166). New York: Hans Huber.

Strunk, W. & White, E.B. (1959). *The elements of style.* New York: Macmillan.

Strupp, H.H. (1980a–d). Success and failure in time-limited psychotherapy. *Archives of General Psychiatry, 37,* 595–603; 708–717; 831–841; 947–954.

Sudman, S. (1976). *Applied sampling.* New York: Academic Press.

Sudman, S. & Bradburn, N.M. (1982). *Asking questions: A practical guide to questionnaire design.* San Francisco: Jossey-Bass.

Sudnow, D. (ed.) (1972). *Studies in social interaction.* New York: The Free Press.

Sue, S., Fujino, D.C., Hu, L., Takeuchi, D.T. & Zane, N.W.S. (1991). Community mental health services for ethnic minority groups: A test of the cultural responsiveness hypothesis. *Journal of Consulting and Clinical Psychology, 59,* 533–540.

Tabachnik, B.G. & Fidell, L.S. (2001). *Using multivariate statistics* (4th edn). New York: HarperCollins.

Taylor, S.J. & Bogdan, R. (1998). *Introduction to qualitative research methods: A guidebook and resource* (3rd edn). New York: Wiley.

ten Have, P. (1999). *Doing conversation analysis: A practical guide.* London: Sage.

Terwee, S.J.S. (1990). *Hermeneutics in psychology and psychoanalysis.* Berlin: Springer-Verlag.

Thornton, H.M. (1992). Breast cancer trials: A patient's viewpoint. *The Lancet, 339,* 44–45.

Tiffany, S.T., Cox, L.S. & Elash, C.A. (2000). Effects of transdermal nicotine patches on abstinence-induced and cue-elicited craving in cigarette smokers. *Journal of Consulting and Clinical Psychology, 68,* 233–240.

Tinsley, H.E.A. & Weiss, D.J. (1975). Interrater reliability and agreement of subjective judgements. *Journal of Counseling Psychology, 22,* 358–376.

Tizard, B. (1990). Research and policy: Is there a link? *The Psychologist, 13,* 435–440.

Todd, D.M., Kurcias, J. & Gloster, K. (1994). A review of research conducted in psychology program training clinics. *Professional Psychology: Research and Practice, 25,* 471–481.

Tracey, T.J. & Kokotovic, A.M. (1989). Factor structure of the Working Alliance Inventory. *Psychological Assessment, 1*, 207–210.

Trierweiler, S.J. & Stricker, G. (1998). *The scientific practice of professional psychology*. New York: Plenum.

Tukey, J.W. (1977). *Exploratory data analysis*. Reading, MA: Addison-Wesley.

van Dijk, T.A. (ed.) (1997a). *Discourse as structure and process: Discourse studies* (Vol. 1). Thousand Oaks, CA: Sage.

van Dijk, T.A. (ed.) (1997b). *Discourse as social interaction: Discourse studies* (Vol. 2). Thousand Oaks, CA: Sage.

Varvin, S. & Stiles, W.B. (1999). Emergence of severe traumatic experiences: An assimilation analysis of psychoanalytic therapy with a political refugee. *Psychotherapy Research, 9*, 381–404.

Walsh, R., Perrucci, A. & Severns, J. (1999). What's in a good moment: A hermeneutic study of psychotherapy values across levels of psychotherapy training. *Psychotherapy Research, 9*, 304–326.

Watson, J.B. (1919). *Psychology from the standpoint of a behaviorist*. Philadelphia: Lippincott.

Watson, J.B. (1931). *Behaviorism*. London: Kegan Paul & Co.

Watson, J.B. & Rayner, R. (1920). Conditioned emotional reactions. *Journal of Experimental Psychology, 3*, 1–14.

Watts, F.N. (1984). Applicable research in the NHS. *Bulletin of the British Psychological Society, 37*, 41–42.

Webb, E.J., Campbell, D.T., Schwartz, R.D. & Sechrest, L. (1966). *Unobtrusive measures: Nonreactive research in the social sciences*. Chicago: Rand McNally.

Weick, K.D. (1985). Systematic observational methods. In G. Lindzey & E. Aronson (eds), *Handbook of social psychology (3rd edn). Volume 1: Theory and method*. New York: Random House.

Weiner, D.N. (1948). Subtle and obvious keys for the MMPI. *Journal of Consulting Psychology, 12*, 164–170.

Weiss, C.H. (1972). *Evaluation research*. Englewood Cliffs, NJ: Prentice-Hall.

Weiss, C.H. (1986). Research and policy making: A limited partnership. In F. Heller (ed.), *The use and abuse of social science*. London: Sage.

Wertz, F.J. (1983). From everyday to psychological description: Analyzing the moments of a qualitative data analysis. *Journal of Phenomenological Psychology, 14*, 197–241.

Wertz, F.J. (1985). Methods and findings in the study of a complex life event: Being criminally victimized. In A. Giorgi (ed.), *Phenomenology and psychological research*. Pittsburgh: Duquesne University Press.

Westen, D., Feit, A. & Zittel, C. (1999). Methodological issues in research using projective methods. In P.C. Kendall, J.N. Butcher & G.N. Holmbeck (eds), *Handbook of research methods in clinical psychology* (2nd edn). New York: Wiley.

White, P.A. (1990). Ideas about causation in philosophy and psychology. *Psychological Bulletin, 108*, 3–18.

Whyte, W.F. (1943). *Street corner society: The social structure of an Italian slum*. Chicago: University of Chicago Press.

Whyte, W.H. (1959). *The organization man*. New York: Simon & Schuster.

Wiggins, J.S. (1973). *Personality and prediction: Principles of personality assessment*. Reading, MA: Addison-Wesley.

Wilkinson, S. (ed.) (1986). *Feminist social psychology: Developing theory and practice*. Milton Keynes: Open University Press.

Williams, J.M.G., Mathews, A. & MacLeod, C. (1996). The emotional Stroop task and psychopathology. *Psychological Bulletin, 120*, 3–24.

Willig, C. (2001). *Introducing qualitative research in psychology: Adventures in theory and method*. Buckingham: Open University Press.

Wilshaw, G. (1996). Adult survivors of childhood sexual abuse: A human enquiry based study of ongoing life characteristics. Paper presented at Second Annual Counselling Research Conference, British Association for Counselling, Birmingham, UK.

Wilson, B. (1987). Single case experimental designs in neuropsychological rehabilitation. *Journal of Clinical and Experimental Neuropsychology, 9,* 527–544.

Wilson, S. (1990). *Tate Gallery: An illustrated companion*. London: Tate Gallery.

Winer, B.J., Brown, D.R. & Michels, K.M. (1991). *Statistical principles in experimental design* (3rd edn). New York: McGraw-Hill.

Winter, D.A. (1992). *Personal construct psychology in clinical practice*. London: Routledge.

Wittgenstein, L. (1921/1961). *Tractatus logico-philosophicus*. London: Routledge.

Yalom, I.D. (1980). *Existential psychotherapy*. New York: Basic Books.

Yalom, I.D. & Elkin, G. (1974). *Everyday gets a little closer: A twice told therapy*. New York: Basic Books.

Yardley, L. (2000). Dilemmas in qualitative health research. *Psychology and Health, 15,* 215–228.

Yin, R.K. (1989). *Case study research: Design and methods* (rev. edn). Newbury Park, CA: Sage.

Young, H.H. (1982). A brief history of quality assurance and peer review. *Professional Psychology, 13,* 9–13.

Young, M. & Willmott, P. (1957). *Family and kinship in East London*. London: Routledge & Kegan Paul.

Young, R.M. (1979). Why are figures so significant? The role and critique of quantification. In J. Irvine, I. Miles & J. Evans (eds), *Demystifying social statistics*. London: Pluto Press.

Zeldin, T. (1994). *An intimate history of humanity*. New York: HarperCollins.

Zimbardo, P.G. (1973). On the ethics of interventions in human psychological research: With special reference to the Stanford prison experiment. *Cognition, 2,* 243–256.

AUTHOR INDEX

SUBJECT INDEX

This book is due for return on or before the last date shown below.

1 3 DEC 2011
1 8 OCT 2012

2 9 NOV 2017

- 9 NOV 2012

2 2 MAY 2014

1 1 JUN 2014
1 8 JUN 2014

3 0 SEP 2015